To Victoria,
with much
love
Stephen
28 Feb 22

Also by Stephen Box

The Odd Patients

PREJUDICE IN LOVE

STEPHEN BOX

authorHOUSE

AuthorHouse™ UK
1663 Liberty Drive
Bloomington, IN 47403 USA
www.authorhouse.co.uk
Phone: UK TFN: 0800 0148641 (Toll Free inside the UK)
UK Local: 02036 956322 (+44 20 3695 6322 from outside the UK)

© 2020 Stephen Box. All rights reserved.
@theStephenBox

No part of this book may be reproduced, stored in a retrieval system, or transmitted by any means without the written permission of the author.

Published by AuthorHouse 25/08/2020

ISBN: 978-1-7283-5471-2 (sc)
ISBN: 978-1-7283-5472-9 (hc)
ISBN: 978-1-7283-5470-5 (e)

Print information available on the last page.

Any people depicted in stock imagery provided by Getty Images are models, and such images are being used for illustrative purposes only.
Certain stock imagery © Getty Images.

This book is printed on acid-free paper.

Because of the dynamic nature of the Internet, any web addresses or links contained in this book may have changed since publication and may no longer be valid. The views expressed in this work are solely those of the author and do not necessarily reflect the views of the publisher, and the publisher hereby disclaims any responsibility for them.

PREJUDICE IN LOVE

Prejudice (1): a socially unreasonable perception, opinion, attitude, or feeling formed without knowledge, thought, or reason especially of a hostile nature, towards an ethnic, racial, social, or religious group.

Prejudice (2): in society the unreasonable attitude and behaviour of people confronted by an older white man in a relationship with a significantly younger coloured woman.

Prejudice (3): intergenerational between an older generation who know they can't always get want they want, but if they work at it they will likely get what they need, and a younger generation who want it all, and want it now.

CONTENTS

Part I. The Journey 1

Part II. The Following 9 Months 365

Part III. 8 Years Later 393

Part IV. 10 Years Later 427

PREFACE

This book contains sexually explicit material intended as instructional

Prejudice in Love is a comment on the social impacts of a generational attitude of 'I want it all, and I want it now'. The advent of social media is intended to be connective. However, it can also be addictive and toxic. Far too many people of the younger generation live their lives through superficial social media leaving little of no time to engage with the real world of their own relationships. Having encountered couples who spend more time sharing their lives through their mobile phones than face-to-face conversation it is easy to understand why such relationships break down without either party really understanding why.

The content of this book, especially Part I, is based on real life experience over some thirty-five years of dealing with relationships that were floundering because either, or both parties are just too busy to engage with the one relationship that really matters to their happiness.

The remainder of the book addresses imperfections in intergenerational human relationships.

PART I

The Journey

Chapter 1 - Sunday

He's restless. Life is passing him by. This does not suit his temperament. It's early Sunday morning, sitting alone having breakfast whilst watching the BBC News Channel. Jane, his partner of some twenty years, has departed for yet another business trip – this time to Singapore - for at least ten days. She left early yesterday so she would be fresh to start her work on Monday morning. Paul was now used to these frequent periods on his own, but this time there was a difference. Jane's cat had recently died after eighteen years and thus Paul is no longer anchored to care for this belligerent moggy. He needs something to do with himself – he needs some focus to his life.

The 8:00am BBC weather forecast warned that storm Lucy, a former hurricane from the Caribbean, is brewing from the southwest of England and will be disruptive to transport systems, cause possible flooding, as well as power line and road transport disruption. Winds could be as high as 90 mph which likely will uproot trees as the ground is sodden after a week of rain. As with any hurricane they expect two waves of this storm, with relative calm between. The first wave is projected to pass over the Midlands mid-afternoon today sweeping eastwards, stretching from Cornwall to as far north as Lancashire and Yorkshire. This would continue into the evening, and the second wave would start in the early hours of tomorrow morning continuing through Monday lunchtime. All the usual warnings were given about avoiding unnecessary travel once the storm starts and expect all public transport to be disrupted both today and on Monday – many train operators were considering not running services tomorrow.

'What to do?' thought Paul as he finished his breakfast. The skies were mostly clear and the thought of being trapped at home alone for two days did not appeal. His mind drifted to Scotland, and the trip he had planned for Jane and her parents over the previous Easter but had to be cancelled at the last minute because of an urgent need for Jane to fly to the Osaka office in Japan. This was very annoying for Paul as some days of research and effort had gone into optimising the route, finding the right hotels to book, and prioritising points of interest along the route. He was particularly satisfied that he had found a little used route along the east side of Loch Ness, instead of the conventional tourist route along the west shore of the loch. The journey would take them to Loch Lomond surrounded by National Reserve forests, then northwest to the wildlife sanctuary at Oban where there are seal and dolphin colonies, then through the magnificent Glen Coe onto Loch Ness, Inverness, Aviemore, and Edinburgh before crossing the border back into England just north of Newcastle where they would walk along a remaining section of Adrian's Wall built by the Romans around AD 125. This trip was to last ten days with Paul driving the 1,000+ mile round trip.

'Why not?' he said to himself, *'there are no storms in Scotland, and if I got started now, I could get past Manchester before the storm arrives. Scotland will be beautiful at this time of the year and should be free of the interminable Viking midges that ruin so many Scottish holidays during the summer months. I can also visit the specialist Scottish attire shop in Balloch to see if I can find myself a new kilt.'*

He still had the details for the trip on his iPad, including the hotels. He quickly looked at the room availability at The Lodge on Loch Lomond Hotel at Luss nestled on the shore of and looking over Loch Lomond. His last-minute hotel search revealed the Carter luxury suite with a separate lounge area, a private sauna, floor-to-ceiling windows, and a private balcony overlooking the Loch at a good price, so he booked for two nights. He packed a wheelie case for two weeks, and then looked at the car keys on the hall table. *'Which car to take.'*

Paul had been forced two years ago through ill health to take early retirement from his long and distinguished career as an International Banker. He had bought himself two cars as retirement presents, a Porsche Panamera 4S, and a Range Rover Sports. He was a keen driver, and even dabbled with rally driving in his younger days. *'The Porsche will be more fun'* he thought, *'but the Range Rover more practical, especially if I want to get off-road into the raw wilderness of the Highlands to contemplate my life without the distractions of so-called civilisation'.*

The Range Rover won the day as he snatched the keys and headed for the car. He then realised that he had not packed any outdoor clothing so put his bag in the back, his carry bag with his iPad, iPod and various chargers and other gadgets, including binoculars and camera in his shoulder bag on the passenger seat, and went back to collect his boots, Barbour, and hat which he deposited on the back seat. As this car was used for his country pursuits, mainly shooting trips, it was already equipped with towels, blankets, and other sundry survival items useful when returning from a wet day in the woods.

He noted he had just a quarter tank of fuel so would need to refuel early into his journey. If he used the existing fuel first a full tank would then easily see him through the 340 miles to Luss. The logical route from his house situated in a small village near Cambridge would be north along the A1(M) highway, and then cut across the Pennines on the A66 towards the M6 motorway. However, it would take some hours to reach the passes across these desolate hills and such passes were quickly closed during severe weather. He decided that it would be faster and less risky to travel west along the A14 highway to the M6/M74/M3 motorways which would take him all the way to Glasgow. He felt that speed was the order of the day to the Scottish border at Gretna Green so he would use the M6 motorway toll road. A final thought to send an email to Jane telling her of his decision and thus he would not follow his routine of calling her between 1pm and 2pm (10pm – 11pm in Singapore) but would contact her when able. It was a little after 9:30am as he pulled out of his drive to head north.

Chapter 2

The traffic on the A14 highway was heavy for a Sunday morning so his route to the M6 motorway took longer than anticipated. He decided to stop for fuel and a last pit stop at the Corley motorway services close to Birmingham airport before escaping the storm. On arrival at the services he decided to get fuel first, and then reverse back to the car park to visit the toilet so that he could clean up as the pumps were usually messy at such service areas. He did not want his hands to smell of diesel all the way to Scotland. He noted that the clouds were dark towards the west, and it had started to rain, but only lightly. Once parked he put his shoulder bag out of sight in the foot well of the rear seats and headed towards the main services concourse. The place was buzzing with people. *'Maybe the usual Sunday evening traffic had decided to move early to avoid the storm.'* He moved directly to the Gent's toilet, washed his hands, and then relieved himself. He was ready for the drive north.

On the way out he was confronted by a woman wearing a hooded coat. She looked up at him. Her face was beautiful, chocolate brown with a flawless silky complexion, and with crystal clear brown eyes. From what he could see she was probably late 20's, maybe early 30's. There was evidence of well-groomed, ebony black hair from the sides of her hood. She politely, but nervously asked him if he was travelling north as she was trying to get home. He asked where she wanted to go. 'I want to get to Edinburgh' she replied, 'but if I can get to Manchester airport, or Glasgow then it's easy for me from either place.' He noted that she was out of place in this building, and clearly able to pay her way if she could afford to fly from Manchester.

He was generally averse to hitchhikers, especially lone females, as he had a bad experience in the past. Also, he was a keen driver so focussed on the road. He did not like chatty passengers, as Jane knew all too well so always took a book, or just absorbed the scenery when they travelled any distance together. He always chose the music, the volume, and the cabin temperature. And unscheduled pit stops were to be avoided. He only stopped to eat or refuel – passengers had to take full advantage of these stops.

He looked long and hard into her beautiful brown eyes which were begging him to say 'yes'. But what to do? He noted that she was carrying a rather expensive travel bag. *'Better groomed than the average hitch-hiker'* he thought. 'Why are you hitch-hiking?' he finally asked.

'I've been staying with my sister and her family in Birmingham this weekend, but they fly to the Caribbean this morning. I thought I could get a flight to Edinburgh but there are no flights until late afternoon – storm permitting. I thought if I could get further north, I would have a better chance of getting home today.'

He thought again. At least he could see why she was out of place in this motorway services. 'Alright. I'm going to Loch Lomond, so I can drop you at either Manchester or Glasgow.' She smiled with obvious relief. 'However' he continued, 'I don't want conversation, the music is my choice, the cabin temperature choice is mine, and if you think that you'll need a toilet in the next few hours, now is the time'.

She looked at him quizzically thinking *'is he for real*?' but felt strangely comfortable with this clearly aging man with very clear blue eyes. She noted that he was still in good shape in his shirt, jeans, and fading blond hair. 'Okay' she said. 'I'll comply with your wishes, including the pit stop if you would kindly watch my bag.' She dropped her bag at his feet and was gone towards the Ladies toilet before he could say anything.

Some minutes later she emerged, but now with the hood down and her coat open. She had the most beautiful arabesque face with long flowing wavy ebony hair, and her clothing revealed expensive and fashionable taste. Paul handed her travel bag to her (he had a thing about carrying other people's bags, especially when heavy. If Jane was any form of measure half the weight would probably be her toiletries bag).

Paul, whose pace took no account of her high-heeled shoes, lead her to his car. The rain was a little heavier, so he wasted no time in using the remote to unlock the doors, the front lights indicating that the message was received, understood, and obeyed. He went straight to the tailgate and opened it so that she could put her travel bag next to his case. He then went to the passenger door, opened it, invited her to remove her coat which he placed on the back seat behind her, and then closed both doors.

Having removed her coat, he could not help but to notice that she had a stunning figure in her designer jeans and sweater. As Paul went around to the driver's door and got in, she thought how amusing his 'ways' were. But she felt comfortable and relaxed in the luxury of such an expensive and powerful car. She had chosen well. If any vehicle can get through a storm, then this is the car of choice.

After Paul had settled and fastened his seat belt she said in a very clear and cultured voice 'My name is Felicity. Most of my friends call me Cis'.

'I'm Paul' as he extended his hand towards her.

She took his hand as she smiled and said 'Nice to meet you Paul, and thank you'.

'Nice to meet you Felicity, or can I call you Cis?'

'I'm happy with Cis.'

'Get comfortable Cis, we have a long drive ahead of us.'

Prejudice in Love

At that he fired up the 3-litre engine, moved the auto-shift into reverse, and eased out of the parking bay. As he made his way back out onto the M6 motorway he asked which of the two drop points she would prefer.

'Glasgow would be great, thanks.'

She kicked off her heels and settled down. She observed that the cabin temperature on the driver's side was set to 19.5°C whereas the setting on her side was 22.5°C. *'Someone who occupies this passenger seat does not comply with his rules'*, she thought.

Chapter 3

Conversation over they both settled down to the next part of their respective journeys.

It was now raining, and the clouds indicated the weather coming more from the west than the south-west. Within the hour they had successfully completed the M6 toll road, but they were now back on the normal M6 motorway with far more traffic. The intensity of the rain was starting to cause problems for drivers, especially those Sunday drivers who should be at home, and certainly not on the road in this weather. They were driving into the path of the storm. By the time they reached junction 14 the traffic was stop-go, struggling to reach speeds over 40 mph at any time, and the windscreen wipers were struggling to keep the windscreen clear, even on the fastest speed. They were still some way south of Manchester and conditions were getting worse.

Some 20 minutes later he broke the sound of the rain lashing against the car. 'This is not good, and not getting any better. I don't think we'll make it today. This traffic could easily become a pile-up, or fully stationery at any time'.

Just then there was a lightning flash, followed some seconds later by a mighty crash of thunder. She responded to this by quickly pulling her legs up to her chest, wrapping her arms around her legs, and burying her head into her knees. She was clearly distressed.

'Okay Cis, time for evasive action. I'll pull off at the next junction, park up, and see what our options are. You clearly have a problem with the thunder and lightning so let me see what we can do'. All she could say as she maintained her screwed-up position was 'Okay, you're the driver'.

Some 10 minutes later, and several further thunder and lightning events, they were off the motorway, parked on the hard shoulder near the top of the ramp at junction 16 with his hazard lights on. He retrieved his iPad and iPhone which he used to create a private Wifi spot for his iPad. She looked on from behind her knees fascinated that this older guy was as slick with this technology as her nephew in Birmingham.

'What are you doing?' she asked inquisitively.

'I want to view a local map of the area to see where we are, and what options we have.' It was now a little after 1:00pm, the light conditions looked more like 7pm, and there was no sign of let-up in the storm.

He switched on the radio and tuned it to the local traffic report. 'Heavy rain: flooding: thunder and lightning all the way up to the Lake District: traffic chaos as roads get waterlogged and clogged with traffic', came the reports.

'Okay, this is unfortunate for both of us, but I feel that trying to fight our way through is not worth the risk. I think I should find a decent hotel nearby and wait for this storm to blow over. I have no need to get to Loch Lomond today, what about you?'

She was now frightened out of her wits by the ferocity of the storm. She did not like storms. Thunder and lightning for her was hell on earth.

She finally spoke quietly, but directly to him. 'I'm okay to stay in a hotel, but not on my own in this storm. I'm too scared to be alone.'

He looked at her in amusement but could clearly see her anguish. Jane was hopeless in a storm. No sleep for either of them as she would leap out of her skin at every thunder crack, whereas he could quite happily sleep through the worst of storms on his own. He had experienced hurricanes, typhoons, electric storms over the north pole in a 747 plane where the plane was being thrown around so much that it looked like the wings were flapping.

He gently gave her a reassuring pat on the knee, 'you're safe in here so please try not to distress yourself too much.' He resumed his search on his iPad. He could see that the iPhone GPS had locked into their location, so started his hotel search app. He needed time to think what to do. He could see that she was in some distress every time there was a lightning flash or thunder crack. He switched his thought to the search results which showed a country house hotel about 2 miles away.

'There's a hotel just a few miles from here so I'll check availability' he said reassuringly. He could see that it was quite full but there was an executive suite that was on offer for £75 for the night plus breakfast.

'They're quite full, but there is an executive suite so I think we should go for it.' He was trying to keep her involved but just as he said okay there was another very loud thunder crack which had her hanging onto her legs in total fear.

'Okay' she timidly replied.

He quickly completed the booking in his name and keyed the co-ordinates for the hotel into the car satnav. 'Okay, let's go and seek refuge from this storm before you become totally distressed.'

It took about 15 minutes to find the entrance to the Crewe Hall hotel which sat some 200 metres from the road in what looked like parkland. As they approached, they could see lights, and then the outline of this majestic Jacobean house. Its solid structure looked like a castle. She became calmer, sitting upright peering out of the windscreen at her new sanctuary.

'Right', he said in a very assertive, but not aggressive way – just enough to snap her into action, 'get your coat from the back seat. I'll pull up as close as possible to the entrance. You get out as I flip the tailgate and grab both bags. Go inside while I park the car.' He pulled the car as close as he could to the entrance. A doorman appeared from inside with a golf umbrella, albeit too windy to be effective.

'Change of plan. You get inside and let the doorman take the bags.'

She jumped out of the car into the arms of the doorman who guided her inside. Then he returned and Paul triggered the tailgate release. The doorman quickly took the bags inside and returned to close the tailgate. He shouted that Paul could park about 20 yards away to the front of the building. Having parked the car, he grabbed his Barbour and gadget bag and made a dash for the entrance.

Once inside the doorman guided them to reception. Paul slipped him a gratuity.

At reception there was a little confusion with his booking as it had not yet been forwarded by the agent. He showed the booking confirmation on his iPad and explained that he made the booking just 15 minutes ago. All was soon good, and he completed the check-in process. He noted that the place seemed empty as he asked about dinner arrangements. He was informed that people should be arriving throughout the afternoon as there was a conference scheduled for the following day.

They made their way to their executive suite on the top floor. On the way in the elevator he wanted to break the silence. 'This trip is turning out to be quite an adventure, and now we are at our castle retreat I hope that we can relax and let this horrid storm get fed up with attacking us and go away.'

She looked up and gave a little smile, but she was still clearly uncomfortable.

Chapter 4

Paul inserted the cardkey into the door lock and opened the huge door. They both stepped inside together but were stopped in their tracks with the sheer size and elegance of the room.

It had a seating area to the left, and a huge four poster bed to the right. There was a real wow factor. He wondered what the normal rack rate would be for such a room – must be at least double what he paid. They looked at each other in amazement.

With a casual air he said, 'if you have to wait out a storm, you might as well do it in style.'

She responded 'You're pretty good with the technology stuff. I would not have had a clue how to find this place. Thank you for rescuing this distressed lamb.'

He looked at her. 'Thank you, kind lady. I thought your generation were totally into social networking, Facebook, email, text, and all that.' Mockingly he added 'in my day we had to use paper maps, a compass, and find a telephone box.'

She laughed 'did you have electricity in those days?'

She was notably calmer, even though the storm continued relentlessly. They put their bags on the baggage rack and she found a cupboard to hang her coat, and then asked him for his coat which she hung in the cupboard and closed the door.

He looked at her for the first time where his mind was not elsewhere. She was truly beautiful and held herself with a gentle grace not often seen with the current generation. She was about 5ft 8in tall with long slender legs.

She looked at him, detecting that he was staring at her. He quickly thought how to prevent any embarrassment and retorted 'You really look very nice when you're not cowering from the storm.'

She smiled 'And you look pretty good for your age.' They both laughed.

'Okay lady, how do we do this because I am, as you have noted, too old to sleep in a chair, especially with a long drive tomorrow. I'm very easy and straight-forward. I'll sleep on the left side of this palatial bed leaving at least two people spaces for you to select, the outer space being a good metre away from me. Alternatively, you can sleep wherever else you feel comfortable. I can reassure you that you are safe with me as I have rules about chivalry and honour towards damsels in distress. If we can get this detail out of the way, then I suggest that we relax and enjoy our beautiful shelter from the storm with a nice dinner this evening.'

She thought about this little speech for a moment and realised that he was very uneasy about this situation but was also being very straightforward with her, and she felt reassured. 'I accept your kind invitation to dinner, and to share your bed. I do feel safe with you, and I thank you, kind sir.'

'Good. Let's find out how this room works, and maybe we can take a look around this place to see what's on offer.'

She suggested that she would like something to drink so he skipped the room survey and they went down to the lounge area.

Chapter 5

Paul was informed that afternoon tea would be served in about half an hour if they could wait. This sounded good to both so decided to look at the spa arrangements. He guided her to the concierge desk where he picked up a guide to the hotel.

'It would appear that the activities part is in the dungeons. Shall we start there?'

She dutifully followed him, albeit he had already forgotten that, although she walked elegantly in her high-heel shoes, she could not move very quickly.

He stopped, waited for her, and offered his arm. 'Sorry, forgot about the shoes.'

There was a wide staircase down to the lower floor, and at the bottom of the stairs they were confronted with large glass doors which he pushed open. They were in a very modern complex of swimming pool, gym, beauty care, etc. Once inside she grabbed his arm with one hand as she used the other to remove her shoes. 'Don't think they would be happy for me to walk on these floors in these heals.'

There was no sign of activity, but the lights were on so they took a look around. The swimming pool was not large but adequate. 'We could have a swim before we leave tomorrow. Loosen up for the drive' he suggested.

'Luckily I bought a new bikini from the fashion gig I attended on Thursday, so we are okay to put this on our list of activities for tomorrow.' She was keen to get as friendly as possible with him knowing that he was still not totally at peace with her demand to share his bed.

At the end of the pool area there was a lounge area and a hot tub. Beyond that there were small saunas, showers, and a steam room. Labels on doors indicated 'Massage', 'Beautician', and 'Hair Salon'. Then they saw the gym. Again, not large but well equipped.

With a teasing look she said, 'Maybe we could use a little time in here as well to keep you in good shape.'

He just looked at her and walked on. She caught up with him 'seriously though, you look in good shape. Do you go to the gym, or play any sport?'

He stopped and looked at her 'I have my own gym which I use as the mood takes me, and I play tennis. What about you?'

'I do the gym because that's the trending fashionable thing to do, and I like to swim. Quite fancy tennis, would you teach me? I do move quite well and have good hand-eye co-ordination.'

Paul looked down into her playful eyes 'You have just extended our adventure by about a year.'

Just at that moment a young man wearing a track suite and sneakers pushed his way through the glass doors carrying 2 bundles of fresh towels, no doubt to replenish the changing rooms for the expected arrivals. He smiled 'can I be of any assistance?'

She quickly piped up with her charm 'We're exploring the facilities to decide how we could spend our morning tomorrow.'

'We expect to be busy first thing, but it would be quieter after 9 o'clock when the conference starts. If you need a masseur or beautician, it would be better to book early as the hotel is full.'

'Is it possible for a facial and manicure later this afternoon?'

He examined the bookings sheet 'You could have a facial at 4 o'clock followed by a manicure and pedicure if you wish.'

She accepted all, and was booked in.

She turned to Paul 'I'll pay for these services as they would help me to relax.'

As they left the spa, she did not bother to put her shoes back on, preferring her bare feet which, he noticed, had a much lighter pigmentation around the base of the foot. He had often wondered why this was as he had noted it with coloured people all his life, but now was not the time for such questions.

Chapter 6

They returned to the lounge area which had now been set out for afternoon tea. He selected a table where he could observe what was happening throughout the reception area. The table had a two-seater couch and two chairs opposite. He sat on the couch where he could get the most panoramic view, and she sat next to him, wanting to stay as close as possible.

Prejudice in Love

She quite fancied something to eat 'Paul, could we eat something. Breakfast was early today, and light.'

He ordered two full afternoon teas with Earl Grey for her and Afternoon Tea for himself. She studied the hotel guide while he observed the now constant flow of people arriving at the hotel. He noted that most of the people were middle-aged businessmen, probably some executive conference.

After some minutes, their teas arrived. A triple stack of finger sandwiches, scones, cakes, and chocolates. She looked at the contents voicing 'yummie' as she started to pour tea for both.

'Do you know that they offer a wide range of massage services from Thai, Indian through to a deep sports massage. They either have an army of masseurs or have to call them in as required.' She noted that he was apparently not listening to her. She followed his gaze to the reception area. She moved closer to his ear, 'what has captured your attention?'

He snapped out of his concentration and looked at her 'sorry, but I like to watch people and I've noted some interesting situations with these people checking in. For example, do you see the older man with a younger woman checking in next to him? They came in together. They obviously know each other but are trying to look as though they are not connected. They are both using their own credit cards to check in. What's the betting that they have adjoining rooms, and she is his most personal assistant during the conference. The rooms will have been pre-paid, so they will only use their credit cards for extras. Any extras that he does not want to appear on his card will go onto hers, and he will compensate her, or even pay her bill in cash when they leave.'

She looked at him bemused. 'Are you a detective or something?'

'No, not at all. It's a game I used to hone my observation skills during the interminable hours spent in airports over the years. I got to a point where I could tell you not only the country of origin of someone but, in some cases, the actual region of that country. In many cases I could tell you their likely occupation and background. Proved very useful during my professional career.'

He returned to his observation of the man and younger lady who had now completed their respective check-in and were on their way to the lifts. He wanted to see if they were on the same floor, which he could detect by only one of them reaching for the floor buttons.

She watched him with some amusement. She remembered how his sharp blue eyes had penetrated hers at the motorway services place when they met. *'He was analysing me'*, she thought. *'I wonder what he saw that convinced him to take me with him? He clearly does not miss any detail that is useful to his analysis.'*

She sat for a while just watching him watch everyone else as she munched through the delicious goodies on the table. He barely touched anything so there was much for her to enjoy.

After a while she thought that he was not very chatty. He had barely spoken to her since they sat down for tea. Perhaps his no conversation rule in the car extended to anytime. It was now 3:45 in any event and she wanted to change her shoes before going to the spa for her treatments.

'Paul, could I have the card key to our room as I want to change my shoes to my house shoes and get my purse before going back to the spa.'

He looked at her. 'Sure, here it is. Keep it with you and I'll get another. See you in the room when you've finished. How long do these treatments take?'

'About one and a half hours should be more than enough time', she responded.

'Enjoy, and I hope you feel better afterwards.'

'Thank you' and with that she was off to their suite totally bemused by her saviour.

He had shown little interest in her or the food throughout tea. *'Who is this man, and why so interested in observing others when she was sitting right next to him? But he has saved me from the storm and has brought me to this castle to protect me. That must make him my valiant knight, and I should be grateful for his kindness. Sir Paul of Crewe'* she thought. *'Doesn't quite roll off the tongue. My valiant knight will have to do'.*

She changed her shoes, grabbed her purse, and off to the spa where she was met by a very nice lady ready to start her treatments. The thunder and lightning persisted but she felt safe in this castle retreat so she could relax, be pampered, and forget the stresses of the day.

Chapter 7

He finally decided that he had enough information to determine the range of delegates for the conference, and the nature of some of the covert liaisons that would play out over the conference period. He secured a duplicate card key from reception and went back to their suite to find out more about the progress of the storm, which was quite audible, even inside this thick-walled building.

He returned his thoughts to information about the storm. He found the TV remote and clicked the large flat screen TV into life. He navigated his way past the 'Welcome' screen and the videos about the facilities and amenities on offer at the hotel. He found the BBC News channel which was reporting the progress of the storm. The weather people had got this one wrong. It was worse than expected with 90 mph winds lashing many areas with heavy rainfall causing havoc and chaos throughout the country. Worse still they did not expect it to ease to the first lull for at least another 3 - 4 hours, starting in the west. He called the hotel in Luss to tell them of his predicament. He still intended to stay there but it would be tomorrow, but still for 2 nights. They were very understanding and agreed to revise his booking accordingly.

After digesting the bad news his mind wondered to his current situation. *'How did this happen? What game is fate playing? Just a few hours ago I was sitting alone at home having my breakfast, not planning to go anywhere. Now I'm in a hotel sharing a room with a beautiful woman whom I picked up at a motorway service station. Where is this going?'*

He was clicking randomly through channels and found a favourite movie, El Dorado, starring John Wayne and Dean Martin, was about to start. He parked himself on the brown leather couch, switched on the lamp on the side table next to him having taken a beer from the bar fridge, and a glass.

When she returned to their suite, he was still relaxing watching the movie. He was wedged in the corner at one end of the brown leather couch with his feet on the coffee table. She noted that he had a can of beer but was drinking it from a glass not large enough to hold the contents of the can.

'I'm back' she shouted above the movie.

'Hi Cis. How was it?'

'Great thanks. The therapist was really nice, and I feel much better.'

'Come and chill while I finish my movie. They are just getting to the showdown between John Wayne and the hired gunslinger. This is where sensationalism overrides reality as John Wayne, suffering from the effects of a bullet pressing against his spine paralysing his right side, jumps off a wagon with a Winchester rifle in his left hand, landing on his right side, shooting the gunslinger off the bounce under the horses. Totally nuts as landing on the floor would completely paralyse him, but it's a movie and we need a dramatic end. Would you like a drink?'

She was now standing behind him. 'No thanks, but can I close the curtains as I don't want to see what is happening out there?'

'Sorry, how inconsiderate of me. I'll close them now.'

Prejudice in Love

As he started to get up, she put her hands on his shoulders 'It's okay, I'll do it. You finish your movie'. She closed the curtains.

She decided that she would finish her notes relating to the fashion gig a few days earlier as she would be expected to submit her copy article to her magazine editor by Thursday evening. She found the switch for the lamp on the table at the other end of the couch, found her notebook, and sat with her back to the arm of the couch with her feet on the couch.

As she was making her notes she could not help but observe how calm and relaxed he looked. Despite the extraordinary events of the day he appeared totally at peace with the situation. She found this very comforting and reassuring. He would stay calm for her, and thus keep her calm.

The movie finished but was immediately followed by a news bulletin. She put down her notebook and sat beside him as the devastation horrors caused by the storm played out on the screen in front of them. Over 1,000 homes flooded, more than 250,000 homes with no power, roads and rail lines blocked, all English airports closed, including Manchester.

'Oh my God' she exclaimed, 'those poor people without a home or power, and another storm on the way. I'm so glad that I'm not out there. What will happen to those people?'

She had her hands up on her cheeks. He noticed her newly varnished fingernails. They were more rounded than the typical pictures in fashion magazines, and not as long. They were varnished in a white, no, ivory colour which suited her skin colour. He had already noticed her white gold wedding band when she first got into his car in Birmingham. She had no detectable makeup on her face, but she looked stunningly beautiful.

'We should think about preparing for dinner. It's now 6:15. Dinner starts at 7pm. You are welcome to use the bathroom first.'

She went to the bathroom door and opened it. 'Come look at this', she said, 'it's magnificent'. He went to the door and looked over her shoulder. They both moved into this lavish marble palace with a large shell bath, double sinks, walk-in shower big enough for two, separate toilet area, and lavished with towels, robes, and toiletries. 'Do you mind if I take a bath' she asked, staring at the elegant bath.

'Go for it and enjoy.' She grabbed her fully laden toilet bag and, without further ado, off she went.

About 6:50 she broke his thoughts by emerging from the bathroom wrapped in a very lush bathrobe looking radiant. The colour and silky complexion of her beautiful skin radiated against the white of the bathrobe. She was smiling, and relaxed. 'I feel much better now kind sir and will be ready for dinner in 15 minutes.'

'No rush, I want to take a shower. If you need a dress code, I don't have anything with me for dinner other that what we call smart casual.' With that he grabbed his toilet bag and made his way to the bathroom. As he went through the door, he turned to ask her if she needed anything from the bathroom in the next 10 minutes.

'Just my hairbrush, thanks. Trousers or skirt' she asked.

'Feminine would be nice – no jeans.'

'Strange man', she thought. 'How does "feminine" answer my question? He's older generation so I guess skirt or dress. Okay mister, I'll not disappoint.'

She rummaged through her travel bag to find fresh underwear, a thigh hugging skirt, and a blouse. She decided that it was okay to get dressed as he was in the shower. Makeup could wait until he finished his shower. It felt good to get into fresh clothes, and she felt good about her choice when she looked into the mirror. Brushing her hair to its full, free-flowing length took years off her age. Tights? Stockings? It was very warm in this hotel, and after all, her brown legs did not need such accessories except for warming purposes.

He re-emerged from the bathroom in a bathrobe carrying his clothes. He looked as though a load had been taken off his shoulders, and she noticed the colour in his cheeks, and those big blue eyes were brighter.

He looked at her, smiled, and said 'beautiful, truly beautiful'.

She smiled and went into the bathroom. 'Just a few final touches good sir and I'll be ready.'

He found shirt and slacks and proceeded to get dressed. He had not been in a situation like this for years, but he was relaxed, amused, and treated it as an adventure – after all she was obviously less than half his age so she was not going to be interested in him other than as a fatherly protector. As he put on his shoes she reappeared from the bathroom, gave him a twirl for approval, and asked if she was feminine enough.

'Perfect. Would you join me for dinner beautiful lady?'

She slightly curtsied as she replied, 'It would be my pleasure'. She slipped into her shoes. These were no ordinary shoes. The heels were so high that she was almost his height. He had heard about these shoes. Jimmy Choo was a name that came to mind. He walked close to her, looked her in the eye, and in a playful stern monotone, 'you are very tall in those shoes.'

She moved her nose closer to his and in a low monotone, 'so I can look you in the eye.'

'And what do you see?' Holding the monotone.

'Someone ready for dinner' she responded in the same monotone.

They both laughed.

It was nearly 7:30pm as he guided her to the door and into the corridor. He offered his arm which she took, and off they went to the elevator.

Chapter 8

As they walked into the dining room, they could not help but notice how wonderful it was. Strangely contemporary, but with elegant style. The tables were well spaced and mostly occupied by mainly men in their 40's and 50's. The noise level was a low hum, and a piano stood in one corner. He noticed the man and woman, acting suspiciously at check-in, were sitting at the same table with four other people. 'A bit obvious' he thought.

He asked for a discrete table away from the gaze of these men, and away from windows. The storm was still ravaging outside and, although the robustness of the building essentially dulled the thunder cracks, he did not want to reawaken the distress seen earlier. It was as though she had forgotten all about the impact of the thunder and lightning, and he wanted to keep it this way.

The chosen table was a solid wood round table about one metre in diameter with an art deco edging, polished to a mirror shine. It was positioned in an alcove, very quiet and intimate. As he suffered some hearing loss in his left ear he ensured that he sat on her left side at 45 degrees, rather than opposite, on the grounds that they could both see into the dining room rather than one of them looking at a wall. He was interested to see if the older man and younger woman with him left together.

There was a table flyer advertising a special Prosecco as recommended drink of the day. 'Would you like a Prosecco?'

'That would be very nice, thank you' she responded with a smile.

They studied the menu in silence as they sipped their Prosecco. After ordering dinner he felt out of his comfort zone as small talk was not his thing. Even if he could start, he lost the will to live very quickly. But he must start a conversation, and refrain from his pet subjects of geo-economic and geo-political debate. He did not know her well enough to move to controversial subjects like sex, education, and religion. So

Prejudice in Love

somewhat awkwardly he looked at her and blurted 'shall we remain strangers in the night, or can I encourage you to tell me about yourself?'

She playfully responded with 'I thought that you did not want conversation.'

He smiled. 'I'm no longer concentrating on safely negotiating traffic, and although my senses tell me much about you as a person, I would be interested to learn more about you. It would appear that fate has thrown us together in this strangest of scenarios, and it would be a shame to not at least know a little about how such a beautiful lady needed to be rescued today.'

'Are you sure that you would not prefer to observe all of these interesting people in the restaurant instead?' she replied playfully.

'I'm sorry about tea, but I wasn't ready to engage in conversation. I hope that you didn't think me rude, but I just needed some space to rationalise this situation, analyse the possibilities so that I can react positively to whatever is thrown at us. Your anxiety with this storm did give me cause for concern as I have no such fear so understanding your obvious distress is not easy when I know nothing of your circumstances. I just needed some time with my thoughts to ensure that, having taken responsibility for your safety, I can deliver you safely home.'

She detected the uncertainty that he felt and was very touched by his obvious concern. He was ready to engage with her, so she decided to take the initiative now that he had opened the door. 'I'm so grateful for your concern for my safety, and I appreciate your explanation. My name is Felicity Duncan. I'm a life-style writer. Married for 2 years to Andy, a businessman who spends more time travelling than he does at home. He's building an import and distribution business. We live in Edinburgh, his place of birth. My parents live in London, and I have a married sister living in Birmingham, currently on their way to the Caribbean. Your turn.'

He wanted more than this. 'Wait a minute. You've given me an abstract summary, but nothing about who you are, and why you were at the motorway service place. I need more.'

She wanted to lighten the discussion. 'We're on a mysterious adventure together' she said playfully, 'so we must move step-by-step revealing just enough to progress the mystery.'

He was perplexed. 'Are you sure that you're a fashion writer, not a mystery adventure writer?' He paused. 'Okay, my name is Paul Fulton. I'm retired – early. I live with my much younger partner, Jane, and until recently suffered the intrusion into my life of her cat. Jane works for an international company, travelling extensively looking after their offices scattered throughout the world. We live in a village near Cambridge nowhere near our respective families. Back to you.'

She pondered this specific information about the age of his partner, Jane. *'Much younger partner'* she thought, *'hmm.'* 'Have you guessed my age yet, because I think I've worked out yours, especially now I know you used paper maps and a compass?'

'Hmm, cutting to the chase, eh. Obviously, natural curiosity means that I have given the subject some thought, albeit of little importance in this situation unless you are less than 16 years old. However, you did throw me when you appeared in your radiant glory from the bathroom earlier. On balance, I'll go with what I saw in the services place where I met you. Therefore, with a great deal of trepidation, and moving to a safe distance, I'll suggest that you are 28 years old.' He shuffled away from her as he suggested her age.

'No, no, no, come back. I cannot have my brave rescuer showing signs of uncertainty. I need my valiant knight to be strong and confident for me in my hour of need – especially when he is precisely correct.'

Feigning wiping his brow, 'Phew. So, I'm your valiant knight? You must be my damsel in distress. I hope to live up to expectations.'

Prejudice in Love

She, more seriously and putting her hand over his 'So far you have been great. I feel safe in your company, and your relaxed attitude to all of this is very calming for me. As you see I hate storms, especially with thunder and lightning, so you will never know how grateful I am that you chose to stop and come here. And what a place! This place is a fairy tale castle. I love it.'

Now feigning writing on his napkin, 'Noted, skilled in the art of diversionary tactics. Your valiant knight would still like to know who you are. What makes you tick? Likes. Dislikes. Preferences. Dreams.'

She looked him in the eye. 'You strike me as someone well able to analyse people dear sir – I felt you probing me at the service place when you were deciding whether or not to take me with you. So, what did you see that convinced you that I was okay?'

He thought for a moment, *'more diversion.'* 'Okay I'll tell you what I see if you agree to correct me if wrong. And then co-operate to fill any gaps and expand as required to know you.'

'Alright, I'll go with that.'

He started, 'I had a bad experience with a lone female hitch-hiker in the past, so my first instinct was to ignore your plea. Then I sensed you were not a regular hitchhiker, so I did probe you. Under that hooded coat of yours there were crystal clear brown eyes looking for someone to rescue her, and the tell-tale evidence of a well-groomed woman revealed by the hair protruding from the sides of your hood which caught my attention. Your attitude when you spoke was courteous, and unassuming, albeit trying to hide a high degree of anxiety. You were clearly not a regular hitchhiker, so I asked myself what you were doing there?'

'When you returned from your pit stop with your hood down and your coat open you revealed yourself as very well groomed, and clearly not comfortable with where you were. You readily accepted my terms which most people would consider odd. You have shown your insecurity with storms, but you did not lock the bathroom door whilst you took your bath. You have not phoned anyone since we met to tell of your plight thus not expected anywhere, nor does your husband appear to be concerned about you. I now feel comfortable that you accepted my hospitality in the way presented, as this situation did give me cause for concern.'

She looked startled. 'Wow. I'm thankful that you came along. I had been at that service place for over an hour looking for a suitable ride. Before you came along, I only felt comfortable approaching one woman who clearly considered my plight as an inconvenience. When you came into the building you were only interested in locating the toilet and looked like you wanted out of there ASAP. But you were not agitated. You were calm, just navigating your way without any interaction. I felt that neither of us belonged there and thus my approach. I thought you were going to refuse, especially when you probed me. It was a great relief when you blurted out your conditions which actually gave me comfort, and I was off to the toilet before you could change your mind.'

She continued 'I feel that everything you have done since has caused you some conflict, but you have always been considerate to me. I left the bathroom door unlocked because I didn't feel any need to lock it. And I'll sleep in the same bed as you tonight without any feeling of disquiet, not least because I imposed this situation upon you. Bottom line - I trust you to look after me.'

'What made you think of hitch-hiking as an alternative to the lack of flights? There is public transport from the airport to Birmingham New Street railway station from where you can go to Manchester, or even Edinburgh.'

'Besides the fact that trains are much slower than planes, I had no idea what trains would be available on a Sunday, and how quickly they are disrupted in a storm. Can you imagine what I would be like if I were stranded in the middle of nowhere in this storm? Last year I suffered an eight-hour delay on a Eurostar train back from Paris where we were stuck in the Kent countryside. There is nowhere to go in that situation. I thought that if I could quickly get a ride north, even just to Manchester,

I would escape the worst of the storm. What made you drive to Scotland today? You must have known a storm was coming.'

'Good question, and long story. Suffice it to say that the decision was impulse based on finding myself alone for 10 days, and on poor information from the weather people.'

'I would like to hear that long story sometime as I think our meeting is fate.'

With a little sarcasm, 'Superstitious, are we?'

A little hurt in her voice, 'If you mean that I think everything that happens has a meaning or purpose, then yes. But I don't avoid walking under ladders, I'm not afraid of black cats, or believe horoscopes.'

Having sensed the hurt, 'Sorry, I was not being cynical. My philosophy is that we are defined by the decisions we make, and the events we experience.'

Quietly accepting the apology, 'My valiant knight is a philosopher'. They both laughed.

'Think about it' she started, 'my nephew looked for flights for me last night on the internet, but no availability until late this afternoon, well after the storm was scheduled to hit Birmingham. Can you imagine me stranded alone in an airport in this storm?' She paused. 'So this morning I had to make a decision that would not take my sister out of her way as getting a husband and 2 kids organised for a flight to the Caribbean at 11:00 o'clock this morning is no mean task, without me being a nuisance. What to do because I didn't want to get caught on my own in a storm. Going to my parents in London does not take me away from the storm, and I would not have my big sister I could crawl in with for comfort as I did as a kid. I couldn't think of any friends that I knew well enough to impose my anguish. Therefore, I had to get away from the storm. I've already told you about my experience on trains. So, my decision this morning about 8 o'clock was for my sister to drop me at the motorway services to get as far north as possible as quickly as possible. That hooded coat belongs to my sister as I attended a fashion gig in London last week, so I had no hitch-hiker clothes with me.' Pause. Looking him square in the eye 'so when did you make the decision to go to Scotland?'

A little agitated. 'A little after 8 this morning.'

'Don't you think that is more than a random coincidence. We are both making major decisions at the same time which will put us on a collision course to meet. My guardian angel saw my distress and looked around for a valiant knight to save me. She found you sitting having breakfast with nothing to do, and not wanting to ride the storm alone. And now my valiant knight has me safe in his castle.' She smiled at him.

He looked her straight in the eyes 'So what do you think is in store for us on this adventure?'

'I've no idea. All I know is that I'm very grateful for this fateful coincidence, and I'm not afraid to just go with it. I have no events in my diary that cannot be moved a few days, and I can write my articles wherever I am. Andy will not be back before next Saturday, earliest, and if he gets back early enough he'll go to the rugby match, and then on to the pub with his rugby mates, getting home after 11 o'clock.' She thought for a second and continued 'The only downside for you is that you are stuck with this damsel in distress who needs to stick to you like glue, even in your bed. How will you cope with that?'

He thought for a second. 'If we go back to your fateful coincidence theory my decision was based on not being on my own during the storm, but for different reasons. So I guess be careful what you wish for. Other than my concern for your distress you have been no trouble so far, and I'm surprised that we are having such an open and easy conversation. Therefore, your valiant knight will endeavour to keep you safe until he can get you home, whatever adventure is in store for us.'

She raised her wine glass for a toast 'Let the adventure begin'.

He clinked her glass wondering what was happening to him. He felt totally out of his comfort zone, but very relaxed at the same time. He was having an interesting conversation with this total stranger less than half his age about fate, valiant knights, and damsels in distress; genres in which he had little or no interest. She was clearly intelligent and cultured, but he still knew very little about her.

She left him to his thoughts as he stroked the stem of his glass and looking into the wine as though into a crystal ball looking for answers. After a few minutes of finishing her dinner she interrupted him with 'would you like desert?'

He returned to the moment 'no thanks, just a coffee. But please feel free'. The last thing he needed tonight was a reflux attack, a hangover from the over-prescription of powerful pain killers some years ago, so no desert.

She attracted the waiter, which took no effort as he had not taken his eyes off her from when they arrived. She was by far the most attractive person in the room, and her easy manner made her a magnet for such people. He came to the table and dutifully cleared away the plates and brought her the dessert menu.

Paul could not remember much about eating his food. He had ordered a fillet mignon with creamed spinach and new potatoes in their skins which had been grilled to brown them after they were cooked. This reminded him of a similar dish that he had modified from a Jamie Oliver '30 minute' meal. Jamie cooked the new potatoes, drained them until dry, put them in a flat pan, gently crushed the potatoes so just breaking the skins, then added cloves of garlic and your typical Jamie slug of virgin olive oil before putting it under a grill. He did not like eating whole cloves of garlic so changed the recipe to cook the potatoes in whole leaves of fresh mint, and when drained and dry, still put them in a dish and slightly crush them, but then covering them in a slug of olive oil that had been warmed in a pan with chopped fresh rosemary leaves before putting the dish under the grill. Both Paul and Jane were keen cooks and preferred to entertain at home rather than visit restaurants.

She had ordered a fish dish. She wanted a white Bordeaux wine, and he wanted his preferred red burgundy, so they ordered by the glass.

His thoughts were interrupted again by 'How do you like your coffee?'

'Strong black with brown sugar or zero-calorie sweeteners please'. He hadn't noticed the return of the waiter to get her desert order. The waiter then asked if he wanted anything with his coffee such as a port or a brandy. 'No thanks, I have a long drive tomorrow' as he smiled in appreciation of the offer.

She interrupted his thoughts. 'You've been lost in your thoughts for some minutes. Can you let me in to them, especially if anything is troubling you?'

He thought how to respond and then, using a little deflection of his own, 'I can't help thinking that I drifted into a daydream this morning, and expect at any minute to wake up and find myself in my kitchen finishing breakfast.'

She reached out and touched the back of his hand 'this is real, and we are really here.'

'What shall we do after dinner as the night is still young?' He went to look at his watch, but it was not on his wrist. He stopped wearing a watch on a regular basis since he retired, and certainly hated anything around his wrist whilst on a long drive. Thus, it would not occur to him to pick it up this morning. 'What time is it?' he asked.

'A little after 9:30' she replied.

'Okay, what about we have a snoop around the rest of this castle and see what delights they have for us?'

'Good idea'.

He gently nudged her and asked her to get her doting waiter to bring the bill. He looked at it and could see that his discount on the room was being quickly eroded by the generous pricing of their food, but he had enjoyed the dinner so scribbled a good tip, signed it, and handed it back to the waiter.

'Ready?' He said. The doting waiter quickly moved to help her from her seat. He found this attention quite interesting, wondering what he thought the relationship was between them.

Chapter 9

The restaurant was now nearly empty as most of the occupants had adjourned with their after-dinner drinks to the deep armchairs in the lounge area.

They explored the ground floor which had a library, and what they called a 'Quiet Lounge'. They guessed that this was for people who wanted to quietly read as the tables where covered in neat rows of various magazines. As they looked at the covers, she pointed to the magazines that published her work. He was surprised to see the range of genre from fashion, health & beauty, house and garden, and more general magazines such as 'Q' magazine. 'I thought you told me you were a fashion writer. Do all of these magazines carry articles on clothes?'

'Who said anything about only clothes? I write about fashion, any current fashion, be it lifestyle, clothes, beauty, food, house decoration, even pets. I write about whatever is in vogue as lifestyle.'

'I'm impressed. I realise that you're intelligent and cultured, so why am I surprised?' as he shrugged his shoulders. 'Probably my ignorance as I don't follow fashion, no matter how many times Jane prods me about it.'

'But you dress okay, not high fashion, but very sure, and you look good in what you wear. If I were to dress you, I wouldn't push too far away from where you are. I don't know what your overall wardrobe looks like, but I suspect it's a mixed bag of your old favourites, and well-cut perennial favourites. I don't like men who try to use clothes to look much younger, especially if they look ridiculous or uncomfortable. You should be comfortable in your skin, including the clothes you wear.' She grabbed his arm 'No, I like what I see. It's part of the calm and security that you exude.'

'Well, thank you for that vote of confidence. I would be interested to go shopping with you to see what you would choose for me.'

She looked him in the eye 'we'll add this to our adventure. I would love to do that with you.'

Having exhausted their expLauration of the building they slowly made their way back to their suite.

Chapter 10

His first act was to click the TV into life, anxious for an update on the storm. It wasn't good. Parts of England were still being battered. All airports in England were closed, motorways were at a standstill with people stranded in their vehicles, and most train services had been suspended, and would be all day tomorrow whilst trees and other debris were cleared. Flooding had put many people out of their homes, and tens of thousands were without electricity. Once again, she looked on in horror with both hands on her cheeks. 'My God. Those poor people.' She whispered almost under her breath 'thank you guardian angel.'

It was around 10:30 and he was ready for bed. 'I'll quickly use the bathroom, and then it's all yours for as long as you need.'

'Okay. I won't be long in any case' she replied.

While she was in the bathroom he got undressed and got into bed. He slept naked, and was not about to change, but he had brought a robe from the bathroom and dropped it at the side of the bed. He switched off the TV and all the main lights just leaving a bedside light for her. He arranged his pillows and settled down.

It wasn't long before she appeared from the bathroom wearing what he thought was a cream coloured satin baby-doll top with shorts. She was carrying her clothes which she carefully arranged on a chair before moving towards the bed. The bedside light revealed a picture of feminine beauty. Her breasts were perfectly sized and firm enough not to need a bra. The satin top almost hung off her nipples. Her hair hung elegantly over her slender shoulders. She would make a natural model if women with curves were put back on the catwalk.

She got into bed, adjusted her pillows, said goodnight, and switched off the light. The storm had reduced to normal rain, without any thunder and lightning. Both were soon asleep.

Chapter 11

It was around 2am when the first thunder crack occurred. The storm had returned with a vengeance, and rain was beating against the window. Cis jumped out of her skin, awake and terrified in the darkness. He was deep in sleep and would not awake on his own. She sprung across the bed towards him. He was facing towards her. She grabbed his right arm which was draped on top of the bedclothes. She hung onto his arm like grim death, so hard in fact that he started to stir from his sleep.

Jane often moved him around in bed if he was sleeping in a position that caused him to snore, but he knew nothing of it. She had even told him that she had spoken to him and he'd replied, but he couldn't remember anything.

Eventually he came out of his deep slumber, but not quite awake, to find her gripping his arm. He was used to this as Jane was also not happy about storms and was such a light sleeper that any noise would wake her. He knew how to calm her down and get her back to sleep holding her either in a full armchair position with seat belts configuration, or if this failed, a cuddle whilst stroking her back.

Almost in remote control, he pulled her towards him with her back to him, bent his legs up so that he resembled a chair, sat her tight in it and then wrapped his arms around her, just like seat belts, so that she was firmly locked into position. Another crack of thunder, but she could not move which somehow was reassuring for her. She had not yet noticed that he was naked, being too concerned with her current distress. She tried to speak with him but all she got was a sleepy 'It's okay, you're safe, go to sleep'.

He knew that he wouldn't get back to sleep until his charge had settled (still having not registered that his charge was not Jane), but he also knew that if he let himself wake up he would not go back to sleep even if she did. If he fully awoke, even after just a short sleep, he was awake, and would not sleep again for some hours.

He became aware that something was brushing against his face, and it was not pleasant. He tried to blow away whatever it was, but it continued. Slowly but surely this irritation was bringing him out of his slumber until he eventually realised that he was *compos mentis* and that the irritation was hair. Jane had long hair, but it was straight. She knew that it irritated his face so if she opted for the armchair position, she gathered her hair and put it between her neck and pillow so that it was out of the way. The hair in his face was wavy and voluminous. He moved his hand from its seatbelt position and tried to smooth this irritation away. As he stroked it away, she spoke. It was at this time that he realised that this was not Jane. He turned his head towards the ceiling to get the hair out of his mouth and nose and opened his eyes. The room was jet black, and he registered the next flash of lightning through the curtains, and then the imminent crack of thunder some seconds later. Having seen the flash, he quickly replaced his arm into the seatbelt position which means that his elbow is on the bed by her tummy and his hand on at the top of her left arm.

'Are you okay?' he whispered to her.

'I'm sorry I woke you' she whimpered as she responded to the thunder crack.

'Let's not worry about that. Let's see if we can get you comfortable and settled.' He realised that her bottom was just below his waist. If he could move her deep into his groin her hair would be below his chin level and thus no irritation. 'I'm going to move you down so that your hair is out of my face' he whispered, 'can you use your hands to bring your hair down where it's comfortable for you?'

'Okay' she whispered.

He moved her down deep into his groin so that her bottom was directly in his lap hard into his groin. She bought her hair down and tucked her head below his chin. Perfect he thought. But no sooner had this firm warm bottom hit his penis than the dragon was awakened, and he could feel the start of an erection. 'I'm afraid that your warm bottom has awakened the dragon, so you'll feel him grow up your back. Just give him some room, let him do his thing, and then he'll go back to sleep.'

By now she could feel what he meant and giggled. 'You're naked' she exclaimed.

'I always sleep naked.'

Then she burst out into uncontrollable laughter. He didn't know what to do until she spoke 'my valiant knight has drawn his sword to protect his damsel in distress', continuing her laughter.

He was going to respond but realised that she had completely missed the last crash of thunder. He now had a full erection and she wiggled her bottom to give him some room, still giggling.

She turned to face him. 'I can understand why you think this position is comforting, but can I just cuddle up to you and find a position that works for both of us.'

'Okay, where do you want to be?'

She rolled him back a little so that she could tuck her head into his shoulder and still breathe, with his left arm behind her, and with her breasts against his torso. After some manoeuvring, she asked him if he was okay with where she was. This was a normal cuddle position with no hair in his face, so he was happy. 'Now put you right arm around me', she said. Paul complied. 'That's good' she murmured as he felt her relax.

After some minutes of just lying there he started to stroke her back. It proved difficult for him to hold a static pose with the right arm in this position. In any event Jane loved her back to be stroked, and this would cause her to drift off to sleep. The difference was that Cis was wearing a top so when he started from the nape of her neck moving down her spine there was a jerk as he hit the neck of her top.

After a few minutes she murmured 'that's so nice. Is this what you do with Jane?'

'Yes, it really works with her' he whispered back.

'Does she sleep naked as well?'

'Yes, why?'

'Your skin to skin stroke is so delicate it doesn't really work through my top. Anyway, I need the toilet'. With that she popped off to the bathroom.

When she returned, she stood by the bed pondering a decision. *'Andy has not really touched me in months. This man has a natural touch that electrifies me. Is it okay to let this man touch me some more?'* She then lifted her top over her head and dropped it on the bed. She crawled back into the cuddle position. Paul started to stroke again realising that her top had gone. She murmured 'that's better'.

He had two stroking techniques. One technique is used to put his partner to sleep and involved a gentle stoking action from the nape of her neck down to her waist. The other is intended as a form of sensual arousal and involves stimulating the energy

Prejudice in Love

lines referred to in yoga and oriental massage as Sen energy lines or chakra with added stimulus to the energy centres. This starts with her back from the base of her skull to her buttocks, but then will progress anywhere on the body with the ultimate energy centre on a woman being her clitoris. There is a delicate difference in touch between a sensual stimulation and a tickle, and he was proficient in ensuring that he aroused, not tickled.

When he stroked Jane, he would stroke with the pads of his fingers all the way down to the base of her spine, around the cheeks of her bottom, and then stroke her rib cage on the way back. Cis was still wearing her shorts which stopped at her hips, so he figured that the top of her shorts was the demarcation line. He stroked down to the top of her shorts but under the band into the top of the cleft between her buttocks, turned his hand so that just the back of a fingernail glided along the line of her shorts until it was time to start the return stroke. This was not a continuous stroke in that he would periodically stroke her neck and shoulders and use a five-finger stroke covering all four energy lines in her back. She clearly liked this as she snuggled in even closer with her breasts now pressed firmly into Paul's chest.

Some time passed, and he hoped that she would go to sleep. Then a soft voice came up from his chest 'You should patent your finger style. I've never had a man touch me with such electrifying deliciousness. I could have you stroke me all day.'

It then occurred to him that he was not using a 'go to sleep' stroke, he was arousing her. Now what to do as she clearly wants more? But she has not reacted to any of the thunder and lightning raging outside.

'I like to stroke beautiful bodies. I like to feel the response. It's like a delicate act of sensual pleasure.'

'You can say that again' came the murmured response, 'I want more.'

With this she rolled onto her back and put her hands on the pillow in a submissive mode. He started at her left shoulder, and with all four finger pads, gently glided downward feeling the start of her breast and adjusting his middle two fingers so that they would glide each side of her left nipple. She purred as his fingers slipped over the top of her breast just glancing her nipple, and then continuing down slowly to the line of her shorts. Then he glided all fingers over her belly, but then changing to a scoop hand just skimming her body with the side of his little finger until he reached the right breast at which time his whole hand glided over her right breast with the side of the little finger glancing over her nipple, finishing at her right shoulder. She arched her back and gave out a sigh as his hand scooped over her breast. He repeated the process but in reverse with the finger pads moving over the right breast and the scoop over the left breast. He repeated this process with the odd variation a few more times.

He knew they had crossed a line, so he must keep control of this situation, especially as he had a throbbing erection. However, he knew that this stroking was infinitely more pleasurable without the interference of bed clothes, and she was really enjoying this attention. He eased himself up onto his left elbow, and gently moved the bed clothes from her upper body. She did not move. He started the whole process again. After a few minutes, when her skin temperature had dropped a little making the skin more responsive to touch, the stroking was getting more and more reaction. He decided to widen his stroke to cover the energy lines in her face, and glide over her shorts onto her thighs having moved the bed clothes down to her knees, knowing cold feet would be a turn-off.

Now she was at a point where a gentle stroke across her abdomen would cause spasms in her tummy muscles. He wanted to show what he could do with a naked body. Jane loved this passive sensuality. He decided to test the water. He did a full stroke all the way down to her right thigh, but instead of moving to the left thigh he moved his forefinger to the insider of her thigh and gently and slowly stoked upwards so that he made contact with the lips of her vagina following the curve to the top of her clitoris, and then opening out his fingers to skim over her tummy and both breasts at the same time.

She rolled over and kissed him on the cheek. 'Where do you want to go with this?' She whispered.

'I want you to let me stroke your body in any way I want. If you find something unacceptable just quietly tell me. When you want to stop, just say so.'

'What about sex?' She asked.

'We are nowhere near that yet, and in any event, you would have to make the first move. There are rules. The first time must be you to initiate, and you on top.'

'You and your rules' she giggled, 'why me on top?'

'Because in that way you have total control. You can back out at any time; you have control over penetration – it's just better all round.'

'Okay, I buy that. Can we get back to stroking?'

'Okay, lie back, close your eyes and enjoy.'

Paul removed her shorts, albeit it in total darkness. He placed her legs open to completely expose her inner thighs and re-covered her feet. After a few minutes of stroking he decided to test the next step.

This time on the up stroke on the inside of her thighs he glided along the lips of her vagina but then stopped and pushed backward opening her lips to reveal the juices of arousal. He was surprised to feel how well-groomed she was, hardly any pubic hair, just how he liked it. He caressed the inside of her lips whilst she just murmured with pleasure. He located the line of her clitoris and started to gently caress it.

'Hmmm, a man who knows how to touch a woman.'

He continued working her clitoris until he sensed that she was starting the build to a climax. He then moved his finger up to her belly button, stroking just below. This aroused a different purr as her tummy started to spasm.

She was in a dream world of pleasure. Too many times over recent months she had to rely on fantasy to satisfy her desires, but this hand in the dark was taking her to places even she had not imagined. The heat in her loins were causing her to sweat. The feelings that surged through her body made her feel excitement and anticipation of what she would experience next as his hand moved around her body stimulating all manner of emotions.

He moved his finger back to the line of her clitoris and started to massage again. This time she built quickly. Within a few minutes she would orgasm. Without any warning she moved her right hand down to find his erection. Her groans indicated she was now in a state of total pleasure. He could feel the spasms growing in her loins but kept the tempo of his stroke constant to slow the build and maximise the impact.

The first spasm of orgasm came. Her breathing was faster, groaning on each breath. The second spasm came, then the third, then rapid spasm until she exploded, her whole body in spasm. She clamped her legs together as the extreme pleasure screamed through her body. She grabbed him with both arms and held him close to her until the spasms had subsided. Then she just lay back on the pillow total spent – totally satisfied. He gently restored the bed covers to cover their bodies.

He could not see her face but wondered what was going through her mind. After a few minutes he whispered, 'A penny for your thoughts.'

'A summary would be what a difference a day makes. Who are you? You've done so much for me, and now you're the first man ever to successfully masturbate me, and wow, how good are you? You make my body sing with pleasure. You take your time. You know how to bring me up, and then let me drop back a little knowing that when I orgasm, I'll explode. And you

Prejudice in Love

demand nothing in return. Long live this adventure. You can stroke me anytime, anywhere, anyhow.'

'It will be a little time before you can settle down to sleep so how about we use this darkness to talk a little more.'

'I totally surrender to you, what do you want to know?'

'Can you tell me about your relationship with Andy as I get the feeling that you two are not as close as you should be?'

'If he could touch me like you can, he would be my Adonis. We know each other from University. He's your typical sporty type. Played rugby for the University but didn't succeed in making any of the national teams. If I'm brutally honest we eventually got married to stop the commutes between London and Edinburgh to see each other. I had already made my mark in the fashion industry, which of course is in London. He's building a distribution business in Scotland, and is fiercely loyal to Scotland, so will not move. In fact, I gave up my position in London to move to Edinburgh and thus why I freelance now. But it's good. I have good editors who always want my work, so I earn very well.'

'What about starting a family? I know it's fashionable for career women to want to establish themselves before having children but at 28 you are starting to limit your options.'

'We've been trying for a family for 2 years, but without success. The situation is so desperate I now monitor ovulation and try to ensure that we try whilst I'm ovulating, but without success. Andy's so fed up with the failure that we only have sex when I push. Something must be wrong with one, or both of us. I've tried to get Andy to a fertility clinic to have us tested, but he keeps putting it off. I thought of going on my own but that would be a mistake. We should do it together.'

'Now we hardly see each other. He's constantly in some far-flung place organising products he wants to import, or I'm in London or Paris. Hence your astute observation that we don't contact each other. I don't know what will happen to us.

Perhaps this adventure will open my eyes, as one thing is for sure, I need more of what we had tonight. Not just the sex, but the intimate company and companionship.'

'Do I assume that both you and Andy are the first serious relationships, and you rely on each other to find what works for you in your sex life?'

'Yes, but I don't think we're very good if after just two years he will not touch me. Do you mind if we try to get some sleep? This conversation is a depressing way to end such a wonderful experience.'

'Not just yet. You cannot go to sleep thinking about such things. I need to find something to give you nice thoughts so that you sleep peacefully now the thunder has passed.'

'How about you cuddle me again, and just stroke my back. That will certainly give me lovely thoughts.'

He reached out for her, got her settled in his arms, stroked her back but in go-to-sleep mode, and she was asleep in minutes.

Chapter 12 - Monday

Paul awoke, as usual, around 7:15am although he was never totally awake until under a shower. If Jane is at home, he has to get her off to the station for London by 6:30am so he would crawl out of bed around 6:15 in autopilot to get her eggs and fruit smoothie ready for a quick breakfast. He would then either go back to bed or sit in his study to listen to the news on Radio 4 until between 7am and 7:30 at which time he would start to get up.

This morning he realise that his left arm was completely numb from the elbow down, and she was still firmly up against him. Shades of light were streaming through the edges of the curtains revealing her profile with the backdrop of the white pillows and sheets. It was still raining, albeit no longer with any ferocity, but the cloud cover meant that the light was not strong. As usual the first thing he needed upon awaking is the toilet. He realised that he could not lift her with his numb arm, so he moved his shoulder upwards and round her head so that she lay on the pillow so that he was free to slide out of bed.

He saw the robe on the floor and thought *'we're way past the need for a robe'* so stepped over it and made his way to the bathroom. Once inside he quietly closed the door shielding his eyes from the light to give them time to adjust, and then made his way to the toilet. He sat down, as usual in the morning as he did not trust his aim before his shower. When he'd finished, he sat there waiting for the numbness in his left arm to subside. His left shoulder joint was also quite stiff.

Once the pain had all but diminished, he arose, flushed the toilet, and moved to the nearest wash basin where he turned the tap lever all the way to cold and started the water flow. Putting his hand under the water flow waiting for it to get as cold as it could get, he moved his head towards the basin and splashed the cold water into his eyes. The bedroom was warm and dry causing him to suffer from dry eyes in the morning and splashing them with cold water gave them the jolt they needed to rehydrate. Once he felt they could now open and fully focus he wiped them with a towel to dry his face. Having then taken a few swigs of water to get his mouth working he made his way back to the door, switched off the light, and waited a few seconds for his eyes to readjust before moving back towards the bed. He stopped on the way to put his head through the curtains to see for himself the intensity of the rain. It was okay, the worst was over.

He tried to crawl back into bed, lying on his back, but she was so close that he could not help brushing against her. She responded by somehow rolling over his arm, head back into his shoulder, but still asleep. Once she was settled his thoughts started to reflect on what had happened in the early hours of the morning. It was very nice, and he had certainly not crossed any lines in the sand as far as Jane was concerned. Earlier in their relationship they both travelled so much that they had a pact about flings whilst travelling, and he was nowhere near the boundary of that pact. But his thought then turned to guilt. Had he taken advantage of this damsel in distress? Did he use her distress to his own ends? She certainly enjoyed the experience, but had he broken trust with her?

He was brought back out of his thought by her stirring in his arms. It was a little lighter now, especially as he had left the curtains slightly open. He could see her face as her eyes opened. She looked at him and took a little time to assess the situation. She registered that she was naked under the bedclothes. She moved her head closer to his ear and in a calm sweet voice she whispered, 'I had a wonderful dream, but now I think it wasn't a dream'.

'What did you dream?'

'That I was being stroked all over my body by a wonderful hand that made me feel soooo good' as she wrapped her arm around his chest to get closer.

He used his free hand to gently stroke her back. 'Something like this?' he whispered.

'Hmmm' was the reply. 'You were very nice to me.'

He felt her breasts press against his chest, and his hands were going the full distance along her spine, down along the crease in her buttocks, and around the cheeks of her bottom before making the ascent back up to the nape of her neck. He could feel an erection coming, and before he had concluded another full sweep of her back, he was fully erect. She was trying to expose more of her back to his touch so tried to get flatter on his chest by swinging her leg over his thigh which brought her thigh directly into contact with his erection. She moved her hand down to find this erect penis and ran her finger around the exposed head. 'I think it's time we became acquainted' she whispered.

She raised herself up and sat astride him. She then moved her hand down to hold his erection whilst she manoeuvred her thighs to line her vagina with the head of his penis. She lowered herself onto the head. Paul could feel that she was so wet that she just slid onto him. He was now fully penetrated deep inside her. She rotated her hips a little and then whispered, 'what a big boy you are'. He could see the outline of her beautiful breasts firmly protruding from her chest. He reached up to stroke them and cupped them in his hand. She leaned forward a little as though offering her breasts to him, and then started a gentle rise and fall, rising to about three-quarters of his penis length before descending back to full penetration. She had her hands on his chest and moved around a little pushing backwards on the up stroke trying to find the angle of maximum sensation for herself.

Insisting that a woman goes on top for the first act of intercourse was not only a rule for him, it was also the time for him to observe at what angle she got maximum pleasure so that he could ensure that he could emulate the best position on future occasions.

Her rhythm started to get faster and more intense. She had found her spot and was about to indulge in unfettered fun. Her grip on his chest was getting stronger. He slowly ran his hands from her knees, along her thighs, round her buttocks to her waist and then upwards to her breasts where he gently but firmly pinched her nipples which were now fully extended.

'More' she said as the intensity was now at fever pitch.

He pinched her nipples again, this time gently pulling them towards him. She erupted in multiple spasms and an involuntary 'ahhhh' as her orgasm reached its peak. She pushed back to full penetration. He could feel her spasms through his groin.

She held her grip on his chest until the spasms had receded. She then started to rise to decouple, but he stopped her.

'No, no' he said gently, 'just lean forward flat onto my chest.'

She did as he asked still fully penetrated and putting her head to one side on his shoulder. He started to gently stroke her again.

'Try to stretch your legs out, one at a time, on either side of mine without losing penetration.'

She carefully obeyed until the weight of her pelvis was now firmly on top of his. He now stroked her all the way down as far as he could reach. She was purring like a satisfied cat. He had not ejaculated so he could hold his erection a little longer.

Holding the top of her hips, he started to gently rotate her pelvis in the hope that her clitoris was in contact with him. Within seconds the spasms started again, and she climaxed for a second time. He could feel the warm juices from her vagina running down his shaft onto his testicles. She was totally submissive, just letting him stroke her and move her as he wished.

The heat from her loins was now having the wrong effect on his erection, and he could feel himself slowly but surely retracting from within her. She did not move. Soon he was all but out of her and decided to roll her back beside him. Again, she just did as he wanted except that she kept her head firmly in his shoulder.

After a few minutes of silence, she whispered, 'that's the only way to start the day' and kissed him on the cheek. 'My dad always told me never to have sex with a man on a first date. How wrong was that?' Silence again. Then 'I need the toilet, don't move.'

She scrambled off the bed into the bathroom. When she returned there was enough light to see her naked body in its full glory. She was like a marble Venus. She took her time knowing that he was feasting his eyes with her. She liked the way he looked at her.

When she was back in his arms it occurred to her that he had not ejaculated. She looked at him. 'Did I come too quickly for you?'

'No. I was unsure about coming into you – could be dangerous.'

'It's okay', she said reassuringly. 'I check myself for ovulation, remember, and I'm not ovulating right now.' She reached down to find his limp penis and started to play with it in her hand. He soon came to life with her sensual touch.

'Time for me to return the pleasure you gave to me last night.'

She pushed the blankets back, and whilst still holding his penis reached down to plant her mouth over the head, gently swirling her tongue around the base. She continued to use her tongue and lips until she felt that the erection was strong, and then started to slowly masturbate him. Her head was now on his chest as she watched herself in action. He stroked her neck with one hand and reached for her breast with the other. Her touch was perfect, and her stroke was slow and sensual. He could feel the waves of pleasure as she started to get a positive response. Then the waves of pleasure turned to the spasms of orgasm as he felt the burning pleasure of pre-ejaculation. She kept the stoke rate constant as he pinched her nipple. A gush of semen landing over his hand and her breast, and then another more intense landing at the top of her arm. Spent, he indicated for her to stop. She looked up at him and said 'Mr Fulton, I can confirm that your sexual function is in good working order'.

She bounced off the bed to get a towel with which she dried both of them.

'Okay big boy, what is on the agenda for today?' as she lay back in his arms.

'As the bar has now been truly raised can I suggest as follows. Firstly, we take a shower together where we will bathe each other. Then we'll prepare ourselves for breakfast and adjourn to the breakfast lounge. Having completed breakfast, we'll get an update on the situation out there to see whether it's safe to continue our journey north. Then much depends on whether I drop you in Glasgow, or I steal you away and take you with me to Luss.'

Lifting her head off the pillow 'Are you inviting me to come with you to Luss?' She said cautiously.

'That's what I implied.'

'Can I have a moment to consider' short pause feigning deep in thought 'of course I will come with you. Our adventure could not possibly end here.' Pause. 'I don't have suitable clothes for Luss, and I'll need more underwear.'

'Then we need to add a shopping excursion to our trip north. There must be a decent shopping centre somewhere around Glasgow.'

'There is', she responded with excitement. 'Braehead Shopping Centre is just a few minutes off the M3 motorway. I go there with a girlfriend when I visit her in Glasgow, so I even know the shops I need. I want you to choose my underwear. Do you prefer sexy Ann Summers or the naughty La Senza?'

He smiled at her joy and enthusiasm and said that Ann Summers would be fine. She held him so tight he thought he would break. He smacked her bottom playfully 'well let's get to it, we have a long way to go'. She grabbed his hand and dragged him off to the shower.

Chapter 13

She put towels on the rack next to the shower and started the water. 'Do you like it hot, or not so hot?' she said without looking at him.

He was certainly looking at her in full light thinking he was in a dream standing here with this naked goddess. 'Not so hot please. Do you want your hair washed?'

Prejudice in Love

She moved closer to him, grabbed him around the waist, and looked into his eyes 'I have messed around in a shower before, and Andy and I have baths together, but I get the feeling that what you have in mind is different, so could you please give me directions.'

He looked at her and smiled at this innocent beauty 'If you want your hair washing then I start with your hair. Then I bathe your body, the full works, except for your face as how women bathe their faces has always been a mystery to me. Then before I rinse you down you repeat the whole process on me. We then rinse each other off and towel each other. If you want body lotion, I will apply this for you. There's no sex – too dangerous in a shower. What we do is to sensually pamper each other. Are you ready?'

'Yes, and I would love you to wash my hair. I have my own shampoo. Let me get it.'

He was standing close behind her whilst she stood under the shower head wetting her hair. When it was completely wet, she turned to him and he applied the shampoo slowly massaging it into her head and then running his fingers through her hair. She held him around the waist throughout as he worked his way through the sheer volume of her hair needing to recharge with shampoo twice more. He then eased her backwards under the shower head to rinse away the shampoo. She was totally compliant with what he wanted her to do.

Having finished with her he made sure that she was suitably wet and then moved her out of the water flow, turned her to face the wall and asked her to support herself with her hands against the wall, arms straight, and legs apart. He primed both of his palms with shower gel and started on her shoulders gently washing her, moving down first one arm, and then the other. He then recharged his palms with gel, reached under her arms and cupped her breasts and started to slowly massage each breast, and then moving up to her shoulder, finished at her neckline. Another recharge of gel and he reach round under her breasts again slowly massaging her rib cage, her tummy, and then down to her loins. Although his hands were wet, he could feel that when he parted the lips of her vagina, she was totally wet.

He asked her to turn around and hold him around the neck. She said nothing, just a big smile on her face. He recharged his hands with gel and started to caress her back. Then down to her buttocks including running one finger down her crease to her anus. Then another recharge, asked her to let go of his neck, and crouched down to wash her legs getting her to put one foot on his knee while her washed it including putting his fingers between her toes, and then the other.

When he stood again, he said 'your turn'.

She put him under the water to douse him. She gently washed his hair. She washed his front facing him washing his chest in circular motions, and then moving down to his ribs and stomach area. She then recharged with gel and went straight for his penis which was already standing to attention. She was gentle as she paid attention to every curve before progressing to his legs, and feet. She turned him around and repeated the process on his back finishing by grabbing him around the waist and using her breasts to scrub his back which he thought was a nice touch.

The rinse down was equally as sensual for both as they did not leave one square centimetre of each other's bodies untouched. Paul gave her hair a final rinse and then switched off the shower. He used his hand to gently wipe the excess water from her body and wring out her hair. He wiped the excess water from his own body and reached for a towel. She still said nothing, just kept smiling while he towelled her and wrapped her hair in a smaller towel. She took a towel and gently and lovingly towelled him. She reached up to his neck, pulled his head down to her and kissed him 'Thank you.'

'Do you want body lotion?'

'Will I desperately want sex straight afterwards?'

'Possibly.'

'Then let me do it on this occasion or else we'll miss breakfast.'

'Can I dress you for breakfast?'

'Whatever you want. Tip out my bag and see what you can find that is still clean and suitable.'

With that he left the bathroom, got himself dressed, and then turned out her travel bag onto the bed. She was right, the clothes she had with her were more city than country. He found underwear but only needed the panties for what he had in mind. He found a very suitable designer jumper top, but all he could find in terms of lower garment was her designer jeans which would not be his first choice with more clothes to choose from.

He went back for a shave just as she was completing the chore of hair drying. She brushed out her hair which shone beautifully. 'Just makeup now and I'll be ready to be dressed. Did you find anything?'

'Stuck with the jeans, but after our shopping trip things will be better. Not too much makeup – in fact, bare minimum. I would prefer a raw country look.'

She looked at him wondering what he had in mind, but she had no complaints so far. *'Let's see what he wants.'* She thought it rather special that this man was so interested in pampering her after so many months of famine.

She walked into the bedroom where he was sitting on the edge of the bed with her clothes beside him. 'Come here'. She stood in front of him waiting for the next instruction. He picked up her panties and put his hand through the legs so that his hands would be holding her buttocks and the thumbs opening the front. He reached down and asked her to put her feet into the panties. He then slowly raised his hands just gliding the back of her legs.

'It's that touch again' she thought, *'so nice.'*

As his hands got past her knees, he kissed her tummy and then brought the panties into position with his hands still inside, so his hands were touching her buttocks, and his thumbs were on the front of her hips. He then slowly removed his hand. To her surprise, he put two fingers through the front of the panties moving them down over her vagina to ensure that they sat properly in that delicate region. She felt herself explode with pleasure.

Satisfied that her panties were properly in place he picked up her jeans. 'Not so easy' she said, 'so you may need my help.'

She put her legs into the jeans but had to help him get them over her hips. He then picked up her top.

'Where's my bra?'

'With such beautifully pert breasts a bra can only do you an injustice. I would like you to wear this top without a bra. It's heavy enough not to show your extended nipples. I would like to see your natural beauty.'

'Okay', she said as she put up her arms to take the top.

He looked at the finished product. 'Jeans are not the greatest, but I like the rest.'

Not wearing a bra did give her a more natural shape, and he showed her this in the mirror.

Off they went to breakfast. 'Eat well' he told her 'it might be dinner tonight before we eat again.'

Chapter 14

After breakfast they strolled back to their room. When they were safely alone in the top floor corridor, she turned to him 'It's a real turn on with my nipples rubbing against this top, but you're right, the jeans are not good with my pussy so volcanic. I'll have to wear something else for the drive.'

'Sounds good to me', he smiled.

Prejudice in Love

Playfully 'Can I hire you to put on my panties every day?'

'I would be delighted.'

As soon as she got into the room, she rid herself of the jeans, staying in her top and panties. Paul had the TV news on to see what was happening out there. He switched through news and traffic channels to find that the M6 motorway should be running freely by noon. He phoned the hotel in Luss to confirm that he could travel.

'By the way', he said to the hotel receptionist, 'I have just looked at my booking confirmation and notice that I had some finger trouble. I seem to have put 1 adult, 1 room, where, of course it should be 2 adults, 1 room. Do I need to revise my booking with the agency, or can you make the change?' The response was 'No problem sir we just need to add another breakfast; the room rate is the same.'

'Great', Paul replied, 'we'll also need dinner this evening. Say around 7:30pm but give us a little latitude as it's still a long drive.'

'No problem sir, we'll see you later today'.

'Thank you so much' and he terminated the call.

She listened to this slick operator – *'so smooth'*.

She started to put her clothes back into her bag trying to decide what she would wear for the journey. She decided to stay with the bra-less top but found a skirt that would be appropriate for both a long drive and a shopping trip. She then went to the bathroom to pack her toilet bag. When she returned, he was sitting on the end of the bed. He looked deep in thought, as if questioning something. Thinking he may be having second thoughts about her going to Luss with him she went to him, standing directly in front of him.

'What is it?' She asked gently.

He looked up at her but said nothing. He just stared at her.

Eventually he reached out and held her hips. 'There's something I would like to try, but I don't know if I'm up to it. Something that has bothered me for some time.'

She could see the doubt in him, so she reached out and stroked his cheek tenderly. 'Just tell me want you want me to do.'

'Take off your top.'

She did so without delay throwing it on the bed. He still had his hands on her hips, but now moved them so that his hands moved up inside her panties in the same way as when he put them on her and slowly removed them. Her knees were already shaking in expectation. He then stroked the lips of her vagina as he gently kissed each breast. He stood, removed his clothes, and sat back on the bed, but further back.

'I want you to get on the bed and stand directly in front of me with your feet either side of my hips. Use the canopy as support.'

She did as he asked. Her vagina was now right in front of his face. She wondered what would come next. He kissed her halfway between her midriff and her vagina. Then he did what she would never have expected. She felt his tongue following the curves of the lips of her vagina. His tongue then separated her wet lips and she felt his mouth gently sucking her. His hands were now firmly gripping both her buttocks. His tongue then started to flick at her clitoris. This was nice, she could feel the heat in her loins as she automatically curved herself to give him better access. He was working her with his lips and tongue. She was buzzing with electric sensations.

He kissed her vagina, and then stopped.

'Lower yourself slowly into a squat position without moving your feet. Use my shoulders for support and I'll guide you down with my hands.'

She obeyed and slowly moved down knowing where she was going. As she approached his groin, he guided her vagina to meet with the head of his now throbbing penis. She felt contact and knew she would easily slide onto him into his lap. Once she was sitting in his lap, he slightly adjusted the position of her heals to give her leverage. 'Clasp your hands behind my neck.'

'I'm going to open my legs and drop you into my hands to achieve full penetration.'

'Use your legs to push out and I'll bring you back.'

He looked her in the eyes, kissed her on the lips, 'I want you to control the rhythm. Tell me to go faster or slower, and whether to thrust harder or softer.'

She nodded and started the first push.

They started slowly to get a rhythm. They were quickly connected as she upped the pace a little. She felt her body relax giving move flexible motion to her loins. He felt this and added a little rotation to the thrusts. He also felt her make slight adjustments to the angle of penetration as she found the best angle to stimulate her. There was a wayward look in her eyes as she whispered, 'faster, harder'. He responded and could feel the heat and fluids flowing inside her. Her head went backwards as she helped him to thrust into her even harder. He felt the first spasm in her loins, and then another as she forced the pace even faster. The spasms grew rapid until she exploded with a long gasp of pleasure locking her legs around his back at full penetration, and wrapping her arms around his neck, pulling herself as close as she could to him.

He was breathless. The support he needed to give her when the frenzy started tested all the strength in his arms, back and legs. He felt like he had a workout. But he was smiling with satisfaction. He'd done it, he had maintained a full erection throughout the whole process, a problem that had dogged him for a few years. The feeling of his hard erection fully penetrated inside her felt satisfyingly good.

As the spasms subsided, he decided to lift her back into his lap to take the weight from his arms. She realised what he was doing and moved her body just enough to sit low in his lap but maintaining as much penetration as she could. She could feel that he was still fully erect, and this gave her added pleasure as it throbbed inside of her. She held her grip a while longer and then whispered in his ear 'Was that as good for you as it was for me?'

'It was great for me.'

She moved her head back so that she could look into his eyes looking for something and then kissed him before moving her head back over his shoulder.

He could feel his erection waning so moved closer to the edge of the bed and stood up lifting her with him. She used her legs to grip around his waist not ready to let go. He moved around to the side of the bed and slowly put her down on the bed and lay with her. They were now lying locked together, each in their own thoughts. As she came out of her daze, she moved her head so that she could see his face. 'Did you get what you needed?'

'Yes, and thanks.'

'What was it that you needed because you get 11 out of 10 for effort, my pussy is still throbbing with joy.'

'It's a long story, but you have helped me with a problem that has bugged me for a while.'

Playfully shaking him 'tell me, tell me. I like long stories, and this is the second time you have used the long story routine. I want to know about this person who gives me so much pleasure. I want to know you.'

'Okay', he said, 'but ask me at dinner tonight, or better still, in the darkness of the night when we're wrapped up with each other.'

She looked into his eyes to see if she could see any pain, but all she saw was calm satisfaction.

'Can I ask a favour of you' she said meekly.

Prejudice in Love

He looked at her 'sure, this is not a one-way street.'

'Sometime over the next few days will you make love to me?'

'What do you mean?'

'You have a special way with me, a way I've never felt before. You don't approach sex in any way I've experienced before. You have a special feel and touch. What did you say in the shower? Sensual pampering. Yes, whatever you do to me I feel pampered with tenderness and affection. I want to know what that feels like when we really make love together.'

He looked her in the eyes 'That's really raising the bar, are you sure that your relationship with Andy can take such betrayal?'

She looked at him, 'you see, always considerate. The bar was thrown out of the window when I jumped you this morning. Okay you say what we just did helped you with a problem, but you must have felt the total togetherness. You're giving me experiences I've never felt before. For God's sake, we only met yesterday but I feel like we've been together forever. I've had 4 out of the 4 non-solo orgasms that I've had all year in this room with you. You clearly like to play with my body, and I willingly give you free reign without question to do want you want – not even Andy gets that liberty – he cannot make me feel the way I feel in your arms.' She paused as if struggling to find the words. 'I want more, I want to know what it is to be loved by you.'

She stopped. He thought about what she had said. It made him feel good. This woman made him feel alive, why would he not agree.

She spoke again somewhat meekly. 'Have I raised the bar too much for your relationship with Jane? Am I asking you to betray her?'

He looked at her smiling 'we are nowhere near the limits of the bar as far as Jane goes. I have one small infringement, but I assessed the risk and see no problem.'

Quizzically she asked, 'what infringement do you mean, and can you tell me the height of the bar?'

'The infringement is not using a condom, but I know your history so not a problem. The bar is that you do not bring anything home except memories, no repeats, just memories. If you want more, don't come home.'

'Wow, that is liberal. It would freak Andy out if I even suggested such an idea.'

'But what about where we are now? Do you think you would have stopped at me just touching you? Can humans control their emotions so precisely? What Jane and I have makes sense, and incredibly I know that neither of us takes much advantage of our liberty in any event. I haven't done anything like this in some years. Sometimes freedom reduces the need to explore. A bit like kids; you tell them they can't do something so what do they do? If you tell them it's okay, they can't be bothered as the excitement and intrigue have gone.'

She looked at him meekly 'I'm way over the line, but I don't feel any guilt at all. I want more – is that shameful?'

'No. You're finding yourself, and what you want rather than what is expected of you. I don't want to be a marriage breaker, especially as I have no intention of breaking my relationship with Jane. But I'm free to go where you want to go and will only stop when you think you need to.'

'This is truly a strange liaison. So, will you make love to me?'

Paul looked at her with a big smile on his face. 'We do need to raise the bar before then if it's to work.'

'What do you mean?'

'We need to add kissing to our repertoire' he said smiling, 'I have never considered that kissing was my strong point and have never rated myself as a good kisser.'

She pushed him onto his back, got on top of him, and said 'close your eyes and enjoy. In this department I know a thing or

Prejudice in Love

two. Other than submissive response you only do something if I tell you to.' She then proceeded to tenderly kiss him on his forehead, and then each eye, the tip of his nose, and then gently brushed his lips. She kept coming back to his lips, each time more intensive and prolonged than the previous kiss. Her tongue flicked along the length of his lips, and on the next visit she eased his lips open with her tongue. He could feel the heat of her breath on his lips as he submissively allowed them to part. She explored the inside of his lips with her tongue, and then gently took his bottom lip between her lips and pulled his lip into her mouth as she massaged his lip with hers. He could feel the intensity in her, and he found it infectious as the full kiss arrived. She was delicious as he savoured every moment of her sensuality.

She raised herself 'With a little practice we should have you in good shape.'

He noted that she was excited to be in the driving seat, and he liked it. He glanced at the bedside clock. 'Come on lady, it's nearly 11 o'clock. We need to hit the road.'

'Just a minute' she said, 'don't move.' She disappeared into the bathroom and re-emerged a few minutes later with two flannels and a towel. She planted herself across his legs and started to clean his now deflated penis. Paul had his hands behind his head looking on with some amusement.

'Do you ever consider that Andy plays away on his trips?'

'I think about it sometimes, and especially when he went off sex with me. I used to encourage sex when he got home so that I could take a good look at his willy for any signs of activity. Look here at your willy.' She gently pulled back his foreskin and was pointing to the skin just below the head. 'These slightly red marks indicate that you've been active. But I never found any signs on him. Maybe he's embarrassed about his sexuality, as he certainly prefers a bar or pub.' Having dried him with the towel she raised her hips from his legs and used the second flannel to clean herself, and then dry herself with the towel.

'Okay lady, dressed, packed, and out of here.'

Cutely 'Just one more thing. Will you put my panties on? In fact, I would like you to be in charge of my panties for the rest of our time together.'

He laughed. 'Okay, let's find your panties and get you dressed. If you need a pit stop now is the time.'

She took the flannels and towel back to the bathroom and returned a few minutes later to find him already dressed. She neatly placed her top, skirt, and panties on the bed and stood ready to be dressed. Paul repeated the process with her panties, much to her delight. He then picked up the skirt and looked at it.

'Is this over the head, or step in?' he asked.

'There's a zip on the side and then it's step in.'

He undid the zip and reached down for her to step in. Once both legs were in, he gently raised the skirt to her waist, zipped it closed, and hooked the eye at the top. Sitting back to inspect his work he made a small adjustment so that the skirt sat properly on her hips and thought 'job done'. He then picked up her top, stood up and let her slip her arms into the sleeves before placing it over her head. She lifted her hair from beneath the top whilst he ensured that it sat well on her.

'How did I do?' he asked.

'You're hired' she said with some aloof.

'Okay, get your things together and let's be on our way.'

She finished loading her bags, and took one more look in the bathroom to make sure she had everything. She slipped into her shoes and went to the cupboard to retrieve both of their coats. She grabbed her bags and reported 'ready for inspection m'lord.'

He liked her playfulness, looked at her, 'you'll do', and guided her to the door.

Chapter 15

At reception he settled the bill and they headed for the entrance. It was still raining. 'I'll get the car and bring it to the door.'

She put on her coat with hood up 'don't be silly, it's only over there' pointing to his car. 'We can make a dash for it.'

They both dashed for the car, He clicked it open as they approached. He quickly lifted the tailgate, bags in, tailgate down, into car, coats off. He kicked the engine into life and keyed the "Braehead Shopping Centre" into the satnav. '244 miles to Braehead, about 3 – 4 hours. It's almost midday, so we should be there around 4 o'clock.'

'Why do you need your satnav? I know where the shopping centre is' she said.

'Firstly, I need to get back to the motorway, and then you are right if you know all of the road works and traffic jams we may encounter. The satnav has a live feed to the traffic centre and will warn me if there is trouble ahead, and even guide me around it. The storm will have left its mark, and I want to avoid any problems if possible.'

She sat in her seat looking out of the window feeling chastised 'clever stuff this modern technology'.

He looked at her, gave her a reassuring smile. 'Are you ready to go shopping?'

She smiled back 'when is a woman not ready to go shopping'. With that they started for Scotland.

Chapter 16

The drive to Braehead Shopping Centre was uneventful. The rain had stopped as they passed the Preston exit of the M6 motorway, and by the time they were passing along the edges of the Lake District the sky was clear, and the sun shining. He drove the 244 miles in just 3 hours 20 minutes.

He had prevented any interruption to the drive by Jane as she would normally text him around 2pm to see if he is available for a call. He had pre-empted this by sending her an email whilst Cis was getting herself together telling her of his delay so email if she needed anything, otherwise he would let her know when he was not on the road.

Cis spent the whole trip deep in here own thoughts trying to rationalise what was happening to her and tormented by the betrayal of Andy and their marriage. *'What am I doing? What would my parents and friends think about me philandering with a man more than twice my age? But this is no ordinary man. He's been kind, tender, loving, caring'* – she could not run out of superlatives to express her experiences with him. The sex was driven by her desire for intimate attention, and it was good sex. *'Why don't I have such intimacy with Andy? When we were students our sexual exploits were rampant, and after university weekends together were filled with sexual activity',* but she could not remember the tenderness she felt now. *'What happened after we got married? Why, after only two years, does Andy not yearn for my body, especially because we spend so much time apart in our daily lives? Why............................'* She was interrupted by a voice in her ears saying 'Cis, we're here. Where's the best place to park?'

She came out of her deep thoughts, sat up 'Are we here already? What time is it?

She guided him into the car park being the first words spoken since leaving the hotel. When he had parked and switched off the engine, he released his seat belt, looked at her, and reached for her hand.

'You have been deep in your thoughts since we left our castle. Did you rationalise anything? Have you changed your mind about Luss?'

Prejudice in Love

She released his hand and unclipped her seatbelt and looked him straight in the eyes. 'Kiss me.'

He reached for her, as she moved towards him. When their lips met it was just a gentle connection, and then he held her closer for a deep lingering kiss which sent a pulse of warmth through her body. When he released her, she considered for a moment, and then, adopting a schoolteacher tone 'We're not finished yet, more practice required.' She then smiled 'My bum is numb. Let's go shopping.'

They put their hand luggage into the back out of sight, and she took his arm and guided him into the shopping centre. She told him that she needed a toilet, and he did as well, so they followed the signs to the nearest toilets.

'What about your panties?' he whispered playfully, patting her bottom, as they approached.

'Public pit stops will have to be an exception lest we get arrested' she smiled.

Chapter 17

As Paul re-emerged from the toilet area onto the main concourse, he noticed an ATM cash machine opposite. His impulse decision yesterday at breakfast meant that he was not financially prepared for a trip, so needed cash. He thought for a second and then withdrew £400. 'Should be enough for a few days', and some special purchases he intended to make, but would not look good on a credit card statement. *'Take nothing home'* he reminded himself.

As he wondered back to the toilet area, she re-appeared bouncy and bright, looking for him. *'How could anyone not want to make love at every conceivable opportunity to this goddess of a woman?'* he thought.

When they reconnected, she pointed along the concourse 'Ann Summers is just along there. I can't wait to see what underwear you choose for me.'

'How many pairs do I need to choose?'

'At least three, but more if you wish. I'll make this visit look like I came with my girlfriend, and we're not shy to shop when we come here. This place has lots of nice shops.'

As they entered Ann Summers, he was reassured to see that it was just like the store he visited with Jane. The front section had all of the regular underwear, and garments became ever sexier and intimate the deeper you went into the store.

'Okay' she said 'go for it. I'll be right behind you.'

He looked around to see what he would like to see her wearing. 'What bra size do I need to look for? He had already seen in her panties labels that she was a size 10.

'You find what you like, and I'll check the sizes as my bra size is different between a soft bra and more supporting bras' she whispered.

'You don't need either' he whispered back.

She gently pushed him forward 'just go and find me some nice underwear or we'll be here all day.'

After much deliberation and intrepidation he found 2 sets of what he would call full panties with firmer bras. He just picked the size 10 panties and handed them to her. She was impressed with his careful choices, so she hunted for the correct bra size. Then he found an almost transparent bikini set with a soft transparent bra. He found it a little strange looking for underwear for a woman with such dark skin as he needed to consider completely different colours to those he would choose for Jane, who was mostly paste white. The bikini set was sheer black which would work as it would look like she was not wearing anything – he held that thought.

There were many thongs, but he did not see that thongs were particularly a man thing. He felt that they were more to do with panty lines under outer clothes. He moved further back to the more glamorous, but skimpy, underwear and found 2 more sets where he liked the panties, but not the bras. He gave the panties to her but told her not to pick the bras.

He then noticed a beautiful silk camisole with French knickers. It was ivory in colour with discrete lace edging. He could visualise her looking ravishing wearing it so picked a set in size 10 and handed it to her.

'Will that do it?' as he looked back at her.

She had a large soft grin on her face. 'You really do want to dress me, and I love your choices.' Looking through his choices 'we have enough but if you see anything else then please feel free.'

'I want to go look at some things at the back of the shop' and off he went.

She knew what was at the back of the store; and realised that he did. *'What has he got in mind for me?'* she thought as she followed him.

The sex toy part of Ann Summers was discretely set so that discerning lovers could choose the toys they would like to put a little alternative spice into their sex lives with a little privacy. It was always manned by a vigilant assistant whose presence was to deter the types who just were not mature enough for such toys. He always found these assistants to be knowledgeable about the products on offer, and not the least judgemental. He immediately looked for the place where there were sample products not in their packaging so that, for instance, you could test the various vibrator modes. He knew that, when you really know your woman, that even small variations in vibrator frequency or pressure can be the difference between great pleasure and no pleasure at all.

Stephen Box

The assistant came to his rescue. 'Can I help you?' she asked politely.

'Yes please' he replied,' I'm interested in vibrators with, and without rabbits'.

Realising that her client knew what he wanted she pointed him to a shelf under the counter where he could see the demonstrator models. She then pointed to one set and told him that there was a new vibrator range which came in 3 sizes. 'If you buy the two larger models then we have a promotion where you get the third smaller one free, and with all the appropriate batteries, for a special price of just £39.99. Also, there is a new vibrator with a rabbit which is proving popular, and it comes in two sizes. The vibrator has 10 programs, and the rabbit has 6 speeds including a pulse mode, and batteries are included.'

All this information was being imparted in a very matter of fact mode but Cis could only look on totally bewildered with what was happening. *'He could be buying a pair of shoes'* she thought.

Paul thanked her for her attention and told her that he would like to test them before choosing. The assistant retreated a discrete distance saying that she would be glad to assist further if necessary.

When the assistant was at a safe distance away Cis looked at him quizzically 'Has our sex already reached a low point where we need sex toys?'

'Certainly not'. He picked up the larger of the new vibrator range and started through the vibration programs. 'Do you have any of these toys at home?'

'Yes', she said, 'I have a vibrator.'

'Does Andy know about it?'

'No', she answered shyly.

'So you use it only as a substitute for sex?' he suggested.

'You'll make me blush with such questions.'

'Lovely dark beauties like you do not blush, well at least not visibly', and at that moment lowered the tip of the vibrator onto her top exactly where her left nipple would be having chosen what he thought would be the most electrifying vibration mode. She winced.

'Don't move', he said as he danced the vibrator around where he visualised her nipple would be. 'Nice?' he asked.

'You're a very bad boy teasing me like this, but yes it's pleasant, but I wish we were somewhere more private.'

He lifted the vibrator and changed the frequency and whilst distracting her with 'we can have a lot of fun in addition to great sex with such toys' moved the vibrator down under her skirt and touched her crotch.

'Stop it' she whispered, 'I get the point. You've given me so many new experiences that I guess I can only believe that I'm about to witness more pleasure.'

He looked into her eyes lovingly 'Worry not, beautiful lady I only want to show you a different way to openly enjoy a more playful sex life with your partner.'

'You're the master, and I your willing student' she whispered and kissed him.

He tested the other vibrators whilst she, having now got over her shock started to look at the other toys on offer. She picked up a cock ring with a vibrator positioned where her clitoris would be if he were wearing it during intercourse. She interrupted him to show him what she had, 'and what about a toy for you' as she showed him her find.

'Okay' he said 'but, please, not pink'.

She looked at it and teasingly retorted 'I think pink would suit you' and giggled. She swapped it for a blue one and handed it to him. He had made his decision and indicated to the assistant that he was ready to choose.

'What have you decided', said the assistant.

'I would like the set of 3 vibrators, the larger of the rabbit vibrators in pink, this cock ring, a spray can of your best cleaner, a pack of plain condoms, a bottle of good quality massage oil, and a tube of your best lube – no sensation stuff, or coloured, smelly or otherwise, just your best aloe vera-based gel'.

Again, Cis looked on totally bemused by such exact instruction. 'What am I in for?'

The assistant assembled the products requested, 'and please include this underwear' pointing to the items on her arm.

'No', she said 'I'll get these'. The assistant piped in to say that she could not take payment for the underwear at her counter, so he suggested she go to a cashpoint till whilst he finished his purchase, which she duly did.

After she had gone the assistant asked him if he was aware of vibrating panties such as the Dr Berman version. He said that he had heard mixed reviews as the 'one-size fits-all' only really worked if the woman was the perfect size for the panties. She told him that a new product from Germany had far nicer panties, came in all standard panty sizes, and the vibrator was far more powerful.

'What about the noise level' he asked.

'I'm wearing a pair now' said the assistant quietly as she retrieved the controller from her pocket. She switched it on to reveal no sound.

He looked her in the eye and asked what it sounded like if set at a setting that would start to cloud her eyes.

She looked at him to assess her situation and gave him the controller. 'Try it' she said.

He started to increase the strength of vibration until she was visibly uncomfortable with what was happening to her. He could not hear anything, so switched it off. She was clearly relieved.

'Interesting job you have' he said smiling.

'I'm very selective who gets that controller' she responded.

'Thank you for your trust. What do the panties look like?'

'I noticed the panties that your partner was carrying so I would suggest these' as she took a package off the shelf, size 10 I believe.

'Correct. What's the deal?'

'They're normally £29.99 but they are on promotion at £24.99 with 2 pairs of panties.'

'Sounds good, I'll take one. Could I also have 3 of those chiffon restraining scarves.'

The assistant completed the purchase which he paid for with cash, and all was bagged before Cis came back to find out why he was taking so long. He held her hand and guided her out of the store.

Once outside he asked, 'Do you know a decent coffee shop in here, I could use a drink and a nibble?'

'Good idea' she responded, 'this way'.

Chapter 18

They selected a range of savouries he had a pot of tea and she still water. She looked at him with her chin resting on her hand, with elbow on the table. He waited for her to speak.

'You're having fun with this situation, aren't you? She finally whispered.

'Yes, I am' he responded, 'but only because you're such a dream partner. This adventure is taking years off me. I hope that you're really feeling the affection I have for you, and the care I take to ensure that we do nothing to cause you any harm whilst giving you the opportunity to explore your inner wishes and desires'.

'I haven't felt such attention, care or affection in years' she replied, 'but just when I think I have the measure of you and think we'll settle into a loving situation where I know what to expect, you blow me away again. What you have in that bag is a whole new world to me with a man. Sure, I've played with such toys with the girls. We had a hen party where one of the girls worked for a company importing such toys and brought a box full to the party at a friend's house. After a few drinks, those toys were well used. But never has a man used such toys on me.'

'Are you afraid of what I might do to you? The same rules apply to these toys as to everything else, when you want to stop, no questions asked. If you want me to leave them in the car, no problem. I can do things to your body with vibrators that will give you sensations like my stroking. These toys will be used more to caress your body than for sexual penetration. How did you feel when I touched your nipple with that vibrator?'

'I felt good, but not in a shop', she responded.

'Think what that sensation would be like without your top in the way.'

'You have a thing about my breasts, don't you?'

I think your breasts are sensational - pert, firm, perfect size for your frame. I would love to photograph you, especially in profile.'

'Are you into photography?' she asked.

'Yes, very much so, and have won amateur competitions with my work. When I was much younger, I even had some glamour shots I took published in a magazine called Mayfair'.

'Wow, I know that magazine, for men isn't it?'

'Yes, it is, but not smutty'.

'No, no', she assured him, 'they must have been good for them to be published.'

'The woman went on to be Mayfair queen of the year, but the magazine used their own photographers for the shoot. She was in, I was out.'

'Now I understand why you look at me the way you do, you are looking at me through the eyes of a photographer, an artist. I have no problem being totally naked around you, totally relaxed'.

'If you were my wife, I would restrict you to a maximum of 2 pieces of clothing when we are alone around the house. So much beauty needs to be savoured.'

She moved her elbow supporting her chin much closer to him 'so what would you have me wear?', she whispered.

He whispered back, 'never a bra, just a revealing top and panties, or just a longer top and no panties - except for special occasions.'

'And what about special occasions?' she purred.

'For special occasions I would find something so silky and smooth that, just to touch you, would electrify both of us.'

'I think I would enjoy living with you. No-one has ever suggested such a sensual dress code, let alone savour me.'

'Why don't we finish our shopping so that I can take you to Luss, and savour you.'

'Can't wait, let's go.'

When they were back on the concourse, she said that she just needed a few clothes more appropriate for Luss, rather than her existing bag packed for London, and knew the shops where they could get what she needed. She bought a couple of sweaters, a pair of trousers for evening wear, a looser pair of daywear pants, a T-shirt type top, a pleated skirt (his choice) with 2 matching tops, some thick black tights, and a pair of flat day shoes in case they went walking.

They had been in the shopping centre now for over an hour, and he was keen to finish the last 30 miles or so to Luss which he thought would take about 45 minutes, meaning that they would not get to the hotel much before 6pm. She felt his need to get going so she surrendered her shopping urge, albeit only with the thought to look nice for him, and they made for the car.

Once out of the car park he looked for a filling station as he thought it better to refill the car now rather than spend time finding fuel once north of Glasgow. He found one before they reached the M3 motorway, filled the tank, and they were on their way. Now the satnav was needed to direct them to the hotel, not that it proved difficult to find.

Chapter 19

They reached the hotel car park just before 6pm. Paul felt suddenly exhausted as he let his adrenalin levels start to fall as he relaxed. They collected their bags and purchases and made for the reception desk of the hotel.

He immediately noticed the look on the face of the coloured male receptionist as he realised that they were together, an older white man, and a much younger coloured woman. He could sense a mixture of prejudice and envy cross this man's mind. As he had booked the expensive Carter Suite, apparently named after a visit by Jimmy Carter when he was the President of the USA, he gave him a challenging look to which the receptionist responded by getting back to the task in hand. He knew that they would face these problems, but he was not going to allow any of it to get to her.

They were soon checked in, and in their suite. They both dropped their bags, kicked off their shoes, and collapsed onto the bed. She cozied up to him and they just lay there.

After some time, each in their own thoughts, he felt the need to turn to her and hold her close. She readily responded. 'I want to thank you for coming here with me' he started, 'this trip has taken some interesting turns, but I could not imagine finishing it without you.'

She looked at him 'it's me who should thank you, my valiant knight'. They kissed each other in a long, warm, deep kiss which said so much more than words. They were as one, and neither of them wanted anything different. They continued to kiss as if two lovers sharing their love for each other.

She finally came up for air and quietly asked what he wanted to do as it must be nearly time for dinner. He looked at the bedside clock, and then at her and said 'I would like us to take a shower together to freshen up, then I would like a fashion parade of everything you bought today, and then we'll decide what you wear for dinner. How does that sound?'

'Hmmm. I can already feel the pleasure of your caresses on my body in the shower, and you'd better be able to control your lust during the fashion parade as it will be sexy, but I would like dinner before you take your pleasure out on me.'

He put his free hand up her skirt and squeezed her buttock. Shall I remove your panties now ma'am?' He whispered.

'Yes please,' she purred.

He encouraged her on to her feet by the side of the bed. He removed her top to reveal those delicious breasts. He sat on the bed and located the hook and eye on her skirt and then unzipped it, nudged it over her hips, and let it drop to the floor. Looking up at her he reached behind her with his hand locating the leg holes of her panties and slipping his hands underneath until he was caressing the cheeks of her firm bottom. She smiled at him with her tongue between her teeth savouring every move he made. He moved his hands around so that his thumbs met in front of her vagina, and then inserted his thumbs under her panties so that he was in direct contact. He then slowly moved his thumbs down keeping contact with her but ensuring that her panties would not snag in the crease of her thighs and her loins as he removed them.

Having satisfied himself that the crotch of her panties was now free of snagging he moved his thumbs up, still inside her panties, so that both his hands and thumbs could remove the panties from her body, and then slowly move them downwards until she could remove her feet. He sat up on the bed and admired this naked vision in front of him, looked up at her and quietly said 'I've waited all day to cast my eyes on this vision of beauty.'

She reached down and kissed him on the cheek and moved towards the bathroom. 'I'll get the shower started', she said as she flicked the light switch and opened the door.

This was not the same as their castle, but still a separate shower which they could both get into with a squeeze – more intimate she thought. As she found a shower cap and attempted to fit her voluminous hair within it, she thought *'why don't Andy and I do this? Bathing together is such a nice thing to do. Pampering each other is a natural demonstration of affection.'* They had taken baths together in their early days, but it was so long ago. She relished the feeling of his hands so lovingly soaping her body, and the closeness. No time was wasted preparing towels before the task of how to start the water to flow.

Opening the shower door, she figured how to set the temperature and turned on the water. She laid a shower mat on the floor while the water came up to temperature, grabbed the shower gel from the pack of complementary toiletries, and got under the water. She then felt him step in behind her and close the door. She leaned back against him and handed him the shower gel. Although a more cramped space than the spacious shower at the castle she enjoyed the pleasure of this selfless act of pampering and could happily adopt this way of taking a shower every day. Even if she had to get up earlier to allow the time needed to fully enjoy this process, it would be worth it in terms of feel good to start the day.

After he had finished towelling her down, no moisturiser required, she went through to the room, closed the curtains, switched on the lights, and went through her shopping bags to put all of her clothes onto the bed. She decided to start the show with just her new shoes so quickly removed all the packing and put them on her feet. 'Ready', she called out. He came out of the bathroom to see her posing completely naked other than her new shoes. *'What a lady'* he thought using his hands like a director framing a scene in a movie. 'That picture would certainly sell those shoes.'

She laughed 'you've not seen anything yet.'

She removed the shoes very elegantly and slipped on a pair of the bikini panties. Perfect he said quietly clapping his hands. It was obvious that she had been around the fashion catwalks because her poise and elegance shone through. She went through all her purchases much to the enjoyment and pleasure of both of them, keeping the camisole until the end.

She asked him to turn away and not to peek until she tells him. She slipped into the French nickers and then slipped the sumptuous silk over her head. *'This is definitely one of his special occasion numbers'* she thought. It felt fabulous on her skin. She looked into the mirror observing how it followed the curves of her body, and the top seemingly supported on her extended nipples. She posed herself and said 'Okay, you can look now'.

Paul turned around and with a gasp of delight 'wow, can I take a picture on my phone camera? This is a picture I must have.' He got his iPhone and found the best angle he could find with the available light to capture this vision.

'Can I see', she asked.

He took it to her. She could see, even with a phone camera, he knew how to compose a picture, and she was happy with it even with her bulging nipples.

'You like this?', she said flirting with her body.

'*Like* is nowhere near the picture I see.'

'You have very good taste, and you certainly choose clothes that make me feel very good. Thank you.'

'We now have to pick an occasion when you can wear it, that is until we think it has served its purpose.'

'It's okay, I'll surprise you with it.'

'I look forward to that.'

'So, what do I wear for dinner?' She asked, 'what would you like me to wear?'

Looking at the pile of clothes on the bed Paul thought for a moment. I think the trousers would be appropriate until we know the temperature around here. She picked up the trousers and put them neatly at the end of the bed. He picked one of her tops which she put above the trousers. 'What about underwear. Are you happy without a bra in this outfit?'

'Not really' she said. 'I would not feel comfortable in this part of the world without a bra with either top, I would have to wear a sweater.'

'It's okay. You have to feel comfortable, so I choose that bra and panty set' pointing to one of the sets they purchased today. She picked up the bra and panty set and put them on top of her trousers on the bed. She stood by the bed 'I'm now ready to be dressed good sir.'

He loved this game, albeit he now had a bra to contend with having not even removed one from her thus far. He thought that he should get off to a good start with the panties so picked them up and went through the established ritual which she so enjoyed. He then picked up the bra opened it out so that she could place her arms through the shoulder straps. Thank goodness she had already adjusted the straps as part of her fashion show, so he just had to get her breasts sitting comfortable in the cups. He had carefully watched how she manoeuvred her breasts after clasping her bra during the fashion show, so he just had to remember the technique. He stepped behind her, but instead of taking the straps, he reached around and held each cup with his hands and slowly moved them over her breasts from a position a little lower than her breast line thus cupping upwards.

She looked back at him with a smile, and he gave her a quick kiss. He then moved his hands around the cups towards the straps without losing contact with the bra until he had the straps in his hand. He moved backward a little so that he could close the straps. Of the 3 rows of hooks he settled for the middle row hoping this was the preferred tension. He then tried to copy how she settled her breasts into the cups by gently scooping the top of her breast to move her nipples higher in the bra. He moved around to her front to see if all looked okay.

'Is that okay?' he said.

'Very nice' she said. 'Not many men know that a little adjustment is necessary after clasping the bra.'

He then considered whether trousers or top next. Would she tuck the top into the trousers, or leave the top outside? He sat pondering this choice when she spoke 'top inside trousers please' as if reading his thoughts.

'Thanks', he said. He took the top and placed it so that she could put in her arms, and then over her head. He did an over-production number to smooth it out over her body to maximise the contact.

'Dinner is waiting' she smiled.

He picked up her trousers, found the zip on the side and reached down for her to step in ensuring that the whole of the leg of the trouser was past her foot before she lowered her leg. Then the same for the other leg. He grabbed the waistband of the trousers at the sides and then started the move upwards ensuring that his hand skimmed the side of her legs all the way up. Once around her waist he moved his right hand around to the zipper and closed the zip and the top eye. He smoothed her down, lifted a little of the top above the waistband of the trousers, and sat back and admired his work. 'I think ma'am is now ready'.

'Give me a few minutes for makeup and we can go.'

He dressed himself in slacks and shirt, still pinching himself to see if this was all real. He used the time to put the clothes piled on the bed into drawers, or on hangers in the wardrobe. He wanted a clear pitch when they returned from dinner. He also found a drawer for the toys he had bought as they would need a clean before he could use them.

She came out of the bathroom and immediately noticed that everything on the bed had been put away. 'Thank you' she said.

'Just using my time productively.'

She slipped into her shoes, reached for his hand, and off they went to dinner.

Chapter 20

The dining room was spacious with tables for 2 or 4 overlooking Loch Lomond – more country style than elegant. These tables were closer than allows for intimate conversation, so he asked for a quieter table. They were shown to a window table for 2 at the end of the restaurant. 'What a difference a day makes' she smiled. 'We should get the best out of this place when we open our doors onto the balcony in the morning. We're right on the shore, and the view is supposed to be very beautiful across the loch. Also, the food here is highly rated, so let's be surprised.'

As she took her seat, she decided to set the agenda for the evening. 'How about we have dinner, have a little walk around, and then an early night. I'm in need of some TLC.'

He was feeling tired from the early morning activities, and the long drive. 'Let's eat and get out of here. What would you like?'

He felt a shoeless foot rubbing up his leg 'thank you.'

After they had ordered just a main course, a bottle of wine, and some water he thought that he still did not know much about this beautiful woman sitting opposite him. 'I still don't know very much about you so how about a little game while we await dinner?'

She giggled 'And what game might you have in mind, and do I keep my clothes on?'

He now knew her playful side, and really liked this aspect of her personality. 'It's very simple. We take it in turns to pick a subject, state our preference, and then the other party states their preference. For example, I might ask about your favourite drink, tell you mine and why, and then you tell me yours and why. No rules, your answer can be short, or informative. Any questions?'

She looked at him a little bemused 'a bit like the games we played on long journeys as a kid. You start.'

He started 'What is your favourite drink? Mine is a good cognac, which goes with my philosophy that the great pleasures in life are a good woman, a good cognac, and a good cigar. All need to be savoured to be enjoyed.'

She looked at him a little startled 'great start. Love the philosophy. I'm up for this game. My choice would be a good red wine. Aged, mature, with a rich, fruity character. Goes with my man of choice.' She giggled again. 'Do you smoke cigars?'

'Not any more. Your question?'

'What is your favourite food?' Seductively she continued 'Mine is a juicy fillet steak, red-blooded, steeped in tenderness, succulent, and delicious on the tongue.'

'My favourite meal would be a good English breakfast; a wide variety of taste, texture, and colour. But overall, I guess my general choice would be Italian. Tasty, with a wanton, brazen attitude.' He smiled at her as she realised the double entendre.

She looked at him with a wry smile 'I need to smarten up in this game. I can see how you construct your answers. This is fun. Next question.'

Which is your favourite place that you have visited, and why? Mine is Karnak in Egypt. Built over 3,000 years ago, I'm amazed at the vast size, sheer majesty and vision of what was built. It's a truly spectacular example of man's capability.'

Not a fair question. You've probably travelled extensively. Within my limited travel I would say Paris. There is a richness of culture which oozes life and love.'

'I don't want to stop the game, but I find your answer intriguing, and you speak of Karnak with passion. Can you tell me a little of this place because I don't know it?'

'Okay a brief description. Karnak is a vast city on the River Nile sitting between Luxor and Abu Simbel built over 3,000 years ago by the ancient Egyptians. The road from the landing site on the river Nile is 2km long and is lined with statues every 3m which are some 3m tall. Theses statues are essentially identical and carved out of single stones. The stiles of the main buildings are some 40m tall, and one can only marvel at how they built this place. There are many TV and computer animations of this place, but you only get the feel for it when you walk amongst these fantastic buildings and realise the sheer dimension of the place. You should visit this place.'

She sensed his real feel for Karnak, but she took a different view of such places. 'Surely these ancient monuments were built with slave labour, with many deaths during construction.'

Paul sensed her concern with slave labour. Was this because of her colour? He made a mental note to try to find out from where her parents originated, and were they a product of the slave trade? 'Why limit your concern to ancient monuments? When you stroll around the centre of Glasgow what do you think of the architecture?'

She thought for a moment trying to work out what he was implying. 'There are some beautiful old buildings. Why?'

'Do you realise that much of Glasgow was built in the 18th and 19th century from the proceeds of the slave trade. The area around Buchanan Street, Queen Street, Jamaica Street, Virginia Street, and Trongate were built directly from the proceeds of the slave trade.'

At this point their food arrived, and once served he wanted to get back to the game. 'Your question.'

She was still reeling from his knowledge, and the fact that he'd crushed her prejudice regarding such historic monuments. 'Okay, what is your favourite animal? Mine is a jaguar. Black, sleek, fast afoot, and delicious to stroke, just like me.'

He smiled as he could see that she was getting better at this game. 'Mine is Baloo the bear in Disney's Jungle Book. Big, strong, and cuddly with the philosophy that the bare necessities in life are free.'

She bent over the table to look him straight in the eyes 'Isn't that just the naked truth, especially when your paws are involved.' They both laughed.

Okay, what's your favourite style of popular music? Mine is progressive rock, with Pink Floyd and Led Zeppelin as my favourite artists. They took Blues and Folk music and orchestrated it into raw and wild emotional energy that snubbed conventional wisdom and rocked the Establishment off their pedestals. It invokes raw animal sex in every bar.'

'Wow, who is this man? Where are the wild clothes, long hair, and rock guitar? I can see why you like this game. I'm a girl of the 1990's so my music was Duran Duran, Bon Jovi and Spandau Ballet. But I cannot say that I have the passion for these bands that you clearly have for Pink Floyd and Led Zeppelin. I'm still learning about raw animal sex, but I think I have found a good teacher. Until now I listen to the radio, but my choice for playing at home would be classical for my sex. Do you like classical music?'

You're off the game again. I love all good music be it classical, opera, big band, smooth, jazz, whatever.'

'What is your favourite musical, whether stage or film, or both? Mine is the raw passion in Les Misérables as a stage production, and the elegance of My Fair Lady as a film production.'

'This one is difficult.' She pondered. 'I haven't seen the stage production of Les Misérables, but now it's your first choice, I certainly will the next time I'm in London. My Fair Lady is really good, and I agree with the elegance, but I prefer the raw passion of West Side Story as a film musical. Stage musical would probably be Phantom of the Opera – but not selected from a wide choice as we don't get much major theatre in Edinburgh. Going on my own in London doesn't appeal. I think the theatre experience should be shared with someone.'

She continued 'What's your favourite colour? Mine is red because it symbolises the dangerous and red-blooded passion that I have for our adventure together.'

He could sense that she liked the more seductive version of this game and wanted away from subjects where her experience was seriously lacking compared with his. 'Blue is my colour. It is by far the most expansive colour we have being the colour of both the sky and the sea. When we have a clear blue sky, we feel refreshed and energised, and the blue seas symbolise boundless energy. Give me a warm blue sky, and warm blue water, and you'll find our age difference evaporate.'

'A super-charged Paul. Could I deal with such a man? Could my poor body take such punishment? Why don't we go find out?'

By now they had finished dinner, so he ordered a coffee while she finished her wine.

'Could we continue with this game when the opportunity arises. It's good fun the way you like to play it. Tantalise would be a good word for this game.'

'Sure', he said, 'but we've finished dinner and I would like to walk a while'. He signed the tab, and they left the restaurant.

'Where do you want to walk? Outside may be a little cool here, but we can try it if you wish. It's only 8:30.' They stepped out and found the shore of the loch. She hugged in against him as they looked at the lights glowing across the loch.

'This is supposed to be the romantic loch' she offered.

Prejudice in Love

'It's very beautiful here. We can stand here and watch the moon rise over the loch at nightfall, and then watch the sunrise the following morning. I stayed here some years ago and was very taken with the natural wild beauty around here. I was introduced to my favourite red burgundy here, – Chevrey Chambertin.'

He continued 'The forest on the other side of the lake provides a natural feel of raw wilderness. If you've never been here before you may be in for a pleasant surprise in the morning.'

'What do you want to do tomorrow' she asked.

'We wake up, we decide when we get up, we eat after we get up, and then see how much of the day is left, and how we want to fill it. The only place I would like to see here is the restored village and the craft centre. I also want to visit a specific kilt shop in Balloch.'

'Do you fancy a kilt?' She asked.

'I can legitimately wear a kilt, and indeed used to when I belonged to the London Scottish Club.'

'I would like to see you in a kilt, you have the legs for it.'

'Maybe we can answer your wish tomorrow.'

'That would be a photo for my album' she teased.

They wandered back inside, looked at the general layout – they have a spa she noted.

When safely back in their room, she put the 'Do Not Disturb' notice on the door and attached the security chain. He cut the lights to just his bedside whilst she got out of her trousers and hung them in the cupboard. The exhaustion from events to date was evident in both of them as he kicked off his shoes and lay on the bed, and she joined him. He did not even bother with the TV. But he remembered that he had his iPod with him, and he noticed that the sound system in the room had an iPod dock on the top.

'How about a little music?'

83

'Nothing too busy.'

'What genre would you like?'

'Do you have anything classical that is gentle and romantic – no vocals?'

'Of course, I do. Any preferred composer? How about Tchaikovsky's 1st Piano Concerto as starters?'

'Yes', she replied, 'that sounds good. Did you ever see the film 'The Music Lovers' about Tchaikovsky – haunting, but beautiful music?'

He continued to find his iPod as he answered 'Yes, the movie is great, but with a score written by Tchaikovsky, how could it fail?'

He found it and pressed it on the iPod dock having selected Tchaikovsky's Piano Concerto, waited to check the volume level, and then returned to the bed. She snuggled in beside him. They both enjoyed being together as they listened to the music.

After the first movement she asked him to pause the music. She got off the bed, went into the bathroom, and returned about 5 minutes later. She removed her top and bra and crawled beneath the sheets. He started the second movement. She reached over to him and started to undress him. He co-operated with her, and soon he was naked. He went to the bathroom to prepare for bed, and then crawled in besides her. She immediately wrapped herself in his arms. His left hand was around her back and naturally fell to her bottom. He noticed that she still had her panties on. He snapped the elastic in the top of her panties. 'You still have your panties on' he whispered.

'The service here tonight is a little slow' she whispered.

He smiled. 'Okay, I'll use the lying down technique tonight.'

'I have a man for all seasons ', she giggled.

He shuffled down in bed until his face was level with hers, and without any warning he brought her very close in his arms and kissed her with such passion she felt swept up in the emotion and just wanted the kiss to last forever. She held him tightly and tried to join her body with his. When they surfaced, he whispered 'how am I doing coach'.

'You just graduated' she murmured and moved in for another kiss.

There was something in these kisses which told her that they had crossed another line. They left her as emotionally charged as sex. She was so close to him that his erection was up against her tummy, her breasts were pressed against his chest, and her heart was pounding with expectation.

The kissing was now intense. He had his hand inside her panties pulling her towards him. Her loins were on fire. She wanted so much to be joined with him.

He reached down with both hands and started to remove her panties. She helped him to kick them off. He moved his hand between her legs and stroked her feeling the heat and the flowing juices. Her breathing was now laboured, she wanted to get lost in the passion of the moment.

He rolled her flat on her back, still frantically kissing her, and cupped one of her breasts, and squeezed her nipple. She arched her back in response to the electricity she felt with his touch. He rolled over on top of her between her legs. She reached down, grabbed his erection and guided it to her erupting volcano, and encouraged him into her. She spread her legs wide as an invitation to take her.

He started to thrust into her. It felt so good to him. It was a long time since he had felt so much passion, and it revealed itself in the power and throbbing he felt in his erection. She was moving with him, lifting her loins to pull him back into her. He could feel the muscles in her loins caressing his erection. They were locked together in a singular and uncompromising passion. She was gripping the back of his arms pulling him towards her.

She started to groan as the pleasure swept across her whole body. This is what she craved. She was totally uninhibited in her expression of desire.

The explosion of orgasms was simultaneous and volcanic. Both uttered involuntary sounds of extreme joy and pleasure. She grabbed his buttocks pulling him deep into her, he on his elbows trying not to crush her, but too breathless to kiss her. She was also panting, seeking air to breathe. They just lay there feeling the power of love they had just shared together.

Eventually her spasms of ecstasy subsided, and they looked at each other. They said nothing, just continued their passionate kisses.

As his erection subsided, they rolled onto their sides, still locked together, feeling the togetherness they both craved. He noticed that tears were flowing from her eyes. He moved a hand to her face and tenderly wiped them away.

'Why do you cry, did I hurt you?'

'I cry with joy', she whimpered. 'You made love to me, and I've never felt so much uninhibited and spontaneous pleasure. I thought that we were both too tired for sex tonight. But sheer desire defeated our tiredness, and I feel so satisfied that I can only cry with joy. You have awakened the desire in this maiden, and she wants to soak in all of the love and pleasure that you give to her.'

He kissed her again with a deep, passionate display of love.

They were oblivious that the music had finished, as they were too wrapped up in each other to notice anything in the outside world. She pushed him on his back, tucked her head into his shoulder, and unconsciously started to stroke his chest. There was nothing to say, or that needed to be said. They were both lost in the pleasure of the moment, and the warmth that flowed between them.

Eventually they both fell into calm and peaceful sleep.

Chapter 21

It was about 4am when she awoke. She needed the toilet so disengaged herself and made her way to the bathroom. When she returned, she stood by the bed and saw the peacefulness in his face in the light of the bedside lamp, which was still on. She felt so much love for this man, she never wanted to let him go. He had awakened her as a woman, and she knew that her life would change from now on. What was in store for her, she did not know. But she knew that she had been asleep with convention for too long, and it was time to express herself as a passionate woman, to break the grip of status quo and duty.

She got back into bed and snuggled up against him. She could not bear to lose contact, even whilst asleep. He stirred. 'Oh no, I've disturbed him.' She still didn't know that he could easily survive on 5 – 6 hours of sleep. They had slept since before 11pm so he was no longer in deep sleep. He opened his eyes and saw that she was awake.

'How long have you been awake?'

'Just a few minutes, I needed the bathroom.'

He realised that he also needed to relive himself, so he sat on the edge of the bed until he was awake enough to be steady and made his way to the bathroom. Afterwards he splashed his face with cold water and rinsed out his mouth.

As he walked out of the bathroom back to his side of the bed, he could not help but notice that she was lying flat on her back with the blankets across her waistline. Her pert breasts were such a turn-on for him. It had been many years since he last had a naked dark woman in his bed, and she was classic in her build and stature, oozing the confidence of someone at peace with her own natural beauty.

He slid back in besides her. She appeared to be deep in thought. She was recalling events a few hours earlier. They had made love, not sex, but love. The kissing gave pleasure to her lips, and she could still feel the pleasure of the love making, she still had a warm glow in her loins. She knew that by any measure of morals, she should be ashamed of her behaviour. Her family were devout Baptists, although she had not been to chapel in years, but she had the moral values of faithfulness to your chosen partner instilled into her from an early age. But were these moral values the chains that constrained her from experiencing a truly loving relationship? Given a choice today her chosen partner would be the person lying next to her. He had cast away her chains and shown her that her desires were not something to suppress and feel guilty about. He was engaged in a long-term relationship which he clearly had no intentions of sacrificing for her, but he felt no betrayal towards his partner. Their relationship openly accommodated the needs of each of them, without compromising their own loving relationship. He was not wittingly taking advantage of her or abusing her. She knew of his commitment to his partner from the start. Yet she felt so much love, love that if she ever felt this way with Andy, it was long forgotten. Was this just infatuation, and the excitement of these new experiences? Would reality slam the door shut on her tomorrow as she returned to her normal life? This adventure was not over. She had entered this labyrinth of emotional confusion and needed to find her own way out on her own terms.

'A penny for your thoughts' came a whisper in her ear.

She turned to face him and put both arms around his neck moving her face towards him. 'You made love to me, and I was replaying the wonderful feelings and emotions that flowed through me. Even your kisses stirred the fire within me – not bad for just one day of practice' she quipped with a smile.

She thought for a moment. 'I hope this doesn't sound silly, but if I have ever felt so connected in love before, I cannot remember when. In the past, no matter how passionate I thought my lovemaking I can now see that there was always some inhibition, belief, or doctrine in the background. What I felt last night was total unadulterated abandonment of any inhibition. I wanted you with such fervour that I would do anything to enhance the pleasure for both of us, and the satisfaction that flowed through me during the aftermath exhaustion was exhilarating. I felt totally liberated. I don't even have to throw you the typical movie line "and how was it for you?" because I could feel that you were totally committed to the moment, and your love and passion came flooding through you into me. Am I making any sense or is this just emotional blubber from a confused little girl?'

'Not at all', stroking her hair. 'What happened last night between us was totally spontaneous. It wasn't planned on my part as I was exhausted by the events of the past two days and could only think of sleep. But what did happen was very special, not least because it just happened, driven by forces beyond our conscious control. You asked me yesterday morning to make love to you. I found that a little absurd because you don't contrive making love. I believe that the difference between sex and making love is the conscious and the sub-conscious. We consciously have sex with a clear objective to give and take pleasure from each other. Making love is a spontaneous reaction that we do not plan or have any control over – it's a total uninhibited expression of feeling and love between two people.'

'For me, events of the past two days have regenerated feelings that I haven't experienced for some time, notwithstanding that I do love Jane, and would not consciously do anything to betray that love. However, I feel exhaustingly reinvigorated by you if that makes any sense. But for you it's clear to me that you are grappling with a whole range of emotions and beliefs, challenges to your moral values, prejudices, and loyalties. I feel somewhat responsible for opening this box of confusion for you, and thus do not want to send you back out there until you have understood the dilemmas that you are now facing and have some idea about your future. Somehow, we need to conclude our adventure with a positive outlook, and fond memories.'

She hugged him tight, moving cheek to cheek and whispering in his ear 'I don't have any problem or reservations about what's happening to me. I just need to understand how this re-educated me translates back into my daily world. You have opened my eyes to so much, so I need to learn to see things as they are, and deal with these realities. For too long I've been sleepwalking through my life, and you have awoken me. And for that I'll be eternally grateful.' She kissed him on his cheek, and just relaxed in his arms thinking about what he had just said to her. *'This sage of worldly wisdom is my whole world at this point in time, but I need to take this wisdom and use it to reshape my life'*, she thought.

He moved her down a little so that she lay across his chest with her head in his shoulder. He reached over to switch off his bedside light, and then stroked her back until she was asleep. He drifted back into a peaceful sleep thinking how grateful he was to this lovely woman. Maybe fate is playing out some game with them.

Chapter 22 - Tuesday

They re-awoke around 8am. She was now by his side but with her head still in his shoulder. He was surprised that he could sleep in this position as he would normally roll over and sleep on his side. But he found her closeness exhilarating. He felt so needed by this woman.

The sunlight was beaming through the curtains indicating that the sun was rising over the loch. She rubbed her eyes and looked at him with her usual beaming smile.

'Good morning my valiant knight, she said. What time is it?'

'Around 8 o'clock'.

'Hmm', she snuggled down again – 'too early'.

Prejudice in Love

He stroked her hair and kissed her on the forehead. She looked up again, still smiling 'I feel absolutely great doc. Whatever you're doing to me, I want more' reaching up and kissing him.

'And what particular medicine would you prefer this morning my bonnie patient?' he whispered.

'Plenty of love potion please' she beamed.

'Okay, let's add a different flavour to this treatment.'

She looked at him quizzically. 'What do you have in mind doc?'

'I want you to start to talk to me.'

She looked even more quizzical.

'I want you to tell me what you want me to do. I sense that this may be lacking in your sex life, yet it is the most frustrating aspect of sex for a man – a woman who cannot tell her man what pleases her, and what she wants at any particular point in time. I want you to guide me through what you would like us to do.'

'He's right' she thought. *'Other than nudging Andy to have sex with me when I'm ovulating, and indicating in bed that I would like sex, I just let him decide what to do. New territory again.'*

She thought about it. 'On the basis that you're right can you give me pointers how to start?'

'Let's start with the basics. Did you ever play doctors and nurses as a kid, essentially to get undressed to be examined by some lucky boy, and you do the same to him – natural inquisitiveness?'

'Yes, but not after puberty.'

'What a sheltered life you lived.'

'Probably my Baptist upbringing' she retorted defensively.

'Okay, I want you to think where you have a make-believe pain anywhere on your body that you want rubbing, stroking, or kissing better. You will point to a place on your body and I'll decide how I want to relieve your pain.'

She looked at him 'You're serious, aren't you?'

'We can get far more sophisticated as you get the hang of asking for what you want. Where do I start? How 'ill' do you feel? Can you stand-up, sit, or are you so ill that you need to lie down.'

'Oh, really ill', she feigned.

'Then lie on your back, or on your front.' She rolled over and lay on her back.

He threw back the blankets to reveal her whole body. 'Okay Cis where does it 'hurt'?'

Gingerly she pointed to her right breast.

'Is it the whole breast, or a particular place?'

'The whole breast' she murmured.

Paul reached over and gently examined her breast with his hand. Then he started to knead and caress her breast. She could feel the pleasure of his treatment. He decided that he would limit each treatment so they could cover as much of her body as possible in a short time.

He stopped and asked 'next?'

She pointed very specifically to her left nipple. He moved down with his mouth and initially licked with a flicking action around the base of her nipple until it was fully extended, and then put his mouth around the nipple and sucked it into his mouth, held it for a few seconds, and then started to suck it as would a suckling baby. As he was resting his hand on her tummy, he could feel the response in her body.

'Next', he asked.

She pointed to her tummy.

He started to stroke her tummy in a circular motion, sometimes softly, and then as a massage.

Cis was no longer watching what he was doing, her head was back and her eyes closed soaking up the pleasure of this game.

Prejudice in Love

'Next' he said.

She pointed to her vagina.

'Outside or inside' he asked.

'Outside' she responded.

He stroked along the lips and, responding automatically, she opened her legs.

'I need a closer look' he said as he got between her legs. He again stroked her, but this time opened her lips to reveal the wetness inside. He went down on her with his mouth caressing her vagina with his lips as though kissing her. She purred and raised her hips to give him more access.

'Next'

She pointed again to her vagina, 'I think the pain is inside' she said.

'Okay I'll insert a probe to investigate.' He already had a throbbing erection so it was easy to enter her as if probing the inside of her.

She was now visibly feeling very good about this game even though he was not dwelling anywhere for more than a minute. After a short probe he removed his erection from her.

'Next.'

She pointed to her vagina again.

'Where?' he said.

She pointed to her clitoris.

'More specific' he said.

She moved her other hand down to open the lips on her vagina, exposing her clit and pointed to it.

'Got it', he said.

She removed her hands. He used his hands to spread her vagina lips and then flicked her clitoris with his tongue. She spasmed in delight. He then went into a licking motion on her clitoris with his tongue which generated groans of pleasure from her. But then he stopped. She looked at him.

'Please more.'

'I think this problem requires a wider investigation. Can you help me?'

She looked at him with glazed eyes and shook her head.

He took her hand and placed it over her clitoris. 'I need you to massage here whilst I continue my investigation.'

He started to move her finger to get her started, and then let her continue. The juices were flowing out of her vagina directed to the crease in her bottom. He used his index finger to gently use her juices to massage her anus. She bent her legs to reveal more of her such that she was fully exposed.

Her work on her clitoris was starting to produce results. As he felt her starting to build for her orgasm he simultaneously inserted his thumb into her vagina, and his index finger deep into her anus and then gently moved this hand backwards and forward in rhythm with her so that he was moving in and out of her. The groans were getting louder as she moved towards climax.

He waited until he knew she was about to explode and pushed both his thumb and index finger in deep. The explosion lifted her loins clear off the bed. She held this position whilst she milked every last spasm out of her orgasm, and then collapsed on the bed naturally removing his fingers from her body.

He moved back to her side watching her enjoy the moment. She was somewhere else in her ecstasy.

He reached for a tissue to wipe his fingers before touching her.

She looked at him.

'Fuck me please.'

He moved into position and easily penetrated deep into her thrusting his way to full orgasm and ejaculation, and then collapsing onto her.

She held him tight kissing his face, neck, shoulder and anywhere she could reach. They lay together spent.

Paul rolled off her onto his side. She immediately rolled over to face him. With her loose hand, she held his face. 'What are you doing to me you lovely man? That was fantastic. Your finger in my bum made such a difference to my orgasm.'

'How did you feel about directing me around your body, and then masturbating yourself for me?'

'A very self-conscious start, but once we started, it was great. If that is just the intro, I can't wait to start the real lessons.' She was still recovering putting her head into his shoulder to catch her breath. After a few moments she came up again to face him, 'I need a drink.'

'I'll get it, just stay there and relax.'

He went to the minibar. 'Just water will do' she gasped.

She sat up to sip her water. He lay beside her again, but not touching her. She reached past him to put the glass on the bedside table, and then kissed him deep, with longing, with both hands behind his head pulling him into her.

'When you get yourself composed, how about a shower, and then see what they have to offer for breakfast'.

'Nice, but just hold me for a few minutes.'

Holding her was never a problem so he just scooped her up into his arms and held her close.

Chapter 23

Cis wanted to talk about what had just happened between them as she had questions but did not want this conversation in the dining room. She broke with the normal tranquillity of the shower. 'You say that I should instigate sex, but how do I start such a process without a dance of the seven veils, or a striptease?'

He laughed at her. 'Surprise is the nature of the game. There are two modes to this game. The mode we just played is where you are trying to instigate sex with some innocent request which should lead to other things. For example, the most used ploy by woman familiar with this art is the breast examination. You are sitting watching TV with Andy, and you feel a little perky. If you're wearing a bra, leave the room and get rid of it. Come back to the sofa and tell Andy that you have a pain in your breast. Could he take a look and see if he can feel anything. If he responds, sit in his lap straddling his legs, and remove you top. But hold the ploy reaching for one of you breast as if trying to find a problem, and move his hand, if necessary, to replace yours. Ask him to feel around to see if he can feel anything. He'll take this as a serious request at the beginning. When he doesn't find anything suggest that your breast probably just needs a kiss to make it better. If that doesn't get the show started you don't have a red blooded male. You even whisper to me the slightest hint that I have access to these beautiful breasts' as he was caressing them with shower gel 'that's all I need.' She looked up at him and kissed him. 'You just need an innocent ploy.'

'What about the other mode?' She asked.

'This is part of the intimate relationship between two lovers. You have code words between you that are personal to you and are clear signs of desire. For example, I think that you like me to masturbate you. What about if we were somewhere where I could discretely masturbate you, but not have sex with you. We would have a code that you would whisper in my ear such as "I need to be stroked" or "pussy needs a stroke". It doesn't matter so long as you both know exactly what that code means. The exact nature is important as you may have a different intent when you whisper "pussy needs attention" which means that you just want him to touch you inside or outside of your panties, as against "pussy needs feeding" which would indicate full sex. Code words like "fuck me" do not work as everyone knows what they mean and thus are not a code. Do you see?'

'I would be too embarrassed to say those things to Andy' she retorted.

'Would you be too embarrassed to say them to me?'

She looked at him and thought about it 'No, I think it would be easy to whisper such things to you. Already I've wanted you to touch me but didn't say anything, but now I would – especially now you've told me I can.'

'What is the difference between me and Andy?'

'Where do you want to start?'

'No, no, break it down to the most basic difference.'

She thought for a moment 'Desire' she answered.

'Exactly, so you need to create the desire between you, and the rest is just creating your code words.'

She turned to him 'can we create some code words between us so that I can get some practice?'

'There you are, a good ploy for more sex, but yes, that would be nice. What would you like me to do to you, and what codes would you like to ascribe to each desire?'

'Can I think about it over breakfast?'

Chapter 24

Breakfast was a real Scottish affair. He went for a full Scottish comprising bacon, eggs, black pudding, haggis with toast, while she had a combination of fruit, cereal, yoghurt, and croissants.

She had something she needed to discuss with him, but not keen to break the flow of their relationship. The past days had changed her whole outlook on life, but there were realities that needed to be addressed, and she needed to face these realities today.

The most important reality was the article on the fashion show she attended last week, and which had to be filed no later than Thursday afternoon. Although she had her written notes, and a clear idea what she wanted to write, she still needed to sit down and write it. She had her Apple notebook computer with her, but Paul would be too much of a distraction. She could not resist living in his arms, and concentration would be a major issue with him within touching distance.

She also did not want this issue to be a distraction from what was happening to her for one minute longer than it needed to be. She had battled with this problem to find the best solution for both of them. Paul would want to move north tomorrow, but she felt she needed to go home, and he could not go with her. If he moved north the time to get back to Edinburgh would be much longer, whereas if he took her back to Balloch, just a few miles back along the loch, she could get back to Edinburgh by train within 2 hours as she would need to change train in Glasgow. If she left tomorrow morning, she would have the afternoon to finish her article which should be enough, and to get herself more organised for the remainder of the trip. She was also agonising over whether she had to be back in Edinburgh Friday evening, or whether she could risk Saturday morning.

Finally, she decided to confront this demon. 'Paul, I have a practical issue that I want to discuss with you.' He looked up from his breakfast and became attentive. 'I have an article to file no later than Thursday about the fashion show I visited last week. After much soul searching to find an alternative solution, I think that I must go back to Edinburgh tomorrow, and then re-join you some time on Thursday. I cannot work when I know that your arms are within cuddling distance. Also, I could do with changing my wardrobe to clothes more suitable for the Scottish Highlands. I don't want to do this, but

Prejudice in Love

there is the reality of my job to consider. The only unknown for me is where you'll be on Thursday, and how long it will take me to get back to you.'

Paul could see in her eyes that she had struggled with this, and she clearly did not want to go, and he certainly did not want to lose her for one minute. But she was right, and it might be good for both to spend some time apart to reflect on the past days.

'Would you like me to take you to Glasgow tomorrow morning?'

The relief in her face was visible. He had understood her dilemma and was already planning how to help her. 'No, you can take me just the few miles to Balloch. I can get a train from there.'

'Are you sure that will work?'

'Yes, no problem. Balloch is a commuter station.'

'The issue for me is where you'll be on Thursday.'

'My original plan was to spend a day around Oban, then drive north along Loch Ness to Inverness taking another day, then to Aviemore for two days, before coming down to Edinburgh for two days. I think that plan got squashed when I invited you to join me. So, I've planned to drive from here directly to Loch Ness to test a route along the east side of the loch, and then across to Aviemore, as I already know Inverness quite well. But Aviemore is too far from Edinburgh, it will take hours by train.' Paul thought for a moment. 'There is one place I've always wanted to visit, and I think that its only about one hour by train from Edinburgh – Gleneagles.'

She agreed that he was right about the distance from Edinburgh as she had been to Gleneagles before.

'What about if I stay in Aviemore tomorrow night, and drive down to Gleneagles on Thursday morning and meet you there?'

She reached over and kissed him. He had made this whole issue so simple for her. 'My valiant knight has rescued me again.'

That issue out of the way she asked what he had planned for today. He had already told her about his desire to see the regenerated village of Luss and the craft place attached to the church. But she also remembered him telling her that he wanted to find a new kilt.

'I think our first task is to visit Balloch to see if we can find me a new kilt.'

'Okay let's go there first and see what my valiant knight looks like in a kilt.'

They finished breakfast, went back to their room, and readied themselves for shopping, and then exploring Luss.

'You can tell me what code words you want to use whilst we drive.'

She had forgotten about this task in her deliberations about her article but relished the thought of this task.

What did she want him to do to her, and what codes could she use? Certainly stroking her with those lovely hands would be top of her list. But how many different ways could this be done? He said the codes must define exact actions. The type of stroking would depend on where they were, and the level of privacy. This is not straight-forward she thought. *'Okay, I want him to stroke my back. Stroking my legs and thighs would be another. He pats my bottom all the time, so we don't need a code for that. What about intimate? Do I want him to just put his hand up my skirt and stroke my pussy, or do I want the whole orgasm? I think both would be the safest, after all I don't have to use these codes if I don't want to. I like the code "pussy is hungry"; just the thought makes my juices flow.'*

She suddenly realised that she could use these codes for other things that she liked him to do such as undressing her for no other reason than she liked him to do it. She could have a code for removing her panties, just to have the pleasure of him putting them on her again. "I want to get naked" – bit obvious but she had no problem telling him this. A variation would be "Let's get naked". Just thinking about these codes was giving her feelings that she would have to suppress while they were out.

As they walked through the hotel reception, she had formulated her list.

Chapter 25

As they drove to Balloch, Paul asked her for her codes.

'I'll start with six, with the option to add more later.'

'Okay let's see what you have.'

'Obviously I want you to stroke me anytime. It's too difficult to break it down into body area so I have one code that means please stroke me, back, legs, breasts, with consideration to where we are. The code is simply "Stroke me". Not really a code but easy to remember.'

'My next is "It's time to get naked" which means we need to leave wherever we are and go somewhere where we can be alone.'

'"I want to get naked" means that I want you to undress me.'

'I have three pussy codes. "Pussy needs attention" means I want your hand in my panties. "Pussy needs stroking" means I want you to stroke me to orgasm. And "Pussy is hungry" means I want sex.'

'How's that for starters?' She asked.

'Pretty good, but what about your breasts, no treats for them?'

'Don't need any, they get more than their fair share of attention from you already.'

Paul laughed 'is it that noticeable?'

'Noticeable? My breasts stand to attention every time you look at them in expectation of the imminent attention. It's my

Stephen Box

bras that are sulking as you have no use for them.' They both laughed.

She stroked his arm playfully, 'what codes do you have for me?'

'Hadn't really thought about any', he said. 'but it might be an idea for you to hear some from me, especially ones that you have not yet experienced; broaden your vocabulary and your experience.'

'So what do you have in mind my lover?' She asked.

He looked at her 'obviously we have the converse of your codes. We would both use "It's time to get naked" and "I want to get naked". On the pussy codes the converse of "Pussy needs stroking" would be "I want to stroke pussy", and for "Pussy is hungry" the converse could be "I want to feed pussy". I have a couple of other ideas, but I would have to show you what they mean when we get back.'

'Can't wait', she smiled.

Paul found the shop he wanted and was able to park directly outside.

They entered to find a labyrinth of Scottish dress compartmentalised into discreet sections. Paul immediately noticed on one wall near the counter rows of folders with names on them depicting the full range of existing tartans shown within.

Cis went straight to the ready-made kilts section. Looking at the range of tartans on display, 'now what tartan did you say you are entitled to wear', she asked playfully.

'Clan Frazer of Lovatt' Paul answered, 'but I don't particularly like the tartan, it's predominantly red, so the colours don't particularly suit me. A blue tartan would go better with my eyes', he quipped.

She went off to find an assistant. Paul was looking at the different types of clothing that they had from formal dress to hunting clothes. He had no idea what she was discussing until she attracted his attention and asked, 'dress or hunting?'

'Formal dress' he answered and off she went again with the assistant.

As he looked at the range of Lomond tweed jackets she was back again '5 yards or 8 yards?' she asked.

'8 yards is traditional for a man' he answered.

'I need you to come over here while I measure you. I have to give this nice man all of your measurements in imperial inches.'

'Good to see that some traditions do not die.'

She had acquired a tape measure from the assistant, insisted to him that this was something she wanted to do under instruction. The assistant had a clipboard with a list of required measurements.

'First, we must start with the kilt' he said. she held the tape measure ready to spring into action having removed Paul's coat. 'Waist'

'38 inches, maybe 39 inches to accommodate dinner' she smiled.

'Widest part of the hips' was the next instruction. Cis played with this one a little moving her hand around his bottom and clasping the tape to make the measurement right over his penis. She replied '45 inches' and then rose up to Paul's ear and whispered, 'needed to make sure that we had room for your sword.'

Navel to knee was the next measurement request. 'Okay my dear let's find your navel. Stand to attention', and with the end of the tape firmly pressed into his navel she extended the tape down to his knee. She looked up to him, 'above the knee, or below, sir?' The assistant piped up with some bemusement at what he was witnessing and told her that the required measurement was to the point on his knee where if the bottom part of his leg was bent backwards at 90 degrees, the kilt would just cover the visible knee.

'Bend your leg' instructed Cis. He obliged, shrugging his shoulders at the assistant. 'twenty-two and a half inches' she reported. 'That's all I need for the kilt' said the assistant.

'Your good lady has chosen a tartan for ye as it would appear that ye find yer Clan Fraser tartan too red, is this correct sir?'

'I have a Fraser Lovatt dress kilt but I don't feel comfortable with so much red. I prefer more natural country colours with a blue base.'

'Not a problem sir. Could I show ye what yer lady has selected?'

Paul took one look at the very modern tartan that she had selected, and thought *'no, this is too young for me'* and was about to say so when he checked himself.

'What are you doing?' he thought to himself. *'This is her show and you're railroading her. She's having so much fun, and she's in the fashion business, but now you want to push her to the edges.'* He looked at her.

'Is this the tartan you would like me to try?'

She had noticed his reticence and looked at him feeling that she was no longer in charge and replied 'yes, but only if you like it.'

He could tell in her voice that she clearly felt anxious.

He smiled at her lovingly, stroked her chin and said 'well you better select all of the accessories that your experienced eye thinks will make me worthy of your choice. I need a kilt belt, sporran, sgian dubh, and hose. Go to it.'

The smile came back to her face and off she went with the assistant.

Paul looked at the tartan again thinking he would have chosen a more conservative blue as the blue in the kilt that she had chosen tended towards purple in colour. Jane was always saying that he was too conservative and looked good in more modern colours and styles. But he had to admit this tartan has a discreet elegance about it, was a fine weave so would not be so heavy on and did look like it would be easy to wear.

Cis and the assistant returned with the accessories that he needed, so it was time to try it all together. He was wearing a white undershirt so this would give an overall impression.

As Paul started towards the changing room the assistant stopped him in his tracks. 'I sense from yer lady that ye are looking to buy yer kilt.'

Paul looked at him quizzically 'Yes, that's why I'm here.'

There's a problem that ye need to know. This tartan is called the Spirit of Bannockburn and is registered to a major clothing hire company. This is why we have a range of sizes already made up in our hire section' pointing to where Cis had found the kilt. 'We're only allowed to hire this tartan, we canne sell ye a kilt.'

He looked at Cis who was looking at the assistant with hurt disappointment.

The assistant saw the look on her face 'I'm sorry missee but I didna know ye wanted to buy as ye were in the hire section.'

She looked at the assistant a little coldly and asked what tartans they had close in colour to the chosen tartan that could be purchased. Paul decided just to hang back and see how she handled this situation as she was clearly not amused.

The assistant selected a selection of folders from the rows of available tartans and went through the possible choices, but nothing appealed to her. The assistant went to a back room and reappeared with an armful of rolls of tartan material, but again none satisfied her. She was becoming despondent. Paul was starting to feel sorry for her as she clearly wanted to be part of this process, and second best would not do for her man.

The assistant was becoming a little frazzled himself as he fought for ideas to please this exacting woman. He looked at her in desperation for a moment, and then had a Eureka moment. 'Wait missee, I think I may have just what ye want.' With that he disappeared into a back room again and returned a few minutes later with a roll covered in brown paper. He opened it onto the counter to reveal a very elegant blue tartan which she immediately liked. The colour balance and weight were perfect for her man.

She looked at the assistant cautiously 'What's the story of this tartan, and can we buy it?'

The assistant explained that it was a special weave tartan commissioned by a German industrialist nearly two years ago for some occasion whilst he was touring Scotland. This industrialist had paid a deposit for the initial weave of twenty-five yards but, other than a few yards used for samples, had never used it, or paid the remainder of the invoice although he had paid for the registration of the tartan. The registration did not preclude anyone from wearing this tartan.

Paul interceded at this point as this story interested him. 'So' he started 'what you are saying is that this tartan was commissioned, woven, and registered, but then the originator lost interest and, to date, has not settled the outstanding invoice.'

'Yes sir, that be the current position.'

'Can you tell me the name of this person so that I might contact him to see if he is willing to sell me the rights to this tartan?'

'Let me first ask my manager' at which point he disappeared into the back room again. He returned followed by a very sturdy Scotsman in his 50's and who introduced himself to Paul and Cis. Paul reiterated his interest in the tartan and the manager looked at the notes in his file.

'The German gentleman is a man called Herr Walter Schwitzer.'

Paul immediately cut in 'Do you mean Walter Schwizter of Schwitzer Industries in Stuttgart?'

'Yes sir. Do you know him?'

'My goodness, yes. As a banker I've participated in transactions for Schwitzer Industries and know Walter Schwitzer very well. Do you have a contact telephone number for him?'

The manager looked at his file again 'Yes we do.'

'Could I please have it' as he retrieved his iPhone from his jacket. 'I'll call him now and, maybe we can satisfy all of our needs.'

Paul dialled the number. As soon as the call connected all that the manager, the assistant, and Cis heard was 'this is Paul Fulton. Could I please speak with Walter Schwitzer' as Paul turned to find a more private space for this conversation.

Paul returned some minutes later with the phone still in his hand and gestured that the manager should take the phone. Paul quickly briefed the manager that he had agreed a deal with Walter to settle the outstanding invoices, and to take over ownership and registration of the tartan. This would be confirmed by Walter to the manager now verbally and confirmed in writing by email.

The manager introduced himself to Walter, and then just listened. He then acknowledged to Walter that he was satisfied with the arrangement, and as soon as he received email confirmation, he would take care of all the details. Walter confirmed that the email was in process as they spoke and would be with the manager within minutes. He also apologised for the delinquency regarding the outstanding invoices, but that Paul was a worthy man to assume ownership. With that the telephone was handed back to Paul.

Both Cis and the assistant just stood there astonished at what they were witnessing. How was it possible that they had found a unique tartan commissioned by a German industrialist, and Paul knows him! Amazing.

Having returned Paul's phone the manager went to a shop computer terminal and started to tap the keys that would load emails. By the time Paul had concluded his conversation with

Walter the manager had found the email, and turned to face Paul 'You are now the owner of this tartan, have the right to change the registration into your name, change the name of the tartan as it has not yet been used, and impose any restriction on its future use. When you have settled our invoices and the variation to registration fee, this roll of tartan belongs to you to be used as you direct.'

'Walter told me the existing name of this tartan and would like me to change it.' Her looked at Cis 'any ideas?'

Cis was still reeling from what she had just witnessed. She stuttered 'Fulton Blue covers the events that got us here.'

'Sounds good to me' responded Paul turning to the manager for approval.

'It's now your tartan, Mr Fulton, and I'm happy with your chosen name. Any restrictions on use?'

'Fulton family and descendants only.'

'I'll get a Registration Variation form and we can complete it now. Then I'll ensure that it's properly recorded.' At this the manager disappeared into the back room.

The assistant was in his own little world involuntarily flipping the corner of the tartan backwards and forwards looking blankly at what he was doing.

Cis turned to Paul and quietly whispered 'who are you Mr Fulton? This is surreal.'

He just smiled at her. 'Now that you've persisted with your professional skills and loving touch to select a fine tartan for me, how about we put the rest of the package together.'

Cis bounced back a loving smile 'yes sir. As you wish my master.'

With that she distracted the assistant from his stupor and asked him if they could now put together a suitable dress package for this fine tartan. She also put her hand over his hand still flipping the corner of the now renamed Fulton blue tartan and

Prejudice in Love

thanked him for remembering that this tartan existed, and available.

The assistant was still a little dazed, but thanked her, and was pleased that she liked it.

We'll need to change some of the accessories missee to do justice to this tartan but let's deal with the main items first.

Cis invited him to direct the process.

He turned towards Paul who was still looking on with some amusement. 'Now for yer jacket and waist coat. Would sir like the tradition Prince Charles jacket and waistcoat?'

'Yes please' said Paul.

'Would ye like 3 or 5 buttons on the waist coat?'

Paul thought for a moment, 'probably 5 would be better.'

'And would sir prefer traditional square buttons, or crested round buttons?'

'Square please, but not chrome.'

The assistant selected a box of blackened pewter square buttons. 'Perfect' acknowledged Paul.

Cis was standing there listening to this exchange thinking Paul really does know his kilts. Andrew got married in a kilt, but she had no part in its selection, but she did know that such selection was treated very seriously. As she came out of her thoughts the assistant was saying 'just one more thing before we take yer measurements, what type of kilt pin would you like as we have a wide selection?'

'I want the traditional knotted dagger in pewter' Paul responded without even looking.

'Good choice' replied the assistant.

Cis stood ready with the tape again. 'Chest' said the assistant. '44 inches.' 'Arm length from shoulder to wrist'. '24 inches.' 'From the back, missee, please measure from his collar to his waist.' '22 inches.'

'Would sir like a short, regular, or long fit for yer jacket?'

'Regular please.'

'Does sir need a shirt?'

'Yes' replied Paul.

'Ghillie or dress?'

'Dress please, 17 inches collar, with black bow tie, but not silk.'

'We have a woven bow tie in keeping with yer jacket sir.'

'Excellent' said Paul. 'I also need shoes, hose, and flashes. I think navy blue hose, and my normal shoes size is 11, but not ghillie brogues, I would prefer dress shoes.'

'Yes sir. We would always ask ye to try yer shoes with yer hose to ensure yer comfort.'

It was decided that Paul should use the hire kilt until his new kilt could be made as everything else was standard sizes. He could then return the hire kilt upon receipt of his own Fulton Blue.

When Paul asked about the length of time needed to make his kilt, he was stunned with the four to six weeks answer. The assistant explained that it took two days just to fold the pleats in the material. He pressed to see if there was any way to speed the process if he was prepared to pay extra. After some deliberation, and a phone call from the assistant to their factory, it was agreed that the tartan material would be collected within the hour, and the factory would work the hours necessary to complete the kilt and flashes as quickly as possible with a view to Paul collecting these items before driving home. Paul would stay a few days longer if necessary. With this Paul moved to the dressing room with the selected attire, and the hire kilt.

It took him some minutes to get into the outfit Cis had selected having sent out for the next size up in the shoes. He adjusted the kilt to centre the weave pattern on the bib, adjusted the sporran belt to sit nicely on his hips, and decided it was time to reveal himself.

He walked out of the changing room into the gaze of Cis. Her face lit up.

'My valiant knight looks fantastic' she gasped. 'Wow, you do look sexy in a kilt. Turn around, let me see all.' He slowly swirled for her. 'A little faster please, I want to see the kilt swirl.' He turned a lot faster so that the kilt really belled out. She went to him, held his hands 'Would you invite me out one day wearing yer kilt, ye handsome man?'

The assistant waited patiently whilst this banter took its course. He had originally thought the tartan too young for this older man, but he had to admit that he carried it very well, and she knew what worked for her man. Even the black fur dress sporran with black tassels and traditional top knotted plate looked very good on him. Again, he would not have considered such a choice for an older man.

The kilt length was a little too long, and he noted this on his measurements for the kilt makers. Kilts of this quality have too much material and weight to simple pin them up, but his experienced eye knew exactly how much the hem line of this kilt need to be raised to fit perfectly on this gentleman. All the other parts were made for him.

Paul looked at her again 'So you're sure that you would accept a date wearing this rig?'

She looked lovingly in his eyes and teased 'I love what I see. In fact, I want a photograph.' She extracted her phone from her bag and took his photograph.

The assistant offered to take one of both of them. She passed her phone to him without hesitation and stood with her arm around her kilted valiant knight.

As Paul went to the changing room he turned to Cis 'while you're waiting could you go look at those jackets over there and decide which one I should buy. You know my size so let me try a regular and a long length in whatever you choose.'

She smiled, now feeling part of this process again, and off she went.

She chose a Lomond Gillie jacket, and a traditional Harris Tweed jacket. Paul liked both but did not let on to this.

He whispered to her 'part of the pleasure of buying is the negotiation of the price. Can you do this, or would you allow me. And by the way is there anything that I can get for you as I would very much like to give you something to remember our trip?'

She whispered back 'We're not here, remember, so as grateful as I am for your offer I must decline.'

He felt frustrated, but knew she was right.

He did not have to haggle well as there was clearly a discount for such a large sale. He took both jackets, and they left the shop with just the jackets and the shoes as they would collect the remainder later that afternoon after the buttons have been sewn onto the jacket and waistcoat. The assistant also offered the correct carry case for such a fine outfit as part of the sale.

They both thanked the assistant for his wonderful help and fortitude, and Cis danced her way back to the car hanging on to Paul's arm. 'I have to write this whole experience down for an article. It's so surreal. And you'll look stunning in your new tartan – the Fulton Blue, the clan of my valiant knight.' She was certainly full of the joys of spring as she got into the car ready for the drive back to the village of Luss.

Driving into the old village proved a delicate affair as the Range Rover was large for the narrow streets with even the one-way streets having cars parked just leaving enough room to pass. Paul found a space to park just off the small street leading to the jetty on the loch.

They walked along the small street bordered by single-storey stone houses renovated as a social project, and now boasting small, but beautifully crafted gardens most of which were in bloom. Paul thought it resembled a pretty picture postcard miniature village as each house was barely the size of a double garage.

He explained to her that legend has it that the village takes its name from the heraldic flower, the iris, or Fleur de Lys. According to the legend a local girl married a high-ranking French officer in the 14th Century. She died in France, but her body was returned to be buried by Loch Lomond. Fleur de Lys strewn on her grave by her husband are said to have taken root and grown here ever since and thus Luss, the Scottish sound of Lys. He added that today it is a popular wedding destination, and they even have a specific tartan called the MacKessog tartan which can be worn by people who get married here. She asked about the colour of the tartan, but Paul couldn't remember, but there should be evidence of this tartan at the Pilgrimage Centre attached to the church.

Once at the jetty they found a craft shop, but it didn't take long to realise that the 'crafted goods' were not local, but factory made.

Paul had noted in his research months before that there was a Pilgrimage Centre attached to the church, and that this centre was the home of local crafts, and provider of the MacKissog kilt. He could see the church spire, and saw a track leading in the same direction.

Within minutes they were standing outside of the Pilgrimage Centre, the purported home of MacKessog tartan, amongst other crafts. The Pilgrimage Centre was a white single storey building, again renovated as a social project during the redevelopment of Luss. However, it did not resemble the thriving craft centre that Paul had observed on the web site, and indeed was closed.

With an air of disappointment, they slowly wandered back to the car and return to the hotel taking in the pretty simplicity of this village but noting the absence of any enterprise.

She was hanging onto his free arm as they strode the short distance from the car park to their apartment. 'You look great in your kilt. I want a show when you get it all back this afternoon. I want a private viewing, and I shall check under the kilt to ensure that you honour tradition.'

Smiling at her, 'don't you think that wool can be a little harsh on such delicate parts, could put me out of action.'

'Those few minutes could be rewarded with some very nice action for both of us. Just the thought of it gives me erotic ideas.'

'Naughty girl.'

Chapter 26

They returned to the hotel around 12:30 and went to their room to deposit his purchases. She took the jackets, removed the sales labels, and hung them in the wardrobe.

'You were going to tell me about your codes for me.'

He looked at her wondering if she was ready to go to another level. The discussion on the way to Balloch was a form of erotic foreplay so she would be easy to rouse. 'Okay' he said 'the first is on a very practical level and can occur anywhere at any time. If a man tries to deal with it himself it will easily draw attention to himself, and for people to get the wrong idea. Let us code it as "the snake is coiled". Sometimes a man's willy, as you call it, gets itself into a coil inside his underwear. Should anything cause a little arousal in him, his willy cannot get itself out of this coil, which is unpleasant. What you would normally notice is a man with a hand, or even both, deep in his pockets seemingly playing with himself – people call it pocket billiards – but most of the time all he's doing is to try to unwind his willy so that it can do what it needs to do without such discomfort. An accomplished lady can relieve this situation whilst distracting away any notion of what is happening. What you need to do is to lower his zip, reach inside his underwear, straighten his willy, and then withdraw and re-zip without anyone noticing. Can you do this?'

'What about if I got hold of his willy, but refused to let go?'

'I suppose it depends on where you are, and how brazen you are. You could also use this technique to arouse your man whilst out in public to encourage him to go somewhere more private.'

Paul returned to the point 'What do you think a suitable act of distraction could be?'

'I could kiss you.'

'No, people would automatically lower their eyes at such an intimate act.'

'Tell me' she said.

'You need to be playful, such as nuzzling your noses – something amusing, a little noisy where people would automatically look to see what is happening, and then hold their gaze. The back corner of a lift is a classic place for this activity. You would use your body to shield any evidence of what your hand is doing and distracting any attention from any other angle. Have you ever done this?'

'No, not even in private.'

'Do you want to try?'

'I thought you'd never ask.'

She came in close to him.

'Now try to shield your activities leaving enough room to enable you to do the job in hand without any obvious movement of your arm.'

She started to nuzzle him, including teasing kisses, and he could feel his zip being lowered. She did not find it easy to get inside his underwear without moving not only her arm, but also her body.

Having finally got hold of him she realised she had failed.

'Okay, what did I do wrong?'

'Take you hand out of my underwear and re-zip me and we'll start again.'

'Told you I wouldn't want to let go' she giggled.

'Okay, forget the distraction for a minute as you clearly have that covered. Let's concentrate on the job in hand.'

'Puns included' she quipped.

'Undoing the zipper is all in the wrist. I'll hold your arm, and do not want to feel it move.'

He held her upper arm. 'Now lower my zip.' She managed this effortlessly. 'Good. Now think what I do to you when I put your panties on in ensuring they sit correctly over that lovely pussy of yours.'

'In through the side', she said. 'Got it.' She reached in and went into his underwear through the side and grabbed his now erect penis.

'Now remove your hand ensuring that my underwear is correctly positioned.'

She did this successfully.

'And now zip me up again.'

'Got it' she said looking pleased. 'I never realised that men playing with themselves are just trying to straighten their willy.'

'Okay, what's next master?'

'Playtime' he purred.

'Okay, what does "playtime" mean?'

He went to the drawer where his bag of sex toys was still lying untouched. He selected the vibrator set, rabbit vibrator, cleaner and lube and took them all out of the packaging and loaded with their batteries.

Cis looked on a little dubious.

'Come Cis, help me prepare the toys we need for playtime.'

She followed him to the bathroom. He handed her the two larger straight vibrators and, having sprayed the smaller vibrator and the rabbit vibrator with cleaner, handed her the cleaner. Both then washed the cleaner from these toys and dried them.

When they returned to the bedroom Paul put down the vibrators and held her. 'I know you are anxious about these toys, but would you let me show you how you can use these just for fun, or as a pre-cursor for sex. You'll see that they can be used for many more things than a penis substitute. Indeed, they're better used for arousal than vaginal insertion. If you think about it the act of intercourse takes a few minutes. Arousal can take at least an hour if you know how.'

'Your hands are enough to arouse me.'

'Ah, but not everyone has the knowledge to enable them to stroke you as I do. Starting with sex toys can very often show the techniques for touch and stroking which then take over from the time that no toys are readily available.'

'Paul, I trust you completely with my body, and my well-being. If you think that playtime will work for me then I'm your willing student. But be gentle with me.'

Paul lifted off her sweater revealing her T-shirt with her bra-less pert breasts surging through it. He also undid and removed her slacks that she had purchased in the shopping centre. 'As you are a little anxious, I want you to sit on the bed with me and close your eyes. As I touch you, I want you to tell me, not how you feel, but any sensations you feel. Talk to me.' She sat in front of him cross-legged and closed her eyes.

He started the medium sized vibrator onto a faster setting and gently touched her cheek with the edge of the vibrator. This vibrator was about 10 inches long and a little over 1 inch in diameter. He moved it around her cheek and then backwards along her jaw line until it was gently straying down her neckline just behind her ears.

'It tingles.'

He brought it forward along her cheek line, under her chin, and then progressed slowly to her neck just behind her ear on the other side of her face.

He moved to the muscle between her neck and shoulder and gently moved it along this muscle. She reacted by slightly stooping her shoulder.

'That's nice' she said.

He moved it out along her shoulder, slowly moving down the outside of her arm to just above her wrist, moving to the inside of her arm and moving upward towards her armpit, but stopping short of the armpit. 'The objective is sensation, not tickling.' When he arrived just below her armpit, he moved the vibrator onto her torso, and slowly moved the vibrator down the side of her body to her waist. Again, she reacted.

She was visibly starting to relax. When he got to the top of her pantie-line he moved it across her tummy with just enough contact to feel the sensation. She contracted her tummy as the vibrator passed over to the other side where he reversed the process back up to her neck.

'Okay?' He said.

'It's quite nice' she responded with surprise in her voice.

He lifted the vibrator from her body, and then moved it across the top of her breast. This caused more than a stir, even through her T-shirt.

'That sent sensations through my body.'

He could see her nipples extending, so he repeated the touch on her other breast. Same reaction. Then he touched just below her extended nipple. He body jolted slightly.

'God, she said, that sensation is very strong.' He did it again on the same nipple. This time the spasm was stronger.

'You still okay?' he said quietly.

'Hmm, I like it.'

He set the vibrator onto a stronger setting and touched the inside of her open thigh.

'Oh yes, I can feel that.'

He glided the vibrator along her thigh until it reached her crotch where he made sure that it crossed to the other leg at the bottom of her vagina, and then down the thigh on the other leg.

'I could feel that right through my loins.'

'Are you ready for some direct contact with your body.'

'Hmm' she purred, 'my breasts are ready for some attention.'

He lifted off her T-shirt. He left her panties in place as a clear sign that this was not about penetration with these toys.

He now took the larger vibrator and found the same vibration setting as the medium sized. This larger vibrator was the same length, but closer to 2 inches in diameter. He asked her to bridge her legs each side of him and lean back supporting herself on her hands. He started both vibrators and started on each side of her body, from her waist, to move up her and down her body. This was having good effect because she arched her body towards him. He moved the vibrators to the inside of her thighs and caressed her thighs with them right up to her vagina. Then without any warning, he reached forward and put both vibrators across the top of her breasts swaying them gently over her skin.

She started to squirm – this attention was good. He moved both vibrators down her breasts until they simultaneously touched her nipples. This sent a sensation spasm throughout her body. She was now pushing her breasts forwards for more as he moved the vibrators under her breasts and down to her tummy.

He lay down both vibrators on the bed and picked up the smallest vibrator. He set this to a strong throbbing pulse and placed it into her panties such that it covered her clitoris. She tried to close her legs on feeling this sensation, but as she was straddling his body, she couldn't do this. He picked up the two larger vibrators but waited for the throbbing in her panties to have the desired impact. As he knew that she was now fully aroused he started to circle her nipples with the buzzing vibrators. She started to spasm as these sensations stirred her loins. She exploded in a convulsion of spasms throughout her body. He immediately lifted the vibrators from her breasts and recovered the smaller one from her panties.

She just sat there still in spasm, albeit starting to subside.

She eventually opened her eyes and looked at him.

'See, you can have fun without removing your panties', he said quietly.

She let her hands go and fell backwards onto the bed. He let her recover her composure.

She sat up. 'Okay, playtime is good.'

'We haven't started yet. We have taken about 15 minutes to just show you that these toys are for fun. Imagine what could take an hour, and how many orgasms you might experience. Also, it's a two-way street. You can use these toys on me when you know how. Then we use them on each other prolonging the fun of sex between us.'

'I need another pair of panties before lunch.' She went off to the bathroom.

He quickly thought. 'Another pair of panties. She's not quite with it, and I'm responsible for panties.'

He quickly went to the sex toys bag and selected a pair of the vibrating panties. They were black, and similar to a normal pair he selected for her. He put them in the drawer that she was using for underwear, and activated the remote control checking that it worked. He put the remote control in the pocket of his jeans.

She emerged from the bathroom carrying her panties and dropped them into her dirty linen bag. She then approached Paul, kissed him, and told him that she needed dressing for lunch.

He went to the underwear drawer, hid the vibrator panties in his hand, recovered her T-shirt and day slacks and sat on the bed.

She stood in front of him resting on his shoulders. He reached down with the vibrator panties and went through the usual ritual of clothing her with her slacks and T-shirt. He then recovered her sweater ensuring that he kept her distracted from any strange feeling about what was now connected to her clit. The sensations that she was feeling from playtime would help to mask this object in her panties.

'Okay, ready for some lunch?'

Chapter 27

They went to the main restaurant in the hotel. Paul organised a window seat away from the few other people already there. It was not a busy time of the season, especially mid-week, so reasonably quiet. Cis was still looking a little dazed.

He spoke with a little concern in his voice, 'Are you okay?'

She looked at him. 'I can still feel sensations. You never cease to surprise me with what you do. When and where did you learn all of this stuff?'

'I had a good teacher. I was 19 or 20 years old, and she would have been early 30's. Like you she was a stunner, and she knew what she wanted, and what she liked. I had a lovely girlfriend, but both of us were wet behind the ears when it came to sex.

This lady, Jill, took me under her wing and showed me so much. How to touch, how to stroke, how to play, and how to prolong the enjoyment that two people can share in moments of great intimacy. Sex with her was never less than one hour, and more typically two hours. I remember that she would not allow any jewellery to be worm. I left my watch there one night which took a bit of covert recovery before its absence was noticed by my girlfriend the following day. I didn't live with my girlfriend at that time, but she worked in the same group as me, and I had a rather large watch which was always conspicuous by its absence.'

'So, your girlfriend knew nothing of this liaison with Jill?'

'Nothing. It wasn't anything other than me getting an education whilst Jill got her jollies. My girlfriend got much better sex, and she thought that I'd been reading Forum magazine, a popular sex technique magazine at that time.'

'And now you're doing the same for me.'

He chose not to answer.

'What do you have in mind for this afternoon?' she asked.

'I have no plan for any of this. I have so far relied on my instincts, and how you respond to suggestion. I think if I can open your mind to some new ideas you can take them home and get your sex life back where it should be.'

'It's where it should be right here.' Again, he refrained from falling into this trap.

'Actually, I have a little add-on to this morning if you're interested.'

'Okay, what?'

Her reached into his pocket and started the vibrator in her panties at the lowest setting. No reaction. He steps it up to the next level of intensity. Now she feels something.

'What are you doing?' she asked.

'Giving you a little covert fun.'

He stepped it up another level. Now she felt it and looked at him in astonishment.

'What have you put in my panties?' she whispered with some urgency.

'Just another playtime toy which you can use anywhere.'

'You have a vibrator in my panties?' she whispered.

'Cis, relax. Just go with the flow. No-one can hear anything. I'll give you the control if you'll promise me that you'll test it further and see how you feel. Imagine giving the remote to Andy as part of your pre-sex foreplay. Agreed?'

'Okay, but I can stop when I like?'

'No. You can only stop when it gets too much for you. Many people use these toys, so don't be embarrassed or self-conscious. Take the attitude that you have a buzz that no-one else has got, and you are about to enjoy it.'

Paul gave her the remote. 'It's the yellow button to increase intensity, the blue button to change the vibration.'

'I want to change the vibration to a slower pulse.'

'Okay press the blue button, and then the minus button.'

She did as he instructed and found a vibrator level that felt better. 'Now I want to increase the intensity.'

'Press the yellow button, and then the plus key.'

She did as he instructed and immediately felt the difference. After the initial shock, she accepted that it gave her a warm glow.

'Okay', he said, 'press the plus button again.'

She hesitated, but could see his expectation, so pressed it. Now the pulses were slamming against her clit.

'Oh, no, no, no. I don't want to orgasm here.' She hit the minus button to reduce the intensity. She looked at him, 'after lunch we'll go somewhere to finish this. It's better than my vibrator.'

'Glad you like it. But I want you to go the full distance in public at some time. Remember people of your skin colour do not visibly blush so you have no excuse.'

'Where are you taking me with all of this?'

'First, I want to show you what's possible. Then I want you to decide what you want, know how to get it, and how to teach your partner, if necessary, so that you get all of the sexual fulfilment that you desire.'

'Can't I just take you home?'

'Only in your mind, my dear Cis.' He reached for her hands, and tenderly looking into her eyes 'as much as I would like to keep you by my side for ever, we both have other partners. Believe me Cis, if I were 20 years younger, you would not be going anywhere, unless with me.'

'Your age doesn't matter to me. In calendar years there is a big difference, but as you said, in the darkness it doesn't matter. If you only gave me 10 years of what you have given me to-date I would be the most satisfied woman on earth.'

'Thank you. I'm very grateful for such feelings. But we both know that we need to find another way to get you where you want to be. I'll give you everything I know, and the courage to go back and get your life back on track with Andy. That's the best I can do at this time.'

As they picked at their lunch, she was deep in thought. *'He really cares for me as much as I care for him. But there's a sadness in him. Something happened to him in the past. I need to find what it is.'*

She came back to the moment. 'Paul, currently you owe me three long stories. When are you going to tell me? They're part of you, and I really do want to know you.'

'If you can remember the nature of these stories then I'll tell you', hoping that she had forgotten what they are about.

Knowing that he was testing her she responded that one is why he intended to go to Scotland on his own, another is why he needed to use her for a test yesterday morning, and the other relates to his children. He was shocked that she was so precise.

'Wow, now I find myself on the back foot. Okay can I suggest that we use our sauna later this afternoon during which you can select one story, and before then we go for a walk along the loch whilst I tell you another.'

'Done' she said. 'Let's go get ready for our walk.'

They went to their room to get their outdoor clothes. Cis wanted rid of the vibrator panties, but Paul asked her to keep them on, and to give him the control. She had visions of walking bow-legged along the shore as he upped the intensity.

Chapter 28

They decided to walk along the shoreline of Loch Lomond towards the north, away from the village.

'Okay' she said, 'it's story time. What was your issue yesterday morning before we left our castle?'

'In recent years I have suffered some medical problems, probably the result of living in the fast lane for so many years. This all started when I had a routine PSA blood test which proved to be very high.'

'What is a PSA blood test?'

'It is a fairly crude way of detecting the possibility of prostate cancer.'

'I was sent for a biopsy of my prostate. This was a disaster, and I suffered from septicaemia as a result. This took some 4 months to clear before I could have another biopsy by someone more competent. The problem transpired to be prostatitis which was treated with antibiotics.'

'Since then I have had periods of not being able to maintain an erection during sex. I had several tests, and debris was flushed out of my tubes. However, this did not solve the problem.'

'These past years have been a drain on me, never before suffering any major illness. One of the possibilities was that it was psychological, possibly depression because I cannot function properly. Sex with Jane was not really stimulating enough because she works hard and is tired much of the time. You'll also find in later years that keeping your sex life exciting can be difficult.'

'When you unexpectedly jumped me yesterday morning, I was able to easily keep my erection. You made me feel refreshingly alive and having such attention from such a deliciously beautiful nymph was exciting.'

'When we came back from breakfast, and it was clear that you wanted much more attention I needed to know if earlier had been a fluke. You took me by surprise and thus dramatically raising my adrenalin levels which would have helped maintain an erection. But what would happen if I was in the driving seat?'

'My reservations when you came to me were first, did I have any right to use you to test my response, and if it was okay with you, could I perform? Secondly, I wanted to choose a position that would place serious demands on my body as supporting you the way I did would place big demands on my major muscle systems. Therefore, an extreme demand on me.'

'But I needed to know as there would be little point taking you on this journey if I cannot fulfil your needs. So, when you stood there so ready to help me, I bit the bullet and found my answer. Thank you.'

Prejudice in Love

She stopped walking, pulled him close, and kissed him. 'You have never failed me, and it would not matter if you did. Everything you do for me tends to culminate in sex, but sex is not the story, it's just the conclusion. But thank you for telling me.'

She suddenly felt a pulsing throb in her panties. She looked at him with surprise. 'You're playing with that remote control again. God it throbs.'

He switched it to pulse mode so that he could give her short bursts.

'I thought we were out for a walk. If you keep pulsing that thing I will be hopping like a rabbit.'

He sent a longer pulse to the vibrator in her panties. 'You are a naughty boy playing with a naughty toy. Give me the remote.' She reached for the remote, but Paul avoided her attempt.

He reached for her hand. 'Come, lets us continue our walk.'

'You are not going to be satisfied until you cause me to explode.'

'No Cis, I want you to control that. I'm just getting you in the mood. I want to see you use this toy to control how you want to orgasm. All out first time, or take yourself up, then down again before building to an explosion, and build again. Or maybe you'll go for multiple orgasms. I want to see this liberated, wanton hussy please herself. We will walk far enough that you have no fear of being seen or heard. Then I'll give you the remote and let you fly.'

'Why don't you want to control the situation? Isn't it fun for you to see me squirm when you press those buttons?'

'This is not about me Cis. It's about you. When you press those buttons only you know how it makes you feel. You can go places that you have not been before. You can experiment how far you can take yourself before you must surrender to the final explosion. And it's more fun outside rather than in the privacy of our room. If it blows you away and you faint in ecstasy, I'll be here to look after you.'

'So you want me to play with myself using this toy while you watch the show.'

'No, I want you to have some liberating fun. I want to see a liberated lady bring a sparkle to her own eyes because she knows who she is and is not afraid to enjoy herself.'

'Can I have the remote to try out a few settings to see what works best for me as we walk?'

'For sure. And you can tell me what those settings are so that I know the ones you most enjoy. Do you remember when we bought these toys. I told you that it's important to check them out as a setting that provides joy for one woman might do nothing for another. Thus multiple settings.'

She stopped walking, took the remote, and started to play with some of the settings. 'I'm trying all of the different vibration types first, and when I have the best one, I'll play with the intensity.'

She found the vibration which she thought would be good for her. Then she took his hand again and they continued walking.

'I have a setting that probably will not take me to orgasm, but I get a really nice feeling in my loins. I could leave this running for a while. Hmmm, nice.'

She played with different intensities leaving each one for a while to experience the effect. She increased to the next level. It stopped her dead in her tracks. Paul spun around to see her eyes wide open, and her mouth look like she was gulping.

'Whoooo, that one has a kick. That did not caress my clit, it hit it with a baseball bat. Good for triggering a large explosion once I'm ready to explode.'

After a further 100 yards or so there were some rocks where they could sit. Cis said she was now ready to have some fun but would like to be sitting as she could change the position of her legs to give different effects.

He was impressed. 'She's really focussing on how she can please herself rather than where she is.'

'Okay my valiant knight. Get ready to catch your maiden if she falls.'

She adjusted her seating position telling Paul that she could move the vibrator directly over her clit. 'I'm on program 3, and intensity is now 2. This gives me a nice feeling but will not take me to orgasm so let us go up to level 3. This feels a little like the intensity you gave to me on our first night. This would probably give me a slow burn.'

'Now we go to level 4. Oh, yes. That woke me up. This would take me really quickly, but that would spoil the fun.'

'Down 2 levels and move to program 5. This is more a vicious throb than vibration, so I'll pulse this one. It's nice but I couldn't leave this running. This is a bring me up, take me down to bring me back up again.'

'This is fun. I could sit and play with this for hours. Beats my vibrator at home. And I could use it whilst I'm doing boring household chores, and no-one would know.'

'Okay let's see if it can deliver. Back to program 3, level 3.' She leaned against him. 'Tell me when you get bored and I'll up it to level 5.'

He was smiling at her. She had turned the game. He loved her playfulness.

Suddenly her face looked serious. Something was starting to happen. 'Level 4 is definitely the action setting. Hold me.'

He held her close. He could see that she was on the path of no return. Her eyes were not focussed anymore. She was starting to pant for breath. He could feel her body bucking. A spasm went through her body. She dropped the remote. Another spasm, and another. Then a gasp, and a cry of pleasure before she closed her legs tight and pulled them up towards her. He quickly reached for the remote and switched it off knowing that it would get very painful beating against a clit directly after an orgasm.

She collapsed in his arms, gasping for breath. He just held her tight thinking what a courageous woman had been given to his care. *'I would love to keep this lady'* he thought. *'Why can't I be 20 years younger?'*

After some minutes she looked up. She was smiling. 'Did I pass, master?'

'Did you enjoy yourself my pretty student?'

'Oh, yes my master.'

'Then you passed with flying colours. Would you like to keep this toy?'

'Having put them on me, and shown me how to use them, you don't expect me to give them back?'

They both laughed as he held her in his arms.

After a while He reminded her that they would take a sauna so should think of heading back to the hotel.

He switched off the remote control and put it in his pocket. 'Enough of that for one day' he told her in his best schoolmaster voice.

They strolled back, arm in arm, reflecting on the use of such a toy in her daily life.

Chapter 29

When they got back to their suite he switched on the sauna.

'Ready to be undressed.'

He was now getting very used to this ritual of dressing and undressing her, but he was never going to get tired of it. He knew this pleasure would await him when they showered after the sauna, albeit he needed to return to collect his kilt before 5:30pm.

The sauna was ready. Paul whipped the towel from her as she went through the door. She looked back, smiled and went inside. Paul quickly followed.

'So how shall we pass the time in here' she teased.

'Rampant sex I think', came the reply.

'Did you order the paramedics to be on standby', she giggled.

She lay on a bench facing Paul with all her splendour on view. 'Is this pose good for you or would you like me to sit with you?' She was obviously in a playful mood after her sessions with the vibrating panties, but he was going to keep her waiting. He would continue to touch her and tease her to keep the foreplay going, but he had it in his mind to savour her delights after he collected his kilt using it as the final prop in the build-up to her climax. His biggest problem was to keep his penis in check as her flirting was taking its toll.

'How about another long story' he offered 'as we have nothing else we can reasonably do in here.'

She sat up immediately, moved next to him. 'That would be nice. Tell me about your children.'

Paul told her how he had been honey-trapped by a woman in the bank where he was a director. She was already in a middle management position, but she wanted the trappings of a senior high-flyer. He explained that remuneration packages for senior bankers were dreams to most people, albeit you earned such packages. But on top of this came the best tickets to the big events such as the opera, Wimbledon, Henley, etc. In addition, he was a director of one of the international clearing systems so travelled to Board meetings all over Europe. These events were structured to take wives, and they were pampered with shopping trips and special visits whilst the Board meetings and a high-level reception and dinner took place over two days. They were very lavish affairs.

'Anyway, I was taken completely off-guard with her assurances that she was protected, and the next thing I know she was pregnant after just one night of sex. My position was such that I was expected to do the honourable thing, and we were married about a month later. Six months later she took maternity leave, and after a very prolonged birth, James, my son was born. What was interesting to me was that my then wife did not like children, so why put herself in this position? I could afford the trappings of a fantastic nanny, and a housekeeper so my wife did not have much to do with the day-to-day. Once her maternity leave was over, she decided that she liked this lifestyle so decided not to return to work. Her salary was a pittance against mine in any event, so she would only return for the social interaction. Looking back, had she gone back to her work she would not have been able to travel with me on my various trips, nor taken the days off for the likes of Wimbledon. Life was okay, and she decided that another child was needed to provide companionship to our son, so we had a daughter, Sarah.'

'For me this was great because I love kids, and even though I worked, I spent more time with them than she did. No working late, no breakfast meetings. I would sooner have breakfast with the children and read their bedtime story.'

She stroked his arm thinking what a great dad he would make to her children.

'Then I woke up. I realised I was living a lie. She didn't love me, only what I was, a high-flying bank director. This made me very miserable. I put on weight, did not look forward to going home, and we argued all the time. I came from a very cold childhood environment of continual argument and bad feeling, so I didn't want this in my own life. Something had to give. My wife threatened to leave me, making it clear that she would expect me to keep the children. She couldn't wait to shunt them off to boarding school in any event. My mistake was that I said fine, close the gates on your way out. She took this as a sign that her gameplay was not going to work, so asked me to leave but on the basis that I would maintain my relationship with the children.'

'I didn't want to go through a messy legal battle over child support, so I agreed a large settlement with her, premised on my continued relationship with the children who were then 6 and 4 years old. This was another mistake because as soon as she had this settlement her vengeful streak kicked in.' He looked Cis square in the eyes. 'Beware the jilted woman.'

'She turned James against me within four years, and Sarah held out for seven years. As they were both at boarding school, against my wishes, I didn't see them very often in any event.'

'The total alienation against me started after one Christmas visit. I was never allowed to see them on Christmas Day, but on this occasion, I had them from Boxing Day through New Year as she wanted to go skiing with her new partner. We had a great time and when she came to collect them neither were ready, and both expressed their desire to stay longer. She was furious. Within a few weeks she had completely alienated James against me. Sarah held out; but relented some 3 years later.'

'My ex had found herself another golden prospect to marry and so wanted me out of the way. We went to Court, but the Courts are heavily biased towards the mother. I eventually got my order for access, but the kids were over the age of 12 years so their view on access counted. My ex made sure that it was never in my favour. So, I lost all access.'

'I tried on various occasions to regain contact, especially when they were past the age of 16 years, but when found out the black witch would weave her spell on them. I have not seen them for some years.'

She held him in her arms. 'What a horrible story. How can any adult use their children in this way? Come let us get out of here, you need some serious TLC.'

Once out of the sauna she went straight to the bathroom and started the shower. She came back to the bedroom, dropped her robe and towel, removed his, and led him to the shower. This time she started on him first, gently bathing him hoping to wash his bad memories away. She used her body to caress him and tease him out of his dark thoughts. She put him completely under the shower head so that he was being soaked from head to foot, and then moved closer to him with a long, loving kiss while the water flowed over both of their faces. Paul reacted to this. He wrapped his arms around her and lifted her onto her toes as he used her sensual warmth to liberate his mind from this painful memory.

He looked at her. 'As much as you want to know these things, I don't want to waste a minute of our time together with such depressing memories.'

'I'm sorry that I asked. But I'll make it up to you.'

'I'll caress your sensual body under this shower so that I come back to this delicious present, and then we must go get my kilt.'

Chapter 30

They quickly went back to the shop in Balloch. The assistant assured Paul that his kilt was already in process, and they were hopeful of a delivery in their Crieff shop on Saturday. Paul checked that all buttons were placed correct. Cis gave the thumbs up so everything was packed into its carry case and they went back to their room.

She insisted that he models the whole rig for her. Once he had dressed, she started to weave her magic on the final touches. She decided that the kilt pin needed to be set at a different angle, and the sporran needed to be a little higher. Much of her efforts where to get him back into a playful mood as she wanted so much to just bundle him up in her arms and smother him with love. She felt desperate about not having children, but to have them taken away from you in such a foul way must be unbearable.

After much fussing she stepped back to admire her man in his kilt. She liked the picture. His legs were perfect for a kilt, and it sat very well on his hips.

'How does it feel?'

'Good' he smiled. 'Would you accept a date with me dressed like this?'

'Only if it involved you taking me to bed afterwards' she flirted. 'But I have one more little adjustment.'

She had stripped him naked before dressing him in his kilt, so he was commando underneath. She walked to him slowly, bent down, put her hand up his kilt, took hold of his penis and slowly moved it as if to change the shape of the kilt. He spanked her bottom.

She sprang upright, laughing.

'Okay lady, you've crossed the line. You must pay.'

'Oh, m'lord, what punishment awaits me', she whimpered.

'You will be lashed with love until you cry out for mercy', he growled.

'Please have pity on this willing maiden. I'll do anything you ask.'

He stripped her naked, but without any tenderness as he was simulating her punishment. He then pushed her backwards onto the bed. Stripping himself naked, he pounced on her, and quickly determining that her juices were in full flow, rammed himself into her and pulled her buttock hard into his groin.

'Oh master, master', she gulped, 'punish me hard.'

He decided that she liked this, so he pounded his erection into her again and again. She was gasping for breath.

'More, master.' He could feel the spasms growing in her loins. She jolted her body in a final spasm as her orgasm ravaged her body. He squeezed her buttock tight and pulled her tight to him to penetrate her as deep as he could as he exploded into her.

He collapsed onto her. She grabbed hold of him and pulled him so that her breasts were hard against his chest. They were both gasping to find air to breathe as they lay locked together.

Finally, she whispered in his ear, 'have I served my punishment, or would you like to do that again.' Her head dropped backwards in sheer delight at how she felt. She had waited all afternoon for this feeling.

When they were both a little calmer she whispered, 'can we get into bed and just hold each other for a while.'

Paul started to rise to prepare the bed covers. She jumped off the bed into the bathroom and returned with warm flannels and a towel. She wiped and dried them, switched off the lights and crawled in beside her lover. They pressed so close to each other as they locked in a longing embrace, came up for air, and went back into repeated embraces totally absorbed in each other.

They eventually calmed, and she lay across his chest with her head on his shoulder. He was gently stroking her back. She was in no hurry to go anywhere. This was what she wanted, someone to want her, need her, caress her, and love her. She was totally content and satisfied in the arms of this man.

They just lay there in their own thoughts for some time, neither caring about what the world was doing. They were in their own world, and nothing else mattered.

Chapter 31

When they finally decided to move it was after 7pm. They quickly showered, and he dressed both for dinner.

Prejudice in Love

On the way down to the dining room she whispered to him 'you were playing with me this afternoon. Could you tell me why? Not that I didn't like it. The finale was great, but you have your reasons, and I want to learn.'

'Let us get a quiet table, get some food and drink, and I'll fully explain my reasons to you.'

The dining room was not that full, and Paul secured a table at the very end so that he could talk easily with her. They order a main course, neither wanted starters, a bottle of wine, and a bottle of water.

'Okay here starteth today's lesson', he said, sounding like some priest.

She smiled sweetly.

'The great maker of mankind got some things wrong when he created us, or they appear to be wrong. You told me that you have not had an orgasm, except self-induced, all year even though you have engaged in some sex with Andrew. Correct?'

Yes, that's true', she responded.

'Why do you think that is?'

'Andrew does not have your interest savouring me, nor does he have your skills.'

'How were things when you first met at university, and again when you were first married?'

'At university things were a bit rampant. Sometimes I would orgasm, and others not. After we got married the frequency of orgasm was less.'

'What ages were you both when your first became an item?'

'We were both eighteen.'

'So essentially you were the first serious lovers for each other, or did either of you have previous experience?'

'If the past few days are a measure, we were both fumbling in the dark. We learnt from each other.'

'Okay, thanks. Your answers tell me much about where you both are today.'

'The anomaly that I mentioned has to do with orgasm. A man can reach orgasm very quickly during intercourse. He can last no more than a couple of minutes in any event. However, to get a woman to reach orgasm from cold will take at least 5 minutes, if not more. This is why many women don't reach orgasm during sex. Men arouse very quickly, women need nurturing. If a woman is not already at least halfway to orgasm before sex she is unlikely to orgasm. Furthermore, the recovery time between possible orgasms for a man is 20 - 30 minutes, for a woman it can be less than one minute. Not very fair, eh?'

'So how come you can hit the spot with me every time you try?'

'First, we don't have a regular relationship, this is all new and exciting to you thus you are constantly aroused. Second, we're not in a day to day situation. You don't get up and prepare breakfast, do laundry, go to work, etc. etc. We are constantly together as if on a holiday together. Third, you want what I can give you so again you are aroused. In addition, and the subject that we are going to deal with tonight, is that I engage in constant foreplay with you, and do not attempt to bring you to climax until I know that you can get there in a short time.'

'I'm not aware of much foreplay as I know it, other than the showers we take.'

Every time I touch you, stroke you, look at you, pat your bum, dress you, undress you, say something intimate to you, it's all foreplay. Today I introduced you to overt foreplay in the form of toys used to prepare you, but no substitute for the real thing. Thus when I 'punished' you this evening you must have been gagging for attention.'

'You're right. I wondered if you were going to do anything to me, or just leave me wanting.'

'The problem I'm having is that I can't help but touch you all of the time, which does not help my intention. But I wanted to

Prejudice in Love

illustrate to you the significance of foreplay, and thus my more overt methods today.'

'Think about it Cis, with the exception of me driving, what percentage of our time together have we not been in contact with each other, even while sleeping? 1%, 2%, but no more than 5%. This is not normal lifestyle. Thus I had to exaggerate foreplay to illustrate what I want to teach you.'

'What do you and Andy do for foreplay?'

'This year - nothing. Before a little fondling, stripping, kissing. Nothing like you are describing or doing to me.'

'So neither of you engage in any real foreplay. Why do you expect to have orgasms, or even good sex? I appreciate that Andy has withdrawn because of this baby fixation, but in 10 years neither of you have advanced your skills in good sex. At your age I could do most of what I can do today, and I made sure that I found out as much as I could to help me develop and hone those skills. I think both of you are sleepwalking to divorce because neither of you understand how to enjoy each other.'

Cis just sat there down in the mouth as she realised she was being scolded by her lover for not being good at sex. 'Okay', she said, 'I can see that what you say is true, and you can certainly demonstrate your skills. But we are where we are. How do we get to where you think we should be?'

'How much of what I have taught you so far are you prepared to teach to Andy?'

'All of it. I like it, and now have tasted it. Why wouldn't I encourage him to learn how to please me? I want what you give to me, and I lust for the dirty side of this game. Getting Andy into the mood might be a problem, but I guess you'll show me how to do that once I have mastered these skills myself.'

'You are a great student Cis, and I love showing you how to enjoy your body, and good sex. What you need to do is remember how you feel at each touch, each action so you know when you and Andy have it right. You must ask for what you want, and not be afraid to guide your partner to give you exactly what you want from them. I want you to start asking me for what you want, exactly what you want, and how you want it.'

'But I can't teach Andy how to touch me like you do. When you touched me in our first night it was electrifying. And when you stroked my pussy you knew exactly where to touch, and how to touch. You were totally in control, and I would not have stopped you for anything.'

'There is an Indian saying, I think in Karma Sutra, where the Indian man holds that you touch a woman's clitoris in the right way, she's yours. When I touched you that first night any prejudice that you may have had towards me evaporated. There was a hand in the darkness that was touching you as you desired. There was no other contact. That hand could have been any hand so long as it knew how to touch you. I'll teach you to show Andy how to touch you properly such that you cannot see him, and you can fantasise that it's me if that gives you a better experience. It's normal that once the excitement of a new relationship fades, unless the foreplay is very good, orgasm will not always be part of sex. So, you need to get that another way, but not always by yourself, someone else who knows how to handle you well.'

'Where did you learn to stroke a body so well? How did you know how to touch a woman? Was this your teacher, Jill?'

'No. Stroking was a technique I was taught by a lovely lady called Mai in Thailand. It has, as its base, a style of massage called Thai Yoga massage, but it's the stress release version.'

'Okay, I'm listening. Tell me about your lessons in Thailand with the lovely Mai.'

'I was in Bangkok for some weeks creating the first branch of our bank in Thailand. I was already aware of the healing benefits of Thai massage from a few years before when I was playing a tennis tournament in Phuket. I injured myself in practise and was told by our team physio that I was unlikely to be fit enough to play the tournament. The Thai coach suggested I visit with their physio team, which was mainly a group of women. They looked at my injury and suggested I have a massage. But this was no ordinary massage, this was a Thai massage which is performed on a mat on the floor. You do not lie still. You are moved around in harmony with the masseur, or two in my case as they were about 5ft 4ins and me being 6ft 2ins. They bend you, shape you, following old traditions relating to energy centres and the Sen lines which control the energy flows through your body. They paid particular attention around my injury. This went on for around 2 hours during which time I did not recognise one single touching process. However, I did feel very relaxed afterwards, and was told to lie still for about 10 – 15 minutes afterwards with an empty mind. When I started to move around, I felt good. I was told to eat lightly and sleep deeply that evening. I played the tournament without so much as a twinge.'

'Before travelling to Bangkok to start my work there I endured a particularly gruelling 3 – 4 months of travel so was not in the greatest of shape. I decided to find a good Thai masseur. The hotel manager pointed me to a professional healing centre where Mai practised. She was a few years older than me, somewhat shorter than me, but very strong. She could move my body around without exerting herself, and she was very experienced. I got into a routine of visiting with her 2 – 3 times per week for a typical two-hour session.'

'After a few weeks I went to her for a session, but I was very tired and stressed. It was a particularly difficult time bringing many local people together to do things our way, rather than theirs. We were on very good terms by then, and she also helped me to understand Thai culture to help me deal with these people. She took one look at me and told me that she would use a completely different technique to de-stress me. Unlike a normal Thai Yoga massage where I would wear shorts and maybe a loose top, she closed the door and asked me to strip naked and lie face down on the mat spread-eagled.

I initially found this request odd, but the relationship was strong enough to give me the confidence to comply with her instruction. She did not pull me around or dig her elbows into my energy centres. She gently stimulated an energy centre, and then move her fingers along my Sen lines to the next energy centre and repeat the process. She started from the top of my skull and worked on each energy centre in sequence on both sides of my body at the same time, all the way down to my feet. The touch of her fingers on my skin was electric. I was then turned over by her, and she started the process again, but this time she went from my forehead to abdomen, and then feet to abdomen. I could feel a warmth flowing throughout my body. Then she whispered in my ear that I should not be alarmed at what she was about to do, and when she was finished I should allow her to reposition my body, she would cover me, and I should not move until all of the energy that I would feel flowing through my body had settled back to a rest position.'

'She then positioned herself on her knees between my legs, facing me. She took my penis and started to caress it until an erection started. Then she ran her hands up my penis with her thumb in contact with the underside of my penis from base to head, and her fingers would circle the base of the head before starting the process with her other hand. This was not like masturbation. It was completely different, but she soon had my penis throbbing. She got into a steady rhythm, one hand after the other. I could feel the sensations, not only in my groin, but throughout my body. After a few minutes I ejaculated and felt by whole body light up as though someone had thrown a switch in my body. I could feel energy flowing through my whole body, and I was sweating profusely. Without fuss she quickly wiped the semen from my body, closed my legs to shoulder width, moved my arms by my side, and covered me in a warm towel from chin to toes. She quietly reminded me not to move and keep my head clear of any thoughts until my body calmed.'

'After about 20 minutes she invited me to take a shower before dressing. As this whole process had taken a little over 1 hour, and I had booked for 2 hours I asked her to explain exactly what she had done, and why. She explained it all to me, and why the penis, and the clitoris in the woman, are the primary energy centres, and having stimulated all of the main energy centres, and removed any blockages between each centre, an orgasm then causes a massive movement of energy around the system to rebalance the body. The sweat was toxins being ejected through the pores of the skin.'

'She also explained that the general ignorance of Westerners meant that this process was seen as sexual, although not intended that way. Probably why you see in many advertisements for Thai massage in England a message that they do not offer any sexual service. She did admit that women did find the stroking very arousing if the hands were experienced and was necessary in any event to achieve orgasm quickly before the body got cold from the massage. Explains why these Thai masseurs are mostly women to prevent things getting out of hand.'

I asked her if she would teach me how to perfect this technique on a woman. She allowed me to practise on her under her instruction. She would massage me so that I could feel how she was stimulating the energy centres and the Sen lines, and then I would practise on her. Jill had already taught me how to masturbate a woman, so this part was easy. There you have it.'

'Incredible. You get Mai to teach you how to arouse a woman just by the touch of your fingers, and she let you practise on her. Did she let you take her to full orgasm?'

'Of course she did. When I mastered the technique, she was getting a full massage and I was paying for it.'

Did this never lead to sex between you?'

'No. This was a teacher and student relationship. You must remember that the English are real prudes with their bodies. If you go to Germany or Scandinavia and try to enter a mixed sauna in any clothing at all you will be laughed out of there. When we were having some fun just before I left Bangkok she did ask if she could try to masturbate me with her vagina. Thai women are not used to large men in that part of the world and she was interested to see how my erection felt inside her.'

'And what happened?'

'She reached orgasm before me, so we just collapsed in laughter.'

'It sounds like I really need to meet Mai and take Andy with me for lessons.'

It's really a shame that the English have such a prudish attitude as I would love to have somewhere I could get this type of massage. I can get the physical Thai Yoga massage, but not the de-stress version.'

Cis looked at him with her playful look 'But Paul, you could open your own therapy unit for women. I would certainly be a client and would readily recommend you to all my friends. Think about all those stressed-out women in the City. I could write a magazine article about it from first-hand experience. You would have queues around the block.'

With a wry smile on his face 'Do you really think the authorities would allow such a place? And what about when these women are fully aroused and then demand sex? Nice idea but I don't think so; not in England.'

'Anyway Cis, have you had enough to eat and drink? Would you like anything else?'

Cis reached across the table so that she could whisper 'Your story about Mai has my juices flowing without so much as a finger on my body. Any ideas about what I might need?'

Paul smiled 'I have just the remedy back in our room'.

'Well then, let's go.'

Chapter 32

It was still early when they got back to their room. Cis opened the doors onto the balcony. 'It's a really pleasant evening. Why don't we sit out here for a while? We have this lovely balcony, but we haven't used it.'

'Would you like a drink?'

'Just water please.'

He joined her on the balcony, and they both stood watching the lights from other buildings flickering on the water as though fireflies dancing. The only continuous sound was the water from the loch lapping the shore. There was a calm peacefulness about this place that he really enjoyed. He had stayed on this loch some years earlier, and the peace and tranquillity he felt had stayed with him all these years. They both were silent for some time lapping up the moment.

Eventually he turned to her. 'It's been a long busy day. How do you feel about what has happen to you today?'

She thought for a moment. 'I feel overwhelmed with the mix of emotions that I've felt, and our discussion over dinner has brought some home truths to me that have made me re-evaluate my relationship with Andy. I've felt that our problems are mainly to do with Andy not grasping the nettle regarding our desire to have children. I thought he just buried his head in his business and hoped the problem will go away. Now you have shown me that I too am equally responsible for not finding a way through our problems, expecting Andy to find all the answers, and then getting frustrated when this doesn't happen. As you rightly observe Andy and I are just sleepwalking through our lives, neither taking responsibility.'

'You've shown me the reality, now I need you to show me the way forward.'

'Has anything that we have done today caused you a problem? Have you felt used or abused at any time?'

'Are you kidding me? I haven't had so much fun and attention in years. You have shocked me, and embarrassed me at times, but this is my closed mind which is now being prised open. You are taking the lid off my pre-conceptions, constraints, and ignorance, and I love it. This adventure is my voyage of discovery about myself, and I can't wait to continue wherever it takes me. I'm sad that I have to go back tomorrow but heartened that I can return to continue my adventure with you.'

She nudged his shoulder. 'I feel liberated, and now you have opened me up you need to feed me until I'm fully satiated.'

They sat in the wooden balcony chairs next to each other.

'Can you tell me your high points today, and any low points? I need feedback from you to know what you're gaining from our activities.'

'The really high point was when you punished me this evening. That was rough, animal sex and it felt truly wonderful.'

'Another high point was when you shared the story of your children with me in the sauna. You showed me a vulnerability in you that I found very moving. It showed me that my problems are trivial compared with the pain you have suffered, so wake up girl and get your life together.'

'I felt very privileged that you would share such pain with me.'

'Thank you. And how do you feel at the end of this busy day of emotional turmoil?'

She moved over, sat in his lap with an arm around his neck. Slowly she replied, 'I feel loved, wanted, and a very satisfied woman, totally at peace with the world and my wonderful valiant knight.' She then kissed him.

'Come, let's to bed. A big day for both of us tomorrow.'

Chapter 33

They went through their now bedtime ritual of him undressing her, completed their bedtime preparation, and slid under the sheets. He killed the lights thinking 'sleep is what I need. I'm too old for so much sex in one day.'

Cis whispered. 'What would you like to do with me tonight?'

He whispered back. 'It's time for you to take responsibility. Remember?'

She thought for a moment. Hold me close. Paul put his arms around her and pulled her close so that he could feel the warmth of her body against his.

'Kiss me as though it's your last kiss.'

He was amused by such a strange demand but obliged with a deep longing kiss expecting her to start to get urgent for more sex.

When their lips finally parted, she whispered 'stroke my back.'

Within minutes she was fast asleep, and Paul was only minutes behind her.

Chapter 34 - Wednesday

They both woke early.

'Why don't we go for a swim before breakfast?' Paul suggested, 'I could use some loosening of my muscles ready for my drive today.'

'Why not? We have plenty of time, and the pool should be empty at this time of the morning.'

She found her bikini and got into it without thinking about her pantie routine. She gathered robes and towels for them both and was ready.

Stephen Box

When they got to the pool they were not alone as two senior citizens were slowly swimming up and down the pool. But they were in the end channels leaving plenty of space.

He dropped his robe and towel on a lounger, and dived in. The water felt fresh, but not cold. He started to swim thinking he would need about five lengths to loosen up. She was soon behind him and catching him quickly. Once she was with him, she paced herself at his pace until they finished their five lengths. The other two swimmers seemed oblivious to their presence.

Paul was standing at the far end where the depth was 1.5m, just up to his shoulders. She needed to stand on her tip toes to keep her face above the water. He saw her difficulty and put his arm under her armpit and took her weight as she naturally glided towards him.

'The snake is coiled' he whispered in her ear.

She lowered her hand on the blind side of the pool and reached inside his trunks and took hold of his penis but stayed there knowing the code to be a ploy.

She, whispering in his ear, 'pussy needs attention.'

She could feel his reaction to her request as she held him, helping him to full erection with her gentle caresses.

He didn't put his hand down her bikini bottoms, but rather went straight to her crotch and moved her bikini bottoms over such that her vagina was fully exposed. He then started to use his fingers on her knowing this would fully arouse her.

She whispered, 'where's this going?'

He told her to do the same to him.

'A little more difficult with an erection this size.'

'Just ease him out of the side of my trunks, and then move the crotch of my trunks over my balls to expose them. She did as he instructed and found it quite easy.'

'Now I want you to put both arms around my neck and start to raise your legs around my waist.'

'What are you going to do?'

'Feed your pussy', he whispered.

'Here, with these people?'

'Yes, we'll start here and then go get naked.'

As she raised her hips, she could feel him hold her bottom with one hand and guide his erection to her wanton pussy. She easily slid straight onto him, all the way.

He pinned her against the wall of the pool and rotated his pelvis against her clit. She felt wicked. There she was with her pussy full of his erection, and the other swimmers were none the wiser. She relaxed as she started to enjoy the risqué nature of this action.

She reached a point where she knew if they continued, she would likely erupt at which point her gasps would uncover their activity.

'Time to get naked my love' she whispered.

He understood and slowly withdrew from her, realigned the crotch of her bikini and reinserted his own penis back into his trunks.

'You get out first and have my robe ready. My erection is a bit obvious in these trunks.'

She giggled. 'Think you can hold it back to the room.'

'It would be more fun for you to bring him back up when we get there. Don't want to waste energy.'

They quickly got back to their room and were both naked before they got to the bed. She headed onto the bed. He went over to her and lifted her off the bed into his arms, and then moved to the bathroom.

'Where're we going?', she laughed.

'We're going to the shower.'

'But I want to finish what we started in the pool.'

'You will, all in good time.'

'Now what's he planning' she thought.

She started the shower as usual, but when they had finished soaping each other he told her to switch off the water. 'Now open the shower door.'

'Take my penis in your hand and caress it.'

'Now kiss me.'

The kiss was long and hard and the intensity of her caresses on his erect penis grew more urgent.

'Now lead me out of the shower and get down on the bathroom floor.'

They were both completely wet and soapy, but she obeyed her master, lying on her back, legs apart. He got down onto the floor and slid straight into her – full penetration, causing her to gasp with pleasure. He raised himself so that they were only in contact at the point of entry. He started to move her body around on the now slippery floor using his pelvis. She could feel the delicious effect on her clitoris. He started to move in and out of her as he continued to move her. She held his forearms to give her some leverage to increase the intensity of the thrusts.

She felt that warm glow starting in her loins which, for her, signalled the start of an orgasm. Now she was allowing her body to flow with his rhythm. *'This is nice'* she thought, sliding around in the soapy water on the floor feeling his erection controlling her body. She felt the first spasm of her orgasm. He gave a much heavier thrust which caused her hips to buck. She was now on the verge of explosion. She could feel the heat in her loins as he thrust again this time causing her to explode, thrusting her torso off the floor, nearly hitting him in the face with her head as she exhaled a loud gasp of pleasure.

She lay back on the floor with her hand above her head totally submissive to the electricity flowing through her body.

He waited for about 30 seconds before thrusting into her again. Her eyes shot open as she felt this movement on her already swollen clitoris. He increased his speed of thrust. She could feel her clitoris throbbing. As he ejaculated into her, he thrust deep. Her clitoris took the full force of this thrust and she exploded again. She had never experience two orgasms in quick succession, the second being yet more powerful than the first. Her whole body was in spasm.

He looked at her, eyes glazed, satisfied smile, totally submissive on the floor. He kept his position to let her savour the waves of pleasure running through her body without disturbance.

When she refocused, she looked at him, 'You seriously expect me to go back to Andy and lose this pleasure?'

He went down onto his elbows so that he could kiss her. 'My dear Cis, you need to bundle all of this pleasure and take is back with you. Show Andrew how to indulge and rediscover your sensuality together.'

He extracted his now flagging penis from her and got onto his knees between her legs. 'You see we started in a pool of water, and finished in a pool of water', pointing at the water on the floor.

She giggled as she realised what he was saying.

He reached for her hands, 'come on my beautiful angel of desire, let us get back into the shower and get you warmed again. Your butt must be getting cold on this hard floor.'

They got up and back into the shower and the water was once again running warm. She held him around the waist, her head on his chest, warm water running down her back.

He left her with her thoughts for a few minutes as the water flowed over their bodies. 'You okay?', breaking the silence.

'Why am I going back to Edinburgh today and leave all of this here?'

He lifted her chin to look at her. 'There is a real world going on out there, and you need to maintain you place in it. You have a job that requires your attention. We have been in a bubble these past days, but you need to pop out of it for a while. It will also give me a chance to recharge my batteries. I'm getting too old for such a demanding nymph.'

She laughed at him. 'You haven't failed to rise to the occasion once' she giggled, cupping his now quiet penis. She reached up and kissed him.

'How did you feel when I whispered my code into your ear in the swimming pool?'

'Wickedly naughty. I couldn't wait to obey. Once I got hold of your willy and looked over your shoulder at the other swimmers, I so needed your hand on my pussy.'

'What about when I started to feed your pussy?'

'Delicious, but I could not have let you take me to orgasm. I would have died with embarrassment. Have you ever taken a woman to orgasm in a pool?'

'Yes, in an up-market couples holiday resort pool with a German nymph from Munich. I was pinned against the pool wall. She used the rail on the pool wall with her feet on the wall. She made it look like we were fooling around as she pleasured herself much like you did when you jumped me on Monday morning. When she was about to orgasm, she ducked her head under the water so that no-one heard her gasps of pleasure. She told me that her orgasm was more pleasurable at the thought of the number of people around us totally oblivious to what was really happening.'

'Sounds like you have had some fun sex in your time.'

He held her around her waist and looked at her. 'Dearest Cis, I was well versed in everything we have done, and will do when you get back before I was your age. Rampant sex is for the young to have fun, and time is passing you by. I grew up in the 1960's. I was a developed teenager in the most important youth revolution in my lifetime – 1967 through 1969. The pill was freely available, women were liberated, youth rebelled against the establishment, rock music was king, and we had fun. There was no such thing as HIV Aids or the other nasty sex diseases of today.'

He thought, *'if I start down this road, we'll be here all day.'* 'Come lady, let's finish up here before you become wrinkly. We need breakfast, and then I must get you to Balloch. The sooner you get your article filed, the sooner you get back. We can finish this conversation later.'

She washed his penis and her own vagina, turned off the water and they were out of there.

She felt she could not leave the evidence of their activity on the bathroom floor, especially as it also contained some of their love juices, so did a quick recovery job.

On the way to breakfast he quietly said 'Cis, you realise that the variation in the shower today is a good way to win or seal an argument.'

'Are you suggesting that a woman uses her body to win arguments?'

Paul looked at her quizzically, 'Only since Adam and Eve.'

She laughed. 'You wily, naughty man. I shall have to be careful with you. You know too much about the ways of women.'

She, thoughtfully, 'It's a very messy way to win an argument. And always left to the woman to clear up.'

'It's the woman who wins the argument. Small price to pay. Anyway, would you sacrifice such pleasure for the sake of a little water?'

'Now who wins the argument!'

Chapter 35

She was feeling good about their earlier exploits between the swimming pool and the watery floor of their bathroom. How totally naughty they were in the swimming pool. She wondered if she could keep a straight face if she saw the other swimmers in the breakfast room, or would she blush if they looked at her all-knowing like. She didn't really care. It was fun, and she felt exhilarated by the sheer devilment of her actions. That someone could be fully penetrated inside her pussy in public was such a buzz. And then a double orgasm. Never before had she experienced such a thrill.

When they were both seated, having made their selections from the breakfast bar, she was obviously ready to be playful. 'Okay, you naughty man, twice now you have taken advantage of me in public.' And then a pause. 'I want more. It's outrageous.'

Paul just looked at her with a wry smile. 'Be careful what you ask for. We can get much closer to the edge than yesterday and this morning.'

'I trust you with me. So why should I be careful. I've been careful all my life. Now it's time to take a few risks.'

'When you return tomorrow, I'll see what can be arranged. Will that do for now?'

'Oh, now I'm deflated. In the excitement I forgot that I'm going back to Edinburgh this morning. God, I'll miss you.'

'You get focussed on your article. I need you back in my arms.'

'Have no fear. I'll gen up on my notes on the train, and then start to get the words down as soon as I get home. I should finish it today if the words flow well. Sometimes I can file the first version. Other times I might need to edit and re-edit several times before I'm happy with it. I'm hoping that this article will just flow out of me so that I can file it today.'

'Look at the time. We need to get packed and out of here. You have a train to catch and I have about 150 miles of driving across the great glens up to Loch Ness.'

They went back to their suite and packed. He offered to take with him anything that she would have to bring back with her, but she needed a total change of clothes. She would travel in her new slacks, so better just take everything with her and start again.

He checked out, and they were on their way back to Bollach.

Chapter 36

As they approached Bollach Railway Station she became a little subdued.

'I'm really sorry that I cannot come with you today. You're going to a part of Scotland I've never seen. I can't think of anyone with whom I would rather take such a trip. Damn article. Why didn't I write it at my sister's house?'

He watched this turmoil with some amusement. Although he did not want her to go either, he knew that it would be good to have a break. They had not left each other's arms now for 3 days so a little lone reflection for a few hours would be good for both.

He parked the car and helped her with her bag. She bought a ticket to Glasgow Central, and a separate ticket from Glasgow Central to Edinburgh Central. Although this confounded the ticket counter lady, He knew exactly what she was doing. She would ditch the ticket to Glasgow as soon as she arrived there, and then only have the ticket from Glasgow to Edinburgh in her purse. Totally consistent with her trip to Braehead Shopping Centre with her friend.

Paul liked her attention to detail despite her display of turmoil.

As the train was leaving within two minutes, goodbyes were short and sweet. A big hug and kiss and she's gone.

He stood on the platform watching the train disappear into the distance. He was missing her already.

Chapter 37

Paul sat in his car trying to focus his mind on the drive he was about to take. After all he was about to embark on the leg of this journey that had inspired him to plan this trip earlier this year. He thought about some of the stunning natural wilderness that he had visited throughout the world. The Rockies in the USA, the wilderness in the Arctic Circle of Canada, the outback of Australia, Siberia in Russia to name but a few. And then there is Europe with the Alps and the Pyrenees. He had driven most routes through both the Alps and the Pyrenees. He thought about the haunting silhouettes of the misty mountains at dawn on the drive down through Austria towards the Brenner Pass into Italy, the trip across the Splugenpass from Switzerland into the Po Plain of Italy where it can be summer at the start of the winding climb, and winter at the top, Toulouse down to Barcelona through the wild and varied topography of Andorra, or across the lush rugged mountains of the Basque Region of Northern Spain, but none compared to the drive that he was about to start. With all the drives he could remember, they all had one thing in common – he always felt that civilisation was never far away. There is no such comfort for his drive today. The Highlands has one of the sparsest populations in Europe.

Scotland is essentially a country of two parts. The Lowlands nestle between England and the Highlands and is the populous part of Scotland with Edinburgh on the east coast and Glasgow on the west coast. In traditional Scottish geography the Highlands refers to the northern part of Scotland stretching from where he was sitting in his car at the south-west corner of the Highland Boundary Fault which crosses mainland Scotland in a near-straight diagonal line from Helensburgh, a little to the west of where he was parked, to Stonehaven in the east. However the flat coastal lands that occupy parts of the counties of Nairnshire, Morayshire, Banffshire, and Aberdeenshire are often excluded as they do not share the distinctive and spectacular geographical and cultural features of the remainder of the Highlands, a landscape of mountains, glens, lochs, rivers and forests resulting from ancient mountains formed from early extensive volcanic activity, and then huge glaciers carving out the lochs and glens; magnificent in its grandeur of remote tranquillity. Within these Highlands lies Ben Nevis, the highest mountain, and Loch Ness, the deepest lake in Great Britain. It is easy to become mesmerised by the majesty of the Scottish Highlands but ignore the dangers of this unspoilt wilderness at your peril, especially during the winter months.

He reflected upon his amusement that many people do not really comprehend just how large a country is Scotland. He had met many foreigners to the United Kingdom who had the idea that Scotland and Wales were minor appendages to England. This may be reasonable for Wales but certainly not for Scotland. Having driven the route in past years he had noted, assuming Gretna Green as probably the most known border crossing from England into Scotland, that the distance from Gretna Green to John O'Groats, the most northern tip of mainland Scotland, is further than from Gretna Green to London. He had also noted on previous trips that the drive from London to Inverness, considered the capital of the Highlands and nestled in the middle of the Highland at the northern end of the infamous Loch Ness, was further than the drive from London to Zurich in Switzerland, and certainly took some 3 – 4 hours longer as there are no highways in the Highlands.

He looked at the original trip plan that he had compiled on his iPad earlier that year. Today he would drive the full length of Loch Lomond towards Crianlarich. At the end of Loch Lomond his original trip plan would require him to head west to Inveraray on his way to the shores of Oban with its abundance of wildlife on and around the small uninhabited islands along the sheltered shoreline. Here he would expect to see grey seal, dolphins, whales, porpoise, and otters in their natural habitat. In the skies he would expect to see sea eagles, golden eagles, buzzards and peregrine falcons circling in search of prey. And, of course he should not forget the spectacular whirlpools within the Gulf of Corryvreckan. However, this diversion required a whole day, a day he had already used to shelter Cis from the storm.

His mind wandered back to her. Whatever I do I must position myself at the end of today such that tomorrow I can get to Gleneagles within a few hours. If he went to Oban his planned stopover at Dalmally, near Kilchurn Castle, or Tyndrum would achieve this, but he would have to travel across country and miss the best leg of this trip. He had the luxury of traveling alone; no-one else to consider, not even for refreshment or pit stops. Oban was more for Jane than him, with her love of all things wildlife. For him, the rugged landscape of the wilderness was his draw to this country. *'But what about if when she gets back to Edinburgh reality kicks in and she realises that their encounter was an embarrassing mistake and she avoids any further contact. What about if her mind is so distracted as a result of the past three days that she finds the deadline for her article difficult to meet meaning that she would stay in Edinburgh on Thursday. Andy is due back on Saturday so would it be worth her coming to Gleneagles for just one day.'* She was proving a distraction to his desired objective for this trip. A very nice distraction, but distraction none the less. A decision had to be made. If he goes to Aviemore and she does not call tomorrow he is well positioned to explore the Cairngorm Mountains and National Park. He also recalled that this trip was also about him getting far away from normality to take time to look at his life, and where he wanted to go for his remaining time on this earth.

Decision Made. He would skip Oban and instead head across the moors towards Glen Coe. He had previously driven through Glen Coe during the spring when it boasts some of the most majestic scenery in the Highlands, and again during the winter when the moody, mist-shrouded mountains, snow-caked moorlands, rushing burns, and steely-grey lochs can be forbidding, and the road is often closed to other than the most rugged of four-wheel drive vehicles.

His research notes refreshed his memory that Glen Coe is the remains of an ancient super-volcano that erupted about 420 million years ago and is considered to be one of the best examples of Cauldron Subsidence. This volcano, as with all the volcanoes in Scotland, has long since become extinct. The landscape was then further shaped by the processes of glaciation during the last ice age some 10,000 years ago resulting in a U-shaped valley, about 16 km (9.9 miles) long with the floor of the glen being less than 700m (0.4 miles) wide, narrowing sharply at the Pass of Glen Coe about halfway along, and then running roughly west for about 12 km (7.5 miles) before turning north-west towards Loch Leven.

From the north-east boundary of Glen Coe at Fort William he would drive along the lochs of the Caledonian Waterway to the heart of the Great Glen at Fort Augustus, the start of Loch Ness. Here he would move away from the highway leading to Inverness along the north coast of Loch Ness, and instead take a military-built road along the south shore of Loch Ness up to the Falls at Foyers, the part of this trip which is new ground for him, and which he wants to test for both accessibility, and interest. From there he would make his way along the country tracks through the Arctic mountain landscape of the Monadhliath Mountains towards Aviemore at the heart of the Cairngorms National Park.

Having thought through the splendour of his planned route his mind was set to enjoy the tantalising pleasure of today's drive. The sky was blue, the sun was shining; the vista would be in full view. His iPad was switched into hotel search mode in or near Aviemore. There were plenty of choices at this time, so he quickly eliminated any hotels below 4-star quality, and any that did not include breakfast. Of the four choices remaining he selected the one with a spa and pool and booked it. He re-arranged the cabin of his car so that incidentals such as his binoculars and camera were close at hand. The singular nature of highways meant that there was no need for his satnav, or at least as far as Fort Augustus at the base of Loch Ness, so he fired up his Range Rover and was on his way.

The drive along the A86 all the way along the west shore of Loch Lomond took much longer than Paul had anticipated. Once he had driven past Luss the road became less than the 'A' road quality that he expected. The road surface had obviously experienced a lot of water damage at some point, probably in the spring when the water resulting from the melting snow from the mountains ran in torrents down to the loch, crossing the road on its journey. Although the road had been patch-filled it had not been properly repaired. The traffic throughout the summer had obviously lifted the infirm material out of the repairs leaving a multitude of potholes to be navigated. He was thankful that he had not brought the Porsche as some of the potholes were quite deep. This poor state meant that driving speeds were quite slow. But he was not bothered. He knew from past experience that anyone driving through the Highlands to a fixed timetable was on a fool's errand; not quite as bad as parts of Ireland, but the numerous potential obstacles rendered any timetable irrelevant, and would only lead to frustration in this peaceful environment. The lush forestry along the loch was spectacular, and he was enjoying the wilderness feel of the landscape.

After negotiating several road works toward the northern tip of Loch Lomond he finally reached the small town of Tarbet where his original route would guide him on the road to Inveraray as the first stage towards Oban. He reflected on the much-heralded tourist draw that Walt Disney, upon visiting the iconic Inveraray Castle, used it as the template for his famous Walt Disney castle creation. He smiled at the vast gulf between where he was and DisneyWorld – two different worlds.

Instead of turning left to Oban he continued towards Crianlarich which would take him on to Glen Coe through the heather moorlands knowing that once he crossed the small but, to him significant, Bridge of Orchy he was entering his favourite part of the Highlands south of the Caledonian Canal.

As he entered Glen Coe the softer beauty of the landscape rapidly changed. The first vista was the dominating and impressive peak of Buachaille Etive Mor – the great heardsman of Etive from across the bleak expanse of Rannock Moor. The road started to rise some 1,000 feet over the wilderness of Rannock with its craggy rocks and desolate heather moorland, before descending into the glen which runs in an east/west direction with steep-sided mountains on both sides. To the north he could see a stark wall of a mountain known as Aonach Eagach Ridge, a precipitous and craggy knife-edge which is a challenge even for experienced climbers. To the south a series of peaks dominated the skyline, three of which are known as the Three Sisters of Glen Coe and are very popular with hill walkers.

He decided that he needed to stop for a while to absorb the splendour of this rugged and desolate landscape. The authorities had created lay-bys at around 200 yards apart along the glen, and parking was in line with the view to the south-east with the three Sisters of Glen Coe. He picked a lay-by that overlooked a stretch of steely water out of which stood majestic columns of granite sculptured by nature over the centuries but looking as though placed there to add dimension to the landscape. He remembered the first time that he had stopped here all those years ago, and as a keen photographer, had jumped out of his vehicle with his camera and dashed across to get close to these haunting figures only to realise that the grassy landscape was a cruel illusion to the unknowing visitor as he was sinking into the peat bog which dominates this glen. He was soon up to his ankles in cold water but got his pictures.

He could imagine Cis doing exactly the same. Would he warn her? Not at all. It was part of the experience. In any event someone had laid a risen walkway across to the water's edge, albeit tipped to look like it is a natural feature of the landscape and thus not obvious as an alternative to the wet feet experience. He grabbed his camera. The combination of sunlight and broken cloud cast eerie shadows from the granite columns onto the steely water, so he would try to capture this artistic beauty without getting his feet wet.

Having taken his pictures, he sat there for a while realising why he loved this place so much. Even though civilisation was only a few miles away you would not know it from where he was sitting. Man had not tamed this landscape or shown any interest to even try.

At the centre of the glen lies the small village of Glencoe overlooked by the impressively shaped Pap of Glencoe, and which essentially provides the needs of the vast number of tourists who visit this glen each year. His original trip plan would take him north-west a short distance out of the village to the old drover's stop of Clachaig Inn for lunch, but today he wanted to press on. She was now far from his thoughts as he took great nourishment from the sheer magnificence of this intrepid landscape. He had now become totally absorbed in the venture he had planned, and the vista certainly justified the research he had undertaken to plan this route.

Having left Glen Coe he turned north-east towards Fort William. On his right he could see Ben Nevis in the distance standing at 1,344 metres (4,409 ft) above sea level. The summit, which is the collapsed dome of an ancient volcano, was shrouded in mist as it is some 80% of the time. On his left was the shimmering steely waters of Loch Linnhe, now part of the Caledonian Canal.

Lying in the shadow of Ben Nevis, Fort William is known as the 'Outdoor Capital of the UK'. It is the second largest town in the Highlands. It lies at the southern end of the Great Glen, on the shores of Loch Linnhe and Loch Eil. As there is no access to the centre for vehicles, he drove around it into the Great Glen that would lead him to Fort Augustus at the start of Loch Ness. He intended to explore this town on his original trip plan but, again, he was keen to push on to the part of this route not familiar to him.

The Great Glen is a series of glens running for 62 miles (100 km) from Inverness in the north-east on the edge of Moray Firth, to Fort William at the head of Loch Linnhe in the southwest. It follows a large geological fault known as the Great Glen Fault, bisecting the Scottish Highlands into the Grampian Mountains to the southeast, and the Northwest Highlands to the northwest. The rocks along the fault were pulverised and shattered by the fault movements and so have been eroded more easily by flowing water and scoured by ice. A series of long, deep sea and freshwater lochs now remain along its length. The lack of islands in the lochs of the Great Glen and the steepness of the flanking slopes testify to the efficiency of the ice in scouring out this feature, leaving sides that are both too steep and too rocky for anything but forestry. All he could see was vast forests of pine and larch trees.

Fort Augustus has an unusual topography lying very low in a valley and regularly boasting both the highest and lowest temperature recorded in the UK each year. The landscape reflects this oasis of extremes and has a dramatic series of eight staircase locks stepping down the 20m drop from the Caledonian Canal to Loch Ness. Known by the name of Neptune's Staircase these locks were designed in the 17th century for cargo ships to pass and had manual gates until the early twentieth century when the gates had hydraulics added. He could not help but marvel at both the engineering prowess of these locks and at their beautiful elegance with their crafted ironwork reminiscent of trail-blazing engineering projects of that era.

Neptune's Staircase lies at the heart of Clan Frazer country, the kilt of which clan he has the right to wear by birth right. In his original travel plan they would spend some time here, and then remain on the A83 highway which crosses the canal at this point to follow the north-west side of Loch Ness for an overnight stop near Invermoriston on the shore of Loch Ness to savour the rugged vista of this infamous stretch of water, with its tales of a pre-historic monster roaming the depths, before moving on to Inverness. But today he turned right onto a country road signposted Errogie and Foyers. This was the start of the part of the route new to him. After a further six miles he turned left onto a much narrower road signposted Foyers. From here it was a continual climb along a narrow road originally built by the military. After some three miles he saw a small café and a car park. The car park indicated that they had visitors, including a coach. *'Popular place'* he thought as he pulled into the car park. He knew from his research that this was the starting point to the climb down to the Falls.

He stretched his legs on his walk to the café. It was time for some refreshment so purchased a coffee and sandwiches. The counter lady told him that if he waited a few minutes the people from the coach should be leaving. He thanked her and sat on a bench outside to eat his sandwiches.

Having finished his lunch, he looked at his phone to see it was 2:20pm. It suddenly occurred to him that he had not spoken to Jane since he left on Sunday morning. He sent her a text message to see if she was available as it would be nearly 10:30pm in Singapore. She responded within a minute with the hotel telephone number. Using his special, low rate International call card he hit the number she gave and asked for her room number. Jane responded immediately.

'Hi. Where are you?'

'Currently sitting looking over the Falls at Foyers on the edge of Loch Ness. The drive from Luss is much slower than I thought but driving across the glens was spectacular. The military track I found up the east side of the loch is not bad, and the visit is well worth the effort. How's Singapore?'

'As usual. Everybody wants much more than is worthwhile for a 3-year occupation, but we are slowly beating these requirements down to a realistic budget. They don't understand that they cannot expect the same facilities that we have in London because in London we have a 15-year lease and thus amortising costs is over a much longer timeframe. How was the hotel at Luss?'

'The Carter Suite is very nice, not cheap, but worth the spend. Location is fantastic, right on the shore, and the food is very acceptable. I bought another dress kilt, but in a blue tartan. I thought the tartan might be a little young for me at first, but it looks good.'

'Can't wait to see it. Where are you going now?'

'From here I'll continue north, but not as far as Inverness as it is later than I thought to get here. So as soon as I can I'll turn towards Aviemore and spend some time there. I have decided to stop at Gleneagles on the way back to see what it's like as a potential stopover.'

'Good idea. When do you expect to get back home?'

He thought about this answer to give himself as much time as he could with Cis. 'Not before Tuesday. Are you still back on Tuesday evening?'

'Still not sure. Tuesday evening, or Wednesday morning. I have a wait list on the Tuesday evening flight, but a firm booking on the Wednesday morning arrival. I'll let you know as soon as I have a firm confirmation.'

'Okay. I'll make sure that I'm back sometime Tuesday so that I can collect you at the airport if your plane is too late for the train.'

'Great. When will I hear from you again?'

Thinking about the possible return of Cis tomorrow 'Well if you need something urgently then just text me and I'll get back as soon as I can. Otherwise I'll try when I am sitting doing nothing around this time, possibly at the weekend.'

'Okay. Have a great time. Miss you. (kiss) (kiss).'

'Sleep tight. (kiss) (kiss)'

The people from the bus were now returning, and eventually the bus was ready to leave and made its way back towards Fort Augustus. *'Thank goodness for that'* he thought. He did not relish the idea of coming face-to-face with a tourist coach along the single carriageway roads and tracks that he was contemplating to use on his way to Aviemore.

Walking across the road from the café, and collecting his camera from his car, he followed a well maintained but rugged path cut into the landscape leading steeply down forested slopes to two viewpoints overlooking the Falls of Foyers. This is the spectacular 140ft waterfall in which the River Foyers drops into a gorge finally twisting it way into Loch Ness. During his walk he came across several interesting information boards about the falls and the history of Foyers as well as boards each quoting two lines of the poem written by Robbie Burns, the most famous of Scottish poets. He noted that during the Victorian period the falls and gorge were a popular tourist attraction for the gentry, arriving by paddle steamer from Inverness. Adjacent to the falls there were forest and gorge walks, and he noticed the unusual abundance of red squirrels in the trees, and friendly enough to seek gifts of food from visitors.

He was inspired to visit these falls by a poem about the Falls of Foyers written by Robbie Burns in 1787:

> *Among the heathy hills and ragged woods*
> *The roaring Foyers pours his mossy floods;*
> *Till full he dashes on the rocky mounds,*
> *Where, through a shapeless breach, his stream resounds,*
> *As high in air the bursting torrents flow,*
> *As deep-recoiling surges foam below,*
> *Prone down the rock the whitening sheet descends,*
> *And viewless Echo's ear, astonish'd rends.*
> *Dim seen, through rising mists and ceaseless showers,*
> *The hoary cavern, wide-surrounding, lowers.*
> *Still, through the gap the struggling river toils,*
> *And still, below, the horrid cauldron boils.*

Having finally navigated the track down to the falls he decided to sit for a while. He thought the falls may not be as dramatic as they once were in Victorian times, not least because the river Foyers was dammed further upriver, initially for an aluminium smelting plant, and later for a hydro facility. However, he thought that they are still worthy of a visit, and should be included in his trip plan, should he ever make it back here with Jane and her parents.

After absorbing the raw beauty of the scenery around him, and the constant stream of water over the falls swirling into the gorge below he started to let his mind drift. He sat thinking about his relationship with Jane. They had been through much together but had survived. He would not call it a totally loving relationship, more comfortable, but he was not about to challenge it for something he knew in his heart he would like to try when, in his head, it was a non-starter. Cis was far too young for him, and she wanted children.

But why had this encounter occurred? He had experienced all kinds of brief encounters in the past, but this was different. It was far more intense, and there is no obvious end-game. There is something missing, or had he just missed it?

Whatever, she was a stunningly beautiful lady, a great companion, and the sex was fantastic. *'Why am I questioning this good fortune?'* he asked himself, *'Just roll with it and see where it leads.'* It made him feel useful again. He was imparting much knowledge to this inexperienced woman, and she was clearly appreciative. It was good to have a purpose and add real value to this woman's life. He felt needed, something he had missed for some time.

He could hear voices descending the pathway to the Falls. It was a little after 3pm. He decided it was time to work his way north, and then east to Aviemore as he wanted to get there long before it got dark so that he could look around. If she could file her article today she would be on an early train to Gleneagles which would mean an early start for him. Until then he would concentrate on enjoying his drive across this rugged landscape to Aviemore.

Upon return to his car he decided that his satnav would provide a safety net should the signposting prove minimalist, or he takes a wrong turning. This was a lonely place to get lost, especially as mobile telephone signals were a luxury in this part of the world. Even if he takes a turn not indicated on his satnav the immediate re-computation of his route would quickly identify if he could still proceed to Aviemore, or the need to backtrack. He keyed the co-ordinates for the hotel he had booked at Aviemore and waited the few moments needed to compute the optimal route. Interestingly the distance was shown as 43 miles, but the journey time suggested 1 hour 43 minutes. This clearly reflected the type of roads he could expect through the mountains as the final 22 miles, equating to less than 30 minutes, was along the main A9 highway. This information made him feel refreshingly alive as, with his sturdy Range Rover under him, he looked forward to the challenge through this rugged landscape.

Chapter 38

Her journey back to Edinburgh was consumed with internal conflict. She had intended to use the time to look at her notes from the fashion show last week so that she could formulate in her mind what she wanted to write in her article. She needed 1,000 words, polished and filed today. But she looked with glazed eye at the words in her notebook; her mind was completely engaged with her feelings over these passed days. She could not even recall the change of trains at Glasgow Central.

What am I doing? In real life what has happened over the past few days is total madness. I'm a 28 year old married woman having a covert romantic affair with a man more than twice my age. Let's remove "covert" to start with', she thought. *'Everyone who has any contact with us will be under no illusion or confusion as to the nature of our relationship'.* She oozed her feelings for this man, and the brazen nature of her feelings.

'Has my relationship with Andy reached such a low ebb that I must find what I need to fulfil me elsewhere; anywhere?' She could have any man she wanted with her looks, so why this man? She could not use his name in these thoughts because every time she did the warmth and affection he showed to her clouded reality.

She looked out of the train window and noticed that they were approaching Edinburgh station. She got off the train, straight into a cab, and was home in ten minutes.

Andy and Cis had a nice four storey townhouse in Ravelston, one of the more affluent parts of central Edinburgh. Both sets of parents had helped them to put down a sizeable deposit when they got married, and both generated good incomes.

She picked up the post and placed it on the hall table without even looking through it. Then through to the living room and dropped her bags. *'I need to get out of these clothes'* she thought so went up to their bedroom and started to change into her house tracksuit type top and bottoms. She was bra-less and decided she would stay that way. No man had ever actually asked her to go bra-less before, but she liked it.

She needed the toilet. It was also time for her daily ritual to test if she was close to ovulation, not that it mattered with Andy away. She was still so lost in her thoughts that she almost missed the smiley face on the testing stick. It wasn't there yesterday. 'Oh no,' she gasped, 'I'm close to ovulation, and I go back to Paul tomorrow. What a cruel twist. Thank goodness he bought condoms at Braehead.'

She scanned the fridge for something to eat. Not much, a few yoghurts, and some fruit. She hadn't been there for a week so what did she expect, and shopping for food on her way from the station was not even in her mind.

'Okay, okay, concentrate woman' she told herself. 'You have an article to file. This is a must do so sit down and get on with it. You can get a takeaway later.' She needed to insert some discipline into her confusion and absorbing herself in this task should help her to get some perspective.

Her telephone rang. It was her editor. 'Hi Cis. Will you have your article filed today?'

'This industry' she thought. *'No time for pleasantries, just deadlines.'*

'Yes, I'm polishing it as we speak so it will be filed this afternoon.'

'Thanks, Cis. Look forward to reading it. Bye.'

This was the crack of the whip she needed, the reality of the journalist's deadline. She sat at her desk, opened her notebook, booted her laptop, and started to work.

It took about 2 hours to structure her article into a finished, polished product. She was pleased with what she had written, so immediately filed it. Job done.

She noticed that the "messages waiting" light was flashing on their landline telephone. Three messages, one from her mother *'Oh my God, I forgot to phone my mum on Sunday!'* Another was to remind her that she was due a dental check-up, and the other from Andy. He did not call her on her mobile whilst away in strange places because of the horrendous call charges. She listened to his call, 'Hi Cis, things are going well in Turkey so will be delayed until Tuesday evening. Love you, Andy.' Her immediate reaction was *'I'm near ovulation Andy, and I need you here. Tuesday will be too late.'*

Next job, call Mum. Her mother took the phone after just two rings. 'Hi Mum, how are things? Sorry that I didn't call on Sunday, but I was trying to escape the storm. You know what I'm like with thunder and lightning.'

They spoke about her sister escaping to the Caribbean just in time. Her mother wanted to know what she did to avoid the storm. 'I ended up staying with a friend. I've only just got home to see your message.' She camouflaged any further discussion by telling her Mum that she should call her on her mobile if she is not at home. Her mother had still not embraced mobile telephone technology, treating it as some addictive device judging by the way younger people could not leave them alone for even a few minutes, and thus did not want the torture of being shackled to one. Her father had a mobile phone, but her mother would never think of asking him to borrow it. She ended the call by telling her mother that she was away again tomorrow, but will be back on Monday, so will call her then.

She looked around her. The sun was starting to set. She needed to get herself organised for tomorrow. She recovered her travel bag from the living room and tipped it out on her bed. She salvaged the remaining clean underwear, her new bikini which was still damp, and dwelt with her gorgeous camisole and French nickers set. Can't forget these she thought. She held them close to her for a moment feeling the fine silk, remembering his reaction when she modelled them for him. They were special, for special occasions, but only for him.

All dirty linen went into the laundry basket, and she put everything else away.

'Now what do I need for the next few days?' Now that Andy is delayed, she had already decided that she was going to stay with Paul until the very last minute before he started for home. She liked to be wanted and needed, and in his arms she felt alive. *'What did he say his choice of animal was, oh yes, Baloo the bear; not just any bear, but Baloo.'* Cuddling next to him with his arms around her he could easily be her big bear, keeping her warm and safe. How she loved the feeling of being in his arms.

Underwear first, she decided. *'I now know what he likes so let's start there.'* She opened her underwear drawer with neat rows of panties on the left, and bras on the right. She heard herself tell the bras that Paul did not have much use for them, so she would only take two just in case she wore a top needing a bra. 'Check', she said to herself, 'choose tops that I can wear without a bra.'

'What will I need for Gleneagles?' she thought. *'Walks. Spa. Gym. Swimming. Most of the time naked. Clothes that he can easily put on her and remove.'* She liked being dressed, and undressed by him, *'so keep it simple'*. She went through her wardrobes and drawers and put tidy piles of clothes on the bed.

'Hmm', she thought. *'Travel bag will not take this much. Roller case I think.'* Off to the closet to recover a suitably sized roller case and started to pack.

She was hungry. Not the most enthusiastic of cooks, but there were many restaurants within easy walking distance, some of which delivered. She fancied an Italian pasta dish and knew exactly who to call. It was now 7:30 and her dinner would be delivered within 45 minutes. She set herself a place on the living room coffee table and selected a bottle of wine.

Dinner arrived. It smelt delicious. She paid with a good tip for the delivery guy and took the food through to her makeshift dining table. *'TV, or music? I think music, something warm and romantic.'*

She sat down, poured a glass of wine, and emptied her food onto her plate. As she started to eat, it suddenly hit her that Paul was not with her. She reached for her bag and found the card he had given her so that she could phone him in the morning when she knew her plans. *'I already know my plans my darling'*, she thought. *'I could phone you now as you should already be at Aviemore. He could be at dinner. Maybe later.'*

She looked at the card. Paul Fulton it said. She kissed the card, 'you beautiful man'. Then she noticed something at the bottom of the card. It read "Blog: paul.fulton.com". 'He didn't tell me he wrote a blog.' She retrieved her laptop, put it next to her dinner, and hit the boot button. As soon as the laptop sprung into life she went into her browser and keyed his blog address. Up came his latest blog, with the index window on the right side of the screen. *'Nice blog page'*, she thought.

She could see that the index menu was full so looked at the topics. *'Wow, we have politics, economics, banking, finance, energy, world affairs; this is serious material.'* She looked at the dates of blogs. Looks like he writes at least once each week, with

Prejudice in Love

the latest being last Thursday. *'Don't think his followers will get one this week, he's too busy with me.'* She felt a warm glow pass through her.

She could see that he had to date posted 72 blogs, and he had a substantial follower group from all over the world. *'I have to read these. I want to know why he's so popular with such serious subjects.'* She decided she would download all of them and slowly work her way through them. She did a total word count – over 153,000 words in total. *'Maybe I will just select a few to start with.'*

Then she noticed a tab for an 'About' page. She clicked it. Up came his profile and a photograph. She noted that he needs a professional photographer to take a better photo. She read intently. *'This man has a fascinating background. No wonder he is my sage of all knowledge. Senior banker, economist, advisor to Governments, the list is long.'* She clicked for a new window in her browser and keyed his name in the search engine. Up came pages of references. The first that struck her was Who's Who. She clicked on it, and up came his bibliography. Tears came to her eyes, *'my valiant knight is a renowned hero, yet he is so humble with me. He's a giant of a man, but you would not have any problem sitting talking with him. Sure, he is obviously very clever, but very understated and unassuming.'*

She read down to his personal details. *'A son, James, and daughter, Sarah – a great sadness in his life.'* It listed his mother and father, and his ex-wife – *'the black witch he calls her'*, but not Jane. Long-term partners are still not included in such references.

She looked at his date of birth and realised that he was older than she had thought by four years which was a surprise to her. *'He keeps himself in good shape'*, she thought.

Her journalistic instincts kicked in as she decided she wanted to know more.

She finished her Italian takeaway, cleared away the dishes to give her some more table space for a notebook, and her fingers hit the keyboard of her laptop dropping some files down to her hard drive, and selective documents to her printer. By 10:30 she had printed some 50 pages and had numerous other files on her hard drive in a new directory called 'Valiant Knight'.

She started to read the selective items that she had chosen to print. His writing style was impressive, as was the way he could take complex arguments and break them down into basic detail. Anyone of average intelligence could read these articles and understand his argument. She sensed that she was growing ever closer to this man as she delved into his mind through his writing. *'No wonder I feel like a little girl in his presence'*, she thought, *'but he never makes me feel stupid or inferior. And the way he explains things to me are pitched at me, not down to me. I want to keep this man'*, but feeling a little naughty, *'preferably in my panties, although he would probably want to be around my breasts.'* She was feeling a little randy, and could imagine him now undressing her, and looking at her. She liked the way he looked at her when she was naked. Why didn't she have her vibrating panties with her; 'what an oversight this morning.'

It was now after midnight. She looked up. *'I should go to bed. I want to be out early tomorrow to journey back to my lover as soon as I can get there.'*

Although she normally wore a baby-doll top and knickers to bed, tonight she crawled into bed naked. She wanted to imagine being with him, and even turned a pillow and put it by the side of her to pretend that he was there with her. It didn't work. She couldn't sleep.

She thought about events since they met, including how they met. *'What did it all mean?'* she pondered. *'Did fate bring us together, and if so, what for?'* Then she thought about how easy it was for them to start a sexual relationship, completely driven by her wanting attention, and extended by the way he touched her, and loved her. She had completely betrayed her marriage with Andrew but felt no remorse. And she would return to Paul tomorrow with even more desire.

Prejudice in Love

'Why can't I have his children?' she quietly thought. 'Why can't I have his child?' she exclaimed.

She sat up. 'This is what this adventure is about. I'll ovulate in the next 48 hours and I'll be primed to conceive. All the coincidences, including Andy being delayed, have to be a sign that this man is my saviour, the man to give me the child I so desire. But how do I convince him of this? How do I convince Andy that this a God given opportunity for us? After the hard penetrating sex we had before dinner yesterday, the chances are that I have enough of his semen inside me already. It might already be the case that I'll become pregnant in the next two days.'

'What do you want Cis?' she asked herself. *'I want Paul, and I want his child. But he has made it clear that he will not leave Jane. But I can still have his child and love that child as I love him. The one thing that is for sure, I love this man with all my heart, so I'll never do anything to hurt him.'*

'Can I convince Andy that a child from this man answers our prayers? After all Andy does want children and feels uncomfortable that this hasn't happened yet. I haven't used any contraception since we got married, so why have we not been successful? Each month that passes without success drives us further apart. Something needs to happen before we drive each other away. But we were madly in love for years before we got married, so what changed? The desire for a child.'

'Okay. I now know that this adventure is my opportunity to have the child I so desire by a wonderful man that I would readily take to my bosom regardless of our age difference. I cannot have him, but I still love Andy. The solution is a child that Andy will accept as his own. Now how do I convince Paul to help me?'

Chapter 39

The drive through the craggy Monadhliath Mountains was slow but refreshing albeit the roads, in the main, were somewhat better than expected. Such wilderness on an island which, further south in England, is over-populated and over developed in much part. Here in Scotland, nearly the size of England, there was a population of only some 3.5 million people, mostly located around Edinburgh and Glasgow. Inverness, a little to the north of where he was located was a major oil & gas centre, and he had visited there on several occasions for oil & gas transactions. He reflected that on days of no sunshine Inverness looked a very drab and cold place with most of the buildings constructed with the local grey granite. But when the sun was shining it glistened in the sun's rays and looked a far more friendly place. However, such days were few and far between and he had decided long ago that he could not live in a place where vitamin D deficiency is a major issue.

Within the craggy mountains sat flat valleys that were being farmed, and there was evidence that these beautifully natural valleys could be a popular commuter area for Inverness as newly crafted houses with steep roofs more familiar with the likes of those seen in Scandinavia were clustered along the road. This could well explain the quality of the road surface as he approached the main A9 road, being the route into Inverness.

He finally drove out of the craggy mountains into the Cairngorm National Park in which Aviemore nestles at its centre. This is the ski centre of the UK, and very popular boasting Britain's highest Funicular Railway being a more comfortable ride up the ski slopes than the modern ski lifts. In a few more months finding a cut-price quality hotel deal would be near impossible and getting there by road would be 4-wheel drive vehicles only. He had spent a Hogmanay holiday in Aviemore some years earlier with some friends who owned a timeshare chalet there. The main A74 road was closed other than to 4-wheel drive vehicles, but even then, it was a slow drive.

He also recalled driving over a local mountain pass to see walkers ill-equipped for the rough terrain and fast changes in climatic conditions. They noticed a couple walking along this pass in normal outdoor clothing and walking shoes without any obvious protection against the possible difficulties they may encounter. The following morning, they were both found dead; they had apparently lost their way in the forest and died from exposure. *'Why do people from towns and cities think they can go into the wilderness without respect and preparation, and expect to survive?'*

However his reason for visiting The Cairngorms National Park was to observe the wild and unspoilt mountains and forest before they become transformed by a carpet of snow, and to breathe and smell the scent of this wilderness home to Golden Eagles, Ospreys, Parmigan and Red Deer.

He arrived at Aviemore around 5pm, and quickly located his chosen hotel. Within 15 minutes he was in his room getting ready to take a walk.

He found a forest trail. The sun was still up but he calculated that he only had about one hour before he needed to be back at the starting point. He had picked up a guide for the local walks from the hotel reception but wanted to get off the pathway for a while to feel the tranquillity of this wilderness. He found a suitable place on the guide and was quickly on his way.

The forest was wonderful. The summer had created a diverse carpet of colour and texture with wildflowers fighting for the sunlight through the dense foliage of the trees. He sensed wildlife all around him, and the beautiful scent radiating from the various pine trees, their cones and foliage softened by the sunlight creating the nectar from which the scents were released. He found the place where he wanted to get off the track and wander about thirty paces over a shallow brow into the untouched woodland. He found a fallen tree trunk on which to sit, and be still, in an attempt not to disturb anything around him, and then observe nature at work. Having spent much of his youth in a tied gatehouse on a three-thousand-acre estate of woodland, farms, parkland, and a lake he was totally at peace with his surroundings. He was always amazed at the diversity of activities in woodlands, and knew that if he stayed still, activities that had been suspended upon his intrusion, would soon be reactivated as the incumbents forgot that he was there. Having grown up under the direction of an exceptional gamekeeper he was highly attuned to even the slightest of activity and knew how to observe without disturbing anything. Insects were already clambering over his boots and his hand resting on the tree trunk, clearly curious to see if this new addition to their environment brought anything of interest to them.

He emptied his mind and told his body to be still. All he wanted was to allow his senses to absorb everything around him, and for his body to absorb the raw energy of nature that he felt around him. He could taste the sweetness in the air, the perfumes on the breeze were creating enjoyable sensations in his nostrils, and his stillness allowed the sounds of activity around him to amplify themselves in his ears. The diagnosis of his cancer had been a life changing experience, as with most sufferers. He came to fully appreciate that the true majesty of life existed in the diversity around him in places such as this, rather than the humdrum activities of humanity in cities.

After about twenty minutes he felt totally refreshed and exhilarated. He would like to wander further into the woods, but the sun was ebbing over the horizon, and he needed to get back before the light faded. He knew that his original trip plan, providing three days to explore this wilderness, was about right so that he could wander far and deep into this untamed landscape, but alas it was not to be on this trip. He reluctantly made his way back to the hotel.

Chapter 40

Before going to dinner, he had attempted to book an apartment at Gleneagles knowing that there should be better deals on the adjacent Glenmor apartments than the suites in the hotel. Although Gleneagles was probably still quite full of tourist golfers, he knew that most foreigners preferred the familiarity of a hotel rather than a self-catering apartment off by the

Prejudice in Love

lake. The Gleneagles website was not that easy to navigate for last minute deals, and such deals were rarely posted to the usual hotel search sites, so he decided to call instead. He was put through to a very chatty lady who confirmed that they had a Thursday to Monday deal available on a one-bedroom apartment, first floor, overlooking the water. He took it. She then told him about the activities available, and that there was a function on Saturday evening, so the hotel would be busy and noisy. Paul asked for more information about this function to find it was to celebrate Michaelmas Day. This confounded Paul as he knew Michaelmas Day as Christmas Eve, but he asked if it was possible for a table for two. She responded that the tables were for groups of ten people, but it might be possible to find him two places at one of the tables. She then very casually asked him who he was and what he did for a living. Paul, somewhat aghast at such questions, responded that he was a retired City banker linking with his wife for a few days away from the bustle of life. She finally said that she thought that she had just the right table for him but would confirm availability when they arrived tomorrow. With that the call was over so he clicked off his phone feeling that he had just been probed for suitability. He decided to put it out of his mind as all would be revealed tomorrow. For now, it was time for dinner having only had his sandwich at the Falls at Foyers since breakfast.

The dining room was quite lively for this time of year albeit he noted that he was probably one of the youngest guests. He ordered dinner and wine, and then his mind quickly reflected on his journey through the day. He felt fresh; invigorated by the sheer unspoilt wilderness that he had navigated – the magical contrasts between the heather-clad moorlands, the forests, and the ancient craggy mountains had a way of putting man's insignificant lifespan into perspective.

He breathed deeply as though he was standing in the wilderness taking the freshness of the unpolluted air into his lungs. He felt good about his decision to make this trip and would like to spend more time in the Highlands of Scotland north of the Caledonian Canal, especially much further north where civilisation fades into the occasional crofter farm. But then his thoughts changed into reflection of the extraordinary encounter with Cis, and his time with her.

He felt invigorated by this young woman. He had certainly laid to rest the issues regarding his supposed erectile dysfunction. It was not a physical dysfunction. It had everything to do with the state of his mind and his relationship with Jane. Life had never been the same since his cancer and wondered if it ever would return to those heady days when sex was a major part of their relationship. The aftereffects of the cancer treatment had left their marks, but this was not the only reason for his problems.

'But what's this meeting with Cis all about? Why did they meet? Are we solving her problems, which are many? Are we solving my problems, not so many but significant? Or are we two lost souls seeking help from each other?'

'Is she right about her guardian angel? After all, both of us were in the wrong place at the right time to trigger the events of these past few days. Nothing like this would have happened otherwise, even if we were in a hotel bar, far from home, both looking for companionship. The age difference prejudice would have kicked in, especially with her.'

He found himself pleasantly confused, albeit amused with the whole situation. Whatever had prompted him to take this trip; he was happy to be here. He was a natural explorer and adventurer, always convinced that he was born after his time. He would love to have been a major explorer in the 17th and 18th centuries. At only 18 years of age he had set himself a target to explore the World, and he had achieved much of this objective, and was paid handsomely to do it. He had stayed single for most of his adult life to maintain the freedom to explore without the trappings of normal family life. Even when he had settled down, it was short-lived. When he linked with Jane, she did not see any point in getting married as she had no desire for children, so he was still essentially free to do as he pleased. He could go where his adventures took him, and this was a great comfort to him, albeit a sometimes lonely way to live.

What about Jane? What was happening to him that he quite happily and enthusiastically desired to pursue his relationship with Cis? He was not stepping outside of the boundaries that he and Jane had agreed together as part of their working travelling lifestyles. But something felt different about this encounter. His relationship with Cis was not just about sex, it was a whole, all-encompassing voyage of discovery. This was not a liaison where each party would do their work during the day, and then get together in the evening for some mutual, intimate fun. They spent every hour of the day together, she to explore her whole life, and for him to regenerate lost feelings and enjoy the fun of their flirtatious adventures. He felt alive guiding this beautiful nymph through a kaleidoscope of new feelings and sensations, savouring in the delights of her new-found sensuality.

After dinner he went straight back to his room as he was feeling the strain of the physical demands of keeping his young nymph satiated. Considering the activities of the past few days, as well as the long drive, he felt in good shape. But he knew that he needed to recharge if he was to continue to perform for some days yet. He started to watch TV to see what was happening in the big wide world. It was very unusual for him to be so preoccupied that he did not watch, at least, one serious international news program each day. It was not only habit, but still a real interest in the shaping of economic and global events, and his ability to predict outcomes of seemingly unconnected events, and which can only be connected in the mind of an experienced observer. He would then commit his thoughts to paper, and then onto his blog to see what reaction he would get. He had lost count of the number of times that he had correctly connected and predicted the future outcome of a string of events. The initial comments of most people would be to challenge his logic, but then retreat as they saw his outcomes become reality. Those who really knew him would always take his views seriously. Indeed, it had been commented by one senior US politician that a good Harvard graduate would be right at least 85% of the time, whereas he would be right over 95% of the time. However, this accuracy was a double-edged sword. Followers were impressed, but others were envious, but not in a nice way. They looked for the times that he was not accurate and exploited such events to the full.

He was not concentrating on the TV news so decided to retire. He was tired, and his overwhelming thoughts were about his own interesting situation.

So where would this adventure take him? Would this adventure with Cis continue, and would it start a completely new life for him? She had no children, her relationship with Andy was clearly drifting apart, and she would not take much convincing to stay with him. The one downside was her desire for a child. This would tie him down at a time when he wanted to go explore places where he had not yet managed to spend enough time. Could she be persuaded to defer her desire for a few years so that he could take her with him? She would certainly be a fabulous companion.

When he first planned this trip he had a desire to fully explore the Aviemore area before the snows came. Now his only desire was to get to Gleneagles where he could continue to wallow in the insatiable appetite of his lovely Cis. *'Pity that it was not the Caribbean with long days of blue skies and sunshine and where they could frolic along the deserted shores rather than being confined to a hotel room. But anywhere would be good with her, so be thankful'* he thought.

He drifted into a peaceful sleep with the thoughts of what had been and will be when they meet again tomorrow. This adventure had scope for some interesting twists and turns, and he needed to be refreshed to meet any challenges.

Chapter 41 - Thursday

It was just after 8am. Paul was strolling back to his room after a very non-descript buffet breakfast. After the last few days with Cis it felt very strange, if not depressing to be on his own. The location and the vista were fantastic, but she was not by his side. He could not wait to start for Gleneagles and prayed that she would join him there.

As he approached his room, he felt his iPhone vibrate in his belt holster. He quickly extracted his phone. It was a text message from her. His pulse started to race, he kicked into a different gear. He went into his messages.

'When you are awake pls call. Andy not back until Tues. Cis x'
He called her immediately, and she was ready in expectation that he was already awake. 'Cis, my beautiful lady, you have just made my day.'

'It's been a long night without my big bear to stroke me and keep me warm. But my article is filed, and I'm ready to come back to you. I have a choice of two trains. The first arrives in Gleneagles at 10:57, and the next at 13:20. Which one shall I take?'

'I'm about two and a half hours from Gleneagles assuming no delays. It will take me 15 minutes to get out of here. Therefore, it would be 11 o'clock, earliest. Depends if you're prepared to wait at the station for me to arrive. I can easily be there for you at 13:20. What do you think?'

'As much as I can't wait to be in your arms again, I'll take the second train so that you don't take any unnecessary risks on those Highland roads. Don't rush, enjoy the scenery. We have more time together now before you go home.'

'Okay, makes good sense. Shall I organise lunch?'

'No, it's okay. I'll have something before I arrive.'

'When I spoke with Gleneagles yesterday, they told me that there was some formal dinner on Saturday evening that we could attend if we wished. They mentioned something about Michaelmas Day Ball, but I thought Michaelmas was Christmas Eve. Do you fancy a dinner and dance with me? They have a live dance band.'

'My darling, are you telling me that I know something that you don't?' She teased. 'Michaelmas Day is the 29th September. St Michael is the patron saint of the sea and sailors and his saint's day is celebrated, mainly in the West of Scotland. On the island of Barra, a bannock is baked from the first grain harvested in the year and eaten on St Michael's day. Everyone is given a piece to eat. Andy and I occasionally attend such celebrations.'

'So why not? I'll need evening wear. What are your instructions?'

'No more than two pieces of clothing, and if you want you back stroking during the evening then choose accordingly. You will also need a stole or jacket as I've booked an apartment by the lake so that we can enjoy a nice log fire in the evenings.'

'The apartment sounds fabulous. You're a bad boy with that dress code, but I'll comply. What will you wear?'

'The hotel informed me that there's a place in the village where I can hire evening dress.'

She remembered his dress kilt. 'Oh no, no, no. Your dress code is your kilt. I want to go to the ball with my valiant knight in his kilt. If I comply with your dress code, then you must comply with mine.'

'I suppose that you want traditional wear under the kilt', he teased.

'That would be nice', she purred.

'No chance. You would be down to one piece of clothing in that case.'

She laughed. 'We have time to decide these details. I must get on and pack. Do I need any walking gear?'

'Why not? Keep it flexible. They have a spa with pool so maybe we'll get another swim.'

'Okay. I'm on my way. See you soon. (kiss,kiss).'

He was now feeling exhilarated. *'She's coming back to me, and I have her until Sunday at least, if not Monday as well. Must get some fizz on the way to celebrate.'*

Fifteen minutes later he was in his car ready to start his trip to Gleneagles. He set the route on his satnav and found the exit from the hotel car park.

Cis, now with a real spring in her step, thought that she now had time to prepare properly for her task today.

She went to her bathroom and completely removed the little remaining pubic hair around her vagina. She knew that he would really like to see her as naked as the day she was born. She applied soothing cream where she had prised out the hairs. *'No panties until last minute'* she thought.

She then went to her wardrobe to see what evening dresses she could pack. She wanted to shimmer for him. She found a long silver shimmer dress which literally would just hang from her shoulders and would show her breasts to the full without exposing her constantly extended nipples. She slipped it on, and then selected shoes that would have the dress just skim the floor. Looking in the mirror she thought *'if this doesn't turn you on nothing will.'*

Looking through the underwear she had packed she identified the shear transparent black pair that he had selected at the shopping centre. This would make her look completely naked without the dress. She could feel his eyes savouring the delights that she was preparing for him. There was an excitement at the prospect of a real night out with her valiant knight in his full-dress tartan garb.

'What to wear for her plea for his help to make her baby? *This has to be right'* she thought. *'I must be wearing this when I get there as there is no point in having sex and then asking him. If I get naked to change when I get there the likelihood is that I'll not get into alternate* clothes until after sex. No, I must be able to peel down to what I want to wear to appeal to him.'

As she had unpacked her underwear to see what she could wear under her evening dress she had unpacked her camisole and French nickers. *'Perfect'*, she thought. *'This is a special occasion, and one must dress properly for a special occasion.'* The French nickers will also be kinder to her where she had just removed the pubic hairs whilst the soothing cream does its work. A nice skirt suit will also help with the healing whilst on the train, as well as be exactly right to hide the camisole. Should be a good feminine picture for her lover.

She was ready. Her speech, the speech of a lifetime, had been well rehearsed, and she was ready to confront him with the objective of their adventure together.

She called for a taxi and was on her way.

Chapter 42

'She's right' he thought. The drive down from Aviemore passed through some beautiful landscape. *Aviemore* looks east to the high Cairngorms and is walled to the west by the granulite crags of Craigellachie. As Britain's largest National Park, the Cairngorms are the most extensive range of high mountains in the UK, with a vast, tundra-like wilderness plateau, girt with magnificent corries, at the heart of the region. This is encircled by the beautiful valleys of the Rivers Spey and Dee, each passing through stunning landscapes of ancient Caledonian pinewoods teeming with wildlife.

As he left the Cairngorms National Park, he entered Perthshire which straddles the Highlands and the Lowlands, offering a rich variety of scenery. Highland Perthshire is magnificently forested, and the region has become branded as 'Big Tree Country' - a name well deserved. The wide and graceful River

Tay - Scotland's grandest river - flows through the region from its source in serene Loch Tay, whilst great rolling mountains make a perfect backdrop. He remembered that the hidden gems of interest included winding Glen Lyon and beautiful Glen Tilt.

Further south the mountains become heather clad moors and finally billowing hills as Perthshire descends to the fertile farmland stretching from Strathearn to Perth and up to Blairgowrie.

This whole journey is only some 94 miles but the extraordinary transitions in landscape were breath-taking and worthy of a slow drive. He felt that, had she not been waiting for him at Gleneagles, he would make frequent stops along this stretch of his journey to step out and feast his eyes on this gloriously wild landscape.

He reached Gleneagles a little after noon so decided that he would find a shop to purchase some fizz and nibbles. The high street of Auchterarder, the village just outside Gleneagles, was ideal for this requirement.

He then went to the reception at Gleneagles hotel to check-in, find out more information whilst booking the dinner for Saturday night, and unload his luggage into the apartment, putting the fizz into the fridge.

The apartment had a living area with kitchenette overlooking the lake, and a large bedroom suite.

Chapter 43

It was 1 o'clock, time to go to the station to collect his beautiful companion, his adorable Cis.

He was waiting on the platform as the train to Inverness pulled in and stopped. There she was. What a radiant picture of joy.

She saw him, and quickly dragged her wheelie case towards him. They met, she let go her case, and without a word they reached for each other embracing in a longing kiss. They held each other close as only lovers know how.

They looked at each other, both sporting smiles of delight, knowing that they belong together.

He reached for her case and her hand and led her to his car.

They were in the apartment within 15 minutes.

Chapter 44

Having already unpacked his luggage he sat in a chair watching her as she went through her case. It looked to him that she had packed for all eventualities, and he enjoyed watching as she decided where she would put everything.

She knew that he was watching her, and thinking if this is the right time to speak with him? She closed her case, looked at him. *'He's clearly very happy to see me, and he's calm.'* She took off her jacket revealing the camisole that he selected for her.

'That's for special occasions' he thought.

She removed her skirt to reveal the French nickers. She said nothing but moved over to Paul and sat in his lap, straddled his legs, facing him.

She gently cupped his cheeks, and with a seriousness in her eyes that he had not seen before, she started to speak. 'Paul, I have something to say to you. I have something I need to ask you, and I need you to promise to let me finish before you say or do anything. Do you promise?'

He looked at her, studying her eyes for some clue of where this was going. Although she was dressed for it, this was clearly not some foreplay game. 'Okay, you have the floor until you ask me to speak again.'

'Paul, my darling, you are a very clever man, so you must know that I've fallen deeply in love with you. And just so you have no doubt about this I openly declare to you here and now that

Prejudice in Love

I love you with all my heart. I have never met anyone in my life for whom I have felt so strongly.'

He wanted to interject as things had gone too far, but then he could see that there was more, and he had promised to hold his peace.

She looked him straight in the eyes 'but I know that I cannot have you to myself, my darling. So fear not, my love for you will not allow me to compromise your situation. I know that I would lose you and destroy the magic of these past days. But should you ever find yourself in a different situation with Jane, please come back to me. There will be forever a place in my heart for you.'

She paused looking into his eyes to see what reaction she could see.

'Last night I had much sleepless time replaying the wonderful events since I met you, and the inevitable changes to my own life as a result of the teachings of my master, my valiant knight, and my lover.'

'I'm already in your debt for so much, and do not feel that I have the right to ask you for anything. Fate brought us together, and I can only believe that my guardian angel has a plan other than for you and I to be long-term lovers. I have learnt so much and can now face my situation with a completely new perspective, but I think that there is one part of the plan yet to unfold. You did not decide to go to Scotland last Sunday, and take a route contrary to your satnav, straight into the storm, just for our adventure to date. There is more, and I now know what it is.'

'You have given me much to help Andrew and myself get our life back together, but I still have to deal with the reality that Andrew cannot give me the child I so desperately desire. I could try IVF, but I sense that Andrew cannot face this deficiency in his manhood, and it's breaking us apart. My mother had no problem conceiving, and my sister has only to look at her husband to become pregnant. In Andrew's family there was obviously an issue, and Andrew is an only child.'

'This is a real issue for me. Thus a revelation yesterday meant much more to me than normal. I don't think that you have much time for coincidence, but so much of our time together has been rooted in coincidence, and I truly believe that this revelation is the culmination of everything between us to date, and the intention of my guardian angel.'

'Paul, I started to ovulate this morning. My plea to you is to help me make the baby I so desire, and that would complete this adventure with the most lasting outcome either of us could imagine.'

He wanted to speak, but she put a finger on his lips, 'I've not finished my darling.'

He could detect tears in her eyes. He relaxed again, fully attentive.

'I have thought through many of the ramifications of this on the way here, and I want to tell you what I've considered, and how I see things working.'

'First, I have to consider how Andrew will deal with this. He can be such a boy, and clearly the challenge to his manhood will give him problems with someone else making me pregnant. I've balanced this with the fact that our desperation for a child has caused us many problems, but I know that he does love me, and would like a child to complete our family. This is a very quiet way to achieve this end without him having to visit any clinic, or me going through a very public process of hormone therapy, and IVF. Thus, the factor that will probably turn this in my favour will be no challenge to his manhood as only he will know the truth.'

'I have to consider the impact on your life. I would love for you to play some part in the life of our child, but I understand that this will be very difficult for you, and probably for Andrew. All I can promise is that I will never arrive on your doorstep with our child unless things are so desperate that I have no other choice. And I promise that I will never contact you unless with your consent.'

Prejudice in Love

'What I will pledge above all is that I will love our child as I love you. If I cannot have you, then let me have your child to love and cherish as I would love you.'

The tears were now rolling down her cheeks, and he was also welling up inside.

'Paul, please will you help me?'

Paul brushed the tears from her cheeks. She had clearly finished, but he needed to gather his thoughts. Having children had caused him great pain in the past, and now he was being asked to bring another child into this world with whom he would have no relationship. Why has life treated him so harshly? He loves children and has so much to offer them but has not been allowed to participate. Why does this woman want to cause him more pain?

He needed to hold someone close for such a distressing decision, so he automatically put his arms around her and pulled her close. He needed human contact to put some sense into his thoughts. *'There possibly is some reason why they had been thrown together, but this? She could promise all she liked but the legal position is clear; his DNA, his responsibility. He was 62 years old. How would he cope with such a responsibility? What about if Andrew did not co-operate and he found his name cited in a divorce? But this lady not only loves you, she has shown it over and over.'* There is no doubt that he felt, in different circumstances, that he would readily scoop up this woman and wallow in the love between them for ever.

He finally decided that he should say something. She had held him in silence to let him gather his thoughts, and silently praying that he would help her.

'Quite a speech, Cis. Let me start by stating that I want to help you in any way I can to get your life together. Where I have a problem is the pain that you want me to endure when you already know of the pain I suffer with my existing children. Your guardian angel may be looking out for your interests, but she is asking much of me. Allowing me to savour the delights of you for the past days only to then ask me to add yet more pain to my already painful life is a big ask. If all of this goes pear-shaped it will impact other innocent lives. I've never met Andrew so I can only gauge his probable behaviour based on what you've told me.'

She was starting to prepare herself for failure in her quest.

'Besides your declaration of love, which I'll cherish for the rest of my life, I find one important factor in your favour. You could have returned today and said nothing. We would most certainly have engaged in sex, and even made love, so you could have achieved your desire without me being any the wiser. In some ways this would be less painful for me. Therefore, I can only think that your request is a symbol of your love for me – you do not want to cheat or deceive me. Despite your desperation for this child your honestly is most surely a risk that could cause you much pain. So there is pain on both sides of this equation.'

'Let me ask you a question. Is making this child something that you would like us to achieve, or something you want us to achieve?'

She looked at him puzzled with this question. 'What did he mean? "Would like", "want"; what's the difference.' She looked into his eyes and could see that this question was a serious question. She said quietly, but firmly 'I want your child.'

Paul could see and hear this commitment to their love. She wanted a child, his child, to cement their love, and to save her marriage.

He thought for a moment longer. *'If I do as she wants, I get pain. If I don't do it, she has pain. I don't want this wonderful woman to endure pain. She has given me so much joy these past days.'*

'I'll do it. I will help you to make a baby, but..'

She interrupted him with such delight 'thank you my love, thank you, thank you, thank you'.

'But' he continued 'there are rules.'

Prejudice in Love

She laughed in joy as she responded 'and when are there not rules with you. Whatever they are master, your dutiful student will gladly follow them.' She was hugging and kissing him with such joy in her heart.

'If you go to the fridge you will find some fizz, and don't forget glasses. I need to talk to you about this as your guardian angel has overlooked one important detail, and thus we need to plan this campaign to ensure the maximum chance of success.'

Although this might have dampened her spirits a little, she took the view, as always, her valiant knight will prevail.

She danced back with the Prosecco in a cold box she had found in the freezer, and two glasses, put them on the side table next to his chair, and sat in his lap.

'As you have decided that this is a special occasion', pointing to her camisole, 'I guess we should celebrate.'

She gave him a big kiss on the cheek. 'You have made me so happy' she beamed.

He popped the cork and poured the glasses. He handed one to her and picked the other for himself. 'I truly wish you every success in your quest' he said as they clinked their glasses in a toast.

'Okay' he said. 'I know that you're excited, but we don't have much time, maybe 36 hours, in which to complete this quest so we need to get started. But I want to explain to you how I think we need to address this task as your guardian angel could have chosen a much younger steed for such a quest. But I do have friends who have had this experience themselves, and the technique they used did work when all others failed. So listen up because sex is about to become somewhat clinical for the next 36 hours if we are to maximise your chances of success.'

'What do you mean by clinical?' she quizzed.

'Somewhere between normal sex and IVF is as close as I can explain it. Listen up.'

He explained to her the experience he had with some friends in Europe. One Sunday he and Jane were at lunch with them. At exactly 2 o'clock the wife looked at her watch and abruptly said that they had to leave.

He was the son of a major family in Europe, and she was the daughter of a minor newspaper baron. He was a healthy 28-year old, but she was older at 33-years and who had partied her life away until she got married. She smoked and enjoyed a glass of wine or two. They had tried for some months for a child without success.

Both were intelligent people, and she was very determined to breed the next generation for the family. She had tried everything, and thoroughly researched the possibilities to overcome the effects of her previous abuse of her body. She had stopped smoking, limited her alcohol intake, and regularly exercised – all to no avail.

About three months after their abrupt exit from lunch they announced that she was finally pregnant. Some months later Paul met with him and queried the abrupt exit. He explained that they had a very specific routine for her for the two days after the start of ovulation, which was onerous, but it worked. He explained in graphic detail the exacting process of sexual intercourse to maximise the level of success. As they successfully applied the same process for a second child, it was the best information that Paul could use to help Cis.

After this explanation she looked at him with admiration. He was serious about this, and she was grateful for this attention to detail, albeit not the romantic approach that she had in her mind when she asked him. 'You really are an endless source of knowledge', she exclaimed. 'Okay master what do you want me to do?'

'I would like to add one irrational notion to this exercise. I've heard that when my sperm reached your egg that they somehow know whether or not their union is a result of real love between the parties involved. I would like what we are about to do be with love, even if a bit clinical. It's probably an old wife's tale with no basis in fact, but it cannot harm the process.'

She looked at him adoringly, put both arms around his neck and kissed him longingly. 'Whatever we do together will always be with love in our hearts' she whispered in his ear.

He held her tight feeling the warmth that flowed between them.

He lifted her in his arms and moved towards the bed. He knew that they must start now as valuable time had already been lost. According to the explanation he had been given by his friend of the process, two of the six attempts had been lost, although he thought that if they start now, he could reduce this to just one lost. She was already in the right frame of mind, so she would not need much arousal. The room was comfortably warm to be naked, so he asked her to pull back the bedclothes as he held her next to the bed, and then laid her on the bottom sheet.

'You have not prepared me my master', pointing to her camisole. She got up and stood in front of the bed.

He took longer than usual to remove her top as the feel of the silk against her skin was very arousing – something he knew would be essential for him. He was still a little anxious about his ability to perform and knew that the more he was aroused the better the chances that his erection would be maintained through to ejaculation. Her guardian angel was either a big risk taker, or a cruel joker.

Having removed her top, he looked at those glorious breasts standing to attention awaiting his touch. He gently stroked each breast feeling the warmth and the effect of his touch. She looked on with such love, feeling very wanted and needed.

He removed her French nickers with the same touches as with her normal panties as he knew she loved the contact. Her vagina would now be very wet making entry very easy for him.

She reached for his hands inviting him to stand up. She gently eased him out of his clothes, kissed him on his chest, and then moved down his body kissing him as she went. She was on her knees and reached for his now erect and throbbing penis. She kissed the head of his penis and whispered, 'I need your help. Enjoy your quest and be successful. Your lady needs you.' She kissed the head again and raised her body up to full height, put both arms around his neck as she pressed her body hard against him, kissing him longingly.

He turned her and lay her on the bed moving two pillows down in line with her hips. She raised her hips as he slid the pillows under her abdomen with her legs open wide.

With her vagina at this new angle it looked so welcoming, a shrine of fertility. He immediately noticed that she was now completely hairless and moved his head down to kiss the swollen lips of her vagina, using his tongue to open the door to the juices that lay beyond her vaginal lips. He could taste the sweetness of her juices and knew she was ready.

She lay back feeling the warmth of his lips, and the thrill as she felt his tongue delve into her. *'If this is clinical, bring it on'* she thought, *'If only Andy would rouse me in this way.'*

Paul said a quiet pray to himself and mounted her.

The entry was easy, nicely moist and very inviting. She smiled at him as he slid deep into her. He started slowly to ensure that he had an angle for himself to encourage maximum stimulation of his penis and maximise penetration. Although the clinical nature of this process was in his mind the warmth that he felt in his loins soon faded such thoughts. He started to increase the rapidity of his thrusts until he could feel the start of the stimulation that would lead to ejaculation. He had wanted her now for over 24-hours, so ejaculation did not take long. He thrust as deep as is possible and could feel the rush of semen into her, and then a second. He felt satisfied. He had succeeded in the first step of this quest. As per the process he withdrew about one inch from her, but then held his position as she reached for him. 'I felt that' she whispered. 'It felt very nice.'

After about one minute he slowly withdrew from her, checked that her vagina entry was suitably raised by the pillows to minimise leakage. He then moved her legs one at a time so that they were separated by only about her shoulder width and tucked back as far as possible. She tried to use her own muscles to help but he stopped her. She must not use the muscles in her abdomen for the next 15 – 20 minutes he reminded her.

He moved beside her. 'Now you must stay there for 15 – 20 minutes. And do nothing that could push the semen out of you, especially laughing. Just relax. We must give the sperm the best chance to enter your cervix to reach your egg.'

'I just want to hold you close to me' she said.

'I want to do the same, but you must be still. I can't even tell you a joke, not that I'm any good with jokes. I can stroke your brow to keep you calm, that's about it.'

'Okay' she said, 'we can't just lie here for 15 – 20 minutes because it will seem an eternity. Stroke my brow and explain the logic of this process again now that you have my full attention. I was a little too excited before.'

'Remember that I cannot make any representations regarding the efficacy of this process, although I can see the scientific logic. All I can say is that it has worked twice to my knowledge in very difficult circumstances.'

'The point of raising your abdomen is essentially to do with gravity and maximising penetration. If you were lying on the bed your cervix is likely to sit below the level of your womb. Therefore, my semen would have to swim against the flow up through your cervix to your womb. This is probably exhausting, and only the strongest swimmers are likely to get anywhere near the egg in your womb, and then they need the strength to break through the wall of the egg in order to fertilise you. The pillows raise your abdomen in such a way that your cervix sits above the level of your womb. Thus gravity will help the semen to move easily through your cervix to reach your egg as it is a downhill swim. Remember that if I was in my prime, I will ejaculate over 1,000 likely candidates to fertilise you, but only a few will survive the arduous swim to ever get anywhere near your egg. And only the strongest will be able to break into the egg, at which point all other suitors are rejected.'

'What about not letting me have an orgasm during sex.'

'Okay, what happens to you at orgasm?'

'I ejaculate fluids', she responded, 'and feel great of course.'

'Not only do you ejaculate fluids, but your abdomen goes into spasm, essentially pushing these fluids out of you. If my semen is mixed with these fluids what will happen?'

'I'll flush them out', she said. 'I can see the logic.'

'However, I have read another school of thought in some magazine that suggests that your orgasm aids pregnancy by causing the muscles in your groin to tug the penis further into you. The argument was that you orgasm with lovers you want to be with and thus the sperm that you want to fertilise you. I don't buy this argument as I feel you pull on my penis without orgasm, so I think your desire to have me fertilise you causes this pulling action. In any event I'll stay with evidence that was successful, even if only anecdotal.'

'But what about the 15 – 20 minutes of rest?'

'As I understand this bit we go back to gravity. If you should stand up, we create the uphill swim again. Don't quote me, but this 15 – 20 minutes of rest is the time it takes your body to recover from sexual activity and return to normal. That is, you stop generating fluids. At this point whatever sperm is not in your cervix will find there are no fluids in which to swim, and thus will be flushed out the next time you go to the toilet.'

'Wow master professor, I get it. Makes sense. As you say, quite clinical, but better than a hospital table where people are sticking instruments into my vagina to extract my egg, fertilise it with someone's sperm, and then put it back into me. I would not even know the donor. I'm very happy to be here with you and go through this process together. A million times better to be with my lover, knowing who is fertilising my egg, and knowing the love that comes with it.' He kissed her on the forehead.

After 20 minutes he told her she could roll over and cuddle if she wanted to. She did not waste a second to roll into to his arms, moving the pillows from under her abdomen with her foot. She snuggled in close. She whispered a code in his ear 'stroke me.'

She was asleep in a few minutes, exhausted from the long sleepless night of thoughts the previous night. He reached down to find the blankets and pulled them up to cover them. He thought how wonderful he felt and started to doze peacefully with his love in his arms.

Chapter 45

They awoke about an hour later both feeling somewhat refreshed, but neither wanting to get up. 'What time is it?' she asked sleepily.

'About 4:30' he answered. 'You have a date?'

'Only with my lover' she teased. 'When do we try again?'

'We need at least 3 hours between attempts, so later this evening after dinner.'

'Why do we need 3 hours between tries?'

'To give me a chance to recover and generate fresh sperm.'

'Do we get any time to enjoy our sex during this process?' she asked.

'Any time after 3 hours and when we next try', he responded.

'So we could have some fun after dinner, and then clinical before we go to sleep.'

'So long as we don't fall asleep after fun time then this will work. It took just a few minutes of stroking for you to fall asleep, and I mean sleep.'

'I didn't get much sleep last night. My big bear was not there to comfort me.'

'Then whatever fun we choose must be somewhere other than bed.'

She looked up at him 'anywhere you want is good for me', kissing him long and hard.

'What's that for?'

'My wonderful present, our baby.'

'We don't know this yet.'

'Paul, I know that this adventure has meaning, and is for a reason. I'm sure of it. Everything we've done together has moved ever closer to where we are, even Andy being delayed. I know that you wouldn't want me to be disappointed, but I just know that this will work. My sage is preparing me for the road ahead and giving me what I most desire as a reward.'

'I really hope you're right my lovely lady.'

'Will you tell me another of your long stories? Now that I'm to have your child I would like to know more about you. I looked at your blog last night. You're a good writer. You know how complex issues interplay and are very circumspect when stripping out the key elements of what really matters. I've printed them all down and intend to read all of them.'

'How did you know about my blog?'

'You gave me your card, remember, for me to have your mobile number.'

'I also looked at your profile. You're an important man and have held some powerful positions. You're also in Who's Who. I'm a journalist by training. Once I have a lead, I follow it.'

'I was a powerful man, but no more. Now I'm just a retired man.'

'No, no. You write almost every week and I looked at the follower profile. You have followers all over the world. They would not follow you if you didn't interest them with what you write. How many people write blogs in the world, but how many have a following the size of yours? No Paul, you are still an important person because your followers say so. I'm now one of your followers under my journalist ID.'

'I'm at a disadvantage. You now know much about me, but I still don't know enough about you. It's not your professional life that I seek, it's you, the person. Of course, your professional life is part of you, but not the "you" I want to know.'

'The "me" that you want to know is in a state of rebirth, being masterminded by you. I will leave you a different "me" in so many respects that you will know me because you moulded me. You've shown me how to change my life for the better, and I'll use every last morsel of the knowledge and experience that you give to me to do just that. And as our child grows, I'll impart your valuable wisdom so that they can also benefit from their wonderful father, my master and valiant knight.'

'This is getting heavy. Do you think that Prosecco is still cold? I need a drink.'

'I'll get it as she tried to bounce out of bed.'

'No, no. I'll get it, you stay where you are. I haven't finished with you yet.'

He recovered the bottle still in its cold box. It was not as cool as he would like, but it was still cool. He grabbed the glasses and went back to bed. She sat up to drink with him. 'Whoops', she exclaimed, 'I'm starting to leak. Can I go to the bathroom now?'

'Sure.'

When she returned she sat back on the bed. 'Okay which long story do you have for me today? This is just like story time at bedtime when I was a kid.'

'If you looked anything like you do today sitting in bed, I think stories would be very short.'

She laughed knowing that he was referring to her pert breasts now protruding above the bed clothes. 'Does this mean that you would have stroked me to sleep rather than tell me a story?'

'I don't know about stroking you to sleep but stroke you for sure.'

'You naughty man. It's a good job that my breasts actually enjoy your attention.'

She gave him her empty glass and snuggled back into bed. 'Story please.'

He put both glasses on the side table and snuggled down with her. 'Sorry lady, the past has to wait. I need to explore the present and future with you to ensure that you can return to your life fully engaged with what you need to do to protect the future of our child.'

She looked up at him somewhat alarmed 'what do you mean?'

'The current relationship that you have with Andy has to change, and I fear that you must take responsibility for this change. It's you who expects to go back to him pregnant with our child, not his. This is a major responsibility as you have betrayed your relationship with him, albeit not maliciously. But such considerations do not prevail in a battle of such intimate emotions. You must prepare him for your news. He must be receptive to your story, and for this you must rebuild your relationship before it becomes known that you are pregnant. I figure that you have 10 – 12 weeks before you really must tell him.'

'But I'll know within two weeks', she exclaimed, 'I have a pregnancy tester that will tell me.'

Prejudice in Love

'This is where you must discipline your mind-set. You must believe what it says on the box; that such devises only give you an indication. They are no substitute for a full medical examination, and confirmation from a doctor. You must not disclose your pregnancy to anyone until you have seen a doctor 10 – 12 weeks from now. If you need a marker to get you into the sensible frame of mind remember that your body can abort your pregnancy, without your consent, anytime in the first few weeks of pregnancy.'

'You mean a miscarriage?'

'Yes. Do you really want to go through the pain with Andrew if you have nothing to show for it at the end? Also, such distress early in the pregnancy could trigger an abortion. So let your pregnancy become established before telling Andy.'

'In any event it's normal for women to keep quiet about a pregnancy until they are sure that it's established.'

He continued 'But this is all good. It gives you the opportunity to rebuild your relationship with Andy so that he's more receptive to your news. From what you've told me I think Andy already knows that he has a problem. The reluctance to have sex with you gives him a way out – no sex, no expectation of baby. No red-blooded male could resist the opportunity of sex with you, so he knows, I'm sure of it.'

'So, my dearest Cis, we are going to spend our 20-minute rest times, and as much other time as we need to ensure that you are ready to put your relationship back together with Andy. You've shown the initiative to satisfy your desire. Now you must take responsibility to build the bridges that protect the future of our child.'

She looked at him with such love in her heart. *'This man is not only going to give me my desire, he is also going to help me to rebuild my relationship with another man. Why can't I have him? He loves me, he protects me, he comforts me, and more important, he wants me. Why is life so cruel?'* She reached for him, took his head in her hands, and settled into a longing kiss pressing her body close to his, losing herself in the emotions she wanted to share with her lover.

She snuggled back into his shoulder. 'Okay my master, what do I need to do?'

'We're going to confer with a wise sage called Aristotle, and study rhetoric using logos, ethos, and pathos.'

'I assume you mean the Greek Aristotle, so I know who he is, but what is logos, ethos and pathos?'

'The tools that you need to prepare Andy for fatherhood with our child.'

'When do we start?'

'Not now as I would like us to get up, take a shower, and stretch our legs before dinner.'

'Hmmm, a shower with you. That will do nicely, thank you. I'll go prepare our shower oh wise one.'

With that she was off to the sumptuous bathroom to familiarise herself with everything to ensure that her master enjoys his time in there.

He took the fizz back to the kitchen area, found a stopper, and put the bottle back in the fridge.

Chapter 46

After their shower he dressed them both and decided to walk around the lake. It was a very pleasant evening so no need for coats, just sweaters. They both enjoyed walking out together. She could be very playful, simulating pushing him into the lake, and then him chasing her to punish her, winding up in each other's arms.

About halfway around the lake he took a more serious tone.

'I had a long think about this whole adventure last night. If your guardian angel theory is right, your guardian angel

Prejudice in Love

is a very smart cookie. Your guardian angel put you into a situation which is essentially a metaphor for where you are in life; insecure, desperate, and without the experience to give you the courage to do something about it. So your guardian angel picked on me as someone who can probably straighten you out without deflecting you from where you need to be, and without adversely impacting my life.'

She was listening intently, accepting the metaphor description as an interesting observation.

'Let us go through it step by step, and you'll see my thinking.'

'Last Sunday I had no plans to go anywhere, but I had planned a trip to Scotland earlier this year. So, if I could be triggered to go somewhere, I didn't need to sit and plan because I already had a suitable trip fully planned on my iPad. Coincidently this worked well for you.'

'Then I decide to ignore my usual common-sense approach to routes. Both in terms of distance, and with knowledge of the storm the best route for me would have been the A1(M) up the east coast. But no, I choose a route straight into the storm up the west coast expecting to be quickly far enough north to miss the worst of it. Again, coincidently this worked well for you.'

'I had the choice of my Range Rover, or my Porsche. My Porsche is more fun, and was full of fuel having just filled it, and would easily get me to Luss. But no, I have a track I want to explore on the east shore of Loch Ness so the Range Rover would be better, but it only had a quarter tank of fuel, so I would need more fuel. I never use motorway service areas for fuel because it's the most expensive fuel around. But instead of filling at my usual Tesco filling station I decide to run down my existing fuel and refill on route which happened to be a motorway service area. Great for you.'

'I don't like hitch hikers, especially lone females, having had a bad experience in the past. This woman confronts me with her beautiful big brown eyes, smartly dressed enough not to look like your usual hitchhiker, clearly in some distress, and going my way. I decide, against my better instinct, to take her with me.'

'The storm arrives early, and this woman is clearly terrified of thunder and lightning. Being a valiant knight, as you call me, I decide to find shelter from the storm, and agree to let her stay in my room because she is too afraid to stay on her own. We get along surprisingly well considering my dislike of small talk.'

'We settle down to sleep in the same bed, but at a discreet distance from each other. I've been there before, so not uncomfortable with the prospect having set my mind-set that such a young beautiful woman would have no interest in the advances of someone clearly at least twice her age. Your guardian angel did not like this, so a bout of thunder and lightning was triggered in the darkness of the night to force her into my arms knowing I was perfectly capable of comforting her.'

'I used my experience of calming Jane to calm you. You like my touch. Andrew had not touched this wantonly tactile woman in months. Her prejudices about my age, and her moral teachings are dispelled from her mind in the darkness. She wants to be touched so much that she completely surrenders to my stroking of her, all the way to her first orgasm in months.'

'By the morning she feels very comfortable, and wanton. I feel very comfortable with her and want her to stay with me for as long as possible. Big tick for your guardian angel.'

'This relationship grows stronger by the minute, with even talk of love. Her brazen desire encourages me to give her experiences that she has never tasted before. She wants more. This allows me to pursue activities and techniques not used in some years. Guardian angel is keeping us both interested.'

'Guardian angel triggers you to ovulate. You use the strength of our relationship to persuade me to help you to become pregnant. You want us to be together, but your guardian angel has that eventuality well covered. The age differential between us will not work for you in the real world. You must go back to Andrew, as intended. But how do you deal with Andrew?'

'Again, your guardian angel has this well covered. Cis, your guardian angel knows that if you're attentive and a fast learner, I can teach you how to convince Andrew that your pregnancy is good for both of you. I've already given you some of the intimacy tools to help you win him over, and my role is to continue with this process until we part. Your guardian angel even provided more days to us by delaying Andrew's return.'

'Bottom line is that your guardian angel had all the bases covered from the start. You will go home to Andrew pregnant, and equipped with all of the experience and knowledge to win the day.'

'My reward is to have the pleasure of your company, and your magnificent body, throughout this process, which is reward indeed.'

She just looked at him speechless. Eventually she smiled at him 'you've bought into the idea that all of this is part of some grand plan for me to have a baby, and you're okay with it. And you're going to teach me how to square this with Andrew. My valiant knight, I can only bow to the wisdom of my guardian angel finding such a wonderful man to help me.'

She continued somewhat more circumspect 'But if my guardian angel asked me what I want it would be at least 10 years in your arms. If you asked me to stay with you, I would not hesitate despite the real-world prejudice you spoke of. Love conquers all. I would take the knocks knowing that your arms are close by to protect me.'

He held her close. 'My dear Cis, my role is to succeed in the plan of your guardian angel, and I don't like failure.' Holding her away so that he could look her in the eye, 'we must work hard as there is much ground to cover to ensure your future happiness. We'll start with your next 20-minute rest period when we get back.'

She noticed something in his eyes. She was now very attuned to his intense eye to eye contacts with him. She saw pain. *'What is it? Is he putting on a brave face for me? Have I rekindled something* in him that is missing in his life? He speaks of experiences not used in years. Is there something wrong with his relationship with Jane? Is he lonely and our adventure has brought this to the surface? Whatever it is my love I need to find out what is causing you pain. There is no possibility that I'll leave you in pain. To hell with the world, my first choice would be to stay with you forever. I have never felt love as I feel with you and will not part with it freely. My future happiness is with you.'

They were both deep in thought as they walked back to the apartment. He was considering what tools she would need to be successful with Andrew, and how little time they had. Thinking back to their hard, penetrating sex before dinner on Tuesday he was already convinced that if she was ready to conceive then that job was done although he would stay the course they had plotted, if only to have her full attention for 20 minutes each time. There was much to learn, and she must be fully prepared for her confrontation with Andrew. He must show her how to prepare for, and to complete Andrew's acceptance of her pregnancy in just one session.

She was on a completely opposite course. She knew that he brought a dimension to her that completely changed her perspective on life. She could never go back to her old life having these new experiences knowing that she was only at the beginning of this new journey. Who in their right mind would sacrifice what she was experiencing with Paul to return to what she had before she met him? She had detected a chink in his armour. He was feeling long buried feelings for her, and he wanted more. She must exploit these feelings to shake his confidence and start to realise his future happiness is with her; his brazen, wanton, tactile woman. She likes this description of her. She would have been embarrassed to hear such a description of her before meeting him, but now she felt the woman he described, and she loves it. *'I hunger for his want of me and my body. He can have me anyway he wants me, and I'll be right back for more. I've enjoyed more adventurous sensuality and love in these few days than at any time in my life. I want more.'*

Chapter 47

They set off to dinner at the main hotel a little after 7:30pm. He'd already booked a quiet table for them so that he could use the time to start her education.

They ordered their food, and some wine.

'Okay, working dinner tonight, or at least for about half an hour. I know you didn't get much sleep last night, and it's no good filling you with information if you're too tired to absorb it.'

She knew that she had to go through this process with him, even though she had other plans. *'Maybe he'll teach me skills I can use in my strategy.'*

'Tonight, I'll give you the building blocks and show you how they fit together. Then starting tomorrow, we'll examine each of the building blocks until you understand how they work, and more importantly, how to use them. You'll find that you can use them in your personnel life, your business life, and with children. For example, the best, sure way to win an argument with a child is to side-wind them.'

'What do you mean by side-wind?'

'You'll learn that there are three psychological stances you can take in a debate or argument: Parent, Adult, and Child. These are symbolic names, but they describe the stance that you take. All of us unconsciously use all three states in our daily lives. If you know how to use them consciously, switching from state to state as the need dictates, then you can almost always win the argument. For example, the Child in us demands certainty. The Child in us wants to know that day will follow night, mother will always be there, and the bad guy will always get it in the end. The Adult in us accepts that there is no certainty to anything. The Parent uses more judgemental emotion or uses emotion to change the position of an argument.'

'When the Parent or Child in us dominates, the outcome is predictable. When the Adult dominates the outcome is not predictable. In your discussion with Andrew you must not, under any circumstances, adopt the Adult stance. Andrew will most certainly adopt the Adult stance from the beginning. You need to arm yourself with the answers to all his possible arguments, and present them in the Parent stance, using the Child stance were necessary to bring him down into the Parent stance. When he's in the Parent stance it will be easy for you to sell your argument and the outcome will be a predictable success.'

'A side-wind is a Parent stance to offset a Child stance, where the actual child is too young to understand the Parent and Adult stance albeit they will adopt them in their argument. If you directly argue with a child, they will adopt the Adult stance and you will do the same and you will get nowhere, just frustration. A typical Adult stance for a child would be to answer every one of your arguments with "Why?" This is a face-to-face direct encounter. You need to think of a way to distract the child with something that is more interesting to them. If you can do this, they'll soon forget the argument and be on their way. So rather than argue directly, you feed a different stimulus in from the side, hence side-winder. As adults we use a distraction or a diversion to break a logjam in an adult argument.'

She looks at him. 'Now you're a psychologist.'

'No, but I'm a trained negotiator so I know all of the various ploys people use to get their way. As a negotiator I need to move the argument where I need it to be without the other side feeling beaten or manipulated. The best result from any negotiation is a win-win, and I must teach you this in just 3 short days.'

'So you just play games with people to get what you want.'

'Life is a game. What you need is to understand the rules of the game and be clear in your arguments. Knowledge is king.'

'So how long will it take me to understand all of this?'

Prejudice in Love

'We don't have time to generalise, as this would take weeks. I want to be specific with you so that you can deal with your imminent showdown, and to be successful whatever Andrew throws at you.'

'If it's any consolation, your approach to me today was commendable. You knew that you had to get your whole story on the table before you let me intervene. You used rhetoric, with good ethos and pathos. I was impressed. We just need to build on that structure.'

'But I didn't know I was using ethos and pathos. I just knew that if I lost my flow, I would mess it up.'

'You don't know how you currently use you Adult, Parent and Child states, but you use them. When you understand these things, you can deploy them with great effect. My role is to give you a fast-track introduction, and the books you should read to continue your education before the showdown. You have 10 – 12 weeks. You must use this time wisely.'

'What else are you going to teach me?'

'Well if you're a good girl and pay attention to your lessons then I'll also teach you more fun ways to enjoy your sensuality.'

She put her elbows on the table as she moved her head as close to him as she could. 'You have my undivided attention my master. I'll be a good girl in class if you teach me to be a bad girl out of class.'

He smiled at her. *'She'll be okay'*, he thought. *'It should be fun to play these games with her. Blow a few cobwebs off my grey matter.'*

He decided he had given her enough for today. 'Okay let's eat, and then get back to your schedule.'

She raised her glass of wine, 'to my master and all the bad things he'll teach me.'

He responded with his glass and an admiring smile. 'To my beautiful student.'

She decided that he was now probably starting to relax, and possibly a little off-guard. 'Have you done this before', she asked.

'Done what?'

She whispered, 'surrogate father.'

'As a matter of fact, I have, but many years ago when I was a much younger banker working in the Bahamas.'

'Well don't stop there, tell me the story.'

'I was sent to the Bahamas for three months to solve a costly problem in our Nassau branch. Having solved the problem in the first week I was told to stay there for the full three-month term to make sure that the original problem stayed solved, and to check that no other problems existed. This meant that I only went to the office once or twice a week, so I had a lot of time on my hands.'

'I was staying in a suite at the best hotel, right on the beach. It must have been a Wednesday evening at dinner. I was on my own. I noticed this rather gorgeous blonde on her own reading a book. I sent her a glass of fizz and asked if she would like to join me for dinner. She came to join me, and we had a very pleasant evening, which went into night even though she was clearly married. She was a real estate agent from Chicago looking at villas for one of her clients. I went with her on the Thursday to look at villas because I had nothing better to do. We had a good time, not least because I know about real estate so I could tell her how well, or poorly the villas had been built. We had a nice lunch, a little frolic, and then another villa. We stayed together Thursday evening and night. She was due to fly back to Chicago on Friday lunchtime, so we said a very fond farewells over breakfast.'

'I went back to my room to decide what to do with my day. About half an hour later there was a knock on my door. It was her with her luggage. She asked if she could stay with me over the weekend. What was I to say? She left her luggage in my room and went to change her flight reservations. When she returned, we changed and went to the beach.'

'Whereas I was very happy to have her for the weekend I was somewhat intrigued to know why this young married woman was spending her weekend with me rather than with her husband in Chicago. Typically American, she was very open about her position. She and her husband had been trying for some time to have a baby, but without success. She had realised that morning that she was at the point in her menstrual cycle when she would likely be fertile so wanted us to have enough sex to give her a chance to become pregnant. She would then return to Chicago on the Sunday flight, have sex with her husband, and hope for the best.'

'So what happened?'

'No idea. I did have her card, probably still have it. Those were days before mobile phones and the internet, so communication was not that easy. I would have been back in London before she was confirmed pregnant in any event.'

'Hmm, you may have another child out there?'

'Who knows? They would be over 30 years old by now in any event.'

'You're a bad boy, and for many years. No wonder my guardian angel chose you.'

'Do you have more naughty stories?'

'How long have you got? Anyway, I need to understand more about you. The more I know, the more focussed my lessons. There is no point in me teaching you things that are alien to you. I need to know your inner ambitions and desires. Talk to me, this is important information for me. Let us start with your ambitions and desires.'

'You are currently a fashion writer. Do you have ambitions to further this career, say to edit a magazine?'

'When I started of course I wanted it all, especially editor of a major magazine. The more I experienced the cut-throat nature of the business the more I realised that I liked the writing, but not horrible way this business is conducted. The competition between magazines is so intensive that you need to be a real bitch, as a female, just to survive. I'm happy to just be a journalist and, as a freelance, I don't have to engage with the politics. Now that my ambition to be a mother is being fulfilled, as we speak, I feel that my primary ambition is to be a good mother, with my writing to keep me in touch with the fashion world, which I do enjoy.'

'As for my desires I would say that my most important desire is to never let you out of my sight again.'

They both laughed.

'Seriously, I didn't know what my desires were, except for having a child, before meeting you. But now my desire is to have your child, and never let you out of my sight again.'

'Okay I can see we are not going any further with this tack. Tell me about how you live. Have you built a comfy nest for you and Andrew, or do you have one of these trendy designer houses that might look good in a magazine, but does not induce the feeling required for love?'

'You'll need to explain what you mean.'

'There is a big difference between a house and a home. A house is where you live, a home is where your heart is. Too many people today read these ill-considered designer magazines and think that they must furnish their house to look like pictures in these magazines. But when you really look at these pictures, they may have some artistic merit, but they are sterile and cold. Everything must to be in its place, and no obvious signs of anyone living there. You could not let a child loose in such rooms or engage in dirty sex. You would break or dirty everything.'

Prejudice in Love

'If you invited me into your living room what impression would you like me to take from what I see?'

'That I had a good eye for design and colour. The room is modern and bright. It's the home of a young, modern and upwardly mobile couple.'

'And you think this is a good impression for me to have?'

'What do you think you should see?'

'I would want to see that my eye never was distracted from the beauty of the person I could see, and that the room is a place where I could savour the pleasure of your company without concern for breaking anything or marking anything. I want to see books obviously being read, a magazine, some evidence that people really live in the room. A cosy nest where I could happily curl up with you on a cold winter's evening, and we make love together.'

'Would I get this impression from your living room?'

'Wow. No, I don't think so. Our sofas are white, lots of sharp edges, ornaments, no books. But I love the idea of you never taking your eyes of me', teasing him.

'Put your child in that room for 5 minutes, and you'll understand what I'm telling you. Try to have rampant sex in that room, and you'll see what I mean.'

'If you want to build a happy family with our child and Andrew then forget the magazines. Think about a comfortable nest where you can all enjoy being with each other; a home where love and a warm welcome is what you feel when you walk in. When Andrew walks into your home after a hard day at the office he should see you and feel an inviting warmth. Everything else is an unnecessary distraction.'

She is thinking about what he is saying. *'All my friends have similar styles of house. But he's right. When we go to these homes, they look good, but never feel warm and inviting. Perhaps he has a point. Andy and I could not have rampant sex in our living room without destroying the place.'*

He snapped her out of her thoughts. 'Do either of you cook?'

'Not really. Although I can prepare basic meals, I've never had much interest in slaving over a hot stove. And Andy has never shown any interest.'

'That means that both of you lack one of the basic skills of foreplay in a relationship, and how the hell do you intend to ensure our child has a nutritious diet?' Let me explain. You have a particularly fractious day with our baby child so are too frazzled to prepare anything for Andy when he comes home from the office. He has two choices; call take-away or sit you in the kitchen with a glass of wine and prepare something you particularly like for both of you whilst having a much-needed adult conversation. Which is the most romantic for you; Andy picking up a telephone and waiting for the delivery, or you watching him apply love and care to preparing you something special for you both?'

She was initially shocked with this rebuke, but when she considered his question, she had to agree that Andy preparing something for her would instil greater love. She looked at him intently 'you're suggesting to me that cooking for your partner is part of foreplay?'

'Tell me your answer to my question.'

'Okay, I have to admit that it would be more romantic if Andy prepared a meal for me, but how do we make that happen?'

'Let me slam a baseline in here to get your real attention to this issue. You would never win my heart on a long-term basis if you could not prepare a reasonably adequate meal for us, especially as such a meal need take no longer than 30 minutes to prepare.'

'Do I have your attention?'

She was speechless. *'I cannot have my valiant knight if I can't feed him?'* she reeled, *'this is a dimension I've not considered'*. She looked at him attentively 'you have my full attention my master.'

He reassuringly smiled at her and reached to put his hand over hers 'Look Cis, gone are the days when the woman of the house is tied to a kitchen. However, it has all now gone too far and many of your generation eat out more than they do at home because they do not have the most elementary skills to prepare even simple, but delicious meals. This really does mean that one valuable aspect of both courtship and marriage is lost. And when you finally have children you add another important learning curve to an already overloaded curve when caring for a baby. You cannot regularly go out for meals during the initial years of a baby, and then you need to feed your child after it comes off your milk, and then off processed foods.'

'And it's not a female chore. It should be something you both can do so that you can care for each other. Being able to feed each other is a loving and caring act which acts as a bonding of your relationship.'

'As you are both in need of learning this simple, but loving act, you can have a lot of fun with it. I would suggest that you get yourself a copy of Jamie Oliver's 30 Minute Meals as a first step. Study it together and see how easy it is to prepare good meals, and then have fun practising them together. You may get a little dirty preparing them, but this could get dirty in other ways as you have fun. You can intimately feed each other. You may even engage in a little desert of your own invention on, or even under the table.'

She smiled 'I would never have considered cooking as a fun thing, let alone involving sex. So you suggest I could prepare myself as the desert? Would that do it for you, my master?' She said playfully.

'If you could make the main course work for me, I would certainly savour such a desert.'

'You will be telling me next that there is a sex angle to the laundry.'

'Some of my most interesting sex has emanated from the laundry.'

She looked at him in disbelief' 'c'mon my master, pray tell me how the laundry transforms into interesting sex.'

'When I lived in New York in my late 20's I had an apartment in a block in the affluent part of East 82nd Street which was seemingly overpopulated by young, female professionals in search of fun, but without attachment. The laundry was communal and located in the basement. More often than not I could take my washing to the laundry, and leave with a date, initiated by a woman, my washing done, dinner prepared, and a full night of entertaining sex. Interesting days', he reflected.

She laughed 'you were really a bad boy in your time. No wonder you can teach me so much. I feel embarrassed with just how closeted my life is.'

'Sure, you have much to learn, but you're committed to learn now your eyes are open, and you're a very willing student. You will be successful, and soon enjoying the rewards you seek.'

'Would you like anything else as time is marching on and we still have things we need to do today.'

'No, I'm fine thank you.'

Having finished their meal she was wondering what he had in store for her this evening. She whispered across the table 'what fun do you have for me tonight?'

'My dear Cis. I have received a clear message from those beautiful brown eyes of yours. They tell me that you have had an emotionally exhausting day today, and you are tired. I propose a leisurely walk back to our apartment, get the clinical part out of the way, albeit with some added TLC. Then I'll stroke you into a lovely deep sleep.'

'But we haven't had any fun today?'

'Isn't this whole adventure fun for you?'

'You know what I mean.'

'True, but you have added a new dimension today, and I need you fresh tomorrow to start your additional education. But fear not I have a treat for you during you 20-minute rest.'

'What is it? Please tell me.'

'It is a calming technique that will make you feel very good about yourself.'

'Do you mean more stroking?'

'No, it's much heavier than stroking. If I gently stroke you when you're so tired you will fall asleep which is not the objective of the 20 minutes.'

'You'll see what I mean when it happens. All you have to do is lie back and enjoy.'

She saw the loving tenderness in his eyes. *'Whatever this man does to me I will most certainly enjoy.'*

On the way back to the apartment she was visualising the fun that they could have in a kitchen, flour faces, gooey cake and chocolate mix used to paint each other. *'Could have some fun with this idea'*, and sex on the table as desert really did appeal.

Chapter 48

When they got back to their apartment, he asked her to prepare herself for bed. He wanted to put her to sleep as soon after her 20-minute rest as possible.

He was feeling emotionally exhausted himself. He was very happy to have her back in his arms, but the additional requirement of making a baby had seriously challenged his feelings. He knew that this challenge is not reversible, and the outcome is fraught with dangers for both of them. But he had agreed to her request, so he must now ensure that he invokes maximum damage limitation. She must succeed in her quest to gain acceptance from Andrew for her pregnancy and ensure that their child is nurtured in a happy, loving environment. He had seen the impact of animosity in the lives of his existing children, and what it had done to them. This must not happen again. At least one of his offspring should have a normal, loving family upbringing.

She interrupted his thoughts by planting herself, completely naked, into his lap putting her arm around his neck. 'I'm ready my master, but I have one request.'

'And what is that my lovely student?'

'This afternoon, before you entered me, you kissed me on my pussy with so much love and tenderness. It made me feel so good about what was happening. Could you make that part of our clinicals?'

'In that position your pussy was screaming to be kissed, so yes, I'll happily comply with your request.'

She kissed him, 'thank you. You said I should feel the love during these sessions. After that kiss, the love was swimming through my body.'

'Okay my beautiful lady let us go do this. But I need you in a different position this time.'

She followed him to the bed where he whipped back the bedclothes, almost completely off the bed. He put one pillow across the side of the bed and got 2 more draped in a towel ready to put under her.

'I want you to lie across the bed with you head on this pillow, pointing to the pillow on the side of the bed. I need to have total access to your head from the side of the bed during your 20-minute rest period.' He moved a chair next to the side of the bed next to the pillow.

She looked at him bemused but was too tired to ask. She lay as he had instructed. Her head was much lower now she only had one pillow so would not easily observe what was happening to her.

Prejudice in Love

He went to the bathroom to clean his teeth ready for bed, and to get the bottle of deep penetrating massage oil he had purchased at Braehead. He picked up a robe and another towel and went back to where she was lying. He cut the lights except for one bedside light. He asked her to raise her hips so that he could get the pillows under her hips.

'Are you comfortable?' as he got himself undressed.

'Hmmm.' Her dreamy voice suggested that she was feeling good, even in this unbecoming position.

He lay beside her. 'You know the drill although I may need a little help getting a suitable erection tonight.'

'Turn around', she said, 'so that your willy is where I can kiss it. You can play with my pussy while I get you into the mood.'

Just the thought of her using her mouth on him started her juices flowing. His erection was already in progress by the time he had turned, and she had hold of him. She had completely relaxed her legs so that her pussy was on full view in her uplifted position. As she moved her lips over the whole head of his penis, he gently stroked her labia. She had completely removed her pubic hair. *'What a fabulous picture'* he thought as he gently kneaded her mound. Kissing her vagina would now be a total delight as his tongue could explore every crease of this welcoming honeypot.

She was now using her tongue to glide and then prod along his penis. She held his foreskin back so that she could tease the tender part below the head. She would cover the head with the warmth of her mouth, and then gently blow air to create the feeling of hot and cold. *'She's good at this'*, he thought. *'Oral sex must have been part of her sex life at some point.'*

He started to penetrate her with his index finger to find the wetness that he needed to enter her. Her juices were in full flow. His erection was now throbbing, but he was not in any hurry to forego the pleasure she was so masterfully providing.

The further she could arouse him the quicker he could deliver the semen she craved.

He could feel his erection ache with pleasure as it throbbed trying to grow ever larger against the stretched skin containing any further expansion. It was time. He kisses her abdomen. 'It's time my love.'

He moved his body so that he was between her legs. As requested, he went down on her with his mouth and savoured the delight of her sex, and then penetrated as far inside as he could with his tongue moving upward until he could feel her clitoris on the end of his tongue. He stroked her with his tongue and then used his tongue in a staccato motion to prod the head. She moaned with pleasure and he sensed another wave of honey fluids being released to lubricate his way into her. He lifted his body and mounted her, one deep thrust. She gasped and then moaned. Her hips were totally relaxed except that he could feel her muscles take hold of his penis as if pulling him deeper into her. He started his movements in and out of her checking that his position would produce optimum stimulation. *'This is going to be easy'* he thought. The work she did with her mouth had certainly sensitised him.

Within a minute he could feel the point of no return. His task was to ensure that his ejaculation was at the end of a thrust so that his sperm would release as close to her cervix as possible. He could feel the inevitable so thrust hard and deep. He felt the release of his sperm at the bottom of the thrust. *'Job done'* he thought to himself with a feeling of satisfaction. *'Not bad for an old guy.'*

He reached down to kiss her, and then went through the exit routine until he was satisfied that her legs were in the optimum position, and she was ready for her 20-minute rest. He went straight to the bathroom to dry himself and collect a bath towel that he had previously put on the heated towel rail. He put this towel over her legs so that it covered her from her navel to her feet. She could feel the warmth on her body.

'That's a nice touch' she smiled as he put on a robe and sat on the chair behind her head.

'Must keep my baby warm as he reached down to kiss her.'

'Okay, I want you to totally relax. You do not move anything. If I want to move your arms just let them come with me, do not assist me. I'm going to move your hair so that it flows down the side of the bed as I want access to your neck.' He reached under her head and gently slid her hair back so that as much as possible slid behind her pillow down the side of the bed.

'Okay, just close your eyes, lie back, and enjoy. But don't go to sleep. You can tell me what you feel as I move around you. I'll start with your hands.'

He reached for his massage oil, poured some into his hand, and then rubbed his hands rigorously to warm the oil. He then reached for her right hand and lifted it up perpendicular to the bed using her elbow as the pivot. He held her hand between his hands and then started to move his fingers between her fingers in a gentle but firm movement so that her fingers within constant motion with his. He started at the top of her fingers, moving his hand down the length of her fingers spreading her fingers in the process, and then back up the finger closing her fingers again. The hand that he used to hold her hand in position then stared to rotate around her wrist with his thumb between her thumb and index finger. She was totally relaxed and let herself be moved as he wished.

'This is nice' she whispered.

'Thank you, we aim to please.'

He put her arm back on the bed and repeated the process on the other hand.

He recharged his hands with warm oil. Starting with a thumb at the base of her neck on each side he moved down her chest to the top of her breasts and then wrapped his finger around each breast, squeezed gently, and then moved upwards away from her breast just clipping her nipples as his hands left her breasts in unison.

'Oh yes', she said, 'they have been screaming for your attention since I slipped my camisole over them this morning.' He repeated the whole movement to her delight.

Whilst he continued, he asked her why she had decided to wear their camisole this morning. 'I thought we were keeping it for a special occasion', he whispered.

'We did. How much bigger occasion can we get than making our baby?'

'So you were sure that I would agree?'

'I would have begged you on my hands and knees if I had to.'

'You will never need to beg me for anything. I trust you to be realistic about demands.'

She threw him a kiss with her lips.

He recharged his hand with oil and moved down to her abdomen. Starting from her waist he massaged into her tummy, up to the bottom of her rib cage and then out repeating this motion with his fingers pressing into her flesh throughout.

'This is so nice, but my breasts are still complaining.'

He got the message so instead of stopping at her rib cage he moved up and caressed her breasts, and then repeated this action.

'That's better' she said. 'You never fail to make my body feel so wanted with your touch. With the oil on your hands I think you could bring me to orgasm when you touch my breasts.'

The 20 minutes was nearly there so he decided to complete this session with a little surprise. He leaned over the bed without alerting her, moved his mouth down to her right nipple, used his tongue to flick her areola around the nipple, and then dropped his mouth down over her nipple and sucked her nipple and areola into his mouth and massaged it with his tongue. Her upper body jolted, gasping as he sucked in her nipple.

'Hmmmm, again please.'

He repeated the whole process on the same nipple knowing that its sensitivity will have heighted after the first time.

'My juices are flowing, you naughty man, but my other breast is complaining.'

He repeated the whole process on her left breast, fully satisfying her body.

He reached down and lifted the towel from her legs and used it to wipe her body where he had used oil.

'Go to the bathroom if you need and let's go to bed.'

She went to the bathroom and was back beside him in bed within minutes.

Paul switched off the light. 'Let's get you to sleep.'

She reached around his neck. 'Paul my darling, I love you so much. Thank you for today.'

They both held tight, lips met and just dissolved into a longing kiss.

He got her comfortably cuddled and started to stroke her back. She was fast asleep in minutes.

'What a day' he thought. *'What have I done? But how could I say no to this bundle of joy. We have much work to do, but she is certainly willing to learn. Guardian angel, I hope that you really have got this right. You cannot hurt this wonderful lady, not on my watch.'*

With that he settled down to a peaceful sleep.

Chapter 49 - Friday

Cis was awake by 7am. She could hear rain beating against the windows, *'Scottish summer'* she thought to herself. *'No need to get up yet.'*

She unravelled herself from the arms of her valiant knight as she needed the bathroom.

When she returned she slid back beside him. He was still sleeping peacefully. She noticed the smile on his face and hoped his dreams were of her.

Her only desire was to lie there and look at him. She felt refreshed, alive, and more importantly, happy beyond her wildest dreams. Yesterday had been a pivotal day in her life, and her valiant knight had not failed her. He had answered her dream to have a baby, and then applied his mind and experience to ensure that she maximised her chances of success. How could she possibly fail?

She felt wanted, loved, fulfilled, and now she had the child she so wanted. The man next to her had satisfied her every desire and need. This is where she belonged.

Now she needed to find a way to keep him. She tried to imagine Andy paying her the attention that she gets from him. Would Andy ever learn to patiently arouse her before taking her?

She decided that she could break sex into 3 categories. There is hot frantic lustful sex, but this needs preparation. She was not interested in the normal definition of hot sex as practiced in certain countries in Africa where the man will force himself into a dry vagina in order to get maximum stimulation for the man. This results in a very sore pussy, and thus the 'hot' in hot sex. She had experienced this with Andy when he has mounted her before she has generated enough lubricating juices for a smooth entry. The resulting soreness would last a few days, and she would resist further sex until the soreness had gone.

Then there is fun sex which also requires preparation to enable the woman to be ready for intercourse to give her the chance of orgasm. She thought that the movies completely exaggerate the capability of a woman to be fully aroused to orgasm in a matter of seconds.

Then there is making love; a spontaneous overwhelming desire to become one with a lover. By the time that intercourse takes place the arousal is so great that she is fully prepared, and orgasm is likely.

She remembered back to Monday when they spontaneously made love, and how wonderful she felt both during and afterwards. She felt so totally lost in the emotions of being loved and wanted.

Andy's idea of sex was to get to the final act as quickly as possible. She has a great body and looks fantastic. She has breasts which captivate this man lying next to her. Andy barely pays them any attention. Her breasts yearn the attention that they have received over these passed days, and such attention really helps to get her juices flowing. How can she get Andy to show such interest, and use them to build to more satisfying sex?

Every time Paul engaged with her in any sexual activity, he knew how to press all her buttons, and waited until she was so ready for entry that she was practically begging for him to take her. They had engaged in intercourse many times in the past days. Other than a constantly swollen clit she had no soreness or pain in her loins or breasts, just a yearning for more. Even at their most active times as students she never had this with Andy, nor did she remotely feel such satisfaction.

Whilst lost in these thoughts he had opened his eyes to see her looking at him, but obviously lost in thought.

He lapped up the view before his eyes as he thought *'What a beautiful sight when I open my eyes in a morning. Whatever did I do to deserve such a vision on my pillow at my age?'*

He reached up and touched the end of her nose to bring her out of her thoughts. She smiled at him 'And how long have you been looking at me?' she whispered.

'Just long enough to savour the vision lying next to me, and thinking how lucky I am.'

She hooked her arms around his neck and pulled him close to her. 'This vision needs to feel you close to her' as she connected to him with as much of her body as she could.

She felt so warm and inviting that a stiff erection was inevitable. He was still half asleep, but he wanted her. He wrapped his hand around her buttock and pulled her close such that his erection was now throbbing against her abdomen.

'My valiant knight is very frisky this morning', she whispered. 'His damsel is also warm and ready to be taken.'

They kissed tenderly, and then again more urgently. She wrapped her free leg around his hips pulling him ever closer.

He reached for the two pillows not being used from her side of the bed and dragged them down to her abdomen and rolled her onto them.

Their kissing was now very intense, and they could both feel the heat of each other body. Spontaneous combustion was about to ignite them.

He reached for her pussy feeling the heat. His fingers probed inside to find that her juices were indeed in full flow. He rolled over and mounted her in one movement. She purred as he penetrated deep into her. They were locked in uncontrollable union.

They kissed more as he started to thrust in and out of her with the urgency of a lover. He could feel the muscles in her loins grabbing his erection, pulling him ever deeper. These sensations were so powerful he could not hold his ejaculation. He thrust deep as his loins exploded gushing semen deep into her. She groaned as she felt the throb of his erection release its load into her.

Prejudice in Love

She held him tight enjoying the warmth that she felt throughout her body. She did not orgasm, but they had made spontaneous love again, and she knew that this is what she wanted, and this is the man to give it to her. She did not want to let him go and held on to him for dear life.

He eventually came out of his daze; slowly withdrew from her, threw the sheets back to ensure that she was seated well on the pillows, moved her legs into position, and then pulled back the sheets. He wanted to lie with her in the warmth of her body.

She did just as he wanted, still savouring the feelings radiating through her body. When he settled next to her she turned her head so that they were facing each other with such a loving smile on her face. 'You made love to me again. I feel so much love and contentment with you. I love you so much my darling.'

He let these beautiful words brand themselves into his heart and his soul. He felt so good. How could he ever let this angel go? 'I love everything about you. You make an old guy feel young again.'

'Less of the old guy please. You have not failed me once, and I go by the age you feel which cannot possible be more than 40. In any event I love what I feel, see, and touch. That's all that matters.'

'We have 20 minutes to kill. Do you want to do some work, or shall we have a working breakfast? I think the weather allows us to spend the morning discussing Aristotle and rhetoric, and it's really important that you get this right as tone and word selection is everything in your showdown with Andy.'

'Can we start over breakfast? I feel so good, I'm happy to lie here and savour the feelings I get when we make love. This is a new experience for me. The intensity and the wantonness are electrifying. So, if it's alright with you I'm happy to start over breakfast, and then work through the morning with you.'

'For now, I just want to feel the moment, and look forward to our shower together.'

'Okay. I want to look at my emails and see what is happening out there. I'll give you a prod in about 15 minutes.' With that he slipped out of bed, found a robe, and went to the living area and clicked on the TV news.

Chapter 50

Paul returned to find her exactly as he had left her some 20 minutes ago, still in her own thoughts, but with a big smile on her face. He reached down to peck her on the lips. She came out of her thoughts and looked at him.

'Ready for a shower?'

'You bet', as she leaped off the bed into the bathroom.

'Just give me a minute', as she went through the bathroom door.

He waited until he could hear the water flowing from the shower before entering the bathroom. She was already inside the shower. He slipped in behind her.

Instead of leaning against the wall she leaned with her back into his body, and her hands on his hips. She was teasing him with something approaching a lap dance, and she could feel the effect as his penis came to life crawling up her buttocks. She said nothing, just waiting for his hands to touch her waiting breasts.

He could not reach her shoulders which were tucked into his chest, so started with her breasts. She purred as he massaged them with his soapy hands. He wondered what was different today as she was being very brazen about what she wanted. But he was in no hurry, so lingered longer than usual on her breasts before continuing with the remainder of her body.

She was wallowing in his touch. Her thoughts were very much in tune with what she was thinking when she first lay on the pillow looking at him sleeping. *'I will make this man yearn to keep me close to him. I will encourage him to take whatever he wants from* me and make it so nice for him that he'll not dare to leave me. When he makes love to me it's like nothing I've ever known or felt. I want him, and I'll get him. Look how he lingers on my breasts. I want him to linger on me forever.'

When it was her turn to bathe him, she became very rhythmic as though she was moving to music. 'It's certainly more sensual than on previous occasions', he thought. 'Is she adding her own touches to these activities, or is she up to something?'

'Is she just responding to our love making earlier? It was okay but not as good as Monday night. Perhaps she thinks she's now pregnant, and she's showing her joy. Whatever it is I need to get a grip on it. We cannot have a role reversal.'

After their shower she selected what she wanted to wear. He dressed her. It was time for their working breakfast.

Chapter 51

Paul suggested that they get everything they need for breakfast in one go so that once they had started on the working part of breakfast she was not bobbing up and down to get additional items to her complex breakfast ritual. Whereas he took a simple English breakfast of two poached eggs on toast with bacon, sausages, mushrooms and tomatoes with tea and juice on the side, she had a convoluted assortment of muesli, yoghurt, fruit, croissant, honey, juice and water. He chose a table for four so that she had plenty of room to stack her assortment of plates and cartons.

He decided to eat his cooked breakfast whilst it was warm as he was a relatively fast eater where she tended to take her time.

'Aristotle, as you well know, was a great philosopher, but also a great politician. As you also know political debate is usually in the form of spoken debate. Thus the art of persuasion is fundamental to a politician hoping to win the argument. Aristotle studied this art and developed the idea of rhetoric as a means of persuasive dialogue. He came up with the three accepted components required in any speech in order to effectively delivery your message in a way that optimised your chance of success. These components are logos, ethos, and pathos.'

'Aristotle's original work has been tinkered with through the ages to what we have today. My version, and what I want to teach you, uses the following definitions.'

'"Logos" is the essential logic of what's wrong, and what needs to be done about it, for example, "this is the problem, and we need to do something about it". Please note the use of "we" not "I".'

'"Ethos" is the credibility and/or integrity of the speaker to address this problem and propose a solution. For example, "I have studied this problem in some detail, and because of this, I think we should do this". This is the only part where the word "I" is used.'

'"Pathos" is the emotional content to energise people into believing that you are doing this for the greater good and thus they should support you.'

'So you see it's not rocket science. Are you with me so far?'

'Yes' she said attentively. 'Fairly easy really. This is the problem that needs fixing, I know how to fix it, but I need your support.'

'Not quite, but not bad. A few examples will hone you into the specifics. I'll use your showdown with Andy throughout so that we cover as many possibilities as possible.'

'But before we start, rhetoric is used in the form of a speech, so you must get a specific commitment from your audience to hear you out before they contribute. It's very important that your audience agree to give you the floor until you have finished. When you came back yesterday to ask me to help you with your child you were very good at securing my silence and attention before you started, and on the two occasions that I wanted to interrupt. If you allow yourself to be interrupted, your chances of success significantly reduce.'

'Also, time and place are important. You cannot allow distractions such as TV, radio, another engagement, etc. Your audience has to be relaxed and prepared to give you the floor and their undivided attention for whatever time you need.'

'The reciprocity of this is that you must be aware of their attention span and keep your speech within this timeframe.'

'Creating your environment is very important. I would suggest an evening when neither of you have anywhere to go, not expecting anyone to call, or any must-watch TV. End of the day, but not too late, is always better than the beginning of the day for a showdown of this nature. This time of the day also allows you both to sleep on it before taking any impulsive reaction that might be regrettable.'

'Let me ask you a question. Has Andy ever laid a hand on you in anger, and if not, have you ever been concerned that he might?'

'No, never. I don't think he would ever dare.'

'Good, so we can keep it close, just as you did with me, so that you can use your finger to keep him quiet should he want to interrupt.'

'It's maybe a silly question as you were very skilful with me, but do you understand the preparation part of this?'

'I think you are describing and explaining to me what I instinctively did with you. But I was really scared about how you would receive my plea. I watched you very carefully while I was unpacking to see if you were in a receptive mood. I knew I must do it before we had any sexual activity and thought that the camisole would prepare you for a special occasion albeit far from what you might expect. But you are normally very calm so that was a great advantage. Catching Andy at the right time will be much more difficult as he is always on the phone or watching sport, so understanding the process should help me to pick the moment and the environment.'

'Apply that same instinct, but based on what you have achieved with Andy over the preceding weeks. The more he buys into your new sex life together the easier to get his attention, and commitment to listen to what you have to say. The more fun he has, the more he will be prepared to put his phone away and listen.'

At this point the restaurant manager asked them if they could move to the lobby as they needed to prepare the room for lunch. There was no point going back to the suite yet because the cleaning staff would want to restore the room to a normal state.

Paul found a quiet corner of the lobby where they could continue uninterrupted.

As they went through to the lobby, she was deep in thought. *'He's really serious about this learning process, and he's good. I have never really thought about this stuff before, but it all makes good sense. Maybe I can practice on him when he finishes his lessons. If I can successfully apply this knowledge with him, I don't need to worry about Andy because I'll be with my real lover. Eh oh, on we go.'*

After they were seated, he checked that she was comfortable, and ready to continue.

'Let's start with Logos. What do you think the logos of your showdown should be?'

'Something like "I want a child, we have not achieved this, so I have found a solution".'

'Goodness no. You're in Adult mode. Switch to Parent mode.'

'You haven't given me the titles of the books you told me about, so I don't understand the Parent/Adult difference.'

'Okay, I'll give them to you when you can write them down. But we don't need this knowledge for the purposes of understanding this process.'

Prejudice in Love

'The essence of rhetoric is to connect people to a common cause.'

'Let me propose a logos. "Andy, we both want a child to complete our family, and we have tried now for two years without success. You seem reluctant to attend a fertility clinic with me, so I have found a solution that I hope will work for both of us".'

'Note the continuous use of "we" and "us".'

'Does this make sense to you? The problem is defined in three simple statements, and the final statement connects you both to your solution. You are addressing this problem, not just for you, but for both of you. This is important to remember and is Parent mode.'

'I need to write this down. It's so simple when you say it, but I need to see it on paper to grasp it.'

'Okay. Let's go back to our suite and hope the cleaners have finished.'

Chapter 52

The cleaners had finished so Paul extracted the notepaper from the hotel welcome pack and gave it her along with the complimentary pen. They sat at the table in the living area.

She wrote down the logos proposed by him.

'You're a writer, so you understand the structure of statements and sentences. This is an extension of the Who, What, Why, When, How that you learn as a journalist with the addition of connective emotion.'

'In the first statement underline "we both want" and "our family". This is critical to connect Andy with the problem.'

'In the second statement underline "we have" and "without success". This keeps the problem neutral with no blame anywhere.'

'In the third statement underline "with me". This is critical to keeping the problem collective.'

'In the fourth statement underline "I hope will work for both of us". You did not do this for you, but for both of you. At no time should he feel that he has failed you and thus you have gone elsewhere.'

'Can you see the inclusive nature of this phrasing?'

'Now it's staring at me I can see it. A simple, but powerful statement of fact.'

'Okay, let us try to define our ethos. In your case our ethos needs to make the case for how you approached the problem, why you chose the solution that you did, with the added support to your argument that it worked. This last part is beyond normal ethos but does validate your solution.'

'To qualify why you needed to look for an alternative solution you can use a statement along the lines of "After two years we should have been successful, and I know that my desperation for a child is driving us apart, and is not good for our relationship".'

'In developing your ethos regarding approach, you need to add some empathy. So a statement like "I know that you are reluctant to come with me to a fertility clinic" shows empathy towards his feelings. There is no need to expand on why, as it's now history, as you are already pregnant, so "why" is irrelevant.'

'Another statement of value in your argument is something like "having studied IVF treatment I shuddered at the thought of lying on a table with instruments inside my vagina extracting an egg, fertilising it with possibly an unknown donor, and sticking it back in my womb, let alone the horrible hormone treatment." You can be really dramatic here to make him shudder at the thought of such a cold clinical process on his darling wife, thus getting empathy from him for an alternate solution.'

'Still with me?'

'Every word. As soon as we're finished, I'm going straight to my computer to get it all in there which will give me a chance to review it and raise any questions I have.'

'Impressive', he thought. *'She's really taking this seriously.'*

'Once you have validated why something needed to be done and identified solutions that do not suit either of you, you can move onto what you propose to do, or have done in your case.'

'I can only give you some pointers here because you need to decide on how much of our story you want to tell, how to couch it to him, but with a clear observation of his attention span.'

'I'll give you a list of statements, and why I think they are relevant for you to weave into your story.'

"I found myself alone in that terrible storm", gets sympathy. 'Why was he not here for you, or even call when he knew about it to see if you were alright?'

"A much older professional man rescued me. But, because of my reaction to thunder and lightning, he had to stop driving and take me to a hotel for two days to escape the storm. He had to delay his trip because of this silly girl." 'Andy will know about your problem with thunder and lightning, so the story is credible – nice fatherly man caring for his Cis.'

'Whilst at the hotel you felt you could talk to him, and essentially poured out your heart.'

"He started to straighten me out. Told me that we are sleepwalking our way through life because of our inexperience. Time to wake up and grasp life. He taught me so much that I have introduced into our life already, and I hope that you agree that life has been much better for us since, and we are now a happy couple again. Everything that has changed in our life over the past 3 months was instilled into me by this man. A true masterclass in life, and we share the benefits together."

"When I got home two things triggered the idea that meeting this man was fate. The first was your message that you would not be back for a few days longer. The second was that I started to ovulate."

"I took a train, went back to him, and asked him to be a surrogate father. He refused. I begged him to help me. He finally agreed on the basis that he would have no part thereafter."

"It worked. I went to the doctor today. I am 10 weeks pregnant with **our** child."

'He will try to intervene at this stage, so you must remind him that you have not finished.'

She was diligently writing down everything he said. She could see how he builds the story to be a logical progression of one event leading to another with no inference of a potential love affair. *'Clever'*, she thought.

'Now we move to the necessary pathos, as you have just dropped a bomb on Andy's macho pride.'

'The most important message here which you will repeat over, and over again until it is engrained in his mind is' "I did this for us, for our family, for our future together, for our happiness together".'

'And the kicker is "and no-one needs to know anything about it. No fertility clinics, no public IVF treatment – nothing". This protects his masculinity.'

'Now you have finished.'

'There will be a very hurt masculine outburst. Typical questions will be:

"How could you do this to me?" – "I did it for us to complete the family we both want."

"What were you thinking of?" – "Us, and our happy family together."

"And what will you do next time?" – "There will not be a next time. I promise. We have our child, which is what we both want."

"Why didn't you tell me earlier because you will have known weeks ago?" – "I did not want to raise any hopes until I was certain that everything is alright. I saw the doctor today for the first time and the pregnancy is confirmed as good. You are the first to know."'

'Do you see? Short simple statements confirming you did it for both of you, and your future happiness. Do not get into long dialogue on any point. Keep it short and to the point, and never go into Adult mode. If you need a break from interrogation drop into Child mode and shed a few tears protesting that you were only thinking of your happiness together.'

'The argument buster can be a simple beg the question. "Andy, have we been happy for the past 10 weeks? He solved that problem for us. But we still had the problem about a child. So has he not solved that problem as well in a way that works for both of us?"'

'You do not tell him who I am under any circumstances during this discussion. You deflect this question with the fact that it is not relevant as my part is over. In IVF they will not disclose the identity of the donor, and you have promised that you will not disclose my name. In the future if he still insists, but things are stable between you, then you can disclose on the basis that you will have to tell me of your disclosure. This will prevent any further inquiry.'

She is frantically writing all this down thinking *'he has all the angles covered. How can I fail? All Andy's arguments are simply neutralised without confrontation. I must learn more of this approach.'*

'Okay, go digest what I've said and let me know if you have any questions. What I hope that you now see is the necessity of this next 10 weeks of no disclosure of your pregnancy to anyone to give time to prepare Andy using the techniques you have learnt, so that there is no argument as to the value of your decisions and actions.'

'Loud and clear my master. Do you ever lose an argument?'

'I do not argue to win or lose. The objective is to sell your point of view, or to accept an alternate point of view. Argument should not be a contest, but a means to develop new thinking. Your role in the showdown with Andy is not to win, and thus he loses, it is to gain his acceptance of a solution to a problem that you both can share.'

She kissed him on the cheek. 'I hope to aspire to the wisdom of my master one day.'

'By the way, the books you need regarding Adult, Parent, Child behaviour are "Games People Play" by Eric Berne, and "I'm OK, You're OK" by Thomas Harris. Be careful, there are several copycats, so check the authors. Study them in the order that I have given them to you.'

'There is one other bible for conflict resolution, written some 2,500 years ago, but as relevant today as it was then. It is required study by many of the major business schools in the world, but you need to be able to put your conflict into context for it to be useful. It's called "The Art of War" by Sun Tzu, and my preference is the translation by Samuel Griffith. When I was in China a few years ago they were amazed that this work is so popular in the West as they had abandoned it in preference for the manuals produced by Sandhurst Military Academy, the irony of which is that they are rooted on Sun Tzu's philosophy. You do not have to study this to be successful with Andy, but it provides clear and pragmatic solutions for all kinds of human conflicts. I commend it to you if you have the interest.'

'If my master refers to this book as a bible then your humble student will surely take your advice.'

Chapter 53

By the time she had finished her notes, checked them with him, and satisfied herself that she understood the construction of her speech to Andy, it was past noon. She put her notebook away and went to sit in his lap with her arms around his neck and kissed him with three smackers on his cheek.

'Thank you for yet another masterclass. I will perfect it and prepare my speech very carefully over the coming weeks. I just hope I have the courage to deliver it well.'

'You had the courage to ask me to help you although you did not know me well enough to know what I would think. You have ten years of experience with Andy, and you can be very persuasive. You'll be fine once you get started. I have every confidence in you.'

'It's still raining so what about a little fun with your next clinical?'

Now what do you have in mind? When you use the word "fun" I have learnt to be wary.'

He started to tickle her ribs 'Come now. When have I used that word and it did not prove to be the case once you get over your anxieties?'

She jumped from his lap 'You'll have to catch me first' as she disappeared into the bedroom.

He followed her into the bedroom and cornered her, and then tickled her ribs some more until she surrendered. Lifting her up he carried her to the dresser where he kept his bag of toys. He sat her on the dresser next to the drawer, and then opened the drawer.

'You should not be so anxious about these toys. They are for the purpose of fun, not pain. I don't subscribe to any form of inflicted pain as I always want you to feel pleasure and come back for more. There is another position for our clinical intercourse that we have not used, and I would like to combine it with a little fun.'

'And what position are you referring to?'

'Telling you where we'll end up will spoil the fun of getting there, so you must wait and see. However, the logic of the position will be obvious to you.'

'So what do I have to do?'

'You don't **have** to do anything. If you would prefer our normal clinical then I'll exclude the fun part.'

With resignation 'Okay my master, what would you like me to do?'

'Firstly, we need to prepare you. I'll start by undressing you down to your panties. Then I'll bind your hands together with one of these chiffon restraining scarves' as he took then out of the bag.

'I didn't see you buy those. What else is in that bag?'

'All in good time my darling. Are you ready to start?'

She raised her arms to indicate he could remove her top which he did slowly with great care to touch her as he reached underneath her top so that his hands were in direct contact with her torso as he moved upwards never losing contact with her skin until the top was completely removed. The touch calmed her as she was smiling as he put the top to one side. He then removed her skirt with the same gentle touch.

He picked up one of the chiffon scarfs and, starting at the top of her arms, glided his hands along her arms bringing her hands together at which point he wrapped the chiffon scarf around her wrists twice and then knotted it firmly, but not tight.

The next step was to blindfold her. Picking up another chiffon restraining scarf, stepped behind her and applied it as a blindfold tying the knot slightly to one side of her head so that she would not lie on the knot when on her back.

'Now we are in new territory' she murmured.

'How many times do you close your eyes when we are being intimate?' he offered.

'That's different as it's my choice' she responded.

'Just relax Cis. Your valiant knight will always ensure that your wellbeing is protected. If you have a problem when we start, just tell me to stop. But at least try the experience first. We're exploring your sexuality to open new options for you.'

'Do you want me to stop now?' he asked.

'Kiss me' she commanded.

He kissed her right breast nipple gently sucking it into his mouth.

She laughed 'That's not what I meant, but it was nice'.

He kissed her on the lips tenderly.

'That was good, but my left breast is complaining about preferential treatment.'

He kissed her left breast nipple.

'Okay, I'm ready. If I get nervous it means I need another reassuring kiss or two, or even three to avoid complaints.'

She was now in a playful mood, so guided her to the bed, pulled back the blankets, and lay her on her back. The remaining chiffon scarf was attached to the bedhead and then he raised her arms above her head and passed the other end of the scarf between her wrists and tied it so that she was now restrained to the bed. He pulled her a little down the bed so that she knew she was restrained.

It was obvious that she was a little nervous, so he sat on the bed and gently stroked her tummy until she relaxed.

He reached for the smallest of the vibrators and found a vibration and intensity similar to the one she liked in the vibrating panties. He started to touch her body along her panty line with the vibrator. The reaction was instant as she contracted her tummy muscles with each touch. A smile appeared on her face. She was happy with this.

The next step was to start at her navel and slowly move the vibrator head down, under her panties towards her pussy. He probed inside her labia and set the vibrator over her clit, withdrawing his hand so that her panties held the vibrator in position. She moved her hips to make a small adjustment to the position of the vibrator and then relaxed as the sensations started to weave their magic. 'Hmmmm, that feels good'.

He left her for a few minutes knowing that her juices would be responding to the impacts on her clitoris.

He started the largest vibrator, selected the speed that her breasts responded to previously and started to roll it around her breast with the occasional gentle prod on her nipples. Remembering her comments regarding equal pleasure to each breast he ensured that each breast was stroked in the same way. She arched her back as if pushing her breasts for more. Her nipples were fully extended as he gave them more and more contact with the vibrating pleasure wand that she now craved.

Testing her pussy with his free hand he could feel the wetness oozing from her. Putting down the vibrator he caressingly relieved her of her panties and opened her legs wide. Then with the large vibrator he started to nuzzle the entrance to her vagina. As he had guessed it slipped inside very easily. He moved it in and out of her slowly. She was now moaning with desire. Then he increased the vibrating pulse to a much stronger setting. She screamed with pleasure as her hips shot upwards as she felt a deep orgasm crash over her. He removed the vibrator allowing her to close her legs and roll onto her side as the waves of pleasure running through her body needed time to play out.

He picked up the midi vibrator and applied a little lube. The wetness from her pussy had already covered her anus in her fluids. He picked up the mini version and put it back into position over her clit and she locked her knees to hold it in position. He wanted it to tease her with a continued intense sensation before using the midi on her. He chose a low but throbbing vibration as he stroked the cheeks of her bottom with his free hand, before gently sliding the vibrator between her cheeks into her anus. She winced as the tip entered her, but she did not resist. She was in the land of pleasure and her valiant knight was not hurting her. The vibrator intensity was increased as he slowly moved it in and out of her. She was groaning again as he felt her building to another orgasm. She was gripping the mini vibrator tight against her as her body started to shake with the orgasm that was building until she again bucked as her thighs went rigid.

He gently removed both vibrators and left her to roll onto her back totally spent.

By this time, his throbbing erection was desperately trying to free itself from his underwear. He quickly disrobed himself.

In a gentle voice he whispered, 'Can you roll over so that you are kneeling.'

She did just as he said without question. He got behind her and opened her knees to lower her hips so that he could enter her. He held her buttocks and thrust in deep. She groaned as she felt his entry. He started slowly, and then increased until he was ramming deep into her. The groans were now increasing as her breathing increased to a rapid pant. He could feel his orgasm building in intensity until he exploded deep into her. She gasped as she felt the burst of semen deep into her.

Stroking her back and buttock he stayed deep inside her until he could feel her start to relax. Then he slowly started to withdraw from her asking her to stay where she was until he could arrange pillows for her to roll over. Having arranged two pillows covered with a towel next to her hips he asked her to close her knees together and allow him to roll her onto the pillows keeping her knees bent. She totally complied with his wishes.

When she was properly positioned on the pillows, he sat next to her and gently stroked her torso.

'Hmmm, so nice' she purred.

'Are you okay my beautiful lady?' he gently whispered.

'Wonderful' she purred, 'I like fun time.'

'Okay, I'll sit here and stroke you for a while to let everything settle, so just relax and enjoy.'

After some 15 minutes Paul went to the bathroom and collected two warm flannels and a towel. He used one to clean himself, and then opened her legs to gently clean her. She had a big smile on her face as she felt this act of love removing the stickiness from around her vagina and anus. He then gently dried her and removed the pillows.

He released her hands so that she could sit up so that he could remove her blindfold. She took a moment to adjust to the light, quickly kissed him and went to the bathroom grabbing the flannels and towel on her way.

When she returned a few minutes later she was beaming. 'That was lovely. The feelings that went through my body were incredible. Had you just lasted a few moments longer I would have orgasmed for a third time in just a few minutes, unbelievable'.

'Sorry I failed you.'

She grabbed him and held him close 'you never fail me my lover.'

He asked her to sit next to him. He showed her the vibrators he had used on her. She gulped when she realised how easily the largest vibrator had slid into her. And the one that she would have used on her pussy he had slid into her anus, and it felt good.

'Do you see my angel it's all about preparation, after which you can experience so much pleasure without any pain. Had I not restrained and blindfolded you all of that pleasure would not have happened.' Pointing to the largest vibrator he added 'in 9 months from now as your baby slips out you will think this very small compared with the size of a baby.'

Prejudice in Love

She just sat there looking at the sources of her pleasure totally amazed at how they made her feel. But she was quite sure that she could not let Andy loose with these toys. Andy was in kindergarten against the skills of Paul, and he would have to show he understood such toys before even showing them to him. For now, she would pleasure herself with these toys.

'Are you ready for some lunch?' he asked.

'Can we have a quick shower first?'

'Go get it running'.

Chapter 54

After lunch they returned to their apartment and sat for a while.

He looked out of the window. 'It's stopped raining. Let's go for a walk in the woods.'

He decided to drive into the country and then off road, following a track through woodland. After about two miles he came to a clearing. There were no signs of human life, or even that anyone used this track at all on a regular basis.

The car temperature gauge suggested that it was 18°C outside.

He reached over to her and removed her top to reveal her breasts.

'Now what do you have in mind?'

He undid her pants and asked her to remove them. She obeyed her master.

He removed his shirt and trousers.

'Do you want me to come around to your side and remove your panties, or can you manage as he removed his underwear.'

'But leave your shoes', he said.

'Are we going out there?' she exclaimed.

247

'Why not? We can frolic in the beauty of nature in our natural state. Should be fun. Maybe I'll find a suitable altar and sacrifice you to the gods.'

She reached over and touched his forehead. 'No sign of fever', she remarked. 'Maybe I have driven him to madness. The madness of Paul.'

He got out of the car and went around to let her out. The wonderful smell of the forest after rain swamped their nostrils.

'It's quite exhilarating' she said with surprise.

He took her hand. 'Let's go walkies.' She followed his lead. Certainly the chance of other people out after all the rain that day was very low, so why not. It had been years since she walked in the rain without a coat, albeit with clothes, but naked, never.

They moved towards the trees.

'Do you like our walk?' He asked.

'With you I enjoy whatever we do, even if I'm convinced that you are slightly mad.'

They were about 100 metres from the car as the heavens opened. The rain was heavy, but it felt good against her skin.

Paul stood behind her as though in the shower and held her breasts up to the rain so that the raindrops beat directly onto her breasts and her nipples. She looked up at him laughing.

'You crazy man. Who would ever think of such a thing?'

'I think that we have been foiled in my quest to sacrifice you out in the open. We should go back to the car, dry off, and I'll warm you up again. No point in running as we are already wet.'

When they got back to the car Paul opened the tailgate, extracted two car blankets and two towels, threw them over the back seat, and closed the tailgate. He opened the rear door on the passenger side, spread one of the blankets over the seat, covered it with a towel and indicated that she should get in, but dangle her shoes so that he could remove them, and which he put in the front passenger foot well. He closed her door and went around to the other side and repeated the process.

Once inside he asked her to straddle his legs facing him. He quickly towelled her back, and then wrapped the travel blanket around her shoulders whilst he used the towel to dry her front and his own front. He then pulled her close and wrapped both blankets around them.

'Shared bodily warmth' he whispered in her ear.

She looked at him 'so what were you going to do to me out there?'

'I hoped to find an altar upon which to sacrifice you.'

'What do you mean?'

'You know what an altar looks like. A flat rock that I can stretch you across and sacrifice your virginity to the gods.'

'A bit late for that. You stole by new model virginity days ago.'

'The gods won't know. They'll see your tasty body and forgive any oversight.'

'I owe you a treat for presenting me with a naked pussy, and I thought I could give you that treat on an altar in the wilds. Works great in the rocks on a Caribbean Island in the sunshine.'

'Tell me about this treat' she teased as she snuggled closer.

'Me no tell, me only show. But you'll get it.'

'I've never been naked in a car before. It's fun.'

'Have you never had sex in a car?'

'Neither of us had a car in our early days so the situation never arose.'

'But you both have cars now. Don't you ever drive into the countryside and have sex across the bonnet of your car?'

'No.'

'My Porsche is perfect for stretching a woman across the bonnet and giving her a good shafting.'

'Dirty talk now. I can't wait for such a treat with my lover.' She leaned over and kissed him. There was urgency in this kiss.

'So how are you going to warm me?' she said seductively as she reached down and caressed his penis.

'It looks like you have your own ideas about that. Would you like me to take you out there and shaft you in the rain, or do you want your first sex in a car?'

'I'm very happy where I am, thank you, so why don't you test my juices while I finish preparing you.'

Paul reached down and found her pussy. As his finger moved across the flesh of her labia she started to purr in his ear. He penetrated her lips. She wasn't quite there so found her swollen clitoris and gently started to caress the shaft leading to the head.

'Hmmm, that touch. Whoever taught you to touch in this way knows about women.'

It did not take long for her juices to flow. As she was becoming more aroused so did the intensity of caressing on his penis. His erection was now throbbing.

He lifted her bottom and directed her pussy to his erection whilst she kept hold to ensure a clean entry into her. She sank all the way down his shaft in one movement.

'Okay, have some fun.'

She did not need any further encouragement. She threw off her blanket and used the backs of the front seats to give her leverage to move in a rhythmic rotational motion. With all the activity over the past days her clitoris was hyper-sensitive, so her build did not take long.

'Play with my breasts' came her groans.

He used his nails to lightly scratch down the top of her breasts to her nipples. He then rolled her nipples between his fingers, stretching them towards him.

Her breasts were now heaving with the panting of her breath as she was slowly but surely bringing herself to climax.

He glided his hands down her body as he sucked a breast into his mouth, fiercely massaging her nipple and areola with his tongue. She was now moaning with delight.

'I need you to touch my clitoris' she groaned.

He reached down running his index finger from her navel down to her clitoris and then pressed the head. She exploded sending spasms down his shaft. She kept moving.

'Again.'

He repeated the move down to her clitoris and prodded the head again. This time she really did explode, and he could feel the eruption of juices running down his shaft onto his testicles. She collapsed onto him gasping for breath. He wrapped the blanket around her to retain the heat she was generating.

When she finally came up for air, she had her glazed look. 'Warm enough?' he quipped.

She feigned beating his chest, laughing. She laughed so much that they disengaged.

'How was your first sex in a car?'

'Cramped, need more room.'

The rain was still beating down on the roof of the car.

'How about if I dress you and take you back to our spacious suite?'

'That would be nice if you promise to lie with me and hold me when we get there.'

'I think I can manage that. Swing back onto the seat so I can reach your clothes. Use the towel to dry yourself.'

She swung back onto the back seat, dried herself and then Paul. He lay her down on the seat to put on her panties and slacks, and then sat her up to replace her sweater.

'I can understand car blankets, but why do you carry towels with you? Were you planning this, although these are not hotel towels?'

'Unlike the Chelsea tractor people, I have this car for off-road use. I hunt and shoot game, so I need this vehicle to get to places that other cars cannot. Some days it rains so I keep two towels for people to dry off so that my nice leather seats do not get too wet, and I have another towel to dry my guns before I put them back into their cases.'

'Do you shoot animals?'

'Yes, but not in any number. I don't like shoots where you are expected to shoot many birds in one day. I uphold the hunter gatherer tradition of shooting what you can eat and no more. I grew up in the country and have much respect for nature and what it provides for us. I don't abuse it.'

'What do you shoot?'

'Pheasant, grouse, duck, goose, and the occasional deer. I have also shot wild boar in the forests of the former East Germany.'

'Have you ever hunted up here in Scotland?'

'When I was a student, I spent some holiday time up here earning money stalking injured deer. The people who paid big bucks to come shooting deer would occasional just wound a deer, and it would be gone before a Ghillie could finish the job. So, when they came in at lunchtime I would be told where the deer was shot, and I would take a crossbow to finish the job.'

'Why a crossbow?'

'The silent assassin. Does not make a noise and thus does not scare away the deer for the afternoon shoot. Ghillies don't like to leave injured deer on the moors.'

'I don't think I could ever kill a living thing.'

Prejudice in Love

'Not even to survive! We would have no use for cows or sheep if we didn't kill them for meat. And what about spiders?'

Cis didn't like this conversation. He'd stumped her again in any event as she hated spiders and would readily terminate their existence if they were found uninvited in her house.

Within minutes they were making their way back to the road, and back to Gleneagles.

It was still raining when they got back so it was a quick dash to their suite. She stripped off here outer clothes down to her panties and went to dry her hair.

He was lying on the bed with his iPad when she returned from the bathroom. She went to his side of the bed and stood waiting for the removal of her panties. He was somewhat absorbed and hadn't realised that the cuddle would be in bed. He looked at her and immediately realised the requirement so put down his iPad and did his duty. She then scrambled over the bed and got under the sheets.

'Afternoon nap my dear?'

'No, but a proper cuddle please.'

He undressed and got in beside her. She immediately tucked herself into his shoulder and snuggled into him.

'Would madam liked to be stroked?'

'No thank you, I don't want to sleep. I just want to feel warm in your arms. No sex necessary unless spontaneous. I want to replay what happened earlier before lunch as I still cannot believe the pleasure that you reigned on me.'

Chapter 55

Cis went to the bathroom to get herself ready for dinner. They had already showered. He walked in as she was applying her makeup. She was stretching her body over the marble top to get closer to the mirror. This presented a completely different vision of her and he wanted to stroke her now extended buttocks.

He stood by the side of her watching her and reached across to stroke her bottom. She turned to him 'not now, I'm trying to look nice for you.'

He found himself instantaneously furious. Rejection has no role between lovers. He slapped her bottom hard.

'Owwww', she cried, 'what was that for? It hurts.'

'Put down your makeup now', he commanded. 'You've been a fabulous student, but you have just committed a cardinal sin. You listen up because you must never do this again.'

He turned her to face him. 'There is no rejection between lovers. A loving advance by either partner to the other should be accepted above anything else. If I stroke your bottom you welcome it, and even show that you are ready to respond if this stroking is to go further. There are ways to defer, but never rejection.'

She could see that he was angry with her. She had never seen him remotely angry with her before, but she knew this was real. She had failed him and must understand what he's trying to tell her.

'Over dinner tonight we're going to deal with rejection, the biggest put down you can give to your lover, and usually the start of the rot in any relationship.'

'Now finish your makeup, and let's be off to dinner.' He was gone.

She stood there frozen and frightened. What had she done to cause so much offence to her lover? She must quickly finish her makeup and repair this damage.

When she returned to the bedroom, he was sitting on the bed fully dressed. He still had a sour face.

Prejudice in Love

She grabbed the clothes she wanted to wear and put them next to him. She stood in front of him expectantly, but with some anxiety.

He looked up at her.

'Please will you dress me?' she timidly asked.

He picked up her panties and reached down so that she could insert her feet. He slowly brought them up to her bottom. When he touched her bottom she cried 'Ouch, it hurts.'

He left her panties at the top of her thigh. 'Turn around.'

'Now bend forward with your hands on your knees.'

He looked where he had struck her and there was a slight glimmer of a welt. He gently stroked it for a few seconds, and then kissed it. 'Is that better?'

'Hmmm, much better, thank you.'

'Okay, face me again and let's get you dressed.'

He was now calmer, so she was feeling somewhat better about what had happened.

When he had finished dressing her, he stood up and pecked her on the lips. 'Well recovered but let us ensure that it does not happen again.'

She heaved a sigh of relief. My lover is not angry anymore. I need to understand what I did to cause such a harsh reaction in my normally calm and collected valiant knight.

Chapter 56

Once they had finished their main course, he decided it was time to straighten this lady out on rejection.

'Cis, we are going to deal with the impact of rejection between lovers, and why such rejection has no place in a loving relationship. From what you have told me you already suffer from the effects of rejection so it should be easy to show you what you did wrong earlier, and why I reacted in the way I did.'

'You have told me that this year Andy has rejected your advances and has shown very little interest in engaging in sex with you. How did this make you feel?'

'At first very confusing, and later very hurt. Okay I was focussed on a baby, but he has always maintained that he also wants a child. So yes, I feel hurt, dissatisfied, and lonely.'

'Does his rejection make you feel anxious about approaching him lest he rejects you again?'

'Yes. He now assumes that I'm ovulating when I approach him. He makes it look like I'm making demands on him.'

'So, you have no fun sex, and very little else?'

'Yes.'

'Cis, rejection by either party is the biggest cause of unhappy relationships. The comics who use the famous "not now, I have a headache" are voicing a paradox on the most destructive aspect of a loving relationship, the cause of many extramarital flings and divorces. For serious lovers there is never any rejection of advances by your lover. At most, you can defer, usually with something more tantalising than what can be achieved at that moment.'

'Let me try to illustrate. True lovers are continually engaged in foreplay with each other, whether wittingly or unwittingly. But the intent is that, when the opportunity arises, they will engage in sex together. One partner will initiate sex, and the other is already primed to engage. There is nothing that remotely overrides this desire, and the slightest touch can trigger such sex. It's an automatic reaction between partners; and is intuitive.'

'If one partner makes such an advance, and the other rejects, then you have a breakdown in the very fabric of the relationship. The rejected party cannot understand why they have been rejected, and thus lose confidence in reading the intuitive signals between them.'

'Are you with me?' he asked her.

She looked at her valiant knight in awe. *'I've suffered rejection, and know how it feels'*, she thought, *but he can define it so clearly.'* She responded 'Yes, I can see what you're saying.'

'Okay, let's look at what happened earlier. We had enjoyed great sex together. I think we're very close, you've expressed your love for me, and it takes very little to trigger more sex between us. I walk into the bathroom and see a vision of you that I haven't seen before; you were stretching up to the mirror which created a beautiful new profile for me of you to savour that triggered the desire to touch you, and maybe more. I touch your bottom with the intent to stroke you, and this touch maybe would have led to more depending on how ready you were for more intimacy. Your response was immediate rejection in favour of completing your makeup. Yet for me you are at your most beautiful when I open my eyes in the morning and see your gorgeous face looking at me. Your makeup has no relevance to me, only to you. This rejection automatically breaks my confidence in our relationship causing me confusion as to why you did not respond as expected.'

'What you should have done is to stop what you were doing, welcome the attention, and follow through. If there is a pressing need to finish what you are doing then you need to respond positively to the advance, and then defer in such a way as to keep the faith in the relationship.'

'For example, you are getting ready to go to dinner at a friend's house. It would clearly be bad manners to be late. So your response to my touch would have been something along the lines of where do you want to go with this as we have the choice of being late for dinner, or to using a naughty code as soon as possible after dinner to initiate our return and play as long as we wish.'

'Does this make any sense to you?'

'Wow, I didn't mean to reject your advance, but I can see the point you're making. Having suffered rejection from Andy on too many occasions I know how it feels, and it does leave me confused. But how do I overcome rejection from Andy?'

'First you must rebuild your intimate relationship with him so that he is comfortable to actively engage with you as a true lover using the techniques I've explored with you. Once you are in this position, and his problem giving you a baby is out, he will pursue you for sure. Just never reject him and ensure that he does not reject you by keeping him tantalised. You are clearly the driver in your relationship, so use this power to positive effect.'

'There is also no room between lovers for the word "sorry". Sure, if you accidently tread on his foot, you can say you are sorry. But in terms of the intimate side of the relationship there is no room for rejection and then "sorry". If you need to use this word in context of your intimate relationship there is something wrong, so fix it. None of us are infallible so problems can occur, but let them be few, and unrepeated. If you really have a headache then good sex beats the hell out of pain killers, and thus the paradox.'

'I seem to remember you telling me that Andy is sometimes too anxious to wait for you to lubricate enough to take him. For this you use a silent deferral. You teach him, as part of your lovemaking, to test you with his fingers or tongue for good lubrication, showing him the level needed to achieve easy penetration. Also teach him how to increase your lubrication if necessary. He'll enjoy your encouragement to touch you so intimately. De facto, he will not enter you until you're ready.'

'So has my smack brought home the negative impact of rejection, and your responsibility to ensure it does not happen?'

She held his hand, 'for sure I'll never reject you again, and I am sorry for what I did. However, I've learnt so much from the event I'm not sorry it happened. Your smack was so sharp on my bottom it will be emblazoned on my memory if I find myself in such a selfish situation again. What you say about Andy is easy in words, but I know that I need to find a way, and it will not be easy.'

'Cis, your showdown with Andy will change everything. I believe in you to succeed in both the preparation, and your showdown, after which everything will drop into place. The announcement of your pregnancy will completely make or break your relationship with Andy. You will be successful if you focus over the coming days and weeks.'

'My valiant knight has much faith in someone who has been sleepwalking until the age of 28. If I'm as smart as you suggest, why have I not sorted this problem before?'

'Very simple. No-one showed you how, and you did not know where to go look for a solution. Thus the intervention of your guardian angel, who obviously thinks you deserve a chance at happiness.'

'It might be worth remembering that a marriage, or indeed any partnership, is a union between two imperfect people who refuse to give up on each other.'

'And what if my showdown with Andy does not go as you foresee, and it breaks our marriage?'

'Clearly I have to rely on what you tell me about Andy in order to formulate my view, but I sense that, underneath all of the heartache, you do love him, and he loves you, therefore your information about him is good. On this basis you will succeed if I prepare you well.'

'In the unlikely event that your showdown fails then your marriage is over. I would have to ask if you approached the showdown with the will to succeed. In any event we would meet to evaluate the way forward for you.'

'I have to say that my only real concern for you is, God forbid, anything happens to your pregnancy, and you lose the child. But you are strong and healthy, and I rely on your guardian angel to protect you against any such event.'

'And what about us?'

'We are a much needed break for you, a holiday fling would be a good analogy, during which you revisit your life, achieve some important ambitions, and return revitalised to kick-start your new life with Andy, and your much desired child.'

'Do you want anything else to eat or drink as we have more to do this day, and I would like to avoid a late night?'

Cis, a little down in the mouth at his evaluation of their relationship 'I'm finished, thank you'.

'Okay, I'll get the check and we can go.'

Chapter 57

They had a slow walk back to the apartment arm-in-arm, gazing at the stars in the clear skies. The rain had gone, and the air was clean with a taste of freshness.

When they got back, she was still pondering the discussion over dinner. She found it incredible that both as a writer and avid reader she was so inexperienced in relationships. *'It's embarrassing'* she thought.

He decided that there was no real need for another clinical session, but he had unfinished business from this afternoon. Now would be a good time for a treat for her attention to detail regarding her pubic hair.

'Why don't we get your clinical out of the way as I want to show you something else later?'

She immediately presented herself for undressing before she lay on the bed.

He put the usual pillows under her, but she noticed that this time they were set further back under the small of her back so that her pussy was lower but more exposed. She didn't think anything of this after the change in position used at lunchtime.

'He knows what he's doing', she thought 'so let us see what he has in store for me this time, my last time of clinical insemination.'

He stretched her legs wide, with her head slightly backward over the end of her pillow.

He ran a finger from the nub of her neck all the way down to her pussy just to calm her. He then stood to one side of her and knelt beside her.

He kissed the areola of the breast closest to him. Her nipple responded immediately. He used his tongue to rotate around this extended nipple.

With one hand on her tummy he then sucked at her nipple with a slow rhythmic motion.

He moved to kiss her on the lips whilst gently massaging the breast that he just kissed. He increased the urgency of the kiss exploring the inside of her mouth.

He moved to her other breast and repeated his ritual.

Then he moved between her legs and bent down to kiss her pussy. He tenderly kissed the lips of her labia. Once it was clear that she was responding he started to move his tongue to open her labia to gain access to her clitoris. He found it and it was suitably swollen from the activity over these days.

He lifted his head and used both hands to open her labia, exposing her.

He went down again and started to stroke her exposed clitoris with his tongue. He started slowly, and then started to both flick with his tongue, and then apply pressure in a circular motion. He could taste the start of her juices flowing. He wanted her to totally surrender to her situation. She was moaning with pleasure completely forgetting about the purpose of this session.

After a few minutes of this intense attention he could feel her abdomen starting to tense. Her purring was now mixed with gasps as her breathing became shorter. He must be getting close.

He changed his motion to a gentle flick of the end of his tongue to the exposed head, and then a firm lick along the shaft. She was now opening her legs as wide as possible and offering her pussy for more. Her moans were in rhythm with the movements of her hips.

He could now feel that she was fully aroused and decided it was time to bring her to orgasm.

He increased the licking of her clitoris so that the connection was continuous, but still at a steady speed. The first spasm started. Then her hips bucked and she audibly gasped as she experienced the first spasm of orgasm. Then the spasms increased in frequency and strength until she bucked as the flow of orgasmic exhilaration flowed through her body.

He looked at her. Her eyes were glazed. She was somewhere else in ecstatic oblivion.

He sat up to observe her whilst gently stroking the inside of her thighs. He could see her juices flowing out of her vagina down past her anus onto the sheets.

It was some minutes before she opened her eyes and focussed on him.

'Wow, you've done it again. You used your mouth to give me an orgasm. No-one has ever tried that on me before.'

'You can do that to me anytime. It's sooo nice. I could feel the roughness of your tongue moving across my clit – fabulous.'

'Normally I would sacrifice you to the sun gods on a rocky altar on some Caribbean island, but sunshine here is a rare commodity.'

She giggled. 'So when are you taking me to be sacrificed?'

'I wish we were there now.'

'What about my clinicals? I thought this session was your last attempt to make me pregnant?'

'I owed you that treat for the delight you have given to me with your naked pussy. That is the first time in many years that any woman has qualified for a full oral orgasm. As you can see it takes some minutes of concentrated effort on my part, but your attention to detail whilst back in Edinburgh was worthy of a special treat. Such a concentrated effort on a pussy surrounded by pubic hair is not pleasant for me, and there is also the risk of health issues.'

She reached for him. He moved towards her, lying between her legs as she kissed him tenderly.

'For you, my pussy would stay naked for ever.'

'On that basis your pussy would receive regular treats.'

'As for your clinicals we have had four very successful deep penetration sessions, plus the hot session we had before you went back to Edinburgh. On the basis that sperm can survive about four days in your cervix at least one of the thousands of little fellas that needs to make the journey to find your egg must have made it by now, so I think job done.'

She kissed him again. 'Thank you, my valiant knight, my wonderful lover.'

'I have something else I want to teach you this evening, and also to show you how to have some fun, but I think we should relax for a while, maybe watch some TV with a nice drink. Why don't you get me your house clothes and I'll dress you before we settle down for some TV.'

She handed him a pair of loose shorts and a T-shirt which he then used to dress her. He recovered a bottle of Prosecco from the fridge, and they settled down on the couch whilst flicking through the TV channels to see what they wanted to watch.

Chapter 58

About an hour later, at the end of the program they were watching, without saying a word, he lifted her and invited her to sit on his lap, her legs straddling his, with her back to him. He encouraged her to lean back against him and let her settle.

They started to watch a romantic movie. He moved his right hand onto her thigh. She put her hand on top of his.

He whispered in her ear 'The hand on your thigh is not mine or has my experience. But it's yours to do your bidding. Show it what you want it to do to you, and how you want it to touch you.'

She looked back at him in surprise, but then understood that he was encouraging her to show Andy how to stroke her.

She started by interlocking her fingers with his hand and started to slowly stroke her thigh, firstly along the top, and then moving inside. After a few stokes she moved his hand all the way under her shorts to her pussy and stroked her mound. She then changed her hold to his index and second finger using her hand to move these fingers along the opening of her pussy, massaging her labia. Paul could feel her adjusting the pressure of the touch on her as she achieved the desired effect on her.

She leaned back into him allowing her to expose more of her to the touch. She then moved his two fingers into her honeypot where he could feel her juices flowing, although not yet fully aroused.

Having wet his fingers, she moved them up just above her clitoris and then pressed them gently behind the head of the clit and started to move his fingers in a rotating massage motion. Again she spent time adjusting the pressure on her to achieve the desired effect.

After a few minutes she was clearly becoming aroused and she turned her head around to him to be kissed. He obliged with a deep and longing kiss as she increased the rotation on her clitoris with more urgency. She tucked her feet behind his calf's as the tension built in her loins. She stopped the rotation and moved his fingers deeper into her juices before moving them back to her clitoris to continue their work.

Her breathing became shorter; more gasps than breathing, as she was feeling the full effect of this attention to her. He felt her buttocks tighten on his lap, and he could feel the flow of juices as she bucked, and then went into rapid spasms bringing herself to a satisfying climax. She lifted his fingers as she closed her legs as the spasms of delight passed through her body. She then brought his fingers up to her lips and put both fingers into her mouth as she licked her juices from them. She let his hand fall as she turned her head for another longing kiss.

As she recovered, he whispered in her ear 'if it helps in the enjoyment you can fantasia whose hand is touching you. And once you have trained the hand how to fully satisfy you, you only need to start the process and let the hand do the rest. You can be anywhere with any hand because you can only see the hand, not the owner.'

'My lover, that hand could only ever be yours regardless of who owned it.'

Once she had recovered he wanted to show her one other thing before ending the day. He moved her onto the couch and went once again to his bag of toys and extracted the vibrator with the rabbit and some lube and took it back to the couch.

'Stand up.'

He removed her shorts. 'There is one more thing I would like to quickly show you while your juices are still flowing.'

He sat her back in his lap, again straddled across his legs with her back to him. He showed her the vibrator. 'I just want to quickly show you how to get the best out of this device as I think that when you see what it can do you will confine your existing vibrator to the bin.'

Applying a little lube he explained that the curved end of the part inserted into her vagina was supposed to be to hit her

G-spot, if she had one. He then explained the programs on the main vibrator, but the best part was the rabbit's ears. He set the vibrator such that only the rabbit's ears were pulsing. He asked her to insert the vibrator such that the rabbit's ears were either side of her clitoris. 'Now play with the intensity of the vibration of the ears and prod your clit.'

The first time she pressed the ears around her clitoris she bucked. 'Wow that certainly hit the mark.'

She lowered the intensity and then started to gently prod again.

'Not too hard. If the ears touch your pelvic bone they will not vibrate. The trick is to find the spot where they surround your clit but not touch your pelvis.'

She was now rhythmically moving the vibrator in and out of herself gently prodding. 'This is nice. What happens if I have the main vibrator working at the same time?'

'Try it. You only have one battery so it will take energy away from the rabbit's ears thus you will get a reduction of intensity. But you can play with all of the combinations until you find the most satisfying for your needs.'

She started to play with different settings. 'This is fun. My friend told me about these vibrators, but it's the first time that I have tried one. Definitely a replacement for my existing vibrator.'

Eventually she removed it and switched it off. 'I can't believe I'm saying this after a year of no sex, but I've had enough orgasms for one day.'

She turned around across his lap. 'Can we go to bed and cuddle? I'm exhausted.'

Paul was delighted with the progress they had achieved during the day so was happy to oblige, and they were soon both fast asleep in their respective happy dreams.

Chapter 59 - Saturday

It was a little before 9am when they awoke. Emotional exhaustion from the events of the previous two days had resulted in a deep, calm sleep for both. Clinicals were over, project complete, albeit it would be some days before any results would be known.

Cis awoke feeling very good about life, and in no hurry to go anywhere. She felt fulfilled, and was where she wanted to be, snuggled up with her lover.

Paul was looking at her thinking how happy he was with this beauty lying by his side, albeit suppressing an overwhelming need to visit the bathroom. He could hear the splatter of raindrops on the windows indicating that it was raining outside, and which did not help his desire not to have to go to the bathroom quite yet. Looking at her first thing in the morning was like a refreshing recharge for him. The vision of her in his eyes permeated throughout his body and soul and he felt young again. After 5 years of medical torment he felt completely rejuvenated by this insatiable nymph of pleasure.

His thoughts were broken by a sound in his ears 'Good morning my darling', and then felt her lips on his as she kissed him.

'Good morning by beautiful lady. You're a vision to behold when I open my eyes in the morning.'

Cis kissed him again and stroked his cheek. 'We slept well last night. It's quite late.'

'Yes. We should have a shower and go get some breakfast before breakfast becomes lunch.'

'Shall I run a shower for us, my darling?'

'I'll do it as I need to use the bathroom' at which point he slid out of bed and surrendered to his need to relieve himself.

They were settled in the shower with her leaning back into him whilst he caressed her body with no urgency to finish. He was thinking about what they could do today. 'Is there anything that you want to do today?'

These words brought her out of her pleasure zone as she thought about the day. *'It's Saturday'*, she thought, *'dinner tonight.'* Actually, I would like to visit the spa later this afternoon. I think a facial and my hair would be good for tonight.'

She turned to face him 'How about if we have a facial together, and then we have our hair done?'

'Me, a facial', he exclaimed, 'whatever next?'

'We can have a facial together, and you'll feel very good afterwards. It only takes 30 minutes.'

'Are you sure about this?'

'Worry not. I'll organise everything before we have breakfast. My valiant knight needs to be in great condition tonight. A facial and relaxing haircut will be just right for you. Trust your damsel.'

She turned around again to indicate that the conversation was over, and they should continue their shower.

The telephone rang. Paul answered to be told that the kilt shop in Crieff had called to say that his kilt was ready for collection. The receptionist told him that he could not miss the shop in the High Street as it was the only such shop. *'Fantastic'* he thought after returning the phone to its cradle. 'My kilt is ready and waiting for me in Crieff, just a few miles away. We can go and collect it after breakfast.'

Once they were both dressed, they wandered off to the spa where she booked what they needed, and then off to breakfast – but they were too late. Breakfast finished at 10am, so it was off to the coffee bar for a snack, and then off to Crieff to return the hire kilt and collect his new Fulton Blue.

Before wandering back to the apartment, she bought a few toiletries from the shop in the hotel.

Chapter 60

The receptionist was right in how easy it was to find the kilt shop, and thankfully he could park directly outside as it was still raining, albeit a gentle drizzle rather than heavy rain.

The assistant opened the parcel to reveal the Fulton Blue kilt, and a pack of garters and flashes. Cis was first to run her hands along the beautifully fashioned pleats, perfectly in line with the pattern of the tartan. 'It's beautiful' was her involuntary response. She looked at Paul. 'Darling this is a finely crafted kilt. They must have worked long hours to complete such a lovely work of art in such a short time. I can't wait to see you in it.'

Paul quickly examined the waist band, buckles and clasps and was satisfied with the quality of finish. The assistant informed him that there was an additional charge as had been agreed, plus the express courier charge from Balloch to Crieff. He happily settled these charges without debate, handed back the hire kilt and flashes, and they were on their way back to the Gleneagles.

Chapter 61

When they returned to the apartment, he sat on the sofa with his iPad deciding that this inclement weather now afforded time to catch up on his email traffic. She sat in his lap. 'As we have a little time before lunch you still owe me a long story, and I think the one I want to hear is why you are here. Over these past days I sense that you took this trip to take some time out to re-evaluate your life, or at least a part of it that is troubling you. Your suggestion that you would keep me under different circumstances suggests to me that the relationship that you have with Jane is not as strong as it once was or is causing you some concern. Will you tell me this story?'

'Don't you think the day dreary enough without a dreary story? Next time you chat with your guardian angel ask her why it wasn't us on that flight to the Caribbean last Sunday morning. We could have both been going to the Caribbean for a break. You would be sitting next to me. We would have flown through the same storm, and I could have comforted you throughout, and we would continue the relationship in the nice, warm sunny Caribbean where we could have great fun.'

'If that had happened how would I have overcome all of the prejudice that you speak of? It was the touch of your hands in the darkness that awakened my desire. How would you touch me on a plane?'

'Your guardian angel knew how to throw us together in the early hours of last Sunday morning, and there are ways on a plane. It's a ten-hour flight, and you would be amazed at what you can achieve under a blanket when all the window shades are down. I joined the five-mile-high club on such a journey.'

She sat up to look him in the eye. 'What's the five-mile-high club?'

'Full sex on a plane with a complete stranger.'

'What? You have had sex on a plane with a complete stranger? It's unbelievable.'

'It doesn't just happen in the movies. It's possible, if somewhat cramped and uncomfortable. I wouldn't recommend it. Just engage in foreplay on the plane and save the full sex until you're in a comfortable hotel.'

'But where on a plane can you have sex?'

'If you are travelling First Class, or even Business Class on some planes, the toilets are less cramped than in Economy Class. There's enough room. Some people tell me that they managed it in Economy Class, but I wouldn't even try.'

She now held his shoulders and looked at him with stern eyes 'So is this something that you often did when you were travelling?'

'It was a long time ago. I did it once to see if it was possible. Thereafter it was always plan B; foreplay on the plane, sex in a nice hotel. I always travelled in First or Business Class. There are only two seats together, and plenty of room. More often than not there may only be a few passengers spaced around the cabin. Anything was possible. Long flights need a little entertainment.'

'So we would have been in Business Class last Sunday, sitting together. And how much foreplay do you think you could have achieved?'

'With all the noise in a plane I could stroke you to orgasm with you in my lap and head into my shoulder.'

'Wow. Sounds like a fun way to fly. I'll ask my guardian angel why she didn't think of that. But you have deflected from your story. We're not in the Caribbean, we're here in Scotland, in the rain, and I would like to hear why you are here.'

She settled down again in his lap. 'I'm sitting comfortably; you may begin.'

He hesitated but put down his iPad. He was thinking where to start and how much to tell. He had never revealed to anyone the pain he had felt for the past few years since he caught Jane having an affair, and still had not really overcome the breach of trust that he felt. It broke the bond between them, and he was unsure if he could ever trust her again.

'I've never told anyone this story, and I don't even know where to start. But if I do tell you I need to know that it will go no further, or that you'll try to take advantage of this situation as it changes nothing between us. I only tell you because I feel a bond between us and telling you might relieve some of the pain I feel.'

She realised that this was to be the story she wanted to hear so took both of his hands and clasped them firmly in her lap as a gesture that she was there for him.

He started 'As you know I was forced into early retirement through ill-health. Having never been seriously ill throughout my life, not even a broken bone, the past five years have been one problem after another. For someone like me this was traumatic. I don't like to be a bother to anyone, so I essentially hibernated whilst I tried to deal with these problems. This had its impact on Jane. She felt helpless, albeit always there for me. Three years ago, I noticed a change in her behaviour. She was distant towards me and was taking frequent trips which did not fit into the pattern of her work. I was too preoccupied with my difficulties to really engage with my concerns. This went on for a few months until she took a trip which was out on Thursday, back on Monday. She told me where she was going. After she left I did some housekeeping on our various email files as she was notoriously bad at managing her private email accounts. I found her flight confirmations on her private email account. This was odd as they should have been on her business email account to which I do not have access. I looked at them to find that she had lied to me about where she was going and knew instantly that this was not business as there was no company office where she was going. My head and my body screamed with pain. Loyalty and trust in a relationship are very important to me.' He paused.

She could feel the pain in him and wanted to wrap him in her arms. But she knew there was more so squeezed his hand to let him know that she was still there for him.

He continued 'What to do. I felt absolutely gutted. Now I knew that the previous odd trips must be to the same place as they all involved weekends away. I looked back through her emails to find that she had tried to delete the previous flight confirmations, but her lack of computer skills meant they were still in her email trash bin. I sent her a text message to let her know that I now knew of her affair, and she needed to decide whether to come back or stay there for good, as per our understanding. She responded that she would be home on the Monday afternoon. I took this as saying she did not care that I knew, and she was not about to curtail her time with this man and come home.'

'I could not sleep that night, and my body was so racked with pain, especially my chest, that by 11am the following morning I felt that I had suffered a heart attack so went to our local cardiac unit where they kept me under observation for some hours before allowing me to go home.'

She could feel the tension in his body. He was really reliving what he felt.

'That evening, and through the night, I tried to rationalise what was happening to us. I did extensive research on the internet and found that much of her behaviour could be attributed to a mid-life crisis. This gave me an odd comfort as I have experienced a few cases of female mid-life crisis and menopause and thus knew the devastating impact that these afflictions could cause to those around them. I have seen divorces result from such afflictions.'

'I decided to write a paper of my findings about her behaviour patterns. This paper was over 5,000 words long and was both for me to rationalise what was happening, and for her to see what was happening in the hope that if it was a midlife crisis, she would see how to break the behaviour before it destroyed us.'

'Jane returned on the Monday and I asked her to read what I had written, which concluded with various options on the way forward. She read it, told me that she was sorry about the deception, but not the affair. In fact, she stated that she wanted to continue with the affair to see where it would go, and that I was free to do the same as a way of testing the strength of our own relationship. I agreed to think about this, but I couldn't deal with the cold-hearted way that she was dealing with this situation. I asked her to go stay with friends whilst she worked things out as I was not prepared to see her go on any more of these trips. She went straight to her lawyers, and I have to say that the advice she received was not helpful, so deepened the problem. This situation continued for some weeks, albeit she did not travel again during these weeks, not least because after the lawyer business I told her that if she went, there would be no trace of her in the house upon her return.'

This last statement certainly caught the attention of Cis. 'Wow', she thought, 'my gentle giant has a ruthless side when pushed. What happened last night when I rejected him was for real.'

He continued 'As you can probably detect the situation was getting very bad, and every day the pain I felt grew and grew. I have suffered serious pain throughout my childhood, and at various times as an adult, but nothing like the extreme pain I felt in those weeks, both mentally and physically. After a number of weeks I could not take it any longer so approached my mother to help me to put enough cash together to buy her out of our house, and send her on her way. My mother was reluctant to get involved but agreed in principle. So I put it to Jane that it was decision time to stay without any affairs, or go. She told me the following day that she would break her affair, and we would try to put our relationship back together. Since then, slowly but surely, we have put things back together. But I'm still not sure whether this is a relationship of convenience, or whether we can rebuild what we had before my ill health. I still cannot find it within myself to trust her or forgive her as she has never shown any remorse for her deception.'

He turned her to look at him. 'This is why you must tell Andy about the nature of your pregnancy. There must be no deception between you both. And you must do it as we have planned if you are to be successful. What Jane did to me has left a disease of distrust that I cannot find a way to cure. And this is why if our situation was more appropriate, I would keep you. But things are as they are, and we must deal with our respective situations. Our adventure has opened my eyes to a number of issues and has resolved some physical issues for me. So, I'm clearer on a way forward for me but, unfortunately, it cannot include you with a child.'

She could see in his eyes the serious and painful nature of what he was saying to her. This was no time for her to put

Prejudice in Love

any counterpoint into this discussion. This was the pain she had detected in his eyes, and now she knew the source and intensity of the pain, even three years after the event. She felt helpless. What could she do to help relieve this pain? Tears started to flow from her eyes as she empathised with his pain. 'My darling Paul I'm so sorry for your pain. It must be horrible.' She could see tears welling in his eyes. *'What to do?'* she thought, *'my valiant knight is in pain and I don't know how to help him.'*

She moved herself around to straddled herself across his legs so that she could put both arms around him and held him tight. He put his arms around her and held her very close.

Neither said anything for some minutes. But then he started to stroke her back indicating to her that he was coming back to her. She started to run her fingers through his hair. He took her arms and moved her back so that he could see her face.

'No more stories. I don't want to waste anymore of our time together with such sorrow.'

'My darling you have completed the 3 stories I asked for. I can now see the cause of the pain and sadness that I have detected in your eyes over the past days. Thank you so much for sharing them with me. I love you like I have never loved before, and I will always be waiting for you should you change your mind. What can I do to make you feel better again?'

'I need you to smother me with your love so that I can forget the past and get back into the moment.'

She got off his lap, reached for his hand, and led him to the bedroom. She quickly, but lovingly, undressed him and put him to bed. This was no time for undressing formalities, so she quickly undressed herself and got in beside him.

They were quickly locked in a deep embrace, and he could feel the warmth of her naked body against his flesh. She took his hand and placed it on her breast, moving her body so that he could stroke or caress her breast as he wanted. He, instead, moved his hand down to her buttocks, grabbed the nearest cheek and pulled her close to him. She could feel the intensity in his grasp and responded with a deep sensuous kiss which closed the door to the outside world. They were slowly but surely drifting into their own world, becoming as one.

The intensity of their kisses increased with an urgency that quickly stoked the fire in her loins, and she could feel her juices starting to flow in the warmth of her loins. Desire took over as she heard herself whisper to him 'please punish me my master for the pain you feel.'

He instantly responded by spinning her on her back, rolling on top of her, and thrust into her whilst grabbing her buttocks. She yelped as he thrust deep, and then she moaned with pleasure as she asked him to really punish her. 'Take your pain out on me my master.'

He wasted no time in thrusting in and out of her with an intensity that was causing her clitoris to scream with pleasure. She raised her hips off the bed so that he could get a good hold on her buttocks so that he could pull her towards him as he thrust ever deeper into her.

She was holding the back his arms helping to plunge deeper into her. She was now groaning with pleasure as she felt the waves of orgasm growing in her loins. He could feel his throbbing penis being sucked into her, and then grabbed to make his withdrawal intense, causing him to build to an imminent explosion of orgasm. He could hear her begging him to thrust deeper as her hips started to spasm faster and faster. With simultaneous groans they exploded in waves of pleasure as her fingernails drew blood from his upper arm.

They both collapsed onto the bed, gasping for breath. She had wrapped her legs around his waist to prevent him from leaving her. She liked this raw sex and wanted to stay locked together to extract maximum waves of pleasure throughout her body.

As he recovered, he started to caress her breasts. For her this was just added pleasure and would lie back and take as much of this attention as he wanted to give her. As he felt his erection subside, he opened her legs and slipped out of her, rolling her onto her back so that he had better access to her fully extended nipples. He was gently stroking, caressing, and squeezing her breasts, much to her delight.

After a while he moved his hand to stroke the hair away from her face and then gently stroked her cheeks. He could see that she was still in a place savouring the feelings and sensations running through her body. He was thinking that this woman made him feel so good about life. Why can't he keep her close to him forever? He put his arms around her and turned her towards him.

She came out of her place of silent ecstasy and looked at him. Inside her head she was screaming at him to keep her by his side forever. She would certainly smother his pain and sadness with so much love and care that he would never feel such pain again. She knew she could not possibly express such feelings in words at this moment but hoped that the message was projected loudly and clearly from the longing in her eyes.

She looked at him somewhat peevishly 'Has my master forgiven me?'

He smiled at her 'how can I possibly forgive you for all of the conflicts you stir inside me. You have opened a door to my heart that I thought firmly shut after the pain I suffered the last time I did that for a woman. Yet I know that your guardian angel has no intention of letting me keep you despite your willingness to defy your destiny. I have run my race, and now I must pass the baton to you for the safekeeping for our child. The baggage I bring can only be an affliction to you. I want our child to be free of such baggage. You must carry my torch without any baggage and create a good life for our child – the life I did not have, nor did my existing children. I want to leave a legacy for our child that I can be proud of, and I trust you to deliver for me.'

She could not believe the pain that was pouring out of her valiant knight. She sensed that there was much more but was not about to cause him any more pain. All she wanted to do was to find a way to free him of such pain, but how? He had given so much to her, but what could she offer him in return?

She decided to speak. 'Please tell me what I can do to ease your pain. I cannot rest with the idea that you have brought so much joy to my life, without at least easing some of your pain.'

'My darling Cis, you have given me a reason to face my demons. I now know that I need to actively confront some lingering issues in my life and put others behind me. And then I must go do the things that I want to do with the remainder of my life regardless of what others think. I made a spontaneous, unilateral decision to travel to Scotland, just as I would have done before my illness. Now I must revert to my former philosophy and follow the adventures wherever they take me, just as with this week. It's my life, and I must live it as I see fit. So you see, you have opened my eyes to the way forward for me, and for that I will be truly grateful to you.'

'So will you stay with Jane?'

'I don't know. Certainly we need to change our relationship from its current existence as a convenient relationship to something more akin to how it used to be, and I must retake the reins to ensure that it has meaning and direction. If this does not work for her then I must move on. I don't need cosy, I need alive.'

'Anyway, I need some lunch and a beer. How about you?'

She knew that this conversation was now over. 'Lunch sounds great. Do we shower or just clean up?'

'Whatever suits you. I'm happy just to clean up as we'll shower later in any event.'

She was out of the bed into the bathroom 'stay there while I get some warm flannels and a towel.'

Chapter 62

After lunch they returned to their apartment as it was still raining. They had a little over an hour before they were due at the spa. He elected to look at his email traffic and book a hotel in Edinburgh for Monday night.

She decided to look at her email traffic. 'Oh my God, I have to submit a 1,500-word article with pictures by Thursday' she exclaimed.

He looked at her with some amusement 'Real world getting in the way of your fun again?' he laughed.

She looked up at him 'I'm glad I looked as at least I can get onto the fashion houses and see what they have.'

'What is the subject of your article?' He asked.

'My editor has asked me to write about what is trending for the Autumn season. I guess that this gives me latitude regarding fashion, places to go, places to eat, places to be seen, etc, but I need to think about this and then send out for suitable pictures and support material.'

'Okay Cis, I'm happy to leave you in peace until we go to the spa as I would like to catch up on a few things and book a suitable hotel in Edinburgh.'

'I can help you there as it's my hometown.'

'Thank you, but I know the hotels of interest to me. I find that the biggest problem with hotels in Edinburgh is finding a suitable quality hotel in the City centre with its own car park. Most are silent that they don't have their own car parking, and with others it's only the small print that alerts you to the fact that their car parking is a nearby public car park. From memory there are some smaller hotels within the City centre that have private car parking, so I'll try them first. You need to concentrate on your article which sounds significantly more demanding.'

She remembered that he was pretty sharp at booking hotels so returned to her own notebook screen and started to consider to whom she needed to send emails to secure support material and pictures for her article. She was certainly relieved that she had looked at her email traffic as her editor had posted it to her on Thursday having been happy with her article on the fashion show.

For this one hour they were both sitting together on the sofa but, for the first time since they met, consumed in their own respective roles in the real world.

Chapter 63

They were in the spa for their respective bookings. For the first time since the start of their liaison he felt totally out of his comfort zone as they entered the beauty part of the spa. She could see this so held his hand and guided him to the facial area. They had a room with two couches as it was usual for two women to have facials together as part of their therapy whilst their other halves were out on the golf course. Indeed, the spa seemed to specifically cater for the orphaned partners of golf players.

She ensured that he was suitably comfortable on his couch before settling on the couch next to him. Two ladies appeared, seating themselves at the head of each couch. Both ladies, almost in unison, asked what was needed from their clients. Cis, with a large grin on her face piped up 'full facial for two please' and reached over and held his hand. She felt quietly amused that her sage and master was clearly feeling uncomfortable with this new experience for him; a first since they'd met.

Although she kept hold of his hand throughout the facial, and occasionally stroked the back of his hand with her thumb as reassurance, he was very relieved when the beauticians, as stated on their name tags, declared that they had finished.

Although he used a multi-sex hairdressing salon for his haircuts, this salon was primarily female. He now envisaged being dragged into a salon clearly intended only for women. She took his hand and led him out of the beauty salon and headed for another door upon which was printed 'Traditional Gentleman's Barber Shop'. She looked at him and smiled at the relief on his face. 'Now go in there and be a good boy. They already have their instructions. As I'm only having a trim, style, and shine we should take about the same time so I'll see you in the spa reception when we've finished.' She giggled as she pushed him through the door of the Barber's Shop. She was enjoying herself with her lover as they participated in the real world.

The Barber's Shop was decorated in the traditional way and even the middle-aged portly barber wore a traditional striped apron. 'You must be Mr Fulton, sir. Welcome to the Barber's Shop'. Paul was guided to one of the two available chairs. 'Your booking shows a full treatment of wash, cut, shave, conditioner and hot towel so I think we should start with your hair.

He sat bemused by the games of his beautiful nymph, but he was now in his comfort zone, so happy to relax and go with it.

The Barber removed the hot towels and splashed a little more conditioner onto his now shaved and moisturised face as the final act in his treatment. Paulgazed into the mirror. His face glowed where the hot towel had been in contact but he was happy with the overall result. He was glad that he had some cash in his pocket knowing that it's traditional to tip your Barber after so much individual attention, and for not cutting your throat. He slipped the Barber a few pound coins, expressed his gratitude and made his way back to the spa reception. She was not there, but he could see her in the hair salon so sat and waited.

After a few minutes his nymph came bouncing out of the salon, her beautiful long black hair bouncing off her shoulders, and a big smile on her face. He stood to greet her.

'How do you feel my valiant knight because you look great.'

He did a twirl so that she could inspect the whole package. 'Do I meet with your expectations as your escort for this evening, my nymph?'

'I would say that you have reduced your age estimate by some ten years, and you will be the most handsome man at the ball.'

He laughed, she giggled. 'Let us away my valiant knight to our castle and prepare for the ball' as she grabbed his arm and started to lead him back to their apartment.

Chapter 64

They were now back in their apartment feeling somewhat refreshed from their visit to the spa. He was grateful at having survived the embarrassment of being the only male in the beauty section of the spa and was somewhat bemused that she had organised a facial for him, and then a traditional shave and hot towel treatment in the barber shop. Did his face really require so much attention?

He organised a glass of Prosecco for both of them and decided that now was a good time to prep her for the evening ahead as he was a little uncomfortable that they were to join another party of eight for dinner.

'Before we start to get ready for dinner I should brief you on the format for tonight as we are making up a table for 10 people. Apparently the other 8 people are one group consisting of a local family and their 4 American guests. Who they are I don't know, but I was subjected to a minor grilling as to who we are, so I assume that they are significant guests. So tonight, you're my wife. Can you handle that?'

The sound of the word 'wife' certainly got the attention as her pulse raced at the thought of her dream coming true. She propped herself up on her elbow so that she could look at him. She could not help herself wanting to engage in a little mischief with this new role. 'First you were my valiant knight, and you proved worthy of this title. Then you became my lover and you have more than pleased me. Then you added the role of my master enlightening me with your valuable wisdom. Now you want to be my husband. I look forward to your progress in mastering this new role.'

He smiled at the cheeky grin on her face. He would certainly miss the playful nature of this nymph of mischief. 'You're wearing a wedding ring my mischievous nymph, so lovers might not go down well, especially if the American guests are conservative middle-aged people from the Central or southern West of the USA.'

'Why should it matter to them?'

'It might not. They may be perfectly lovely people, but I don't like to take chances, especially as I want us to enjoy this evening. I try never to leave things to chance, and I always plan for the worst, and hope for the best. This way I'm never disappointed but can be pleasantly surprised. The Art of War is very useful in such situations.'

She was stunned by how much attention to detail he was prepared to inject into making this evening good for her. *'How could I ever want more from a man?* So how long have we been married?'

'Let us stay as close to existing truths as possible. Therefore, we will say 2 years. Wait a minute, you would be listed in Who's Who if that were the case. Let us say recently, nearly a year as I file my annual updates each July for the next edition.'

'Let me profile what I think, and then we can discuss any changes or additions that you consider useful.'

'You are Felicity Fulton. You are a freelance lifestyle writer, note: not fashion writer. If need be you can mention that you publish under your professional name of Felicity Duncan, but only if asked. Let us not seed the name of Felicity Duncan into their minds.'

'I'm Paul Fulton, former investment banker, now a writer, primarily on global politics and economics, but with specialist knowledge about energy. This will allow them to rank us – very popular pastime with significant Americans.'

'We live in Cambridge in a detached house on the outskirts of the city. This will impress the Americans as they will know of the name, and of course Cambridge, Massachusetts is the home of MIT. You have only lived there for less than a year so still don't know much about the place as we travel extensively with our work. When you are there most of our time is spent putting our home together. This will block a detail conversation about Cambridge for you. They can talk to me if they want detail.'

'We have no children, although this is a current consideration. Again, Americans like family, so with your current maternal instincts you will win much support with your desire to have children. If pushed, I have a son and daughter from a previous marriage, but they are now both adults.'

'You know enough of my writing career to field questions. If asked about my banking career, just limit your answers to the fact that I had already quit banking when we met 2 years ago, and I don't speak much of it. You believe that my career was at an executive level, primarily with major American banks. This is more ranking information. Anything else, just deflect.'

'Are you okay with this profile?'

She was totally impressed with how he had packaged their profile and could see how he was positioning them to be at least equals at the table. Attention to detail was certainly obvious. But she did not write as Felicity Duncan as she was already established as a journalist before she married Andy.

'I get to play your wife, and you ask me if I'm okay with this? It's my dream to play this part, so I'll relish the opportunity, and treat it as an audition. However, I write under my maiden name of Felicity Chambers, so please make this mental correction my dearest husband.'

He kissed her on the forehead. 'I shall watch your performance with great interest'.

'I don't know how much experience you have with professional-type Americans so let me give you some more background so that you can see how the interactions work. If the men are important people, businessmen or even politicians, then remember that nowhere in the world is it more true that behind every successful man there is a great woman, even if she appears to live in the shadows. Play the same game, win over the wife, you'll win the day.'

'Americans can also ask a lot of questions without a hint of diplomacy. Some can be very personal, and even very close to the bone. Should you find yourself uncomfortable just press my thigh with your hand and I'll rescue you. Also if you find the man next to you a little difficult then use your journalistic skills and ask him lots of question.'

'One more important thing for you to know is what will happen if I detect even a hint of prejudice against you. I didn't mention your skin colour in my discussion with the organisers as it's not relevant in civilised society. If these people are typical Republican deep South they can be overtly hostile. If I detect this, I'll deal with it very early. Please do not interfere in any way whatsoever. If you detect that I'm quietly dealing with any such hostility you just pretend that you know nothing of it. This is important as any interference from you could make it difficult for all to settle down for a good evening.'

She was looking a little perplexed. 'If these people are, as you say, significant guests, do you think that my lack of experience and worldliness will not be good enough?'

'Good heavens, no. There is nowhere that I wouldn't happily take you with me as my partner and be proud to have you at my side. I'm only assuming the worst, and thus preparing you, so that nothing will spoil our evening. You should also remember that only some 15% of Americans have passports, so worldly does not generally figure in their vocabulary.'

'Besides being a stunning woman who will blitz the room with her very presence, you are also very bright and knowledgeable despite your tender years. There is no need for any anxiety or insecurity. Don't interpret my preparation as anything more than alerting you to the possibilities. My plan will hopefully be a wasted effort, but if it is needed, we can quench any issues quickly.'

'Perhaps a little protocol might also help you here if you don't already know of it. After the main course it's perfectly acceptable to move around the table. If there is anyone, especially a wife, that you would like to speak with then just swap places with someone so that you can sit together. If you want to keep me close by then swap places with me which will put you with the lady to my left. None of this is necessary, especially as we are not part of their party, but it does happen, and can be very interesting. As you now know I'm not a social small talk person so I might appreciate a switch if there is someone interesting to chat with.'

'You must go to many of these functions.'

I have a wardrobe that only contains formal attire. Full white tie and tails, 3 black tie suits, a tropical white jacket suit, morning suits both black and grey, afternoon suit, and my Fraser Lovett full dress kilt. Today they get more use than my wardrobe of business suits. I had hoped, in my retirement, to cut down on such functions, but there is no escape from some of them. I'm not really a socialite, but I have to admit that some of the more traditional functions in the City of London are interesting. But I'm well versed in the appropriate protocols, and which can be daunting if things start to happen and you don't know your role or options.

'Do you know why, traditionally, you are on my right if we sit or stand, but on my left if we lie together?'

'Tell me my master.'

Prejudice in Love

'The shorthand version is when we stand or sit you should not get in the way of my sword. But when we lie together you should be close to my heart.'

'But, my master, your sword is on the front of you, and I would gladly impale myself upon it.'

'Are you looking for a smacked bottom?'

'Oh yes please, my master. Punish me, just as you did on Tuesday.'

'It's 6:45 and we should be there by 7:30 so punishment will have to wait. Why don't you get the shower warmed so that we can get this show on the road.'

She moved to get off the bed as he landed another smack. 'Master, are we sure we want to go to dinner?' She looked over her shoulder for a response, gave a curt smile, and with that she was gone.

Their shower was a much longer affair this evening. He spent more time on her than usual getting her into a very comfortable mood for the dinner, and he was required to apply copious amount of body lotion to her after he had dried her. Her mood was good. She was overjoyed at the idea of being Mrs Felicity Fulton, if only for one evening. This was a little step which may advance her cause, and she was not about to fail this audition albeit that she found her brief a little daunting.

It was 7:20 when she finally emerged from the bathroom ready to be dressed. He had already completed dressing in his new kilt albeit with a few issues to be addressed. The kilt fitted perfectly, but he had overlooked that a new shirt would be creased where it was folded and thus would need to be ironed. Thankfully the waistcoat and Jacket hid the creases, so he must remember to not remove his jacket. Also one of the wings on the front of his collar had become rounded in the packaging but, as the Scottish tend to push these wings behind their bow tie, rather than have them sit proud as in English evening dress, this was not an issue. The only other issue was whether he should tie the laces of his dress shoes at the ankle or to criss-cross them up his shins and tie them under the hose flashes, thus giving extra support for his hose. He tried both but settled for the latter as this would give extra support for his hose should he get trapped into any Scottish dancing. He gazrd into the mirror to see whether he needed any adjustments. Everything was perfect, and he felt so much more comfortable in the tartan she had chosen than in his traditional Frazer Lovatt kilt.

'Wow, my prince looks fantastic. My darling you look wonderful. I shall be afraid to touch you in case I disturb anything.' It was the first time he had worn the whole dress suit.

'Thank you, my princess. I can honestly state that I feel so much better in your choice of tartan than I have ever felt in my existing kilt.'

'Can we get you dressed as we should be on our way.'

She only had her panties, dress and shoes so was very quickly dressed. She did a twirl for him. 'Absolutely gorgeous Mrs Fulton. You honour me. Can I escort you to the ball?'

She dropped a few emergency cosmetic items into his sporran, grabbed her stole and they left the apartment.

Chapter 65

When they arrived at the reception area to the ballroom many people were mingling. He had been told that some 200 people would attend this dinner, and most were still outside the ballroom albeit it was clear that the organisers would like them seated. She noticed a photographer who had positioned backdrops to enable the guest to have their presence recorded. She secretly wanted a photograph of her prince in his kilt so guided him across to where the photographer was working. When he saw them he beckoned them over to one of his backdrops that he thought would work as a full height photograph was most definitely the best option for this lovely couple.

He asked Cis to stand on Paul's left side arm in arm and took his first photograph. Then he asked then to get closer with arms behind each other's backs, but still face the camera. He took his second shot but felt he had not captured what he could clearly see – the love that glowed between this lovely couple.

'Just one more please, but this time could you turn a little and look into each other's eyes, holding hands with your loose hand.' He framed the shot, deciding to go for a multi-shot burst as he knew that something magic could happen. He saw what he thought was the glow between then and clicked the shutter. '*Yes*' he thought.

He thanked them for their patience and informed them that the photographs would be on display tomorrow morning in this reception area.

He guided her to a notice board by the entrance to the ballroom to find which table they had been allocated. He found his name against which it was marked as table 17. However, all names were in alphabetic order and thus it was not obvious who were the other people on table 17.

He took two glasses of champagne from a nervous waiter trying to balance his tray of drinks on one hand. He gave one glass to her without taking his eyes off her. 'Okay Mrs Fulton, here's to us, and our first dance together.' They clinked their glasses and each took a sip of champagne.

She didn't need to respond with other than a smile which beamed across her face every time she heard him refer to her as Mrs Fulton, or wife. She would be very happy to get used to hearing these references to her.

He noticed that she was the only coloured woman at the reception. There were two coloured gentlemen, several Japanese and Chinese couples – probably there for the golf. The local gentry were in their kilts, or tartan trews, and there were a few regimental types with their ribbons and medals. This made her stand out, not least because she was such a shimmering beauty. He could see that she was getting the eye from a number of people, some with a clear *'what is she doing here?'*, and a number of men, and some women, just captivated by her beauty.

They made their way into the ballroom looking for table 17. The room was a typical configuration with stage, and a dance floor directly in front of it, and then tables filling the remainder of the room. The decoration was very Scottish, but very elegant. The guest had paid much for this evening and the surroundings were appropriately regal.

At least half of the men were in traditional Scottish dress, even if some did wear their tartan in the form of trews rather than a kilt. Some body shapes did not easily sit with a kilt so compromise was in order. There was a lone piper piping a lament from the centre of the stage to accompany people finding their seats.

Cis was the first to spot table 17 and noticed that it was already populated with the other 8 guests. She felt the first pangs of anxiety as the reality of their venture was unfolding. She grabbed his arm, and he could feel her tension. 'Relax my darling, your valiant knight is here with you.'

They made their way to the two remaining empty seats and stood behind them. 'Good evening ladies and gentlemen. My name is Paul Fulton, and this is my wife, Felicity. I believe that we are to join you for this evening.'

At this point a sturdy and portent gentleman in a kilt stood. My name is Seumas McCulloch, this is my wife, Sandra, and this is my party of guests for this evening. Welcome to you both.'

At this point he helped Cis to be seated, and then he took his own seat. Seumas then completed the introductions. To the right of Cis there was Senator Frank Chapman and his wife Dorothy. To the left of Paul was Laura, the wife of Bob Hartley, the head of the Federal U.S. Marshall's Office in Washington.

Prejudice in Love

Then there was the son of Seumas McCulloch, Duncan, and his fiancé, Jennifer who was a solicitor in Inverness.

All pleasantries over, with handshakes where possible, Seumas decided to engage with Paul to expand on the essential introductions. 'Mr Fulton, what brings you to Scotland, and more specifically to Gleneagles at this time?'

Paul was scanning the eyes at the people on the table to see if he could detect any obvious signs of prejudice or unfriendliness from the other guests as Seumas spoke. He looked at Seumas 'We decided to escape the storm in England over last weekend and take a long overdue visit to this beautiful part of the world.'

Seumas continued 'so you have been here a week so far?'

Paul's honed sense of presence had detected two possible sources of disquiet, one from the senator who was clearly old school Republican, and the other from the surprising source of the son of Seumas who he thought to be around the age of Cis.

'Yes, we started at Luss on Loch Lomond, then moved north to Aviemore, and arrived here on Thursday.'

Duncan McCulloch suddenly spoke to Cis. 'Mrs Fulton you look surprisingly young to be the wife of Mr Fulton. How did you meet? Did you work for him before?'

Paul quickly put his hand over the wrist of Cis to indicate that she should not respond. Paul looked at Seumas with a look of *'will you take care of this, or shall I?'*

Seumas immediately saw the problem. 'Duncan, my son, did you leave your good manners at home this evening? You will please apologise to Mrs Fulton for your ill-consider words.'

'But father I was only interested in how they met' was the startled response of Duncan.

'There are ways, and there are ways, my son, and your way this evening is not acceptable so please apologise and let that be an end to it.'

Duncan was clearly not pleased with the embarrassment he now faced, but he obviously knew that his father must be obeyed. 'Mrs Fulton, I am truly sorry if I offended you with my question.'

Cis nodded acceptance of his apology.

Seumas, not wanting to allow this embarrassment to last any longer than necessary decided to change the subject. 'Mr Fulton, would I be right in assuming that you are the Paul Fulton, the banker listed in Who's Who?'

Paul, in resignation 'you have me there, sir. I am that person.'

Seumas continued 'I'm sorry if I have intruded, but I did ask reception who was joining us, and did find your name listed. I'm truly honoured that you and your wife join us this evening. Your reputation in financial circles is quite remarkable.'

The other people at the table were just spectators during this exchange, all seeming to want to know the identity of their mystery guests.

Paul quickly responded, 'You have me at a disadvantage sir as reception would not divulge your name to me.'

'I'm so sorry. I am McCulloch of McCulloch Machinery. I make motorised machinery for farmers, the horticultural sector, and gardeners. My son, Duncan, is currently being groomed to take over from me as my health forces me to consider stepping to one side.'

'Very pleased to meet you, and on behalf of myself and Felicity I would like to thank you and your guests for allowing us to join you this evening.'

Paul thought that rank had now been established thus it was time to take the awkwardness and formality out of the evening. 'Now that we have all been introduced could I suggest that we drop formality. I'm Paul, and pointing to Cis, this is Felicity. The senator's wife, Dorothy, immediately piped up and said she preferred to be known as Babs, and although her husbands preferred to be called senator, that Frank would get his attention. There was an all-round laugh at the table at her putdown of her husband. Bob Hartley then stated that Bob was good for him, and Laura for his wife. All was now settling down except that Paul still detected the unease of the senator sitting next to Cis.

Seumas decided to probe Paul some more as he knew everything about his other guests, and the Who's Who entry of Paul intrigued him. 'Paul, could I ask you what tartan you're wearing?'

Paul knew that the old clans were very particular about who wore what tartan so he needed to be thorough to ensure that the current calm is not disturbed further. 'In this tartan I might be considered a fraud. I do have the right by heritage of my grandmother on my father's side to wear a Frazer of Lovatt tartan. And indeed, I have a full-dress Frazer of Lovatt outfit at home, and have worn it many times over the years, especially at the London Scottish Club in London. However, no matter how sacrilegious, the very red content of the Frazer tartan does not suit me, and I never feel comfortable wearing it. Having discussed this with a pipe major whose regimental tartan clearly did not suit him, he advised that, as with a suit, the best tartan is the one that you feel good to wear. Tradition should be honoured, but the canny Scots have realised that kilts can be very profitable if introduced to a wider audience. So, on this trip, we went to one of the traditional outfitters in Balloch and sought his advice. My preferred base colour is blue so he went through all the clan tartans, and the universal tartans to find which ones I could wear without causing offence. Then Felicity and the shop assistant went through these to choose one for me, but Felicity did not see any that she felt fulfilled my need. Finally, the assistant remembered a weave that had been commissioned by a German industrialist, woven, and registered, but never used. Felicity decided this tartan was right for me. The shop manager gave me the details of the owner only to find that I knew him well. A brief telephone call to my German friend and the tartan is now mine and re-registered as the Fulton Blue. They worked hard in the past few days to make my kilt, and I collected it this morning from Crieff. So now I have a tartan which I feel much more comfortable to wear, is my own family tartan, and should not offend anyone.'

Babs jumped in at this point. 'Would you mind standing up so that I can see how you look as I did not really notice when you arrived?'

Paul stood, moved his chair back a little so that Babs could see the whole rig. He also did the compulsory twirl so that they could see the rear. Light-heartedly 'My wife chose everything else as well, so the complete package is her design.'

'You chose the buttons my darling' piped in Cis. Everyone laughed.

He shrugged his shoulders 'I did choose the buttons, folks.'

Babs kicked in 'Felicity my dear, you clearly know what works for your man as he is so handsome in that kilt I could wrap him up and take him home with me. We must talk to see if you can give me some idea how to achieve such a result with Frank.' She turned to her husband. 'Change seats with Felicity so that I can get some advice how to make you as handsome.'

At that moment the pipers started to signal the start of formalities with the entry of the festive bannock bread, so Paul re-seated himself and all thoughts of changing seats were suspended.

He took this interlude in them being in the spotlight to scan the people on this table. As an accomplished negotiator he was used to analysing people quickly, albeit he felt at a distinct disadvantage with Seumas who had clearly researched him. In his work he was respected for his extraordinary diligence in his investigation of everyone he was likely to encounter at a negotiating table. Knowing the person meant that he knew how to approach them with argument and knew where their pressure points were.

He saw Seumas as probably in his mid-60's and second generation in the family business. He did not have that withered look of someone who had spent years building a business from scratch. His father had probably taken advantage of the need for intensive farming after the second World War to feed the people, and thus the need for more and more mechanisation of farming practice. Indeed, Seumas looked like he had spent much of his life promoting the company through corporate entertainment, and which would account for his health.

His wife, Sandra, probably late 50's, looked like she was from affluent stock, but lived in the shadow of her ebullient husband. She was clearly comfortable with Babs and Laura but knew her place at this table. She would add little to this evening.

Duncan and Jennifer were the odd couple at the table, probably to make up the numbers. There was no obvious connection between Duncan and the Americans, and Jennifer looked like she was just visiting. Paul concluded that Jennifer probably practiced in the oil and gas sector as Inverness is the heart of the legal profession in this sector and commuting from here to Inverness every day is not likely, thus she must live in, or around Inverness. As she looked to be around her mid-20's she would be recently graduated and thus still learning the business. He felt that she would be happier if Cis was sitting with her, being of similar age, and disconnection from the Americans at the table. But this could be a disaster if Cis fell into a comfort zone with Jennifer and forgot the role she was playing at this table.

Bob was probably early 60's and was wizen enough to suggest that he had come up through the ranks. He was a very stocky man standing well over 6ft tall and was clearly someone who took care of himself before the current desk job took its toll on his girth. He was very comfortable in his own skin and could be considered as someone he could engage with. He thought that probably half of his staff would be coloured so there would be no prejudice from him.

Laura, his wife, was very much the wife of a junior US Marshall, and who had never been called upon to be a socialite for her husband. She was very much the mother of his children, and very comfortable in this role. He saw this as the connection with Sandra, albeit from different social backgrounds.

Babs was certainly the lady of the table. She was early 60's, slightly built, well groomed, and her now somewhat withered, but long elegant fingers suggested good stock. Clearly very bright, educated, and astute, she was obviously very comfortable in any social circle. He saw a resemblance to Nancy Reagan, the wife of former President Reagan, and her manner reminded him of the specific characteristics of a Wharton College girl. She was clearly the power behind the throne of her Senator husband, and he probably owed much of his career to her skills. Although he was happy for Cis to sit with Babs to reinforce her message to Frank, he must not leave them alone for long. Babs was smart and would probe.

Senator Frank Chapman was in his mid-60's and was clearly southern State Republican. He was a tall, stocky man suffering from too much social entertainment, and far too little physical exercise. Although his tone did not suggest gravitas, he certainly liked to exert a presence, but Paul felt that this was a bullying presence rather than one of wisdom. His clearly detectable prejudice toward Cis did nothing to attract Paul to this man, but he did admire how quickly Babs had spotted this problem and dealt with it such that Frank knew he was being told to behave himself.

What he could not fathom was how these people knew each other. He turned to Laura and, in order to break the ice with her, asked her if she needed anything. She thanked him for his concern, but she was fine for the moment. He then thought she would be the least defensive for the question he wanted to ask. Very disarmingly he started 'Laura, how long have you people known each other, and how did you all meet?'

She saw no issue with this question so matter of fact she responded 'We all met on a cruise around the Caribbean about 20 years ago. The men found that they all shared those antisocial male bastion interests of hunting, shooting, fishing,

Prejudice in Love

and golf. So each year they get together, alternating between the USA and here, and drag us women along with them.'

Paul found her answer amusing but did not want to pursue her obvious imposition. 'Do I detect a touch of Virginian in you?'

Laura looked at him in surprise 'Yes, but how did you know that?'

'I'm interested in people. Having lived in America on three separate occasions, I started to get used to the various State dialects.'

Cis was listening to this conversation thinking to herself 'what a smooth operator, and he claims he does not like social small talk.'

Laura now felt connected and turned a little in her seat to better face him 'Where did you live?'

'I have spent 2 periods in New York, and the other in San Francisco, but I used these opportunities to travel around. I have also visited Washington on numerous occasions.'

'Seumas is obviously impressed with your credentials, but what do you do?'

Paul realising that he needed to keep his response low key for this lady 'Before I retired I was an investment banker, primarily for major US banks. But now I'm just a writer.'

'You're far too young to be retired, and I don't think you are 'just' anything.' She turned to Cis who was still listening to their conversation 'Tell me Felicity, what does Paul really do that has so impressed Seumas who, believe me, is a very hard man to impress.'

Cis wanted time to think how she should respond so pushed out her hand in an offer to shake hands with Laura and gently spoke 'Hello Laura, pleased to meet you.' They shook hands. Then Cis continued 'Paul is supposed to be some sort of hero in the international financial community, but this is before I met him, so I don't really understand what all the fuss is about. For me he is my valiant knight, and a real pussy cat.'

Laura laughed at her response. 'So how did you two meet?'

'Cis had now had time to think this through to give as little information as possible but satisfy the question. 'Paul, a complete stranger to me, came to my rescue during a period of real distress for me. He scooped me out of that horrible place, cared for me, and we have not been apart since.'

Laura looked at Paul 'So you really are an English gentleman, and I can see why a valiant knight from the fairy tales. What a lovely story. You two really glow with love, so God bless you both.'

At this point their conversation was interrupted by a volley of waiters serving the bannock rolls, and soup.

Seumas attracted the attention of Paul. 'Mr Fulton would you do me the honour of breaking this special bannock with me as a sign of welcome and friendship?'

Paul responded, 'The honour would be mine.'

They both stood to attention. Seumas picked up his bannock bread, held it in front of him at waist height, and broke it in half. He then handed one half to Paul. Paul took the bread as they bowed their heads towards each other, and then each broke off a little of the bread and ate it. They both bowed their heads again towards each other, and then shook hands.'

Everyone at the table sat in amazement of the solemnness of what they were witnessing. As soon as both men had sat down it was Babs who quickly got excited. 'Okay boys, what was that all about?'

Paul looked at Seumas as if to ask who should respond. Seumas spoke 'Mr Fulton is the Englishman at this table, so he is best placed to explain the Breaking of the Bread tradition.' And then to Paul 'Would you kindly explain to our American cousins what this very worthy tradition symbolises.'

'Breaking of the Bread is as old as time itself. Could I ask you in your normal life with whom you would normally break bread?'

'My family and friends, I guess' Babs responded somewhat bemused.

'Exactly. You break bread with those closest to you. In ancient times people existed in groups that we can call clans or tribes, and who shared everything together. Also bread is the most basic of food so sharing your bread with someone symbolises that you will share whatever you have. If you invite someone to be part of your clan or tribe you break bread with them to indicate that they are welcome and will share with you whatever they have.'

'Today this ritual is still practiced to welcome a new member to a group, or a new member to an extended family. If I join, for example, an Order of chivalry we will break bread together. What you just witnessed is the sincere offer by Seumas for the two of us to be everlasting friends.'

Babs was animated 'I so love these old English traditions. Every true American loves English history and tradition. If only we could have your Queen Elisabeth rather than our Presidents. But I suppose that adding another 340 million Americans to her sovereign territory would be too much for her.'

'Dear Babs, she already reigns over some 1.8 billion people in over seventy nation states throughout the world so I don't think another 340 million would bother her too much.'

Babs, now really animated '1.8 billion people! Is the British Empire still that big?'

'No, unfortunately we had to mortgage much of the Empire to pay for two world wars, but we have the Commonwealth of Nations over which she has dominion, including Canada.'

'That's right. So she's already in our backyard.' She turned to the Senator nudging his arm 'Now that's something you could usefully debate in the Senate. Adopt the Queen as the sovereign head of the United States of America. You would be the most popular man in America.'

There was laughter around the table.

Paul found this attack on her husband amusing. Babs had clearly detected her husband's disagreeable attitude towards Cis and was ensuring that he knew that she would not permit him to cause any disquiet. Paul had met various Senators during his career, and it was invariably true that the wife was the real power.

Babs reverted back to Paul 'Tell me more. Is there something I could take home and practice in Washington?'

'Do you realise that the way we are seated is a tradition from the fifteenth century where every lady has to be flanked by a man with his sword to protect her from any possibility of harm. It is part of our code of chivalry, and until formalities are over we should honour such tradition. Once the main course is finished then we are free to swap places as we see fit. It may seem a little silly these days, especially as we no longer carry our swords. But at least you now know why you are seated in this configuration.'

'But something you could take home and practice. Are you aware of the Ceremony of the Loving Cup?'

'Never heard of it.'

'As it is very fitting for politicians let me try to quickly explain it to you. It dates back to the 8th century and is still very much practiced today in the ancient guilds and liveries. You need something like a two-handed chalice with a lid, and this is called the Loving Cup. At home we have a glass bowl with handles and a lid. I guess it's supposed to hold chocolates, and stands about 9 inches high, and the bowl is about 5 inches in diameter. The content is traditionally spiced wine called "Sack", but any red wine, or even Ruby port will suffice. The content symbolises blood as in blood brothers and should not be confused with the symbolism of the wine used during Holy Communion.'

'The ceremony usually takes place at the conclusion of dinner. The Loving Cup is positioned in front of the host. When the host rises to start the Ceremony of the Loving Cup, the guests on each side of him also stand. The host turns to the right-hand neighbour, usually the honoured guest, and the left-hand neighbour turns so that they are back-to-back with the host. The host, and the neighbour now facing the host bow their heads to each other, and the neighbour removes the cover of the Cup with both hands – important detail. The host holds the Cup with both hands and takes a drink, wipes the Cup with their napkin, and the lid is replaced. They both bow their heads. The person holding the Cup passes it to the person facing them, who then turns through 180 degrees, and their neighbour stands facing them. The host now turns 180 degrees to stand guard, whilst the previous guard now sits again. The process repeats until all around the table have drunk from the Loving Cup. Throughout there are always 3 people standing, one lifting the lid with both hands, one in the centre drinking with both hands, and the one who has previously drunk, now facing outwards standing guard. The reason for the ceremony is to extend the hand of peace and friendship, and the guard is to prevent the recipient of the peace from being stabbed in the back, as was the case leading to the founding of this ceremony. Very fitting, I believe, for politicians who are trying to back stab each other.'

'Bravo' exclaimed Seumas 'well described, although many of the politicians I know should suffer the fate resulting in the ceremony.'

Babs joined in 'sounds wonderful. Before we leave this evening would you run that past me one more time as I would like to introduce this ceremony into our dinners in Washington. It might help when harmony is needed.'

Seumas put his hand on the arm of Babs to get her attention 'It's alright Babs, I know this ceremony so I can explain it when you can write it down. If you want to use it let's be sure you get it right.'

Paul added 'If you search the internet using Ceremony of the Loving Cup you will most certainly find what you need. It is widely used in the City of London.'

Babs sought attention 'Well gentlemen. We have two cultured men at this table who can teach their American cousins some interesting aspects of ceremonial protocols. I thank you both for what we have learned this evening.' She turned to her husband 'We can introduce these ceremonies into our dinners. Make ours stand out from the rest.'

Frank just gave her a resigned look 'Yes dear, very interesting.'

Paul and Seumas just looked at each other with a knowing smile.

Dinner was served comprising wild goose, carrots, and mashed potatoes, or neeps and tatties in Scottish-speak, and wine. This took some minutes before they could settle again.

Conversation became more intermittent, and mainly one-on-one whilst consuming dinner. Paul conversed with Laura and Bob whilst Babs dominated the conversation with Cis and Frank. Cis exercised her journalist skills to keep Babs primed with questions to minimise any interrogation. But Babs got wise to this, so as soon as dinner was finished, she had Frank swap seats with Cis so that they could have a proper conversation, and Babs was a skilled interrogator.

After the main course debris was collected by the waiters, proceedings were interrupted by a display of traditional Scottish dancing and a reading of some appropriate verse honouring Saint Michael, albeit indecipherable to anyone other than hardcore Scots, followed by a lone piper's lament. Then desert was served during which conversations were re-ignited or continued, and coffee and tradition dram of whiskey taken.

Paul kept a watchful eye on Cis as he conversed with both Frank and Bob, generally discussing the situation in the USA.

Prejudice in Love

He noted that although Cis and Babs were in deep conversation, it was a two-way conversation, so he was comfortable that she had remembered his suggestion that she engage her journalist talents to prevent too much probing.

The dance band, which was something akin to a big band as per Glen Miller, started to play as the band leader invited people onto the dance floor. After this intrusion of music conversation was very difficult as table 17 was only two rows back from the stage. Paul took this interruption to recover Cis and take her to the dance floor to see how she was coping with Babs, and to see if she needed rescuing, or any guidance. On the contrary to his concern she was full of the joys of spring, and very happy in her role as Mrs Fulton. She beamed with both outer and inner beauty, and certainly attracted much visual attention as she shimmered around the dance floor.

Around 10:30 Seumas indicated that it was time to leave. This was typical for Scotland from Paul's experience. Whereas the youngsters would party into the night, the older generation would seek out their beds long before midnight. Seumas had a quiet word with Duncan who quickly left with Jennifer without saying a word. Everyone stood to leave, as did Paul and Cis, albeit with no intention of leaving before they had danced the night away, or for at least a while yet. Bob and Laura were the first to say their goodbyes. Then it was the turn of Babs and Frank.

Babs firstly held both hands of Cis. 'It has been a real pleasure to meet you both tonight. And Felicity I will pray to God that your wishes for a child are granted. You will make a wonderful mother.' She let go of one hand of Cis to take Paul's hand. 'And look after this gorgeous man of yours. I still want to wrap him up and take him home.' She turned to Paul 'If you are ever in the States you must come visit with us. I have much to learn from you. And please bring your kilt. You would wow my parties dressed like this.'

Cis responded first. 'You are very kind, and I will most certainly take good care of Paul. He is a special man.'

Paul smiled at these exchanges. 'A consummate socialite' he thought. 'Babs you are truly a remarkable woman, and it has been a great pleasure to meet you. Enjoy your stay in this green and pleasant land, and should we find ourselves in the States we will certainly make contact.'

Frank chipped in 'Mr Fulton, you have enlightened our evening, and I hope we meet again in the not too distant future.' He said nothing to Cis.

Waiting behind was Seumas and Sandra. Sandra made for Cis with the usual pleasantries. Seumas grabbed the hand of Paul. 'It has been a great pleasure to meet you Paul, and I hope we meet again. What could have been an ordinary evening turned out to be a very interesting and entertaining affair, and I'm glad you joined with us. Once again thank you for the discreet way you handled my son. He has much to learn in our ways. I hope that he has not spoilt the evening for Felicity.'

Thank you, Seumas. I think Duncan was just a little clumsy in his choice of words, but absolutely no harm done. But thanks for asking. We have really enjoyed our evening with you and your guests. And we wish you a safe journey home.' At that they shook hands and Seumas guided Sandra out of the ballroom.

They sat down again. 'Okay, my master, how did that go?'

'You were great. A few unfortunate surprises, but my mistakes, not yours.'

She reached for his hand 'What mistakes are you talking about?'

'Primarily the ease at which I was talked into joining an existing group, rather than a table where no one knows each other.'

'But why was this a problem?'

'Seumas took the trouble to find out who I am, and clearly would like to continue a relationship. Unless we actually get married I could not engage with him again, and certainly could not return to Gleneagles. He is obviously well known here and as such I could not stay here without it reaching his attention. By breaking bread with him as husband and wife I have breached trust with him. Not good. However, it's done, and is my fault so let us not dwell upon it.'

'Can I ask you about the situation with Duncan? What happened there? I saw the way you looked at Seumas, but you didn't need to say a word.'

'In polite circles one must always give the host the opportunity to resolve any impropriety. I looked at Seumas to indicate my disquiet, and he was astute enough to deal with the matter. There is nothing more to it. Duncan was expressing inappropriate prejudice, albeit I think his clumsy words were more his need to speak before thinking about how to phrase his question. And I think your response to the same question from Laura was admirable.'

'I have seen that look before from you. You looked at the receptionist at Luss the same way. No words, but he clearly got your message. What is this look you give people?'

'I had hoped that you did not see the problem at Luss. That man was clearly questioning why I was with you and drawing inappropriate conclusions. He had to be stopped and brought back to the responsibilities of his position. As for the look I use, I don't know how to describe it. I'm told that it is like the look of death. Apparently my irises turn black, and the uncomfortable intensity can easily be felt by the recipient. It speaks volumes without words.'

'I shall have to take a closer look the next time you use it to see what it feels like.'

'From what I'm told, you do not want to be anywhere near the receiving end. You have witnessed the reaction, let that be enough.'

'What did you think of Babs, and what was that comment about regarding a child?'

'She is some lady. Clearly the boss in that house, but lovely as well. She asked if we were considering a family, as you had predicted, so I told her that we were trying for a child.'

Did you realise the prejudice that Frank displayed towards you? He was clearly uncomfortable sitting next to you, but Babs spotted it before I needed to do anything. The suggested change of seating arrangements was part of her chastisement of Frank. She let him clearly know that she liked you, so back off and behave yourself.'

'I didn't spot anything specific, but now I think about the fuss she made of me, it makes sense. What is it with people like him?'

'The colour of your skin, my dear. But we can now enjoy ourselves, so what do you say about dancing the night away.'

She laughed at his strange invitation, grabbed his hand, and led him to the dance floor.

Paul was not a competent dancer, but he had good balance, a great sense of rhythm, and he knew how to enjoy himself. They swirled, twirled, jived and laughed through a series of different genre, culminating in the required slow dance at the end of the evening.

They left the room hand in hand, both hot and exhausted but with joy in their hearts and smiles of contentment on their faces. Except for the unfortunate breaking of bread incident Paul was feeling very happy about the evening together with his 'wife'. *'She would make a fabulous partner'* he thought *'why does she so want a child?'*

She floated on air back to the apartment, absolutely thrilled that her audition had proven very successful. She was in the moment as Mrs Fulton and part of his world and was not in any hurry to leave it. As with Babs she was enthralled with the traditional aspects of his world. What a welcome change from the superficial world of fashion. Tonight she really enjoyed traditions going back to the eighth century, and even time itself with the breaking of the bread, in contrast to her world where it was difficult enough to keep a trend going for just one season. *'What an interesting world he lives in. And he was not out of place at their table; he could easily hold his own with these people.'* She really enjoyed her chat with Babs but could not imagine the opportunity to meet such a woman on a social level in her world. This world is fun, and she wants more.

Chapter 66

Once inside their apartment they both kicked off their shoes and made their way to their bedroom suite. He switched on the bedside lamps which just gave a welcome hue to the room. The evening was warm and so the room was at a very comfortable temperature.

She went to the bathroom to remove her jewellery and makeup. He removed his jacket, bow tie, sporran and hose. He could see her out of the corner of his eye reminding him of the vision he noticed at the dinner. He walked into the bathroom, stood directly behind her admiring this vision in the mirror, wrapped his arms around her, and kisses her on the shoulder.

With his chin on her shoulder 'I saw a very beautiful woman at dinner tonight and realised that this vision was my own lovely Cis. It made me feel very good realising that I have not really felt this way for some time.'

She was watching him through the mirror 'I saw you looking at me as though you were a predator, and I felt good about it too. So what do you propose to do mister predator?'

He turned her so they are face to face and kissed her on the lips. She reached up and put her arms around his neck. He pulled her in close and they kissed again, but this time a longing kiss.

He took the opportunity to slowly stroke the exposed part of her back all the way to her shoulders. She cast him a knowing gaze as he moved her slightly backwards so that he can move the straps from her shoulders so that her dress falls to the floor.

As she has no bra she is standing in only the sexy transparent black panties that he had selected for her at Braehead. He looked at her and admired the beautiful lines of her body.

She moved closer and unbuttons his shirt never taking her eyes from his. She slid the shirt off his shoulders and finished the removal without bothering about the cuff links as the cuffs slid off his wrists with ease, and his shirt joined her dress on the bathroom floor. They join their bodies again and indulge in another longing kiss.

Without another word she stepped out of her dress taking his hand and walked him to their bed where he placed her close to, but with her back to the bed. He sat her on the edge of the bed and gently pushes her backwards such that she is lying on the bed with her feet still on the floor. He reaches down and kissed her on her belly as he knelt between her legs stroking her thighs.

He ran the back of his fingers along the top of her panty line as he returned to his feet.

She sat up to undo the straps on his lovely kilt encouraging it to fall to the floor. His erection was bulging his underwear. She ran her hand up from his crotch to the top of his shorts stroking the erection that lay beneath.

She noticed that the head of his erection was bursting out of the top of his underwear. Taking care not to exert any force on the head of his penis she used both hands to pull away the elasticated top of his underwear to remove his shorts whilst lightly kissing the head of his penis. He was standing before her naked, and fully erect.

She now felt an exciting power over her man as she was still not exposed. She stood, running her hand from his scrotum upwards along his stiff erection as she kisses him deeply on his lips as though he had made the grade and can proceed to the next stage.

After this lingering kiss he lifted her and placed her on the bed with her head raised on the pillows. He knew that she likes to watch his penis as he prepares her for love. He parted her legs and knelt between them running his hand along her thighs up to her waist, and then across her belly. He moved one hand down her crotch along the line of her vagina to let her know that he is about to take control.

Whilst gently caressing the area around her vagina he leaned forward and kisses each nipple with suction until her nipples were fully extended. She strokes his hair as he kissed each nipple.

His attention moved to the lower part of her torso with gently licks and kisses as he progresses down to her pantie line whilst gently caressing her breasts with his hands. He moved his tongue along her panty line as he moved his hands down the side of her body, inside the top of her panties drawing them down whilst sitting up to allow her to put her legs up in front of him so that he can remove her panties in one movement.

She put her feet back on the bed with knees raised and her legs open as far as possible to reveal the full wonder of her naked pussy.

He glided his tongue along her vagina wall to check that she is ready for penetration. He lingered until he could taste the love juices that will lubricate their lovemaking.

He moved forward allowing her to take his erection in her hand and direct it to the entry of her vagina. The entry was one gentle slow movement all the way to the base of his penis at which point he placed his hands on the bed just below her arms such that the only point of contact between their bodies was at the pelvic ridge. He rose high on the pelvic area to maximise connection with her clitoris.

He kissed her once more before starting to pleasure her with a moderate rhythmic motion. He is now looking for guidance from her as to the right rhythm for her. She holds his arms just below his elbows to help to guide the speed of motion. The rhythm of their bodies now moved as one.

As she started to show signs of imminent orgasm he maintained the rhythm resisting any temptation to increase the pace of penetration. Her orgasm caused her to spasm violently and he was careful not to interfere with her ability to feel the full force of these spasms. She clasped her legs around his waist to indicate that he should penetrate deep and then stay still whilst she allows the pleasure of orgasm to wash through her body.

He did not move until she took her legs from around his waist and placed them back on the bed to indicate that he can continue.

He now took a lower position which maximises his sensation during sex. He started to penetrate again this time using his own rhythm. What he hoped this time is for both to orgasm together.

When they reach orgasm together, she wrapped her legs around Paul's waist. Paul bent forward so that she could put her arms around his neck. He placed his left hand around her waist and his right hand under her buttock as he rolled her over on their sides, but very tight together and still connected, so that she would not be squashed under his weight. They held each other and kissed, gently savouring the connection between them.

After some minutes they uncoupled, got under the bedclothes and slept their deepest sleep wrapped in each other's arms.

Chapter 67 - Sunday

It was after 9am before either stirred.

She went to the bathroom nearly tripping over the clothes that still lay where they had fallen. She picked them up reflecting on the lovely feeling she had when he slipped her dress off her shoulders, let it slip onto the floor, and then it started. They had made love last night, a tender romantic love with her playing the role of wife, both absolutely absorbed in the moment.

'I have to stay with this man. He makes me feel so loved.'

Chapter 68

They went to breakfast, Paul walking and Cis skipping along hanging on to his arm with both hands. She was full of the joys of spring. She's in love and she was happy to share this information with the world, or at least those who could see her. Even when she was collecting her various items she had chosen for breakfast she bounced from server to server.

When she finally sat, he looked at her. 'You're very bouncy this morning considering the late night we had.'

'And what a wonderful night it was. I danced with my prince, and then he carried me back to his castle and made love to me. A fairy-tale evening.'

He reached for her hand, 'It was truly a lovely evening, and I went to the ball with the most beautiful princess, the belle of the ball. Everyone wanted to be with my princess, but she was mine, she was with me.'

'It's what happened after the ball that won my heart, my prince.'

Feigning loss of memory, 'can't remember that bit, what happened?'

'Magic, just fabulous magic. My poor heart was completely stolen.'

After breakfast they went through the main foyer and saw the photographs from last night. She steered him towards them and started to scan for the photos taken of them as they entered. She found 3 pictures, but one of them glowed at her.

It was a full-length picture of them looking at each other. The picture radiated love. You could feel the glow coming from the picture.

'I must have that picture', she thought.

The photographer came over to them. 'I'm so glad that you two have come back. I'm very proud of one of your pictures. It's the best picture I've taken in a long time.'

She pointed to the one she liked. 'This one?'

'Yes' replied the photographer. 'Did you ever see a picture that radiated such love?'

'I would like a copy, but I would prefer a 10" x 8" size.'

'This picture would also look great on canvas', interrupted the photographer.

'What size canvas?', she asked.

'24" x 16" is my normal canvas size.'

'And how much are we talking for a 10" x 8" and a canvas copy?' she asked.

'The 10" x 8" is £24 and the canvas is £50. But as this picture is so special rather than use my printer for the 10" x 8" I'll print it properly on a quality grade paper. Then you'll get the full majesty of this picture.'

She thought about it. 'Okay I'll take the 10" x 8" and the canvas if you let me have this 6" x 4" now, and a digital copy for my computer.'

He looked at her. 'That will be fine as it will take a couple of days to get the pictures ready. How long are you here?'

'We leave tomorrow morning. Can you post them to Edinburgh?'

'No problem. Just give me your details including an email address to send you a digital copy.'

She gave him her details. She told Paul that she would pay for them, but she did not have her purse with her, so he added them to his bill.

The photographer put the smaller picture into a folder and gave it to her, and they made their way back to the apartment.

'What are you going to do with those pictures as I cannot see Andrew allowing you to put them in the family album, or on the wall?'

'This picture I'll put where it is easily available to me. The 10" x 8" will go into a private album that I intend to keep for our child when old enough to know of their real father. And the canvas I shall store somewhere safe until I can hang it.'

Chapter 69

When they returned to their apartment, they were surprised to see a bouquet of flowers and a bottle of champagne on the table. She went to see if there was a card. She found an envelope and opened to find that it was from Duncan McCulloch. She read it. 'He has sent me flowers and champagne as an apology for last night. How sweet of him.'

He looked at the champagne. 'It's a very good bottle of champagne. His father must have really bent his ear last night. I'll put it in the fridge for later.'

She busied herself removing the flowers from the wrapping and arranging them back into the vase in which they had arrived.

They both went to the living area of their apartment and sat down on one of the leather sofas. She decided that after the fantastic evening last night it was time to make her move on him, using this beautiful photograph as evidence of their love for each other.

She gave the photo to him. 'What do you see?'

'I know what you want me to say, but if I say it then we need a reality check to put it into context.'

'Tell me what you see', she insisted.

'An independent observer would see two people clearly radiating love for each other. But this is without the knowledge that he loves her for one set of reasons, and she loves him for a completely different set of reasons. The only common denominator is that the reasons for both are either directly personal to themselves or attached to connected third parties.'

'And what is that supposed to mean?'

'Come sit with me as it's time to have this conversation. I know what you have been scheming since you got back, and I fully understand why you think the way you do. I'm also very flattered. But let us analyse this situation because it's not real world.'

'Let me have a few minutes to outline how I think things are, and then you can tell me what you think. Is this okay?'

'Yes.'

'Cis, before we met you were in a marriage which was becoming derailed, not because you did not love each other, but because of a common, all-consuming constraint that you wanted a child and he could not give it to you. This meant that you both detached from sexual activity for many months, and a loving relationship fell baron.'

'If you were looking for an alternate mate, and you saw me on the street, but had never met me or know who I was, would you consider me as a potential mate? The answer is "no" because your visual prejudice would not even consider me suitable.'

'Our eyes are generally the first point of contact with other people, and our most prejudicial sense. If you used your eyes only with me before you knew me, would you let me stroke you, would you consider me suitable to sire your children, or even consider me as a mate?'

'With our eyes we can see great beauty, or we can exercise unqualified prejudice. With your cultured voice how many times have you spoken to someone on the telephone only to find that when they see you in the flesh their prejudice against the colour of your skin becomes an issue? This has happened to you hasn't it?'

'Yes', she replied, looking down at her hands in sadness.

'When I look at you I see a beautiful goddess of a woman, where others cannot get past the colour of your skin. When I was a kid they still had segregation in America. If you were on a bus and a white person needed your seat you would have to give it up. Your skin colour expressed prejudice in supposedly the freest country in the world during my lifetime, and it's still an issue today.'

'It was only in the darkness of the night that you allowed other senses to overcome your prejudice against my age. When I touched you all you could feel was a hand touching you in a way which made you feel very good. Your preoccupation with your fear of the storm, and probably the lack of any intimate contact for so long, blocked your normal prejudice. Once my hands started to weave their magic on your body, intended only to calm you, all fear of the storm evaporated, and desire kicked in. The storm raged all the time I stroked your body, but you did not react once to a thunder crash thereafter.'

'When we awoke in the darkness and you accidentally nudged my erection you did not move away. Here was another desire of yours, and it was available to you. You mounted it fully lubricated meaning the dream that you mentioned was clearly a wet dream. You could not see me, and I did not have to do anything other than explore your body with my hands as an added sensation for you. You fulfilled another long overdue desire in the way you wanted.'

'So much so that by the time the day brought light you had experienced two orgasms and so much attention to your needs that you closed down your principal source of prejudice knowing that there were overriding desires that could overlook the age issue.'

'We were lucky in that the opportunity arose to break your natural prejudice. Otherwise you would not be here with me today.'

'But what about the prejudice of others towards us? If we were to stay together let us look at some of the prejudice that we would have to endure.'

'If you were white, people would look at me and form the opinion that you might be my daughter, or I may be your sugar daddy. But you're coloured, so the possibilities are that I'm so sad that I went to another country, bought you, and brought you back to be my sex slave and housekeeper. Very few would look at us and see what you see in that picture.'

'Look at our experience last night. We presented ourselves as man and wife but we still experienced open prejudice from Duncan, and if Babs had not been so astute you would have been made uncomfortable by the prejudice of the Senator. And these were intelligent people. I anticipated correctly and was therefore fortunate to deal with both without incident. Do you want your life to comprise of me having to deal with such nonsense on a regular basis? I tried to make it as simple as possible last night, but I failed, and in doing so compromised my precious integrity. If I were still a banker, I would feel gutted about what I did. As it is, I cannot come here again without you as my wife.'

'And what about your friends? How many would accept a very much older man in your life? How fast would your invitations to dinners and parties dry up?'

'If you came to some of the events I attend many of the people there would not give you the chance to show that you are intelligent and cultured. You would be my bit of crumpet and, because of your great beauty, they would either be envious, or try to get a piece of you. When I first took Jane to such events she got some of that treatment even though she is white, and is far less than half our age difference.'

'I think that it's a biblical reference that the age difference between a man and his wife should be no less than half his age plus seven years. The youngest you could for us to remotely be acceptable as a couple is 31 + 7 = 38 years old. That is ten years more than your tender age of 28 years. I've said to you many times over these past days that if I was just 20 years younger, and thus our age difference just meets the above criteria, your proposition would take me but an instant to consider, and you would not be going back to Andy.'

'I have racked my brain to find a reason how I can keep you. Every avenue but one is a win for me, lose for you. The one avenue that was a win for you is a lose for me. With all my knowledge and experience, I cannot find a single win-win scenario, and this we must have to stand any chance of having a good life together.'

'As appears usual in my life, your guardian angel has given me a brief taste of true happiness, knowing that I'm wise enough to know that I cannot keep you.'

He was now welling up inside and tears were in his eyes. 'Cis, you have given me so much joy in these past days, and it will truly break my heart to let you go. But let you go I must. So please do not make it any more painful than it is already. Please let us enjoy the remaining time together and then go back to our respective lives renewed and refreshed, and with happy, loving memories of our time together.'

She put her arms around his neck holding him tight, begging him not be sad albeit she was crying herself.

She leaned back to look at him, kissing the tears from his cheeks as tears washed down her face.

She whimpered under her sobs, 'life is so unfair for both of us. I feel that we are stuck in a Romeo and Juliet love affair with the whole world against us.'

'You have your whole life in front of you, and now with a child to consider. I'm in my fourth quartile. What sort of father could I be at my age? When this child is old enough to go kick a ball in the park I'll be over seventy years old, older than most grandparents of children at that age.'

She quickly interrupted him. 'But how can I live without you? You're now my life. I'm moulded in your image. I live, eat, breath your knowledge and your thoughts, and by body craves your touch. You make me feel so alive.'

'You need to remember everything between us and set a goal to replace me with Andrew in that photograph within six months, or certainly before your baby is born. Then you'll be satisfied. You'll find the demands of a child distracting from your cravings. But the child will substitute for many of them, and thus why men feel neglected after the birth of a child. It would be helpful for you to remember that you have a husband who also needs attention after the birth. In that way you will balance your needs with that of the child.'

'I have serious doubts that Andrew could ever achieve what you do to me.'

'Go teach him. I had a good teacher who showed me the way. Go show Andrew how to treat you. He now has every incentive to make it good for you. You have removed the constraint between you, so let your beauty be his aphrodisiac. Let your body be his temple of worship.'

He gathered his thoughts. 'Do you have an argument that I should listen to? I don't have the answers to all questions in life, as clearly demonstrated last night. Believe me, if you have something realistic to put on the table I'm listening.'

'No. You have just crushed them all so convincingly. But it's still unfair. I could live in your arms forever.'

He kissed her. 'I would love that my darling.'

Chapter 70

She just sat there for a while, head down, looking at her hands. She had lost her crusade to keep this man, and his pain at letting her go was obvious. 'Why can't the world accept us and our love for what it is? Why are people so prejudiced?'

He broke her thoughts. 'Cis, you have been such a great student, and I think you now have all of the skills you need to make a complete success of your marriage. I think that you should now take over and determine the events for our remaining time together.'

'What do you mean?'

'To date I have determined what we do, and where we go. Now I think you should take that role. You can use it to practice your skills, or you can try new things. You tell me what you want, and how you want it.'

'My only input is that I think that we should leave here tomorrow around 11 o'clock. When we get to Edinburgh we can have a fond farewell lunch, say all our goodbyes, and then I'll take you home where you just jump out as though I've given you a lift. I would just like to see where you live.'

'So you're saying that I can ask you to do anything, even to me, and you will obey?'

'Exactly. But anything strange, like taking my clothes off and jumping into the lake, you have to do as well.'

'Okay my lover. The first thing I need is a big hug to get me out of my sadness while I think of what delights I want from you.'

He scooped her up in his arms and held her tightly.

'Can we have room service this evening?'

'Cis, get with the game. You want room service this evening, then you just say that and tell me if you want me to organise it, or you want to organise it. If you want to organise it then decide what you want, pick up the phone and arrange it.'

'But I want it to be a surprise.'

'Then go to the hotel desk and surprise me.'

'Back in 30.' She was gone.

Chapter 71

On her way back she thought about the day ahead leading to her surprise dinner. To have sex during the day would dampen the impact of what she had in mind for the evening.

What had she learnt about foreplay? *'Seductive, leave your lover wanting, build the anticipation and the pleasure.'*

She changed direction and went to the spa. Having looked what was available she decided they would have a swim, then a private sauna, and then a massage together. They would be naked or near naked all afternoon, but not able to indulge in anything other than touch. She knew she would be ready for her evening plan and thought she would add little treats for him to ensure that he was ready to indulge her desires later. They could even undress each other for both the sauna and the massage. She was looking forward to her dirty, but delectable plan. *'This man wants to send me home?'* she thought, *I'll teach him that love can transcend prejudice. I'm going to treat him so well today, he'll never let me go.'*

She passed through a lounge and decided to sit for a while. There was so much emotional turmoil in her mind. She needed a few minutes on her own to think what she wanted to do. Although she had conceded to his argument earlier, she did not agree with him. *'What did he have to go back to? He may love Jane but there is clearly something missing for him in that relationship to show sadness and loneliness in his life. And Jane hurt him so badly with her betrayal that he has no real trust in her anymore.'*

'Okay, I do love Andy, but we're not happy together. Paul needs me as much as I need him. Is that not an optimal formula for a relationship?

He is much older than me but I'm going to enjoy treating him today to as much foreplay, unadulterated sensuality, and sex as I would any lover, using techniques that he has taught me. I have no visual prejudice towards this man, and I'm well used to prejudice in my life because of the colour of my skin.' 'Everything he used in his argument about colour prejudice is not only correct, but I've dealt with it all my life. So I have to add another layer of prejudice to my life, so what? The love I feel will most certainly overcome.'

The issue she could not rationalise is that of her most certain pregnancy. Over the past few days he had injected so much sperm deep into her that only the absence of an egg could prevent pregnancy. *'He would make an unusually old dad, especially to a son. But Rod Stewart can handle it so why can't he? He's in good shape, and she certainly did not put him at 62 years old before she saw his Who's Who entry.'*

As for her friends, *'what type of friend are they if they cannot accept us as we are? He is a super-intelligent and very experienced man. He could only bring interest to any gathering. So why would we have a problem? In any event we would live closer to London than Edinburgh'*, and she experienced far less prejudice in London than any other place in the UK. London is a multinational, multicultural city with a general acceptance of any flavour of relationship. *'So we live in London which would be great for me in my job.'*

What she did know was that words were not going to win the day. Using words, no matter how well constructed, were not going to win over this teacher of skilful rhetoric. Her only weapon was to get him to feel that he cannot live without her. She must show him that he cannot live happily without her, and that she would be a far happier person with him.

'Okay, he has given me 24 hours to show what I can do. This is going to be a very important time so let's go to it and see what happens. It must be as normal as possible to contrast with our highly sexed days to date. Let me try to show him how good our life would be under a more normal day to day relationship.'

Chapter 72

She had been gone for over half an hour. He was wondering what she was planning as she came bouncing through the door.

'Okay mister get your walking kit on. We're off for a walk, but not here. Let's drive to the village and see where we go from there. Maybe find a nice pub where we can have lunch later.'

He decided to try one of the jackets he bought in Luss selecting a matching shirt and trousers. She was happy with what she was already wearing save for a sweater and shorty coat.

They drove to the village of Auchterarder, found somewhere to park near the High Street.

'So what do you have in store for us today my young nymph?'

'We need some non-sexual exercise to get us limbered up for the evening.'

'Okay' he replied curiously. 'Any other forms of exercise on the agenda?'

'Oh, yes. After our lunch I think we'll go for a swim. I've booked a private sauna for us at 3:30, and then a massage for two at 4:15.'

'No wonder it took you so long. You have been busy.'

'I want us to have a normal Sunday together where we can talk, laugh, play – all the things a normal couple would do on a Sunday. I think we have had enough sex to last for a while, so it will be nice to do something with our clothes on.'

He smiled at her. 'But I prefer you naked.'

'You can have too much of a good thing, my lover' she retorted.

'With you, never' he growled under his breathe.

She smiled back at him. 'It wouldn't cost much to clothe me in your house.'

'Why would I put covers on one so beautiful? It would be like putting a suit on Michelangelo's David.'

'Don't you think clothes can enhance beauty?'

'I'm old school. The woman makes the dress. No amount of fine clothes can turn a poor frame into a beautiful woman. The dress you wore last night does not make you more beautiful, it merely draws one's eye to the beauty inside of it. Look at the way people looked at you last night. You radiated confident beauty. And it wasn't just the men. I felt privileged that I was the one who really did know what was under the covers.'

She held his arm tightly. She wanted to ask him if he could really let that beauty go but chose to heed her own thoughts that she will not win this man with words.

'You say the nicest things to me, and I really appreciate your attention.'

'I don't just say them. I'm not a small talk person. If I take the trouble to speak, I mean it. I was always accused of not complimenting people enough when I managed banks. The current culture expects a compliment for doing something which is expected of them. The contra argument which I use is that if I chose to compliment you then it's from the heart because you have gone the extra mile and exceeded expectations, and thus has value. My staff felt good about themselves if they received a compliment, and would aspire to do even better, and so they grow in confidence and stature. For me that is true management of people.'

'Just like with me. You have encouraged me to aspire to all the things I want to be and given me the confidence and the courage to reach for what I want.'

'Cis, you have been a particularly exceptional student. I want to cry with joy sometimes at what you have achieved in such a short time. You're an extraordinary person and you deserve everything that you desire. All my apprehension about helping you to become pregnant has gone. I'm glad that I can leave you with the child that will bring you and Andy back together, but also remind you of our time together. Our time together will always be precious to me.'

She could feel herself welling inside. *'What is it that compels this man to leave me when it is clear in his words, which certainly do come from his heart, he has no desire for this to end?'* She stopped walking, reached up and kissed him.

'My valiant knight, master, and lover; you are my life. Everything I do or think comes from you. You have given me life, and you have given our child life. I have never felt so loved, cherished and wanted by anyone in my life. I will always live my life as you would expect of me.'

'I have experienced a masterclass in life, and I want more.'

'I would like to give you more, but our time together has already been extended once. I fear that this will not happen again. Perhaps you should send a text message to Andy to check when he intends to return.'

'I'll do it while we are having lunch. What about Jane's return?'

'It wouldn't matter if I were a few days late as she will go straight back to work in London.'

'Okay. A ray of hope', she thought. *'I'll send Andy a text and see if he is still coming home on Tuesday.'*

The High Street was very long for a village and populated with far more shops than you would expect unless you counted the visitor traffic from Gleneagles. Even though it was Sunday all the shops were open as is the norm now in the UK. She found a particularly interesting men's clothing shop. She steered him towards the door 'let's go in and look around to see if there is something that would suit my prince.'

The shop was mainly traditional country clothes, but of a high quality. She already knew his sizes so was quick to scan through the various racks and shelves.

'This is a window shopper's paradise!' She exclaimed. But he was not interested in shopping, so he gently moved her on.

They strolled past a white fronted Tudor building with painted black framed windows. The sign above the door announced the Star Hotel albeit it looked like a former prominent building converted into a pub. They decided this was as good as any for lunch so went in. He went to the bar and asked about lunch. He was directed to a cluster of tables and told to find an empty one and someone would be along to take their order. He found a leaflet, obviously for the hotel guests, informing them about the history of this town.

He told her that Auchterarder is known locally as The Lang Toon - a name derived from its extended High Street. Today, little of the original Burgh of 1200 remains. Indeed, the town dates largely from the 18th Century and is now famous for the quality of its shops.

In the Middle Ages, Auchterarder was known in Europe as 'the town of 100 drawbridges', a colourful description of the narrow bridges leading from the road level across wide gutters to the doorsteps of houses.

Once they had ordered lunch she turned to her phone, and whilst praying that Andy would be delayed again, tapped out a text message to him asking when he would return. It only took a couple of minutes before the response came back. Cis looked at the message and her spirits dropped. Her prayers had not been answered. Her guardian angel obviously thought that her job was now done; time to go home. She looked at him, 'no change, he will be back on Tuesday evening.'

He could see the disappointment in her face. 'We will always have this past week, so don't be sad. Also, you will have some time to readjust your magazine-style house to create your new nest. Put into practise what you have learnt. Tomorrow is the start of a new adventure giving our child a happy home and a good future. I'll watch your progress with great interest.'

'If you're trying to cheer me up you are not doing so good.'

'Cis, stay in the now. We still have some time together so let us not waste it dwelling on tomorrow. You have your plans for us today, and I'm very much looking forward to see what surprises you have in store for me.'

'Okay, my master. I'll give you something to remember this day.'

Their food arrived which cut the conversation for a few minutes. He was reflecting how difficult it will be tomorrow to let her go. But he still could not find a sensible reason to keep her. He knew that she would go to the ends of the world with him and not care what anyone thought. Without a young child this would be possible, but not with a baby in arms. *'Life is such a bitch,'* he thought.

Chapter 73

The changing cubicles were mixed so they found an empty one in the middle of a group of empty ones. She wanted her usual dress/undress routine with maybe a little fun, but not an audience. Once inside she took her bikini out of the bag of things they had brought for the afternoon into the spa and put it on the bench seat. She stood waiting to be undressed. He saw what she wanted and removed her top to reveal those wonderful pert breasts with nipples fully extended. 'And what thoughts are going through your head young lady?' he whispered.

'They always do that when they know you're near, and ready to expose them.'

He reached down and kissed both nipples. 'Does that feel better?'

'Only for now.'

He picked up her bikini top and slid the straps along her arms, turned her around, cupped her breasts with the bra cups, and moved his hand around along the straps until he could clasp them shut. He turned her again, adjusted her breasts within the bikini cups until she looked perfect. 'How's that?'

'Very good considering how little practise you've had this week.' She giggled.

He sat on the bench and removed her slacks, and then used his normal ritual to remove her panties. He would really miss this part of their time together. He slowly slid on her bikini bottoms taking extra time to ensure that they were seated properly. He wanted her to get back totally into their playtime together so that they could really enjoy the little time they had left together.

Before she started to undress him, she put her hands along his crotch to find the expected erection. 'Hmmm, can't let you out there with that. You'll scare everyone away.'

'What do you propose, dear lady?'

'We'll undress you first, and then see what we can do to coil the snake back to sleep.'

She slowly undressed him until he was completely naked. His erection had already started to subside, so she put on his trunks and tucked his penis down telling it to go to sleep for a while. She gathered up their clothes, grabbed a towel each and off they went to the pool.

He was in the pool first as he wanted to get in a few lengths before the inevitable playtime would occur. She came speeding past him halfway along the length of the pool. *'She's a good swimmer'*, he thought as he tried to catch up with her.

After 3 lengths he stopped. He noted that there were only a few people swimming this afternoon so plenty of room to play, but what would she try?

She came storming towards him, only pulling up as she was right in front of him. He was using the rail to support himself as the water was 2m deep where they were. She had a big, naughty smile on her face.

Stephen Box

'What is that naughty grin about? What are you thinking my gorgeous nymph?'

'I was remembering your story in the pool when you had sex. There's a rail here. Maybe we should try to copy that day and see if anyone notices.'

'There was a lot going on in that pool, with diving, jumping and splashing to avert attention. Not a lot happening here until you start bouncing up and down as you get your rhythm, so you'll get attention. Would you like me to prepare you?'

She came in close, and he felt her hand go inside his trunks taking hold of his penis as she kissed him. Then she whispered in his ear 'I want you to stroke my pussy all the way so that I can feel what it is like to orgasm in the water.'

Chapter 74

When they arrived at the sauna there was an outer compartment with a door so that the user could hang their robe before entering the sauna. There was a latch on this outer door which he dropped. He whipped off her towel as she moved into the sauna itself and hung it with her robe.

When he got into the sauna she was already splayed out across a bench ensuring that he got a good view of all she could display. She had not given up on keeping this man and would take every opportunity to ensure he knew what he was giving up.

He was happy with her determination as she would certainly apply it to ensuring success with Andy, and the happy upbringing of their child. She'll be a wonderful mother. He scooped her up and positioned her so that she was laying in his arms. She snuggled in with a cheeky smile until the heat made this connection uncomfortable after which she sat next to him gently nudging his shoulder in a playful way. Nothing needed to be said.

Chapter 75

They made their way to the massage room for two. She turned to him teasingly, 'would you like the male masseur to massage my breasts, and for the female masseur to massage your erection, or shall we play it safe?'

'Do you think that he can massage you breasts as well as I can, or she massage my erection better than you can?'

'No-one can stroke my breasts like you can.'

'Then I propose we use this massage to limber up for us to massage each other later. You take the lady masseur, and I'll take the male. We look into each other's eyes and imagine what will be later.'

'Shhh, my juices are starting to flow just thinking about it.'

'I thought that you said no sex today. Aren't you sexed-out?'

'I didn't say anything about no playtime. A little flirt here, a little foreplay there, should be part of our daily routine. Have I remembered well, my master?'

The lady masseur appeared with shorts for both and said that she and her colleague would be back in a few minutes. They disrobed and got into their shorts.

The massage tables were end-to-end, so she got onto one table face down, He put a towel across her, and then got onto his table facing her. They gazed into each other's eyes like two lovers waiting to see who would get the giggles first. He decided to stare her out, but she crossed her eyes, stuck out her tongue and rotated it. He could not hold his stare at this sight so settled for a loving smile. She stopped her funny face, smiled back and gave him a couple of air kisses.

The masseurs arrived. The woman went to Cis and adjusted her towel asking her if there was any particular area she wanted to focus on or just a normal all-over massage. She went for the latter, as did Paul.

Paul's idea of a massage is to just switch off and let the masseur get on with it. He certainly did not like masseurs who wanted to chat throughout. Spend the time chatting with Cis did not appeal either. This needed to be a quiet time so told her he just wanted to look at her. She was at peace with this idea. She wanted him to fix her on his memory so that he knew where he belonged – with her.

When the masseurs had finished and left the room telling them just to relax for 20 minutes before dressing and leaving, Paul got up from his table and moved over to her. He lifted the towel from her, removed her shorts and asked her to rollover onto her front.

'Now where is he going?' she thought.

He started to massage her buttocks. She looked back at him and smiled. 'They missed some parts, he quipped, 'just can't get the staff these days.'

'He always knows how to add that extra touch that makes all the difference', she thought.

When he'd finished he asked her to turn over and gently massaged her breasts until her nipples were totally extended, at which point he kissed each nipple whilst massaging her pussy establishing that he could take her there and then if he wanted.

'Have I missed anywhere my princess? Please point if you require any further attention.'

She sat up, kissed him, 'I want much more, but not here, or now my lover. Let us go back to our room.'

They dressed and departed the spa.

Chapter 76

When they got back to their suite, she dropped her bag, kicked off her shoes, and went straight to the bed and lay down. She

Prejudice in Love

did not want to get undressed as she felt like sex after his special massage attention but wanted to wait until her big show later. He looked at her. 'What next my princess?'

'A little chill would be nice with my lover. We have an hour before we need to get ready for dinner.'

'She's still dressed' he thought, so he just kicked off his shoes and lay next to her. She immediately cuddled up to him and wrapped her arm around him. He knew this Cis, so he turned part way towards her, gathered her in close, and folded his arms around her. She settled indicating that she was where she wanted to be, and they both fell silent, lost in their own thoughts, but living in the warmth and safety of each other.

She was thinking through the detail of her plans for dinner. She wanted this to be a night for him to remember, and an outrageous demonstration of her newfound sensual freedom. Timing will be everything, and her props needed to be exactly where she needed them so that she could get a flow without the need to find anything. He had given her a wonderful night last night. She wanted to do the same for him. Her mind would study every detail of the plan and hope to God that the food is exactly as she had ordered. They did look at her with some disbelief, but she insisted that they do exactly as she wanted.

He was trying to work out the best way to close out this fantastic week after lunch tomorrow. He had to be strong for her although he would feel gutted inside. At his age in life holding back emotions was not as easy as it was in his younger days. He never used to cry or even well up just 20 years ago, but now it happened often, even just looking at something extraordinarily beautiful. And she was an extraordinary beauty who would certainly shed a few tears when they said their goodbyes. *'Probably better to say goodbye in the car in the car park after lunch before taking her home. Must note to get a parking space as private as possible so she could shed her tears in peace, and I can hold her as long as it takes to settle her into the idea of going home.'*

When he finally surfaced from his thoughts, he noticed it was a little after 6 o'clock. She was still peaceful. He leaned over and kissed her on the forehead. She looked up at him. 'It's after 6 o'clock. What time did you order dinner?'

'We should start to get ourselves together because I want you to wash my hair for me. If you'll undress me, I'll go get the shower ready.'

They got up and he lovingly undressed her. She was still a little relaxed so was putty in his hands as he removed her clothes. Once undressed she kissed him on the cheek and was off to the bathroom. He got undressed and followed her.

She was already standing under the shower getting her hair fully soaked. He joined her and picked up her shampoo ready to run his shampooed fingers through her lovely hair. She made it known that she really enjoyed being pampered in this way, and he did not rush the movement of his fingers through her hair, especially when he was close to her scalp which he massaged as he shampooed.

After her hair was rinsed he started to cleanse her body with oodles of gel to increase the feeling. She clearly was not in a hurry so again he pampered her, paying particular attention to the parts of her body that craved his attention, not least her breasts. She thought this is like making love, rather than sex, and she felt so exhilarated by his gentle touch.

When he indicated that he had finished she kicked into a different gear and started on him, including a hair wash. Everything from now must be perfect, and part of the build to her ultimate climax with her lover later that evening. They had avoided sex all day so tonight could be special.

After they had towelled each other she told him to go relax while she prepares herself, but to tell her when it is 7:15.

Chapter 77

She had organised for dinner to arrive at 7:30. At 7:15 they were both still naked from their shower together, but she had already applied the makeup she needed for the evening and inserted the large earrings she wore which he so liked.

She asked him to dress only in his kilt and waistcoat but stay in the bedroom until she tells him she is ready to serve dinner. He had some email traffic to attend to, and he needed to check his hotel reservation in Edinburgh on Monday night, so was otherwise engaged in any event.

She slipped into her shimmer dress from the night before. *'He likes this dress, not least for how easily he can slip me out of it.'* She prepared the dining table and set the lighting she wanted. His iPod was sitting on the hi fi system, so she selected one of his many playlists that indicated nearly 2 hours of play time.

A knock on the door. The food had arrived. She examined the content with great care to ensure that her instructions had been correctly executed, including the additional table décor she wanted. It was all good. She asked the porter to leave the trolley, gave him a good tip telling him she would leave the trolley outside of the door before they retired for the night. As he left she switched on the 'Do Not Disturb' sign.

She dispensed part of her dessert menu to the fridge, put the remainder out of sight, put her cooked items on a warmer, and set about preparing the table. Even the four chairs needed to be arranged to achieve her objective.

She had agreed with the hotel reception that this dinner be put on a separate bill for her, along with her photographs, so she could indulge her lover without abusing his wallet. She felt that this was the least she could after all he'd done for her although he's clearly not concerned about the cost of this trip.

She ordered a bottle of their best Gevrey Chambertin wine as she remembered him saying that he was introduced to this wine whilst in Scotland, and it had become one of his favourite burgundy wines. The champagne delivered that morning was now in an ice bucket, and the wine had been opened to let it breathe.

Everything was good. Her meal, which was a shared board of vegetables and special meats with a series of different dips, was in position. She wanted a shared menu so that they could feed each other with their fingers. They would have to sit next to each other which would disguise the unusual chair layout.

She poured two glasses of champagne and went back to her lover who was still pouring over his iPad. He had dressed as instructed. She thought there was something missing, so she put down the drinks and went to the dresser to find his bow tie. She went back to him and expertly put it around his neck without any fuss. She sat next to him. He closed his iPad and put it on the dresser.

She handed him his drink.

'Are you ready my gorgeous lady?'

'For you I'm always ready' she seductively responded. She lightly kissed him.

'My darling Paul. As this is our last evening together, I would like to say what a joy and experience it has been to know you. My love for you is greater than any love I've known and will never die. You will always be in my heart. I want to toast the man who saved my life and answered my dreams. To you, my darling.'

They clinked glasses and drank.

'Thank you for your kind words my damsel in distress, my princess. Believe me you have revitalised a derelict wondering what life was all about now he's not in the thick of his career. You have brought so much joy to me over these past days, and you will always be in my heart. To hope that you will succeed is not appropriate because I have no doubt in my mind you will. I wish you every happiness for the future, and great love in your new life with Andy and our child.'

They clinked glasses again and drank albeit, tears were welling in her eyes. The emotion of the occasion was starting to get to her, but she must hold herself together. She wanted to show her lover how much she had learnt from him, with a few added touches of her own using her new-found liberty of sensual expression.

She decided one more glass of champagne before dinner to give her time to compose herself for the brazen nature of what she had planned. She went to collect the bottle and filled their glasses. 'One more glass my love and everything will be ready.'

After they emptied their glasses she stood up, reached for his hand. 'Shall we?'

She sat him where she wanted him, and then sat directly next to him on his right-hand side. She filled their glasses with the Gevrey Chambertin. Paul looked at the bottle. 'You have been busy, and your attention to detail is impressive.' He kissed her hand in appreciation.

'Thank you, kind sir. We're going to feed each other.'

He noticed that there were no knives and forks at the table, no cutlery at all.

She noticed that he had realised the omission. We eat with our fingers tonight. We're lovers feeding each other with all the nourishment required to satisfy all our needs.

She recovered the three dishes of suckling pig, shredded duck, dried lamb with their sauces and put them on the table with the salad dishes.

'And what would my beautiful lover like to eat?' he asked.

'You decide how and what you feed me. Whatever you choose will be delicious served from your fingers.'

Paul thought about what was happening here. *'She's playing the archetype seductress. I love it.'*

He dipped his finger into one of the dips and presented it to her mouth. She took his finger into her mouth without losing eye contact, and seductively licked the content from his finger holding it between her teeth until she had licked it clean.

'OK Cis, let's have some fun', he thought. He picked up a piece of celery that had been filled with cream cheese. He put it halfway into his mouth, and then moved his lips towards hers. She realised what he wanted her to do and moved her lips over the exposed end of the celery until their lips touched, and then she bit off her piece and moved away to chew it.

Cis had realised that he wanted to kiss her, but it's too early in her plan to engage in such intimacy. She wanted much more playfulness first. His kilt would let her know when he was starting to get aroused.

She took a slice of carpaccio, rolled it, dipped it into an avocado moose and then moved it towards his lips. He opened his mouth expectantly. She put it into his mouth allowing her fingers to go with it. He closed his lips around her fingers and sucked in the contents slowly releasing her fingers.

They continued to feed each other using sensual flirting to keep it interesting.

She decided to home in on another plan of hers to get him to see himself living with her in the future. 'My darling Paul tell me more about sacrificing me to the gods. Where and how would you prefer to do this if we had the time and could travel together?'

'Somewhere warm where you never need more than two pieces of clothing. Probably the Caribbean would be my first choice.'

'Any particular island or place you have in mind?' as she prepared him another delicious bite-sized pancake full of tasty duck.

'I know St Lucia very well and have an ambition to retire there some day. All year-round temperatures between 22°C and 28°C, and sea breezes off the Atlantic to keep the humidity under control. I would like to buy one of the old banana plantations and build something very special there.'

'Would you take me there?'

'Do you think Andy would let you come with me?'

'If you invite me, I'll ask him.'

'Okay, I will happily invite you. Let me know when you can make it.'

'How about for the rest of our lives?'

'Hey, don't spoil such a wonderful evening.'

'You have made you choice to have a child. My choice is to use the remaining time I have of relatively good health and fitness to travel to some of the places I have yet to see, and to return to others that I never had the time to see properly. I'm talking about the Andes from Bolivia down to Peru, across to Argentina, and up to southern Brazil. I know much of the north of Brazil, but I've never journeyed south of Sao Paulo. Then there is South East Asia where I would like to travel through Vietnam, and then maybe north-east China. These are all long trips with no end dates and not suitable for a young baby. I can't afford to wait for a few years until a child could travel. In any event by the time they could travel they would be at school, so yet another restriction. Thus my definition this morning that we love each other for different reasons. I would love you as a travel companion, and you would love me as a father to your child.'

'The trouble with people of your generation is you follow the Queen creed of……' Paul began to sing, emulating the actions of Freddie Mercury:

'I want it all,

I want it all,

I want it all,

And I want it now.'

Cis enjoyed this new side of him. 'Now he's a rock singer' she laughed.

'Ah, but you see I'm from a different generation and I follow the creed of the Rolling Stones from their album "Let It Bleed"'

Again, he sings:

'You can't always get what you want,

You can't always get what you want,

You can't always get what you want,

But if you try,

Sometimes you'll find,

You'll get what you need.'

'So you see my darling Cis,' as he stroked her cheek, 'neither of us gets what we want out of this encounter, but we most certainly get what we need. You have your child and a new way of life, and I, a new lease on life from you. Not bad for 7 days of fun.'

He kissed her gently. 'Be happy my beautiful Cis. We had it all for 7 wonderful days and nights, and we got what we needed.'

He fed her again with suckling pig dipped in plum sauce, letting her bite off half of it and then eating the remainder himself. He then fed her a sip of wine to wash it down. He decided to become very attentive and loving to get her back into her seductive mood.

He dipped a piece of pork in more plum sauce, but accidentally on purpose wiped it on her nose, and then reached over to use his mouth to take it from her nose, moving his lips down to meet hers with a loving embrace. She responded with no urgency to lose the taste of his saucy lips massaging her lips.

'Hmmm, that was nice. Do you think you can put more sauces on your lips and let me kiss it from you?'

He used his finger to scoop more sauce. He coated his lips and put the remainder on the end of his tongue. They then moved together until their lips met and tongues intertwined to remove the sauce from lips and tongue. This was a longing embrace. He could feel her building towards more intense activity.

She sensed it was time to move to the desert. She moved everything from the table except for their wine glasses and wiped it clean. She then put a dish of fruits on the edge of the table, a bowl of clotted cream, and a dish of clear honey. He looked on in wonder of where this was going.

She stood up, slipped the dress straps from her shoulder, and seductively let the dress drop slowly to the floor. She then stepped onto the chair she had used to feed him, stepped her leg over to the chair on the other side of Paul so that her pussy was in his face, and then sat on the table in front of him.

She picked up the clotted cream, scooped out four fingers of cream and spread it over her naked mound. She lay back on her elbows, took another scoop and covered her tummy. She then lay flat on the table and coated the top of her breasts and nipples with a mound of cream.

'Please dress me with honey on the cream, and then the fruit in that bowl.'

Paul stood up and moved his chair away so that he could move to the side of her. He used his fingers to dribble honey over the cream on her body, and then proceeded to dress these areas in strawberries, raspberries, and blueberries finishing with a raspberry over the nipple on each breast.

'Now my darling I want you to feed us both with desert using only your mouth, starting with my tummy, and then my breasts, but not my pussy.'

Her head was only half on the table so she could turn her head to meet his lips without the risk of choking her.

He reached down to kiss her. 'This is really great. I would never have expected such a delicious desert.'

'Feed me my darling.'

He reached down onto her tummy using his tongue to scoop the cream from her skin including a piece of fruit and moved to her mouth.

He reached down until he had covered her mouth with his and they shared the fruit between them licking the cream from each other. He continued with this until all the fruit on her tummy had been eaten.

He then moved to her breasts where he sucked the raspberry and cream into his mouth and fed her with it. He went back to the same breast and slowly sucked and licked it dry ensuring that her pert nipple received much attention. This had her purring. He moved to her other breast, and with one large suck, took the raspberry, cream and her pert nipple into his mouth extending her breast, and held it there. She arched her back in delight at the sensations flowing through her body. He slowly let her nipple retreat whilst he devoured the raspberry and cream, and then licked all the remaining cream from her breast.

'Did I do well my darling?' he said with a wry smile.

'Hmmm, you did very well, but now for the final test of how well you can feed me. Please remove your kilt.'

He quickly unstrapped his kilt and threw it onto the nearby couch. His erection was full and ready.

'Now go to my pussy and using only your willy, feed me the remainder of the fruit. When I have removed it from your willy then we will kiss to share the fruits of your labour.'

'What a lady' he thought. *'She is certainly into this game, and what a player.'*

He carefully loaded the top of his erection with cream and fruit and presented it to her mouth. She slowly and sensually took the content from him with her tongue and then invited him to join lips and share the spoils. He would have no problem maintaining an erection during this game.

He did this twice more, clearing the fruit. After the second of these she took his willy into her mouth and gently licked it clean. He stroked her breasts lovingly as she performed her magic on him.

'Now my darling I would like you to clear the remaining cream and honey on my pussy with your tongue and prepare me.'

'She deserves a treat for this wonderful evening' he thought so set a chair in front of her exposed pussy and started to stroke her pussy with his tongue moving slowly but surely to her clitoris. He would build her slowly, then move his tongue around her honeypot before she could orgasm, and then move back to build her again. She arched her back to push herself into his face completely drowning in this pleasure. He lifted her close to orgasm twice before taking her all the way to an explosive orgasm which jolted her hips as she let out a cry of joy as the spasms washed through her body.

He watched her body spasm in delight, and a look into her eyes showed that she was lost in her pleasure. He scoped her up and took her to their bed, wrapped his hand around her buttock and slipped deep into her. She opened her eyes beaming love at him as he started the motion that would relieve his throbbing erection and bring her to another fulfilling orgasm which would leave them both spent, closing yet another adventure that would engulf them as one, in perfect harmony with each other.

Both spent, they wrapped around each other and savoured their satisfaction and pleasure at such a wonderful evening together.

Chapter 78 - Monday

When Cis opened her eyes Paul was lying on his back, deep in thought, looking at the ceiling. Lying on the upper part of his chest she could hear his heartbeat was not at rest so assumed that his mind was wrestling with something. She waited a few moments and then whispered 'a penny for your thoughts'.

This brought him out of his solace as he looked at her. 'Good morning my angel' and kissed her on the forehead.

'You were deep in thought. Can you tell me what you're thinking?'

'My mind is wrestling with the fact that I have to let you go today.'

'You don't **have** to do any such thing if you don't want to. You ask me to stay and I have no reservations about spending my life with you.'

'That's the problem. I want to keep you, you want to stay, but my better, more rational judgement tells me that it cannot be. Sure, in the short-term we could be very good for each other, but you have cells inside your womb that are multiplying as we speak which means that the most important consideration here is the child that you want to bring into this world. You believe that we may be strong enough to deal with all the prejudices that we would face as a couple, but what about a child? Believe me Cis, I've now battled for days trying to find the right solution for all parties involved, trying to find a way in which we can stay together, but I haven't yet succeeded.'

She raised her head so that she was now looking at him. 'Paul don't you think you're trying to apply a perfect scenario to an imperfect human relationship. Since when has emotion been rational? Things happen to humans every day which are not rational, but life goes on and we muddle through.'

'But I don't consider muddle through as acceptable. I've had enough heartache and prejudice with my existing children, and they've also suffered the consequences of poor judgement on my part. This time I must give our child the best chance of a happy childhood and, as much as I would dearly like to be part of our child's future, I don't fit into the best chance scenario.'

Prejudice in Love

'What about if I'm not pregnant? What about if it's me that's infertile? What would you say then?'

'That would be a more interesting scenario.' He moved his hands to her ribs and started to playfully tickle her. 'Then I could ravish you all day, every day, in the safety of knowing that a child would not be part of our thinking.' She was laughing as she fought to stop him from tickling her.

He held her so that he was looking into her eyes. 'My instinct tells me that you are very fertile. So fertile that even an aged guy like me can make you pregnant. And I believe that you are pregnant with our child. This was your desire from the beginning when we first met, and your guardian angel has delivered for you.'

'If I could find a scenario which had a good chance of success for our child between now and when I leave for home tomorrow, I'll be back for you. Maybe in the cold light of dawn tomorrow, when you're not in my arms, my loneliness may trigger an acceptable solution in which case I'll act on it. But until then I must let you go, and you must accept my judgement, not only because I've been right for you so far, but also because you should by now understand my pain at this decision and respect that my consideration is for you and our child.'

'That's not fair. You're using emotional blackmail to argue your case.'

'Call it emotional blackmail if you wish, but I call it pragmatism, and I would ask that you respect my view on this. You came to me to give you a child on the basis that you would go back to Andrew and nurture our child in a loving family home with you and Andrew. If I cannot persuade myself otherwise, then I must hold you to your commitment to me. You cannot change the rules without my agreement.'

She knew that this could lead to their first major argument, and she could not argue with this man. She did commit as he stated. If he cannot be persuaded to change his mind, then she would have to go home to Andrew. She was not remotely successful so far. 'This is not a good way to start our last day my darling, so I'll comply with your wishes in the hope that my valiant knight will find a way for us to stay together.'

'That's better my lovely damsel. You can be assured that my mind is working on it.'

She moved her upper body onto his chest so that she could kiss him. He wrapped his arms around her. She went in for a longer, tender kiss feeling the warmth of the togetherness between them. They were soon lost in the love between them.

She whispered in his ear 'What would you like us to do this morning?'

He whispered back to her 'I seem to remember that you were directing these remaining hours. What would you like to do?'

'I want us to stay wrapped in each other's arms for as long as possible, then a long shower together, before a late breakfast. Then we can work on the remaining time together at breakfast. I've thought of a nice restaurant for lunch. It's on the outskirts of Edinburgh, about 15 – 20 minutes from my house. It's nice, quiet, and discrete so we can say our goodbyes.'

'But until then I want some fun, not with toys, just us.'

He started to stoke her body in arousal mode. 'Okay lady, let's see what we can do.'

She felt his hands, those wonderful hands, starting to work their magic on her body. It would not take long to get her into a different place in her mind. She used her left hand to stroke his body moving further down his torso on each stroke slowly, but surely, in autopilot as her body reacted to his strokes.

She found her hand in his groin stroking a penis which had just been awakened and was slowly starting to respond to the sensations caused by her gentle teasing. She could feel the firmness grow as his erection developed. *'Hmmm, this is nice'* she thought.

He liked her auto-response to his stroking and wondered whether her juices were yet in full flow. He whispered in her ear 'does your pussy need feeding?'

She purred back without moving 'whenever you like.'

'Okay my brazen hussy, mount me. When you're mounted, I want you to put your feet at the side of my ribcage.'

She complied with his bidding lowering herself onto his now full erection and sliding her feet forward so that her full weight was centred at the pelvic point above his penis and her vagina.

'Wow, I can feel you deep inside me.'

'He bent his legs so that his knees were at the side of her. 'Rest your elbows on my knees just enough so you can rotate your pelvis without losing contact with me.'

'Don't you mean massage my clit' as she looked at him with a big smile on her face.

'I mean have some unabashed fun. Take yourself where you want to be.'

She did not need to hear this bidding more than once. She had already found the angle and contact which hit the mark with her, and she was on her way to the land of ecstasy. Her body was in a wayward rhythmic rotation as she purred her way to joy. He could feel the build as he watched her body tense and start to spasm. Her head was sloped backwards as she applied more pressure onto the pelvic connection between them. Suddenly there was a jolt of her body, and a gasp of delight as her orgasm hit its crescendo. She was not finished. She lifted herself and gave one last crash of her clit against his pelvis as her involuntary cry of 'aaaarh' came from her throat. She tried to clench her knees together as she sat still, fully penetrated as the waves of orgasm washed over her.

After about 30 seconds she looked at him with somewhat glazed eyes.

His next bidding took her by surprise, but as usual she responded. 'Move your feet back to a squat position, lift yourself about an inch off my pelvis, and use the muscles in your loins to massage my erection.'

He could feel her muscles caressing his penis as she gently rotated her thighs. This is what he needed in addition to the wonderful visual of her beautiful body, and those sensual breasts standing to attention for him, nipples fully extended.

'Now put your hands on my knees and start to do squats as you would in a gym. Rise to the head of my erection and lower all the way down to full penetration.'

She started to rise and fall. He could feel his erection now fully regained after its temporary loss of fullness as she rested after her orgasm. The sight of her pussy rising from his erection, and then being totally swallowed by her on the down stroke, coupled with her breasts thrusting at him on each rise, generated such desire in him for this woman, this vision.

'Now Cis, I want you to find the angle and rhythm that feels good for you, and then hold my erection tight with your pelvic muscles as though sucking me in on the down stroke and resisting exit on the up-stroke.'

She was in autopilot as she obeyed his instructions, feeling the pleasure she was experiencing. He could feel the effect on his penis as she gripped him, and the sensations started to arouse him. He could feel her making small adjustments to her angle of penetration, no doubt to maximise her pleasure.

She upped the tempo of her squats and he could feel his orgasm starting to build.

Breathing hard, she suddenly gasped 'tell me when you're ready.'

Paul could feel the spasm needed for ejaculation building in his loins. He was there. 'Now.'

She came crashing down with her clit in direct contact with his pelvis and gasped as the impact caused her orgasm to erupt as he ejaculated deep into her. She could not hold her knees in this position so collapsed into a kneeling position as the waves of this second orgasm washed over her whole being. Her head was now hanging down, gasping for breath, and her hands were on his chest supporting herself.

Neither of them moved as they both enjoyed the sensations running through their bodies.

She looked up at him 'what are you doing to me you lovely man? The spasms in my leg muscles suggest I've just had a workout, but the rest of my body tells me that this was no gym workout. I feel full of desire, but I'm exhausted.'

'Come lie with me and get your breath back.'

She rolled off him and collapsed into his arms by his side.

'You did real good, really great.'

After some minutes she looked up at him 'I sensed that there was some motive to what we just did. What was it?'

'I have two strong messages from you regarding your sex life. One is the absence of orgasms with Andy, and the other your seeming reluctance to create your own fun when engaged in sex. On our first morning together you, what did you call it, you jumped me. You enjoyed yourself and brought yourself to orgasm, and then you were happy to just jump off without any regard for me. I accept that you were somewhat in need of sexual activity, and thus your selfishness. This activity was in near total darkness so was this just another anonymous hand in the night? Could you have fun in broad daylight when the provider of the erection can watch you in action?'

'So this morning we have dealt with a number of issues that show me that you can satisfy both of the observations, and you have shown me that you're not afraid to enjoy yourself when being watched by your lover.'

'If you can't achieve orgasm during conventional intercourse with Andy, change your position. If you mount him, take your pleasure, and then give him his pleasure, he won't complain because he gets his jollies without any of the effort.' 'Watching you in action was really sensual and helped me to keep my erection. And you could get a bonus in the form of an additional orgasm, as you did this morning.'

'You only have to remember that inactivity, whilst fully penetrated, can have a detrimental impact on an erection, especially if your pussy is hot. You must maintain activity that holds the erection. After your first orgasm lift off a little to give your now sensitive clitoris a rest but keep his penis active. If necessary, lift off and use your hand to stiffen him again. Also using squats is generally more likely to bring him to orgasm than movement from a kneeling position unless you have very good muscle control in your abdomen. Squats are also very good for muscle tone without going to the gym, and far greater fun. Does this make sense to you?'

She just looked at him for a few moments in disbelief. 'How do you know this, when I have never even considered it? It's so simple when you think about it.' She paused and then looked at him again 'We are on our final day. How much more do you need to teach me, and how long would it take?'

He smiled at her 'If I had a free hand with you, I would take you to an isolated villa on the seashore where the sun always shines, for at least 2 weeks. We would shop for ourselves, and take care of ourselves – no staff, no cleaners, no-one else. There would be no clocks, no structure, no telephones or TV. We would eat, sleep, and enjoy as we pleased, and when we pleased. Only then could I teach you how to be totally at one with each other.'

'Our time together has given you the basics plus what you need to get your marriage back together. But there is much more to explore, and you must do this with someone with whom you feel totally committed in a loving relationship. Much of the sex you now have, but there is so much more to a great relationship. You know that you are at peace with someone when you are together in the same space, but you feel very content with long silences.'

Prejudice in Love

As she was absorbing what he was saying, and the loving way in which he expressed himself, there was a voice inside her head screaming at him to take her away with him and show her how to live such a relationship. She was now really questioning whether the desire for a child was worth losing what this man can give her.

'I would love to take such a trip with you, but it sounds like you would only take someone with you as a final test of your love for each other. You come back either committed to each other thereafter, or not.'

'Interesting observation. I guess you're right. If we went on such a trip it would either cement our love for each other or awaken us to another reality.'

She decided to change the subject. 'Do you have any other last-minute treats for me before we leave?'

'I've not planned any. I only thought of what we did this morning whilst I was thinking over our initial time together. As I've told you before, I can only build a schedule of activities based on what you tell me about your needs. I want to give you everything that I think will help you in your quest with Andy. I need you to be successful for the sake of our child.'

She reached over and kissed him. So much love has passed between them. 'What about our long shower together?'

'That would be nice.'

Chapter 79

Their shower that morning really was a lengthy affair. There was much teasing, sensual pleasure, and togetherness punctuated by long lingering kisses under the showerhead. She wanted to drown in the love of this man, so the water had the effect of completely shutting out any other aspect of the world outside of their embrace. There was so much more she wanted from this liaison, and she was devastated that their time together was nearly over. What was she going to do without his wonderful hands playing magical tunes on her body? Could she ever feel like this with Andy?

When he dressed her for breakfast, she alerted him that these clothes were not for their departure; any of them. She expected to be completely undressed, and then dressed again, including a little farewell pampering that would be difficult in a public place.

Breakfast was more solemn than normal with Paul trying his best to keep her focussed on her new life with their child. He explained to her that, by his calculations, it will be Christmas before she would know for sure about the sustainability of her pregnancy, and probably New Year before the scan that would reveal the gender. Did she want to know the gender of her child before birth? She did, so that she could plan an appropriate nursery.

Did she have any views on the education for their child? She did not want a religious denominated school, and definitely not a boarding school. She wanted her child to be close to her so that she could give and feel the love that they had shared these past 7 days. In any event Edinburgh had very good public schools close to where they lived. She would also teach their child many of the philosophies that Paul had taught her, or that she would learn during her future studies under his instruction. She wanted their child to grow up in his image.

He tried to reassure her that when she had her new-born child in her arms all thoughts of the alternate lust for him would be put to the back of her mind. She had wanted this child so desperately now for over two years, and now she was in reach of her dream. Her guardian angel had responded to her despair.

Walking back to their apartment she wanted to talk about future contact with him. He told her that he would be there for her if needed. He would very much like to see his child during its first year, if possible, so that the child would not have any recollections of meeting him. He certainly would like to keep some sort of record of their child's development, if only the occasional picture. She assured him that she had a good friend who was very good with the internet. She would set up a site just for him and would text him the access codes once it was in place. She would also leave messages for him. She would not write letters just in case of intercept by Jane but would text him with news.

There was a finality about these discussions which was starting to depress her. She had never felt love like this before for anyone. She felt wanted and loved but now she had to give it up. *'Life's so cruel.'* Paul reminded her that it is better to have been loved and lost, rather than never having been loved. She now knew how it felt, so go make it happen with Andy. They obviously loved each other, so now mould Andy to her way of thinking; her new way of thinking. Take control of your life and live it to the full.

Chapter 80

Preparing to leave was a very quiet affair. He gave her the toys that he'd bought. Trying to make lite of the situation she held the largest of the vibrators 'I still can't believe how easily you slipped this into me. I don't think I would dare let anyone else even try.'

He smiled 'When you trust someone enough you can achieve beyond your dreams. They would not make them if they were too large, or even dangerous. Anyone who can get your juices flowing properly can use these.'

'I don't think anyone will ever achieve what you can with my juices. I've never experienced anything like it before and cannot imagine anyone taking your place. You are my one, and only true love. Anyone else will be a poor substitute.'

They went to the hotel reception to take care of their respective bills. Paul noticed that there were no charges for the Michaelmas Ball, but there was an envelope with his hand-written name on the front. He opened the envelope to find a note. It was from Seumas McCulloch. It read:

Dear Paul,

It was a delight to meet you and your wife on Saturday evening. My guests thoroughly enjoyed your company. As I had already booked the whole table for the evening I have decided that you both were my honoured guests so have asked the hotel to leave the charge on my bill.

If you are ever in this part of the world again we would be delighted for you both to visit with us. Have a safe trip home.

Best wishes to you both,

Seumas McCulloch

He handed the note to Cis. 'Darling, it's from Seumas McCulloch. He invited us to dinner on Saturday evening.'

She read the note. 'What a lovely man. We must send him a thank you note before we leave.'

The receptionist told them that Mr McCullock would be in during the afternoon, so we could leave a note for him at reception. He secured writing paper and they went to the reception seating area to write a note. Cis added her own note that she wanted Seumas to thank Duncan for the lovely flowers and champagne. She wanted Seumas to know that Duncan had made amends just in case he did not already know.

They gave the note to the receptionist, and they were on their way to Edinburgh.

Chapter 81

The place that Cis had chosen for lunch was a small country hotel north of the Forth Road Bridge on the outskirts of Inverkeithing. Paul parked in a secluded part of the car park.

He quickly got out of the car and went around to open the door for Cis who had been locked in her thoughts of the sadness she felt that today may be the last she has with him.

He could sense this and was keen that events kept moving to prevent any dwelling on what he still felt could not be. He led her to the restaurant door where he quickly arranged a table by a window. As it was a weekday lunchtime the restaurant was not that busy and thus there were no people at adjacent tables. They ordered food, and he tried to engage her to snap her out of her sadness. 'We're not at a funeral. Indeed, one way or another we're on our way to a rebirth for both of us. Our story is not ending; it has just started for both of us.'

This profound piece of philosophy did capture her attention. She looked at him in shocked bemusement. 'I accept that I don't yet share the wisdom of my master but far from rebirth I feel gutted that I'm about to lose the most important thing I have in this life; you.'

'These past days have been a rebirth for both of us. Now we both need some time and space to reflect on what this rebirth means to us and where we go from here. You certainly have forced me to re-evaluate my life. I now know that things must change for me, but I need some time to decipher the nature of this change. You need to do the same outside of the cocoon in which we have developed over the past days. Do you seriously believe that I would let you out of my sight if my instinct is not telling me otherwise? Come on Cis, you have been a fantastic student. Please don't let me down now that it's time to examine what you have learnt and achieved. We both need to re-engage with the real world and see where we each belong within it.'

'Paul, I know what you want me to do, but I cannot help how I feel about it. I will try to be strong, and you will not be disappointed with me, but please do not expect me to be happy about it.'

He reached across and held her hand and gently squeezed it with a knowing glance. 'If I can find a way for us to work, I'll be back.' There was nothing more to be said. They finished lunch and went back to the car.

He sat in the car in no hurry to fire the engine into life. He smiled and exclaimed 'I know where we are now.'

She looked at him curiously 'What do you mean?'

'We are in the last scene of the incredible movie, Casablanca, where Rick and Elsa are debating if Elsa should stay with Rick or fly away with her husband. We are of course speaking of the Humphrey Bogart and Ingrid Bergman film. The twist in the last scene of that movie made it the classic that it still is. I hope that my decision merits such accolade as time goes by.'

He pondered, still fighting his judgement 'We'll always have Scotland.'

With that he fired the engine of the car and started the last leg of their trip together to Edinburgh.

Chapter 82

On arriving home, she did as he had asked. She immediately got out of the car. He got out to recover her luggage and handed it to her. They said their goodbyes and he got back into the car, but waited until he saw her open the door of her house and walk in. She turned to wave with the most chiselled smile she could manage. He waved back, powered his car into action, and was on his way.

His words that he would continue to consider the options of staying together until he left Edinburgh were still ringing in her ears. Was this just a ray of hope to allow their parting to be easier, or was he serious? She had certainly detected that their parting was as painful for him as it was for here. 'He's a serious man so maybe he is still fighting to reconcile reality and emotion.' She would pray that he returns for her, but she had better prepare for the worst.

She decided that she had two major tasks to complete before the return of Andy on the following evening. She had to remove any traces of Paul from her and her clothes. She needed to clear out the laundry basket, get it all washed and into drawers and cupboards, and she needed to get the house to be more like a nest, just as they did as students. She would also need to do some shopping as whatever was in the fridge was way past its 'use by' date.

She unpacked her case splitting the dirty clothes from the clean and put the case back in the closet. She sorted her laundry basket into piles for washing and started the first load. This would take about one hour, so it was shopping time.

She carefully shopped to ensure that they had everything they needed for the remainder of the week. She knew that she would need to prepare meals at home if she was to have time with Andy to regenerate their sex life. She also decided that she was going to change her dress code around the house to attract his attention to her. Her normal tracksuit type house clothes would be replaced by skimpy attire that would hopefully attract the eyes and hands of Andy.

She also took it totally to her heart that she had to change their house into a home, a nest where they could enjoy each other. She remembered his core marker for a home – when Andy walked into their home nothing should distract his eye from his beautiful wife, lover, and friend. She is the one who should radiate the warmth and welcome that stirs his desire to be there. And nothing should deflect him from playfulness. No furniture that marks easily, nothing positioned such that its breakage during passionate embrace will distract from the moment. Nothing is more important than the unfettered love between them.

She acknowledged that her engagement in the fashion world had seriously impacted the way that their house was packaged. Great for Harper's Bazaar, but not a home or a nest where two lovers can comfortably engage in the love, they have for each other. The white sofas would have to go, or at least recovered, especially with a baby on the way.

She was absolutely convinced that she was pregnant even though she had no way to prove it. She believed absolutely in the fate of her meeting with Paul, the way he had changed her life, and her responsibility to both Andy and her unborn child to set the tone for their future.

Paul had changed her whole perspective, but she fully understood the psychology, and realised that she was as much responsible for the lack of love in her life as was Andy. She could not ask Andy to change and accept her new condition if she did not demonstrate that she was committed to him, and their marriage. Much work was needed in the next twenty-four hours, and thereafter.

She also knew that he was right about the management of the timeline before she confronted Andy with her pregnancy. Using a pregnancy test kit she would know in about ten days if she was pregnant – but only with a 95% certainty as Paul had been at pains to ensure that she understood that such testers can be wrong. She knew that she would be so excited to see a positive test, but she must keep it to herself, not even her mother or best friend should know. This would be very, very difficult for her, but she had promised him to be patient, not least because of the possibility of miscarriage. She needed to use the 10 -12 weeks that she had available to rebuild her marriage and fully prepare Andy for his role in this adventure.

She was also determined to build a portfolio of information about Paul to present to her child if they ever found out that Andy was not their father, albeit she would comply with the instruction not to do this before their eighteenth year. DNA was so commonplace now that it was relatively easy for anyone to check their parentage, or the need for stem cells, or blood could also reveal the truth. But she must not reveal his name until the eighteenth year. She would have contact with Paul in the event of absolute necessity, but any contribution he made would be anonymous. She also wanted the memories of their time together to be at hand when she needed the strength to overcome. She felt a compelling need to write her account of their time together so that she could reflect when needed, and also a more censored version might help her unborn child to understand, in years to come, the love that surrounded their conception.

She reached for her bag where the photograph of their last evening together was lodged in her notebook. She opened the page to look at the photograph. A folded piece of paper fell out. It was on Gleneagles notepaper. She opened it and read:

My Dearest Darling Cis,

I know that your intention was never to need to read a goodbye letter such as this but your guardian angel always intended that your destiny is with Andrew, raising our child.

I can assure you, that had I been just 20 years younger, your guardian angel would have had a contest with me. You are a dream to be with, and I would happily have carried you off to a happy ever after land. However, the reality is that I am too old to raise children, and there are other things I want to do during the remainder of my life which would negate the responsibility of young children. Note plural as I am sure that you would want more children from me.

You will never leave my thoughts, and I hope that you can find a way to keep me informed of your progress, but please do not get caught.

Heed your lessons well, and continue to develop as we have agreed, and you will most certainly prevail with Andrew. You are a fantastic and delightful student, and I have every confidence in you.

I charge you with the responsibility to give our child a good, happy, loving life, and I hold you to your pledge to love our child as you love me, and indeed I love you.

I hope to meet our child before old enough to recognise people, but I will abide by your best judgement in this request.

I will always be there for you.

With all my heart,

Paul

She looked at the photograph and burst out in tears. 'My beloved Paul I will always treasure our time together' she cried. 'I will always treasure this photograph taken of us at the dinner in Gleneagles – it was a special night, and my love for my master, valiant knight, mentor, lover, and father of my unborn child radiates from this picture.'

But where could she hide these valuable memories so that not even Andy would ever find them? She would also set up something privately online so that she could post pictures and news for Paul to view the progress of their child. This photograph would be the first loaded.

Prejudice in Love

After some minutes of reflection, she wiped her eyes. Her guardian angel had given, and taken away, but she was grateful for the experience. She pulled herself together. So much to plan, so much to do. But she had a definite spring in her step, and a new lease on life in her heart. She would prevail, she would honour the good fortune presented to her in that terrible storm. She felt so blessed. Life can turn in a moment. Hers had been completely transformed in just seven days and seven nights of the most concentrated love in her life. *'Thank you, guardian angel, for bringing Paul to me'* she thought, *'you will not be disappointed with me.'* She added a footnote *'I do not thank you for taking him away from me.'*

'If you're listening to me, it's not too late to send him back for me.'

Paul pulled into the George Hotel in Edinburgh where he had booked an executive room for the night. He felt wretched without her by his side. He knew that his remaining hours in Scotland were going to be probably the most demanding and focussed thinking in his life, and far from joyous.

Chapter 83 - Tuesday

Paul opened his eyes. There was no Cis next to him. His heart sank as he realised the enormity of the loss that he felt. What had he done? In his head he knew that he was making the best decision for all concerned, but he was heart-broken that it had to end this way. Fortune had presented him with such a jewel, and she would readily stay with him for the remainder of his life. Why would anyone hesitate at such good fortune? He was not happy with his life. The lack of work and stimulation in his life for the past two years made him very unhappy, albeit he always found things to occupy his time. But his relationship with Jane was more a convenient friendship than a loving relationship. He could not remember the last time that Jane had told him that she loved him.

He just lay there staring at the ceiling challenging his head to follow his heart. He had made similar decisions in the past where two different women, at different times in his life, expressed their love for him and had asked him to marry them, but he had walked away from both opportunities for different reasons. When he did get married it was a honey-trap so where was his head on that occasion? So how reliable is his head when confronted with affairs of the heart? He had occasion to reappraise these previous decisions, and postured what life would have held for him had he accepted either proposal. Indeed, both women were wealthy, so his life would have been very different. So what drives his decision process?

He decided that he should get up, take a lonely shower, and prepare himself for his long journey home. A good breakfast would give him a little more time to think of something that would change his mind.

Cis finally awoke around 8:30 after a long restless night eventually sobbing herself to sleep. She should feel happy with herself now that she was almost certainly pregnant. But she was far from happy. She felt empty. She wanted to open her eyes and see her lover lying close to her in the expectation of a new day of adventure, but most of all feeling wanted and loved. Why has he not come back for her? She could pack within 30 minutes and would never look back.

She reached for her mobile phone to see if he had left a message for her. Nothing. She came to the sad realisation that if he did not contact her by 9am he would be on his way south, leaving her behind.

Paul, having taken a good breakfast, checked out of the hotel and went to his car. He put his bags in the car and prepared himself for the long drive home.

He sat in the driver's seat but did not fire up the engine. His thoughts were again the struggle to leave her behind. He knew

Prejudice in Love

that she would be waiting in hope against all hope that he would return for her. He could not just leave without alerting her to the fact that he was leaving without her. She needed to prepare herself for Andy's return, so the sooner she knew, the better.

He reached for his phone. To call, or text? If he called, he could face a long, tearful debate. A text is more definitive. What to say. He selected the SMS app, selected her mobile number as the destination, and started to key his message.

'Dearest Cis. I still cannot find the right reason to return for you, so I must go home without you.'

'No, no, no. Try again.'

'Dearest Cis. I feel wretched this morning without you but cannot find a solution to keep you. I hope that in time you will forgive me, but your future is with Andrew. I love you and will always be there for you. Paul xxx'

He read this message three times to check the balance, and then reluctantly touched the 'send' tag. Watching the progress of the transmission of his message he felt a great sadness. He thought to himself *'we are defined by the decisions we make. God help me if I have this one wrong.'*

As he fired up the engine to start the journey home, he was resolute that his relationship with Jane needed to change. He felt so energised from his liaison with Cis. This must now be translated into a new lifestyle with Jane.

She heard her phone ping to indicate a new message. She grabbed for her phone and read the message. Her worst fears were displayed on her screen. Tears of despair rolled down her cheeks. 'Goodbye my love' she voiced in her sadness.

Chapter 84

Andy phoned from the airport to say that he had landed and should be home in about half an hour. He had eaten on the flight and sounded buoyant.

'Okay Cis', she told herself, *'you have 30 minutes to prepare for your first encounter with your new life. What to wear? Too much, too fast, will rouse suspicion, so no sexy lingerie. Reasonably snug T-shirt without bra should do the trick, and snug shorts. Panties? No. Maximum two items of clothing is the rule from now on.'*

A bottle of wine and two glasses had been prepared on the coffee table, and the lighting had been selected to provide just enough light to illuminate the beautiful wife that now wanted his attention. The room had been restyled to de-clutter the room into a welcoming love nest. Much more was needed in terms of different, homely furniture, but this could happen over some weeks. The show must start now, with new props added as and when possible.

How to start? Remember back to student days. They could not wait to get naked in those days. What did they do to trigger the lust and desire in those days? She would tease him with her skimpy clothes and ample attributes. Invite him with her eyes to dare to touch her, and then encourage him to take her there and then. They certainly had more sex out of bed, than in it in those days, and this is what she wanted now. Rampant, urgent sex out of bed, slow lovemaking in bed where they could curl up together afterwards and drift into dreamy sleep.

The front door opened. 'Hi Cis, I'm home.'

'In here' she answered. She was curled up on the sofa as tempting as she could, two glasses of wine poured. As he entered and saw her, she jumped up, wrapped her arms around his neck, and kissed him.

He was still wearing his suit, so she took his jacket, and removed his tie.

'Come sit and tell me that you're as happy to be home, as I am to see you.'

He looked at her. *'Who is this frisky lass?'* And he could not help to notice what she was wearing. He sat down, and she removed his shoes. Then she handed him a glass of wine and snuggled in beside him.

'Good to have you home. I've missed you' she teased.

He looked at her, she had changed. No fashion garb, just a sexy T-shirt and shorty shorts. And the room feels warmer. *'What has she been doing whilst I've been away? But this is nice, I like it'* he thought.

She turned to face him so that he could not avoid the sight of her pert breasts staring straight at him under her snug top.

'You're not wearing a bra', he quizzed.

'Do you like it', she teased again.

'You look great' he replied.

She slowly pealed of her top. 'How about this? Does this look better?' She moved closer so that he could easily touch her. *'He's interested. Time to get dirty'* she thought.

She reached over and whispered, 'I also have a nice juicy pussy desperately in need of your attention.'

'Why, are you ovulating?' He asked.

'No, that was days ago. I just need to feel you in my shorts. I need to feel you in my pussy like we did when we were students. Rampant, dirty, and full on.'

He already had a throbbing erection with what he was seeing and hearing. She kneeled on the sofa by his side and sexily unbuttoned and removing his shirt, ensuring her hand touched his erection through his trousers as she reached the last button on his shirt. Her legs were apart ready to take his hand and direct it up her thigh, under her shorts to her pussy. He took no encouragement to go with her. He could feel how wet she was inside her shorts. He used his free hand to reach for her breasts reaching down with his mouth to cup her extended nipple.

She was tempted to remove her shorts but stopped herself. *'He must remove them so that he'll then take the lead from me.'* She needed to switch from temptress to submissive lover. She undid his belt and unzipped his trouser fly, placing herself where he could easily start to remove her shorts. He stroked her butt, and then placed his hand inside her shorts to grasp one of her buttocks. She made sure that he knew that she liked this and wanted more.

He slid out of his trousers and underwear in one move, and gently pushed her back on the sofa. He grabbed her shorts and slid them down her legs. She positioned herself so that her sensual body was on full view to him with her legs open, and with pussy exposed in expectation. He wasted no time ensuring that her attention seeking pussy was fully penetrated. She became totally submissive and let him do as he pleased with her. He became more urgent as he thrust in and out of her, and then exploded into her before collapsing on top of her.

'Oh, Cis', he gasped, 'my beautiful Cis'. He kissed her deeply. 'How about we go to bed and play some more', he whispered.

She lay back with great satisfaction as Andy lay on top of her. In her mind she looked up. *'Thank you, Paul. The journey has started. I think Andy will be okay.'*

PART II

THE FOLLOWING 9 MONTHS

Chapter 85

Over the coming days Andy came home in the evenings, rather than going to the pub with his rugby mates. Cis prepared nice meals for them using the Jamie Oliver *30-minute meals* book Paul had recommended. She found these recipes easy, and Andy liked them. Afterwards sex was regular and varied, albeit not the same as with Paul. But they were becoming closer to each other. They could play together, talk, and enjoy being together. She was very clever in selecting subjects that did not involve the future or children. She always used stories of their rampant life together at university to guide Andy where she would like to revisit in terms of their sexual activity, and he was very obliging.

It was Saturday morning. They had lain in after a very playful evening of sex. However, she knew that she needed to push the boundaries to keep the freshness and interest in their sexual activity together. Although he would most certainly go to the match with his mates today, he would not leave until lunchtime.

Andy got up to go for a shower. She let him get started, and then slid in behind him.

'Would sir like shower service?' as she picked up the shower gel. She started gently on his back, and when fully soaped, used her breasts to rotate around his back in a washing motion.

He turned round to her 'and what's your game ye brazen hussy?'

'Special service at weekends, sir' she teased. She started to wash his chest, slowly moving down to his groin. She refreshed her hands with gel and started on his testicles, gently but sensually. His erection started.

'Would you wash me my lover?' He started to wash her chest facing her. She turned around so that her back was close into him. She looked up at him and kissed him 'easier for you to do a good job on my breasts from this angle.'

He took no encouragement to fully engage with her lovely breasts and made much of the opportunity to caress and squeeze these delicious appendages.

While he was caressing her breasts, she was using her bottom to nuzzle his erection until she knew he was fully extended up her back. To ensure that her honeypot was full ready for action she imagined that she was with Paul, feeling his wonderful hands on her body. It wasn't that Andy couldn't arouse her, but he had a long way to go with his hand technique before she would feel the same excitement and expectation as Paul could give her.

When she felt she was ready to take his erect penis she turned to face him, caressed his erection, and kissed him. She then turned off the water, took his hand, walked out of the shower and inviting him onto the floor. They were both wet and soapy, but she lay flat on the floor smiling with expectation.

'Now what do you want, insatiable nymph?' he teased as he took his position above him.

'I want you' she purred.

He mounted her, and she could feel the same pleasure of two wet bodies locked together at the groin as when Paul showed her this technique. *'This is fun'*, she thought. *'Why have we never done this before?'*

She could see that Andy was enjoying this, using the wetness of their bodies to slide her around on the floor with his groin. Andy took his time with his movement in and out of her. She could feel her pussy starting to react. This was nice. She started to move her loins with his to increase her pleasure. She could feel her orgasm starting to build. At last, a real orgasm with Andy. She held the back of his arms to bring him deeper into her. He could see what was happening to her and worked with her to increase her pleasure. He had seen this glaze in her eyes before, so long ago. *'What a lovely sight she is when she's like this.'* He could feel her build and build as her spasms increased in speed and intensity.

As she exploded, she uncontrollable lifted her torso towards him before she fell back fully satisfied. Andy finished his ejaculation into her and then came down close to her, resting on his elbows on the floor so not to crush her. He just watched her as the pleasure flowed through her body, not wanting to disturb this magical moment for her.

When she finally opened her eyes, she saw him smiling sweetly at her. She reached up and stroked his face, and then pulled it down to her so that she could embrace him with a tender, loving kiss.

'Wow Andy, we should shower together every day. What a way to start the day.'

'I don't know what happened to you while I was in Turkey, but whatever it was, I've never been happier with my beautiful wife. I love you so much.'

'I love you my darling Andrew.' They kissed again.

After a few minutes just lying there enjoying the moment she whispered 'I'm getting a cold bum. Would you please take me back into the shower and warm me through again?'

He picked her up, took her back into the shower, and they bathed each other again, but this time more tenderly, savouring every touch. She showed him how she liked to be touched, squeezed or caressed on the various parts of her body, and how slowly. She bathed him as instructed by Paul, and she was satisfied that she had lifted their love life to another level.

She was five days into her quest, and all was very good, even her first lovely orgasm with Andy for a long time.

When they got out of the shower and saw the wetness of the floor resulting from their activities, they just smiled at each other. Before today if she had seen such a mess on the bathroom floor her reaction would have been very different. She was understanding the need to have a loving home, not a pristine house.

As they dried off, he turned to her. 'How about we go out to dinner this evening?'

'But what about after match drinks with your mates?'

'Okay for bachelors and sad people, but not for someone with such a delicious wife at home.'

The shock brought tears to her eyes. 'I would love you to take me to dinner. Thank you.'

Chapter 86

It was now ten days since Cis returned home. She was desperate to know if she was pregnant. She had started to notice small changes to her mood, but this could also have much to do with her renewed relationship with Andy. Every day got better and better as she, slowly but surely, added her new armoury of activities to their relationship. He was certainly now very attentive, and although he still was not able to give her consistent orgasms, she had no complaints with the way he treated her. She had not yet introduced him to sex toys because she wanted to teach him to excite her body with his hands before letting him loose with the toys Paul had purchased and used so effectively on her. They were still hidden in her closet.

Her periods were generally like clockwork, and she could predict the day that her period would start. This date was today, and no period had started. Andy had left for his office. She was supposed to be working on an article, but she could not resist taking her pregnancy test kit out of another safe place in her closet. She followed the instructions and waited to see the results. The stick turned blue. 'I'm pregnant' she cried with joy. 'Thank you, my beloved Paul, you have made me so happy.'

She picked up her mobile phone. She typed a text message 'P test pos. Cx' and sent it to Paul's iPhone. As soon as she could see that it had been successfully sent, she deleted it.

Paul heard the alert indicating a text message on his iPhone. He read the message, smiled, sent back a smiley face and a heart, and then sadly deleted both messages.

She sat down to her work with a new vigour. Her article was about the stresses attached to pregnancy in the modern world of female professionals wanting it all. She thought *'I want it all, but I know what I want the most.'*

Chapter 87

'Today is the day', she thought to herself. My doctor's appointment is at 3 o'clock this afternoon. It was the 23rd December; eleven weeks into her pregnancy by her calculations. For the past three weeks she felt a little queasy in the mornings but nothing like the morning sickness horror stories she had read on the internet. Once she had something to eat, she was generally okay.

Some weeks ago, she had persuaded Andy that they should host Christmas this year and invited both sets of parents, and her sister and family. Her family would arrive tomorrow, and his parents would join them for breakfast on Christmas morning. Although she thought that she'd planned well for her showdown with Andy she felt that she needed her family around if something went wrong and Andy did not accept the situation.

She had spent much time preparing the house and ensuring that adequate food was available to provide for their guests. She hoped that this would be the happiest Christmas ever with the announcement of her pregnancy. She knew that both of their parents would rejoice with such news and could only hope that Andy would be as happy as she was.

The morning sickness, albeit only nominal in intensity, had provoked her to face this fateful day before it became noticeable to Andy, or any of the female members of the family. Their relationship had grown from strength to strength, and she added new features to their sex life on a regular basis, including code words. She had even taught Andy how to stroke her pussy, primarily because, other than in specific circumstances, such as on the bathroom floor during a shower, Andy still could not give her regular orgasms. She reassured him that this was normal in a stable relationship, but she still craved them every few days. He had really got the hang of how to gently bring her to a good orgasm. They had found a very relaxing position that worked well with her in his lap. This also taught him to ensure that she was suitably ready for him to mount her, which he often did after stroking her.

She enjoyed regular use of her vibrator panties, especially when he was away on business. She had been back to Braehead Shopping Centre with her friend from Glasgow and had bought more pairs of the special panties so that she always had a pair available. Her friend also bought the whole package and was very happy with the result after instruction from Cis. That evening they had swapped remote controls over a bottle of wine and exhausted each other.

Her old vibrator had already been replaced by her new rabbit vibrator, although the vibrator panties was the preferred means of naughty orgasmic activity anywhere she pleased. She had even worn them to do the weekly supermarket shopping. What a difference a pair of panties, equipped with a silent clitoris stimulator, and a remote control in hand, makes to a shopping trip. She wanted to let him into her secret panties but thought she should buy a new set so that they opened them together in order to avoid any questions about her existing sets. Definitely on the shopping list when next at Braehead.

Although she still had much anxiety about the inevitable showdown with Andy announcing her pregnancy, she could not think of anything more she could do to prepare him for the inevitable news. She had rehearsed her speech to him many times using Paul's logos, ethos, and pathos teaching, and even had written it down on her computer so that she could practice and refine it. But she knew that this would be a very emotional event, and timing would mean everything. If the doctor confirms that all is well, she must tell him tonight so that he can sleep on it, and then use tomorrow morning to deal with any issues that she had overlooked from his perspective. Everything must be good between them before her family arrives tomorrow afternoon.

Chapter 88

Andy arrived home around 6pm. She had a nice dinner prepared for them. He had closed his office for Christmas so was ready to wind down in preparation for the frantic days ahead with a houseful of guests.

After dinner they adjourned to the living room with a glass of wine to have a relaxing evening together. Once they were comfortable, she decided it was now or never. She straddled his legs so she could look straight into his eyes. 'Andy', she started, 'the past weeks have been great, haven't they? We have come back together just like we used to be?'

He looked at her somewhat quizzically. 'Yes. Life is great for us.'

'Do you remember saying to me that whatever it was that happened whilst you were in Turkey, the changes are really great? Well something did happen while you were in Turkey and the difference to our marriage is fantastic. We are so close now, and our sex life is great. But there is another step to take, and you must help me to take this step, so I must tell you the story of what happened. I want you to promise me that you will say nothing until I've finished my story because you need to know the whole story to understand where we are. I also need you to accept that whatever I did, I did for us in my love for you.'

Andy put his hands behind her and held her buttocks. 'Cis, the past weeks have been great for us, and if you need to take it to a different level, I'm all ears. You have me a little scared with the promise bit, but I love you for what has happened these past weeks, I see the changes, and feel the love. I'll let you tell your story and promise not to interrupt.'

She looked him straight in the eyes 'this is important to me, so you must keep your promise.'

'While you were in Turkey there was a major storm here for nearly three days. I had gone from my fashion shoot in London to Birmingham to stay with my sister for the weekend. They were flying to the Caribbean for a holiday on the Sunday, so I went to say hello, and help her with the kids while she got things organised. The storm warning suddenly got worse. You know what I'm like during a storm, so I was beginning to get very worried. I did not want to get stuck in such a storm on my own. By this time, on Saturday evening, there were no more flights to Edinburgh. I did not know what to do as even staying at my sister's house would mean me being alone in the storm – not what I wanted. There were no mid-morning flights on Sunday morning, only Sunday afternoon. The storm was due to hit Birmingham about lunchtime on Sunday so the chances were that flights would be cancelled, and I would be stuck in the airport on my own. I elected to be dropped off at the M6 motorway services near the airport and try to get a lift north. It was early in the morning with only a two-hour drive to Manchester. The weather forecast did not expect the storm to hit Manchester, so I could get a flight from there. I borrowed one of my sister's coats, which I must give her back, as I only had my fashion clothes with me. I waited over an hour looking for someone I thought would be okay to get a lift.'

'Eventually this older man came along who was going for a tour of Scotland to plan a route to take his partner and her family. He did not want to know me but could see my distress so reluctantly agreed to take me with him. We had been travelling about an hour when the first thunder and lightning flash happened. You know what I did then, just freaked. Then again, and again. The storm had not only arrived early, but had come from the west, rather than the south-west, and hit all the way to the Lake District. The traffic was now very slow, and the rain beating down, so he knew we could not carry on with me freaking out in his car. He got off at the next junction, used his iPad to find a hotel, and we went there for the next two days waiting for the storm to go away.'

'He was a lovely man, so we talked a lot. I now know who he really is, as he is very well known in high places. We got talking about life, and me, and us. I was so down I just let everything out. He then started to straighten me out saying that we needed to get our lives sorted out because we were just sleepwalking, and we were driving each other crazy after only two years of marriage. I told him about my desire for a child, and the difficulties we were having.'

At this he had forgotten his promise and wanted to protest, but she saw it and put her finger to his lips. She held it there until he acknowledged his silence.

'After he realised that we were each other's first real loves he assumed, correctly, that our knowledge of sex and love was somewhat limited. All of the changes that you have seen in me came from him explaining to me how the intimate part of relationships is not in a bed, it's all around us, if we understand how to interact with each other. I felt like I was a student sitting at the feet of a great master, and I think you have enjoyed what I learnt from him.'

'Andy, this meeting with him was no coincidence. It was fate, and our good fortune. He only decided at breakfast that morning to go to Scotland because his partner had gone to Singapore the previous day on business. He then decided to use the M6 motorway rather than go the way his satnav told him up the A1(M) and away from the storm. Something brought us together.'

'When I got back to Edinburgh, I was very happy with the knowledge that I had gained from him and looking forward to starting to rebuild our marriage together. What I found was two coincidences I could not ignore. First, I listened to your message about your delayed return. The second was I found out that I was ready to ovulate. For me it was a sign that I had to go back to him to solve the one remaining problem in our life together, a child. He had already told me that it was likely that you already know that you have difficulties giving me a child, and that this was the likely cause of most of our problems because you want so much to fill this gap in our life together.'

'I knew where he was going so, the following morning, I got on a train and went to where he was and asked if he would help me make a child.'

She had to put a finger to Andy's lip again.

'He refused, telling me about the pain that he continually felt from losing contact with his own children, and that his current twenty year relationship with his partner was built on the basis that she would not want any children, and he did not want to betray her. His partner is fifteen years younger than him and was still in her prime when he met her.' She became reflective looking down, feeling guilt. 'For the first time I noticed a deep sadness in his eyes. This wonderful man had rescued this silly woman who then caused him to lose two days of his trip because she was terrified of storms. He had to keep her in a hotel and occupy her so that she would not freak out every time there was thunder and lightning. And then she disturbs him again to ask the one thing that causes him pain.'

She looked Andy straight in the eyes. 'Andy, I was so desperate to solve this problem for us that I begged this man to help me knowing that I only had about twenty-four hours of fertility. Again, just like at the motorway service place, he must have seen the desperation in me because he finally agreed to at least try, as he's 62 years old.'

'Today I went to see my doctor. I'm 11 weeks pregnant with our baby.'

'Andy, I did this for us because I love you and want us to be a happy family, and it will be our baby. He does not even know that I'm pregnant, and I had to pledge to him that I'll never contact him unless a dire emergency for blood or stem cells for example, and that I will never divulge his name to anyone, including our child, before his eighteenth year when he or she will be legally entitled to know if they want to.'

'I know that it will hurt you that I did this with another man, but this way is far better than a fertility clinic and IVF. This way only you and I know, no-one else. We don't have to bother with fertility clinic, horrible hormone therapy, and sticking instruments into my vagina to extract an egg, then fertilise it with whoever's sperm, and stick it back. It makes me shudder to think about it.' She shivered her shoulders to add drama to this last statement.

'And we complete our family. With this baby we are complete, and I'll never ask for another, I promise you.'

'I need you to support me in this, and to be happy for our good fortune. Will you do this for us?' She had finished and looked into his eyes for his reaction.

'Jesus, Cis, that is some story. I don't know how I feel, other than sick in my gut. What were you thinking?'

She could see he was angry, but she knew this was a natural first response. *'Just let him feel his way through this challenge to his masculinity.'*

She responded softly 'Us, you and me, and our life together as a family.'

Andy just sat there looking at her, seething.

She started to cry 'Andy, I love you, and only you. I want you to love me. And this baby takes the pressures away from you, your parents, my parents, our friends. It solves all our problems completely.'

She got assertive. 'This man helped me to put our life back together, and it worked. Then I asked him to solve the final problem between us, and it has worked. We have everything we need to be happy. Please be happy for me, for us, and for our baby growing inside me.'

He pushed her away from him. 'I need a drink.' With that he went to get himself a stiff scotch.

He was now pacing the room. She had retreated to the sofa.

'You chased a 62-year-old man to give you a baby', he shouted. 'You couldn't make it up. Who is this man?'

She contained her crying and looked straight at him. 'He is a well-respected, successful man who likes to keep a low profile. He's intelligent, cultured, and was very kind to me. I cannot tell you his name today. If you really must know, and we get through this, then ask me again and I'll tell you in confidence. But I must then tell him that you know. Andy, his name is not important as he has no further role in this family.'

He then jabbed his half-empty glass towards her, 'why have you taken so long to tell me about this? You have all these testing kits. You must have known you are pregnant weeks ago.'

'If you read the box, it says that pregnancy test kits are only an indication. Second, so many things can go wrong in the first 12 weeks. First pregnancies can abort themselves within the first

6 – 8 weeks. I've had no morning sickness symptoms until I started to feel a little queasy this week. I was getting frightened that something was wrong. The only certainty is when you are properly examined and your pregnancy is confirmed by a doctor in the eleventh or twelfth week, and which is what happened this afternoon. Besides my doctor, you are the first to know that I'm pregnant. I haven't dared to breathe a word to anyone else, not even my mother. Do you seriously think I would put you through this pain before I was sure that we had a good chance of having a baby?'

Andy was feeling a desperate frustration that she had good answers to all his anger. 'She's carrying another man's baby, and she expects me to be happy about it. What was she thinking? We can't have it aborted as our families will want to know why. What the hell am I supposed to do? I've been cornered and betrayed by my wife. How could she do this to me?'

Andy continued to flex his anger at her, but she was well-rehearsed by Paul, she had the answers to everything he could throw at her.

It was getting late. He announced he was going to bed.

She just sat there for a while, sad that he was not happy for her; for them. *'He cannot give me a baby so what's his problem? Does he want to go the IVF route? If so, why haven't we started already?'*

She waited long enough for him to be asleep, got herself ready for bed, and slipped in besides him, naked.

Chapter 89

She woke up to see him looking at her. He waited for her to fully awaken. He had been thinking about the revelations the night before. It occurred to him that she did not need to say anything about a surrogate father as they had indulged in so much sex since he returned from Turkey, including the evening he returned, that she could have just said she was pregnant.

But she had told him the truth at great risk to their relationship. She had put everything on the line to solve their problems, yet he did not have the courage at the beginning of the year to tell her what he knew about their dilemma. For ten years she had been his faithful friend, lover, and soul mate, and all he did last night was to doubt and scorn her. He needed to tell her a truth that he had kept from her all this year.

'Cis', he started, 'I think I need to tell you something while we're being honest with each other because it must have taken a lot of guts to tell me you're pregnant with another man's child when you could just have kept quiet. Just before Christmas last year a medical research team came to the rugby club wanting rugby players to help them with some research – something to do with testosterone levels in macho rugby players. About a week later I got a letter telling me that my sperm count was so low that it would be very unlikely that I could give you a baby naturally. I was devastated because I know how much you want a child, and I would like a family as well. I went off sex all together because I felt inadequate. I knew the more we tried the sooner we would have to go through a fertility process which would become public at some point – not good for my ego at a rugby club. I realise that it was tearing us apart, so the last weeks have been a great relief to me. I can't say that I feel very good about what you have done, but I cannot argue that the result is good for both of us; if this man is definitely out of the loop.'

He reached for her. She quickly responded but said nothing because she felt he had not finished. He held her in his arms stroking her hair.

'Cis, you are clearly stronger than me, and certainly more focussed on our future together. I need your help to come to terms with this situation. I really want to be happy for you but give me a little time.'

She smiled at him. 'Take all the time you need my darling. That letter must have hurt you, but why didn't you tell me? Why all

Prejudice in Love

the pain over the past months? We can only work things out together when we share the problem.'

She quickly remembered her master's teachings and decided to take the rebuke out of her last statement 'If it's any consolation to you I felt like I was in kindergarten with this man when we discussed relationships and sex. He opened my eyes to a new world of how we can enjoy each other, and I have shown you just some of what he taught me. There is much more to come, and you will enjoy all of it as we grow together in our intimacy. I so want us to be happy and have a great life together.'

She tucked in close to him and kissed him. He looked at his beautiful wife again. 'I do love you, and I'll try to come to terms with what you've done.' He was quiet in his thoughts for a few moments.

Then, to her surprise he said, 'can I tell my mother the news?'

With tears in her eyes, kissing him repeatedly. 'Of course you can, my darling.'

He pushed her flat on her back, took the duvet away to reveal her naked body, and then kissed her abdomen above her womb. 'We are three' he smiled at her.

They kissed long and hard.

He looked at her 'before I tell my mother how about a shower?'

She was ready to jump off the bed when a thought crossed her mind. 'Andy, we have all of our immediate family here tomorrow, Christmas Day. We will all have breakfast together and then open presents. Why don't you announce our baby after the last present is opened? I guarantee it will be the only topic of conversation for the remainder of the day. And the present is not only for us. It's also a grandchild for our parents. What better present could we give them for Christmas?'

Andy thought for a moment 'great idea'.

She continued 'the only request I have is that when you make the announcement I am standing by your side in your arms.'

'But Cis, this is your announcement'.

'No Andy, this is our announcement, and you are the man of the house. It's for you to make the announcement on our behalf, just as you did for our marriage.'

She continued 'This way we tell everyone close and dear to us together; as one'.

He was thinking, and looked at her 'How do you feel? Do you have any morning sickness, or anything like that?'

'I have started to have queasy periods each day, but none of the horrible symptoms that you hear about. Why?'

He was now fully engaged. 'Okay Cis, you cannot work your arse off in the kitchen on Christmas Day in your condition. I have a plan, as I want you close to me all day tomorrow.'

'I like the idea very much, but what's this plan?'

'I have a plan, so how do you feel about that shower before I go to work?'

She was off the bed to the bathroom. 'I'll get the water warm'.

During this shower he took much longer than usual to caress and stroke her abdomen, and she just lay back into him feeling the warmth that he was showing towards her. And when he knelt to wash her feet her kissed her unborn child again. She beamed with love for him, and the happiness that this child would bring to them. She quietly thought about Paul, her master, her lover. He had been right about everything, and he had taught her well. *'Thank you, my darling Paul for everything.'* She must remember to text him later with the good news.

Chapter 90

Her family arrived together a little after 5 pm. Her parents had travelled to Birmingham yesterday, and had driven up in the people carrier belonging to her sister and her husband.

Their two kids were excited, but the adults were tired from their long drive. She took them all to the kitchen for refreshments, and the inevitable catch-up.

She told her mother that the preparation had been exhausting and could do with a lie in tomorrow. Her mother agreed to deal with breakfast.

Chapter 91

Cis and Andy awoke on Christmas Day morning and indulged in their own intimate start to Christmas knowing that her mother was taking care of breakfast. They could hear the excitement of her sister's children, and the doorbell announced the arrival of Andy's parents. They should really get up, but neither was in any hurry. They enjoyed their shower together before dressing and joining the assembled family for breakfast around 10:30am.

The dining room table, which could accommodate ten people, was very busy with all the excitement of Christmas. Cis and Andy decided not to intrude any more than needed, but quietly had breakfast knowing that dinner would not be until mid-afternoon.

After breakfast they all adjourned to the living room with two over-excited children, and where the base of the Christmas tree was now littered with a vast array of presents. Andy and Cis started to hand out the presents from under the tree.

After all of the presents were distributed, they let the general noise level die a little before Andy rose to his feet and invited Cis to join him. He held her by his side as she had requested.

He turned to the assembled family. 'Could I have your attention please. We have one more present that we want to share with you all.'

Everyone went silent in anticipation of what he was going to say.

He looked at Cis with love in his eyes, and then looked back to start. 'Cis and I have a special announcement to make. My darling wife is now 11 weeks pregnant with our child.'

The room erupted with congratulations and the flashes from cameras.

After the excitement had died down Andy asked for attention again. 'Cis is suffering from a little morning sickness so I'm looking for volunteers to organise Christmas lunch.'

The response was instant. Both grandmothers-to-be immediately offered to take charge.

Cis looked at Andy, beaming at his plan, and he looked at her with the love that said he was now committed to this new addition to the family.

Little did they know that her brother-in-law, Josh, a photographer, had captured the whole speech on camera in a series of high-speed stills taken every half second. Once the excitement had abated, he sat with Cis and went through the frames he had captured. The first frames showed her and Andy preparing for the announcement. But later in the sequence one particular frame hit her like a thunderbolt. She stopped him moving forward to the next frame. It was Gleneagles, but her beloved Paul was replaced by Andy. And just as Paul had said that the picture of them did not reflect the truth, the picture now before her eyes, to an observer, would show radiated love between her and Andy. But she knew that her radiance was the knowledge that, yet again, her beloved Paul had prevailed – Andy was totally committed to their child.

She told Josh that she must have a framed copy of this particular shot, and a digital copy for her laptop. He agreed to drop a copy to her laptop before he left.

She looked around the room. The two grandmothers-to-be were in the kitchen preparing Christmas dinner, her sister was preparing the dining table, Josh was taking pictures of his children playing with their presents, and Andy was engrossed in conversation with his father. She quietly picked up her mobile phone and retreated to their bathroom. She had already received several festive messages that morning, but there was one that she needed to send, and which she had forgotten to send yesterday, – the most important message of that day.

Once she was settled in the bathroom, she activated her phone, went into her SMS app, selected "Paul Fulton, Writer" from her contacts as the recipient and then composed her message.

>"Doc confirms all OK.
>Showdown successful.
>All family delighted with news.
>My VK has won the day. Thx xxxxxxx
>Hope you are well.
>Happy Christmas. Cx"

Cis looked at her message to check that it was as she wanted. She pressed the SEND icon and watched as the progress bar indicated the transmission of her message. She decided to wait a few minutes to see if she would get a response. She did not have to wait long before her phone buzzed to indicate a new message had arrived. She opened it and read:

>"Well done. I'm so happy for you.
>Have a great Xmas. VKx"

Her beloved Paul was there for her. She shed a tear as she very reluctantly deleted both messages. *'Life is so unfair'* she thought in despair.

But life had to go on, so she took some minutes to compose herself before returning to the festivities.

Paul had been in the kitchen undertaking his annual ritual of preparing Christmas dinner for their guests. This was a task he preferred to do alone so when his phone buzzed to indicate a new message, he could just wipe his hands, and then read it in private. The message from Cis took him completely by surprise. Having read it he felt himself welling up inside with both pride and sadness. He was still fighting his decision regarding her. His head told him that he had made the right decision for both her and their future son. But his heart craved her in his arms again. The worst part of his responsible decision was that he was to be a father again, but he would have a child in whose life he would play no part. And this time it was his fault. *'Why is life so complicated?'*

He quickly answered her in case she was waiting for a response. However, he was not prepared to delete either message. Later he would find a quiet moment to go to his study and reflect on this news, and again torment himself with his decision not to take this wonderful woman into his life.

Later, after dinner, Cis reflected on the day. She had watched Andy's ego grow by the minute as a proud father-to-be. He had no way out now. He would be the father figure of the child of her beloved Paul, just as he had predicted. She had followed his teaching without fault, and she was proud of her achievement. The only sadness was in her heart. She would still have preferred her beloved Paul by her side. She would put a copy of the photograph onto her website for him to show him that she had obeyed his instruction and was successful in her quest.

Little did she know that, over 300 miles away, her beloved Paul was sitting in his study looking at her message, reflecting on the news she had sent to him, and the sadness he felt in his heart. The picture he had taken of her during her fashion parade at Loch Lomond was still on his phone. He was not ready to delete her picture or her message.

Chapter 92

All their friends were overjoyed with the news of her pregnancy. This also fed back into Andy's ego. He became very proud of the fact that he was to be a father at last. Nothing more was said about Paul, and this detail became a distant memory.

She ensured that he got involved in all the various stages of her pregnancy. He kept his travels to a minimum. He attended the antenatal clinic with her, he was holding her hand during the scan which revealed that she was to have a son. And of course she would covertly keep Paul informed of her progress, including a copy of the ultrasound scan of their son.

One evening over dinner she had raised the issue about the inevitable changes to their lifestyle that would be imposed by their addition to the family, not least preparing meals. She told him about the Jamie Oliver book that had now been appended by other such books, and they agreed that both should be ready to feed themselves, and their child. Each Sunday they worked in the kitchen learning new recipes together. They had so much fun with this that one Sunday, whilst trying to make pizza, they got so messy that they attacked each other with both flour and dough. This resulted in him laying her across the table, covering her in flour. She only had her T-shirt and panties, and he just T-shirt and shorts. He started to reach under her T-shirt with flour covered hands, and found himself removing her T-shirt, and then her panties. He then took her on the kitchen table, much to her delight. Afterwards they took a shower together to clean off the flour and dough, but this transformed into a something much more. They played together, and then made long, passionate love as the day faded into evening. She had not felt such closeness with him for so long, and she wanted to encourage more of this playfulness in their relationship.

Sundays became their play days with both cooking and loving, even as the child inside her was starting to make itself visible as her belly started to bulge. He would make faces on her bulge with the ingredients they were using, and then enjoy bathing them off her later, usually after sex. They got very used to the idea of staying home and having fun together.

Chapter 93

It was now May of the following year and Cis was well into her third trimester as the expected date of delivery would be around the 28th June. Summer had started so the days were warm. She was looking and feeling very large. He took great interest in her development and would spend time feeling for the kicks of his son.

As promised she had introduced more and more of the knowledge she had experienced with Paul into their sex life, and they were still actively enjoying each other. She decided to hold on the sex toys until after the birth as her body felt too sensitive at this point in her pregnancy for inexperienced hands to be let loose with such weapons of joy – or pain in the wrong hands.

She had planned, and he had organised a beautiful nursery for their son. She often found him standing in the nursery purveying the colours, hanging toys, and the lovely white crib they had bought together. She could see that he was so looking forward to his new role and was clearly going to play his part. He had merged his business with another entrepreneur he knew so could take time out to spend with his darling wife who was finding these last weeks a little tiring. As his new partner had a young family there was much understanding that this new father-to-be needed some space from the office to familiarise himself with his new role, and to help his wife through the birth.

Chapter 94

Andy could feel himself being shaken. He opened his eyes to see her trying to get his attention. Her waters had broken, and she was feeling contractions. It was very early morning on the 29th June. He swung into action. He'd played out this role in his head many times so was ready. He quickly dressed – no time for a shower. He helped her into some clothes. Her bag was already in the car. They only needed to get themselves out of the house into his car. He had to help her as she was clearly not easily able to move on her own. He phoned the hospital to say he was bringing her and informed them of her rate of contractions.

As they arrived at the hospital a porter with a wheelchair came to the car to collect her. He went to park the car before joining her in the maternity unit. When he got to her she was already in a gown and connected to various measuring machines. The midwife told him that all was well, and the baby should arrive within the next 2 – 3 hours.

'Stay with her', said the midwife. 'Comfort her and help her with her breathing.' She looked very matronly at him and sternly said 'I assume that ye went to the antenatal classes with your wife and understand yer role in this birth?'

'Oh yes' he replied excitedly, 'I remember everything they told me.'

'Good' she said, 'Most men just stand there looking gormless.'

The midwife went off to look in on the other patients that she was guiding through the same process.

Andy sat with her, made sure she was okay, and then decided to text his and her parents that the birth was imminent.

Her contractions were becoming more frequent and she was feeling the pain. She would take a little gas to help her through but wanted to resist an epidural if she could as this would detract from her ability to push the baby out.

Stephen Box

After two hours of waiting, but with the continual increase in pain that she had to endure as the contractions got stronger, this event was losing its shine. The baby had turned, and the monitoring showed that progress was good, so why did this baby not come?

Andy had started enthusiastically helping her with her breathing, but now even his throat was feeling the strain. 'Phew, phew, phew, phew, phew', the midwife insisted. 'Help your wife, she needs you. Rub her back if that helps. Hold her hand. Be there for her' were the words resounding in his ears every time this matriarchal midwife came to see them. Quite naturally all focus of attention was on her, but do these people understand the strain on the man feeling helpless to the screams of his wife as the contractions get stronger? He was also feeling the pangs in his stomach of having not had anything to eat or drink since she woke him up.

After three hours he was quite exhausted, and the screams during contractions were getting stronger. Finally, the midwife called for the delivery doctor. The head of their baby had appeared. Cis was a first-time mother so maybe she would need help to get this baby past her slender loins.

The strain on her face was obvious. She too was feeling exhausted, but at each contraction the midwife just told her to push, seemingly oblivious to her expended condition. More gas was being used to help her with the pain. Andy was getting more agitated, but at the same time more excited as he was shown the baby's head just starting to appear.

The delivery doctor appeared, scrubbed up and ready for anything. A trolley of seemingly instruments of torture were put by his side. A very large set of tongs was on this table. Andrew thought that they seemed far too large to breach her vagina, even in her dilated state. He shuddered at the thought of them being used on his darling wife.

The delivery doctor, Dr Johnson, was very nice, but very assertive. He gave his instructions to her in a no-nonsense way. His primary consideration was to get this baby out of her as quickly as possible to prevent any issues associated with pregnancy that could cause difficulties for the child. He also wanted to keep the distress level for the child as minimal as possible. He watched the monitors, even the new monitor attached to the head of his unborn son.

'As soon as your next contraction starts, I want you to really push' he told her. 'Let us see if we can make this the last contraction.' He looked at Andy, 'be really there for her this time and encourage her, as she will feel this push.'

The contraction started. Everyone was at their station. 'Push' he commanded. She pushed with all her might screaming as the pain hit her. 'Again, push' he commanded. 'Good. Nearly there. One more big push, Felicity. You can do it.' She gathered all her remaining strength and pushed until all the veins in her body were screaming at her, and she was screaming back at them, but she felt movement in her abdomen. The baby's head fully appeared; Andy could see it. Now he was excited and held her hand even tighter, encouraging her to push. 'Nearly there, Felicity', she heard as the strain was racking her body into oblivion. 'Good, good' she heard. 'Push Felicity, push.'

Andy watched this rubbery body slip out of her with a little help from the doctor. The doctor quickly gathered up this creature, cut the umbilical chord, cleared the mouth and airways, and handed it to the midwife. She lay back exhausted but was brought back to the moment when she and Andy heard those first signs of life, their baby crying. He still had hold of her hand. They looked at each other in quiet satisfaction as tears of joys ran down his cheeks.

'All we need now is the afterbirth, Felicity' she heard the doctor tell her. 'A little push please to help me.' She responded automatically, and it was out. He put it into a kidney dish, handed it to a nurse, and told her to take it to the lab. She felt her abdomen being checked for damage, and then gently wiped. The midwife had cleaned the baby, weighed him, and then lay him on her chest. She held this little bundle in her arms with tears of joy streaming down her face. She could only think of one thing to say to Andrew. 'We have our son.' He kissed her. 'You were great Cis, I'm so proud of you.'

Although it was still early in the morning; the recorded time of birth being 8:42am, Cis was clearly totally exhausted so it was decided to keep her at the hospital overnight to give her a chance to recover before going home. The hospital staff did their after-birth chores, and then left the room to allow this new family to spend some time bonding together. The baby was now in a shawl having been examined by the hospital paediatrician and given a clean bill of health.

Cis was propped up in bed with their bundle of joy in her arms. He had brought his camera with him so was busy taking photos and short video clips. She was still under the influence of the gas that she had so fully used towards the end but was smiling from ear to ear. He sat down again by her side. She handed her bundle of joy to him. He took this baby boy into his arms. She could see in his face the joy that this brought to him. There was clearly no sign in his eyes that this was not his son. Quite the contrary, it was clear that this father had a son. She was so happy for both. She wanted to capture this moment so picked up his camera, which was now beside her, and quietly captured this picture of love between Andy and their son. This would certainly be a picture that she would post on the secret web site that she shared with Paul.

After about half an hour nurses reappeared. It was time to take her to a room where she could get some sleep. She was told that her baby would be brought to her when it needed its first feed, and a nurse would help her to get the connection between baby and mother's breast. Andy was told to go get some rest and he could come back during the afternoon for a while, and then collect his wife and son after they had both been finally checked for discharge around 9am the following morning.

He had forgotten all about his tiredness and distress. He just wanted to tell the whole world that he had a baby son weighing in at 6lbs 9oz. He sat in the hospital reception calling first his own parents, then her parents, her sister, his business partner, and anyone else in his contacts list that thought might be remotely interested. Having got to the letter Z in his contact list he finally put his phone in his pocket and skipped his way to his car. He needed to prepare for the homecoming of his wife and new son. His life had just changed, for the better, and he was very happy about it.

Chapter 95

Andy returned to the hospital around 4pm to find her sitting in bed beaming. His son was sleeping in a crib beside the bed. Flowers had arrived from various well-wishers. He kissed her so tenderly. 'We have a son. What shall we call him?'

She turned to him. 'I have a name in my head which I would like if you are happy with it. I would like to name him after you, but it would be a nightmare in the house having two Andrews.'

He could see the logic.

'I would like to name him Paul Andrew Duncan.'

He thought about this name. There were no other people that he knew in the family that had the name 'Paul', even as a second name, and it was not a typical Scottish name, but he could see no objection. He was so happy with her that he would accept her wishes. 'Paul Andrew Duncan it is' he said.

She wanted to cry with relief. Her beloved Paul may not be able to share in the life of his son, but he could share in his name.

'We need to go to the Registrar's office to register the birth' she told him. A nurse watched over young Paul Andrew Duncan whilst he helped his darling wife make the short journey to the Registrar's Office, seal the name of their child, and received a Birth Certificate confirming his name as Paul Andrew Duncan, Felicity Duncan as his mother, and Andrew Hamish Duncan as the father. Andrew looked at this Certificate and beamed with delight. 'I am officially a dad' he shouted. He turned to her, 'I promise you I'll be a good father to our son.' Her tears welled as she hugged and kissed him.

When they got back to her room he wanted more photographs as she had now cleaned up, and he wanted to capture her beaming face with their new son. She made sure that her son spent time in his arms as she knew that the sooner they fully bonded together, the less chance that he would remember that he is not the real father of this little baby boy. Her fears were unfounded. There was no doubt in his mind about his role with this little bundle; his son.

When he had left to go home, she sent a text message to Paul.

'Paul Duncan born 8:42am 6lbs 9ozs. Pictures to follow. All is Well Cis x'

Paul saw the message, and with tears in his eyes replied

'Well done. I'm so happy for you. Good luck. Thx'

PART III

8 Years Later

Chapter 96

Life was very good for Cis, Andy, and their young son, Paul, who was now at school, and looking forward to his eighth birthday in a few days' time. It was a Saturday, and as usual this was Father's Day with his son. He had practically surrendered his rugby playing to have this valuable time with his son every week. He knew that this gave his lovely wife a break from the continual boisterous demands of their young son before the days when he started school, but it had now become part of the routine of the week. Andy had now established his business and had other people that could do much of the foreign travel. His partner also shared the load when one of them was needed to travel.

Andy had taken Paul out for the day to do boy's things and would be bringing nanny and Grandpa Duncan back for tea. As he walked through the front door, he immediately could hear the sound of uncontrollable sobbing. 'It's Cis, what has happened?' He asked his mother to take Paul to the kitchen and give him something to drink. His parents immediately saw the concern on his face and quickly and noisily directed young Paul to the kitchen to avoid him hearing the distress of his mother.

He followed the sobbing to the study where he found her, head in her arms on the desk, with her laptop open in front of her. She must have been sobbing for some time because her screensaver of Andy and Paul was visible.

'Cis, what is it?', as he put his arm around her. She looked up, eyes completely red, 'he's dead, Paul is dead' not even thinking that he had no idea who or what Paul was to her. He had never seen her so distraught in all their years together. Instinctively he knew that this was serious, and he needed to find a way to deal with it.

He hit the screen on her laptop. The display restored to the last item she was viewing. It was a news report about the untimely death yesterday of a Paul Fulton. He had died of a massive aneurism in his head whilst on the street in the City of London. He knew the name because his business partner was an avid reader of this man's financial and economic columns in the financial press. But what did this man mean to her?

He lifted her from the desk and spun her seat so that she was facing him. He knelt so that he could hold her with her head on his shoulder, still sobbing. 'My darling Cis, help me here, I don't understand. What does this man mean to you?'

She put both her arms around his neck and held him tight, but she was not responding. If anything, she was now inconsolable in the intensity of her sobbing. He decided just to hold her and let her get this new intensity out of her system.

After some minutes she calmed a little, but still sobbing. 'Andy, my darling, this man was there for me when I so desperately needed him, but no-one was there for him yesterday. He died alone with no-one who loved him at his side. Life is so unfair, especially to a special man like him.' She then went back to her sobbing. He was totally confused as he knew nothing of any connection between her and this man.

'Okay Cis, I'm here for you. Please tell me why the death of this man has upset you so much so that I can help you.' She looked at him for the first time and saw his confusion. This brought her back to reality. *'He doesn't know about Paul.'* He never did interrogate her any further about the father of their son after she declared her pregnancy.

She collapsed into his arms. 'My darling Andrew, this is the man who came to my rescue in the storm eight years ago. He's the man who made us the happy family we are today, and now he died alone. Where was his guardian angel when needed? He did not deserve to die this way. He's a good man, who gave so much to me when I most needed him.' She sobbed again.

He immediately understood that this was his son's biological father. He now knew why she chose Paul as the name for their son.

'Cis, just stay here for a moment while I ask my parents to take Paul with them overnight. Just stay here. Can I get you anything?'

'Just some water please', she sobbed.

He went to the kitchen. He asked his father to come to the living room. 'Cis has had some really bad news. Someone very close to her has suddenly died in tragic circumstances. She's distraught. I need to be here for her. Can you take Paul with you overnight, and we'll see what the situation is tomorrow?'

'No problem son. I'll get mother to go to his room and get some things and go. What shall I tell Paul?'

'Just tell him that mammy has had some really bad news and daddy needs to be with her.'

'Okay son. Give our condolences to Cis, and we'll talk tomorrow.'

'Thanks dad. This is really important to us.'

His father could see that this was a major upheaval, and his son did not want to elaborate any further. He just wanted to get back to her. He returned to the kitchen, announced in his best grandpa jovial voice that young Paul was staying wee nanny and grandpa tonight. 'So let's away.' Paul was happy to stay with them so only interested to know if grandpa would play computer games with him. Nanny went to get some clothes and toys from Paul's room, and they were off.

He returned to her with a glass of water. She was still sobbing. He could sense the deep sorrow that she was suffering. There was much he did not know about her relationship with this man, but he had never seen her like this before. He must find a way to console her.

He started gently 'my parents have taken Paul with them for the night. Now my precious Cis, what can I do to help you through this?'

She looked at him. 'I'm so sorry Andy, but I cannot help how badly I feel. I do need your help to get through this, but please be patient with me. It's been such a shock.'

'Just tell me what you want me to do.'

'I need to grieve for this man, and I want to go to the funeral. I need to say goodbye to him.'

He knelt in front of her and held her hands. 'Whatever you need Cis.'

She looked at him. 'Thank you my darling. I cannot ask you to understand, but this is very important to me.'

'Come with me.' He stood and helped her to her feet and guided her down to the living room where they could sit together. He knew that the sooner they had a plan that worked for her, the sooner she could start to get control of herself.

'It's so unfair', she kept saying to herself. He decided a glass of wine might be more helpful than water and handed it to her.

'Cis my darling, if you want to talk about this, I will let you just talk as long as you want. If you want me to just hold you whilst in your own thoughts, then I will happily do so. I will most certainly take you to the funeral, and make sure that you can say your goodbyes in whatever way you choose.'

'Thank you my darling, thank you. I don't know what I can say, I'm so sad. But I do need you with me.'

No matter what he did, he could not console her. He tried to get her to eat something, but she just picked. He tried to talk to her, but she could not string a sentence together.

Eventually she sobbed herself out. Exhaustion took its toll and she went to sleep in his arms. He carried her to bed, and just held her. He started to understand that he did not really know the real story of those days, eight years ago, when this man changed her life, and she then saved their marriage.

'But this man had died in tragic circumstances, and this had triggered something within her that is now expressing itself in inconsolable grief. What can it be?' He could not deny that life had been very good for them since the intervention of this man. He must respect her feelings and help her through her grief. He must not question her. She must be allowed to express her grief as she chooses so that they can move on.

He looked at her asleep in his arms. *'It's my turn to get you through this distress, my darling. I'll do as you need, and I'll not question why.'* He kissed her tenderly on her forehead.

Other than footwear he did not bother getting either of them ready for bed. He just pulled the duvet over them and held her.

Chapter 97

When he awoke, the sun was up, but she was still sleeping. He unravelled himself from her as he needed the bathroom. When he returned she was stirring. He stroked the matted hair caused by her sobbing out of her face. 'Good morning, my darling. How are you feeling? Can I get you anything?'

'Something to drink would be nice', she gasped.

'Tea? Water? What is your bidding', trying to lighten her mood.

'Tea, please.'

'Stay there, I'll be right back.'

He brought two teas and lay back next to her.

She realised that they were both still dressed. 'What happened last night?' she asked.

'You cried yourself out, so I just brought both of us to bed.'

'You probably think I'm overreacting to his death, but it's so unfair.'

'Cis, I have never really asked you about this man, and I'm not asking now. If you want to talk, please trust me. You have nothing to prove to me, or apologise for, and I'm devoted to your happiness. Your courage eight years ago made us what we are today, and this man is obviously a significant part of our story. I'm ready to listen, and completely accept what you tell me.'

She looked at him with tears in her eyes. 'Andy, have I been a good wife to you?'

'Good would not even begin to describe the love and happiness that you have brought to me.'

'Have I been a good mother to our son?'

'What is this, Cis? Paul has the best mother he could ever hope for. We are by far the happiest and most together family in our circle of friends. Even my parents adore you for the joy you bring to our lives, and they're surly Scots.'

'I want to show you something.'

She went to her pantie and bra drawer, and fully opened it. She removed some of the bras from the back corner to reveal the 6" x 8" photograph taken at the dinner in Gleneagles. Paul was looking at her. She thought that her beloved would appreciate hiding amongst her bras having had such affection for her breasts.

She picked it up and closed the drawer. She then picked up the photo on her dresser taken on Christmas day when they announced her pregnancy and went back to lie with him.

She showed him the photograph from Gleneagles. 'This is Paul. The picture was taken on our last night together at Gleneagles.

Prejudice in Love

Although it was such a late night, and the weather was so bad, we stayed another day because of the long five-hour drive home for Paul.'

He could immediately see how she radiated her love to this man. There was no doubt about how she felt for this man when this photograph was taken.

He looked at her, 'Why did you come back to me? You could not have painted a better picture of two people so deeply in love with each other.'

'Rules, my darling. The very first words this man ever said to me at the motorway service place were', she tried to copy Paul's voice tone, 'alright I'll take you with me but there are rules; no conversation, I select the cockpit temperature, I choose the music, and if you will need a pit-stop in the next three hours take it now'. She tried to laugh under her tears. 'I dropped my bag at his feet so he could not escape and ran off to the toilet before he could change his mind.'

'When I went back to him to help me conceive, he realised from what I had already told him about the difficulties in our life that I would likely fall in love with him during the process as I needed to be wanted and loved. Before he agreed to help me he imposed rules that when it was time to go home that I would do so without fuss, and that I would come home and repair our marriage in preparation for the birth of our child. We did get very close, not least because he wanted our child to be conceived in love.'

'When we saw this photo the following morning, he let me have it, but only as a reminder of what you and I needed to achieve. He told me that now I knew what it was like to love, and to be loved, I must go home and make it happen between us. He told me that if I followed his teaching, within six months, certainly before our son was born, a photo of us would look like this.' She gave him the Christmas Day picture. The tears were now running down her cheeks. He could not help but see the same radiance between them as was showing between her and Paul.

'Andy, this man gave me a masterclass in life, not just relationships and sex, but making a marriage work, preparing a loving home for our child, preparing me to be a good wife and mother. In those few days he opened a whole new world for me which I then brought home to share with you. I have books I had to study when I got home because our few days were not enough to cover everything I needed to know and understand. This knowledge even helped me in my work. I have written at least two features which achieved critical acclaim. But I'm a fraud. They were his words, his teachings. He was my master, and I have profited from every teaching he gave to me.' She paused as she looked at the Gleneagles photo.

'This is the only physical reminder he would allow me to keep of our time together.'

'So you see my darling, it's not that he died, he was 70 years of age. It was the way he died. When I was with him there was a deep sadness and loneliness in his eyes. He was always there for those in need, but rarely was anyone there for him. This may be irrational to you, but it was the way he died that got to me. He was alone. He gave everything but got so little in return. We took so much from him, but what did we give him in return?' Her tears were now streaming down her cheeks. 'I hoped that one day you and I could visit with him and show him what he did for us, and how grateful we are for his guidance and love. I need to make my peace with him and thank him for what he gave to us. Does this make any sense to you?'

He could see the real sadness in her eyes again, and the uncontrolled grief pouring out of her. 'You tell me what you want us to do, and we'll do it.'

'I would like to keep this photo close to me. It will never leave this room or the study until we go to the funeral. When we come back, I'll put it back in the drawer, I promise.'

'No problem. Thanks for showing it to me. It tells me so much about your feelings for this man.'

'We need to find out when and where the funeral is to take place. We must be there.'

'Okay. Why don't we get up? Can I run a shower for us, get you into some fresh clothes, and then I'll get us some breakfast? I'll find out the funeral arrangements and make all of the arrangements needed for us to be there.'

'Thank you, that would be great' she whimpered.

Chapter 98

Andrew found the funeral arrangements, along with his Who's Who entry, and other details about this man. *'His credentials are impressive'*, he thought. The funeral is in a village near Cambridge on Friday 29th June, his son's birthday. Although he did not want to miss his son's birthday, he was now committed to taking Cis to this funeral. She needed him, and he was not about to add the conflict on this date to her grief. He decided that Paul should stay with his parents until this situation was over.

She was in no fit state to fly, so he must drive which would mean travelling on Thursday. He sensed that they would travel back, at the earliest, on the Sunday. He would stay near to the grave for as long as she needed to say her goodbyes. He wanted her to come back with this distress behind her. He now understood that she had unfinished business with this man, and that he can help her by being there with her, as this relationship is the essence of their relationship, and what she always intended one day.

He found her in the living room, deep in her own thoughts. He sat next to her. She looked up at him.

'Okay, the funeral is on Friday near Cambridge. I've found us a hotel near to the church. We'll drive down on Thursday to get the lie of the place and be sure to be there. We'll stay there until you tell me that you want to come home.'

'What about Paul's birthday. Oh my God, it's his birthday on Friday. It's so unfair.' She started to cry again.

He held her, 'It's okay. Paul can stay with my parents until all this is over, and we can give him a very nice party when we get back. I don't want you to miss the funeral. That cannot be changed, but we can delay a birthday treat. I'm sure that his grandpa and nanny will spoil him rotten.' She laughed under her tears knowing that this most certainly would be the case. They loved their grandson so much.

'I'll pack some things for Paul and go over to see them later and explain our plans. They can stay here once we have gone so Paul will be here to greet us when we get back, and his mammy feels better.' Tears welled in her eyes again. 'You're so good to me my darling.'

She thought about what he had said and planned 'The funeral is five days away. What happens between now and then? I cannot be without my darling boy, the son who reminds me of my beloved Paul every time I look at him. This could be both distressing and a comfort at this time.'

'Andy', she started, 'although I'll want time on my own this week, I don't want to be alone. I need my family around me. You need to work, and Paul must go to school. Could I ask you to see if your parents can come and stay here so that they are around during the day and can do the school run if I don't feel like it. I realise that it could be difficult for Paul to understand why I'm so sad, but he'll be such a comfort for me.'

He thought about this change. 'It will be difficult. But he can work knowing that she has two loving in-laws around who both adore her. They can certainly deflect Paul and entertain him when necessary. And he would see his son in the evening. *'On balance she's right'*, he thought, as was usually the case.'

'Okay, I agree with your thinking. But I'm not going to explain this over the phone to them. I'll go and explain this situation to them and ask them to come later today. I still want to spend some time with you to ensure that I have taken care of everything you need before starting to think of others.'

'What about if I come with you to stay with Paul while you explain things to them?'

No Cis, I want you to stay here and think this through to the last detail. What do you want out of this week, and how do we achieve it? Every last detail, including what you will wear, and what flowers you need. You are good at these things, and I need you to focus before we have a houseful.'

She knew that he did not want her to break down with Paul away from our home, but he had a point. It would take him between one to two hours to drive there and back including the time he needed to explain what was happening to nanny and grandpa. She could use this time to plan what she wanted to do for her beloved Paul.

Chapter 99

Andy arrived at the home of his parents around lunchtime. His parents were sitting in their garden, and Paul was playing football against a wall upon which grandpa had painted a set of goal posts. When Paul saw him he cried 'daddy, daddy' and came running into his arms. There were lots of hugs and kisses. Then Paul looked around 'where's mammy?'

He sat with Paul in his lap. 'Mammy is not feeling good, so she stayed at home. But you'll see her later. I want to speak with nanny and grandpa for a few minutes so can you go and play. You can show me afterwards how good you are with a football.' 'Okay daddy', and off he went.

He looked towards his parents. 'You know that Cis has had some really bad news. Someone very close to her has died suddenly in very tragic circumstances. This person is not family in the normal sense, but he is real family and mentor to her. I've never seen her so distraught, but I now understand what this person meant to her. I'm not going to even try to explain anything, but I need your help and support to get through this.'

His father put a warming hand on his son's arm 'whatever we can do to help, ye can count on us.'

'Thanks Dad. We have to go to the funeral which happens to be on Friday.' His father piped straight in, 'but that's Paul's birthday. Surely nothing outside of the family can be more important than her son's birthday?'

His mother cut across him. 'Hamish, how could ye say such a thing? Ye are talking about Cis, the loving wife of our son, and adoring mother of our grandson. Do you seriously believe that she would go ta this funeral if it were not very important to her? Have ye been listening to what Andrew has been saying? Shame on ye.'

Andy listened to this chastisement of his father and fully understood why Cis is the boss in his home. It's the way he grew up, with a very strong woman as a mother.

His mother looked at him. 'What do ye need us to do?'

'I want you to come stay with us until this is over. We need to leave for Cambridge on Thursday and won't be back before Sunday. Before we go Cis wants to have time to grieve, but she does not want to be alone in the house. What I need from you is to keep things going around her, including taking Paul to school, but not interfering in her grief. I'll be there as much as I can.'

'She does not want to talk about any of this with anyone but me, not even her own mother, so I must ask that you don't probe. Just allow her to drop in and out as she wishes. Clearly Paul will need careful management. He should have access to his mammy when she wants it but let her be when she grieves this terrible loss.'

His father looked at him. 'My son, I'm proud of the way you are taking care of Cis. Mother is right, she is a wonderful woman,

Prejudice in Love

and I apologise for what I said.' He put a reassuring hand on his father's arm.

Andy felt himself welling up inside, and it did not escape his mother and father. 'Now I understand why she's so distraught I can feel her grief.'

Nothing more needed to be said.

'When do you need us to be there?' asked his mother.

'Around teatime will be good. I want to complete all our planning with Cis before you arrive. I need to get her focussed on what she wants out of this week, and make sure that she gets everything she thinks she needs to get her through this.'

His mother could see what was needed, including getting Andy back into focus. 'You better get back to Cis. We'll deal with Paul and prepare him for when we arrive. Go do what you need to do for her, and we'll do the rest. Go now. We need to pack.'

He shouted to his son, 'see you later son. Love you.' And he was gone, back to his grieving Cis.

Chapter 100

When he arrived back home Cis had a writing pad in front of her and had scribbled some notes.

He came to her, kissed her, and told her that everything was okay. They would be here around teatime. They had enough time for them to plan their trip to the last detail.

Andy got tea for both. 'Have you eaten?'

'Not really hungry.'

He looked at her 'I'll get some nibbles and you will put some in your mouth, chew, and swallow, in autopilot mode if necessary. I need you strong for this challenge. You are our rock, and you need to show me the way to get you through this to make you happy again.'

She smiled at him. He could see that she had been crying again.

'I don't feel much of a rock today, my love.'

Having put a plate of nibbles on the living room coffee table within her reach he decided to bring some order back into this situation. 'What have you got so far?'

'I don't have anything suitable to wear for a funeral, so I must go shopping.'

'Okay I'll come with you.'

'No Andy, you have a business to run. Your mother can come with me. She always likes an excuse to go shopping without your father. Probably good for both of us.'

He remembered that in all this grief he had not called his partner to tell him what had happened, and what time he needs for her in the coming week. As soon as she finishes her list, he must phone him.

'I know what flowers I want so we just need to find a florist near to Cambridge to order them. I want to take these flowers to his grave when we can go on our own. I need to be alone with him to say what I need to say. I want only you there with me.'

'I don't want a wreath because I cannot declare who we are.'

'I can't think of anything else. I have to call my editor tomorrow to say that I can't write this week.' Fortunately for Cis her editor knew what Paul did for her so this will be an easy call.

'What about your mother? Are you going to call her tonight? If you're still grieving, she will press you for detail.'

'I hadn't thought about that. I can't face a grilling from my mother today. Can you call her and tell her I'll call in the week when I'm a little more composed?'

'No problem. Anyone else needs to de deflected?'

'Perhaps you should call my sister. If she calls and catches me at a bad moment, she will worry my mother.'

'I can stop all calls. I'll switch the landline to automatic answerphone. Then we can filter calls. If you give me your mobile phone, I'll set that direct to message service. Once my parents are here you don't need to use the telephone at all.'

She held his hand. 'I would like to tell you more about Paul now he's no longer with us, and just how much he did for me, and us, so that you can get a better understanding of my grief. But it's all too tender for me at the moment. I need to get through this sorrow first.'

'Cis, I have known you for nearly 20 years as my best friend, my lover, my wonderful wife, and devoted mother. You've always been there for us. I've never in all that time ever seen you remotely so distraught about anything. I know that there is something very special going on here, and I also sense that it is not totally to do with you and me, but something you shared together with Paul. You probably felt his sadness and loneliness but could do nothing about it. I think that developed an empathy with him, but you feel guilty that you did nothing about it or could do nothing about it. And now it is too late. Maybe you think that you failed him, just like everyone else did. But you are clearly walking in his image, as you have done since you met him, so he will never die because he still lives on in you. He changed everything for you, and you changed everything for us. Is that not success? I think he would be very proud of you and satisfied with what you have achieved.'

She reached for him and sobbed openly in his arms.

Chapter 101

Later that day they heard the door open as nanny, grandpa, and her darling son arrived. Having agreed with Andy all the arrangements for the week ahead she had tried to compose herself as she did not want to upset her son.

Paul came running into the room to see her, jumped up on the sofa crying 'mammy, mammy' and wrapped his arms around her. She was so glad to see him that she nearly squeezed him to death. It felt so good to have him in her arms. She closed her eyes, and it was her beloved Paul comforting her.

After many kisses he looked at his mother. 'You've been crying mammy. What is the matter? Nanny told me you are sad today.'

'My darling Paul, mammy has had some very bad news. A very good friend has died, and mammy will miss him.'

'Who is he?'

'No-one you know my darling, but he was very good to me, and I never said thank you to him. So now I feel bad about it.'

'Mammy, you tell me that I should always say thank you.'

'That's right, and you must always do that. It's just that my friend suddenly died before I could say thank you to him.'

'So what will you do?'

'Daddy will take me to his funeral so that I can say thank you to him at his graveside. Then mammy will feel better.'

'Can I come too?'

'You need to be at school my darling. And mammy needs to do this with daddy. We will be there a few days because it's a long way away, so nanny and grandpa will stay here with you and spoil you', as she tickled him. He reeled in uncontrollable laughter as he always did when mammy tickled him.

Andy could see that she was right about needing her family around her. She was clearly feeling much better. He reflected how this young boy had brought so much joy to their lives, and he was exactly the medicine that she needed right now to bring some sunshine to her darkness.

Chapter 102

The following days were hard for Cis. She needed to keep her composure as far as the family was concerned as Andy must never know just how close she came to leaving him to be with Paul. But she felt so wretched that Paul had died alone. He was her true love and although she had buried her feelings for him over these years, they had now all come flooding back. Every time she closed her eyes she could see him, feel him, and so wanted him to rescue her again. *'Why had this happened to him? Why wasn't I there for him?'*

She had told her editor about the nature of Paul's death. As she knew of the feelings Cis had for Paul she had every sympathy for her trying to cope with the distress, and even offered to come and spend time with her. In any event she could take as long as she needed to get over her loss. She was not in need of visitors, she only wanted to grieve for Paul.

Whilst her son was at school, she would sit in her study replaying those days together in great detail. She had recorded those days, one uncensored version, and another edited version that she would give to her son at the right time. Both versions sat in her 'Valiant Knight' directory which she had password protected so that no-one could read anything in this special directory, including all of the pictures she had loaded onto the web site, and those of her naked that she chose not to load, but did show to Paul during one of his visits after their son was born.

She would have periods of fond reflection, and others of uncontrollable sobbing. Although her in-laws could hear her sobs, they did not cross the boundary into her study. They always waited for her to emerge at which time they would feed and talk to her but complied with the wishes of her son not to probe. There was a general feeling of sadness in the house as they felt her grief.

They had never seen her in such a state from the day their son had first brought this beautiful angel to see them when they were both at university. What they did know was this was a very serious situation for her, and they were thankful that their son loved her enough to help her through this terrible period in her life. They certainly knew that she was a wonderful wife and mother, and their support for her was unconditional.

Cis did not engage in the school run once during those days. Her face was such a mess from her sobbing that she did not want any inquisitive questions from other mothers, and sunglasses would certainly be a giveaway. Andrew took Paul to school, and grandpa was there to collect him in the afternoon. Cis always composed herself to greet her son from school and spend some time with him. Little did Paul know that all of the hugs, kisses, and squeezes were his mammy remembering contact with her beloved Paul; his real father. Paul lived on through her son, their son, and this was a great comfort to her.

Andy was always home before 6pm to take time to play with their son before his bedtime. Sometimes Cis felt guilty that this family unit had closed ranks and were standing steadfastly by her without any requirement of explanation for her grief, completely unknowing how close she came to leaving them for Paul.

On the Tuesday she asked her mother-in-law if they could go shopping for something to wear for the funeral. They went into Edinburgh City centre looking for something for her to wear. She did not want black as she did not want her beloved Paul seeing her in such clothes. But she wanted to be respectful so eventually found a grey skirt and jacket suit which she thought Paul would approve. This would be a special suit just for Paul as she knew that, with this jacket, she could be without a bra, although she would not do this with Andrew present. She would also choose underwear that Paul would have chosen for her and wear the earrings that she wore that wonderful Saturday evening when she was Mrs Felicity Fulton for just one precious day.

Chapter 103

It was Friday, the day of the funeral. It was a bright and sunny June day with just the hint of a breeze.

Andy had driven Cis down the previous day, and he had booked a room at a small hotel about a ten-minute walk from the church and cemetery. They had walked to the church yesterday just to see the church layout and decide where they would sit. It was only a small church, so she could be part of the service wherever they sat.

As they walked around the church and the cemetery, she thought that this would be a nice resting place for her beloved Paul. The church itself was of a very solid Norman architecture type, built of stone with the usual shape of a cross design with sturdy buttresses holding the walls in position. It was well maintained so she assumed that the local congregation were affluent and interested in maintaining this piece of hallowed history.

The cemetery surrounded the church on three sides and had headstones dating back to the 1700's. There were well maintained trees, gravel walkways threading around the graves, and the grass was well manicured. She thought of it as a picture postcard type church, very traditional English village. She was satisfied that this place fitted the dignity of her valiant knight and master. Yes, it was a place for a valiant knight to rest, and she felt calm in this place.

The service was at 2pm. Cis thought that this late time would be to allow people from far and wide to get there. She expected a large crowd. She told Andy that she wanted to be there some fifteen minutes before just in case there was a greeting party. She wanted to be inside before any such greeting party got into position by the gateway. She most certainly did not want to introduce herself to Jane, or any of the other family members.

His view was that this was her day of remembrance, so he just went along with whatever she wanted. He had ordered the flowers requested by her, but she did not want to leave them until they came alone on Saturday, so they would collect them on Saturday morning.

When they got to the church people were already mingling around the church area. The roadside was full of cars, and parking would be a problem for latecomers. They got through the gates into the church grounds a few minutes before she saw a lady dressed in black stand by the gate greeting people as they arrived. She could see that this lady must have been in her late 50's or early 60's but still maintained a good figure, and the little she could see of her facial features under her hat revealed a good looking woman. This must be Jane she thought, the woman who had so pained Paul with her betrayal of him yet stood between their happiness together.

She did not really know what she felt about Jane. After all it was Paul's decision to go back to her, or was it Paul's decision that she should go back to Andy? She could not, after these eight years, fathom why they did not stay together. It was the obvious outcome of their liaison. But he did not come back for her. She wanted to weep at this sadness but thought she needed to be a little controlled until the service started where her weeping would not be considered out of place.

More people arrived, and it was nearly time for the funeral to start. A hearse arrived at the gates to the churchyard. 'It must be Paul', she thought. Tears started to fill her eyes. She wanted to rush over and hug the coffin but knew that she had to hang onto Andrew to stop her losing control. He could feel the tension as she increased her grip on his arm. He put his arm around her to reassure her that he was there with her.

Everyone moved inside the church. They had picked seats about two-thirds back from the front, but from where she would be able to see everything during the service.

The funeral procession started. The organist was playing a very powerful piece of music which she found out later was Siegfried's Funeral March from Götterdammerung by Richard

Wagner. The coffin bearers walked very slowly down the aisle followed by Jane and two younger adults who she thought must be his children, James and Sarah. Why couldn't their son be part of this?

The service was a traditional funeral, and the vicar gave a lovely eulogy about Paul. Someone she did not know spoke of Paul's time in the City of London, and the changes he made to the way the financial markets worked. The whole thing was very fitting for her valiant knight, she thought, and she felt a peace and calm in his presence. She was so proud to have known this man, and to have shared his love and compassion.

At the end of the service the coffin was carried out of the church to another Wagner piece; Siegfried's Idyll. She did not know of his affection for this music, but this second piece was so soothing and light that she was uplifted by its beauty.

Once the coffin was again outside of the church on its way to the grave that had been prepared for him, everyone filed out of the church making their way to the graveside.

Once assembled at the graveside the vicar voiced more prays as the coffin was lowered into its final resting place. Tears were now streaming down her face, but she was sobbing in silence.

The crowd started to disperse, but Cis had chosen a spot where they could just stand, essentially unnoticed, and wait for everyone to leave.

When she was satisfied that the main party had left she led Andy to the pathway running past the final resting place of Paul Fulton. Two men had appeared to refill the grave that had been prepared for him and were busy shovelling the earth to complete their task in this funeral. They stood on the pathway facing the grave. Andy heard her speaking 'My darling Paul, I have Andrew with me to say thank you, and goodbye, but we will come back tomorrow as I have much to say to you on this saddest of occasions'. With that they made their way back to the hotel.

Chapter 104

Andy would never forget that night at the hotel. All of her grief for this man's passing came pouring out of her again. Having been to the funeral he felt swept up in her grief and could easily empathise with how she felt. But if this outpouring was needed to get her though this tragedy then so be it.

Chapter 105

It was 8:30am before Cis awoke. Andy had been awake for a while but he decided to let her sleep after her outpouring last night. There was no rush to get anywhere as they only had to collect the flowers she wanted, and then go to the graveside for her to make her peace with Paul Fulton.

Although he had mixed emotions about the intensity of her grief, he did feel that once she had visited the grave, and said what she wanted to say, she would feel much better allowing her to return to some normality. She had spoken at the grave yesterday as though Paul could hear her. Although he thought this odd, he knew that coming to the funeral had been the right thing to do as she needed to be in close proximity to him in order to say what she wanted to say and get this loss out of her system.

He was intrigued to hear what she wanted to say to him. They had only known each other for a few days, but they obviously developed a very strong bond and a lasting relationship. To his knowledge they had not communicated with each other since then, so would Paul even remember her? Did this man know about the son he had given them? His suspicion was that there was much he did not know about this relationship, but he did think that some communication had continued, but kept from him for obvious reasons. Perhaps she confided in him, and he mentored her long after they parted. She had certainly brought much to their relationship; knowledge that would be expected to take more than a few days to accumulate. But he was sure that she was loyal and true to their new life with their young son. In any event this man was now dead so could not be any form of threat to their life now. Perhaps today would reveal the true nature of her relationship with this man albeit he could not complain with the difference that it had made to him and his life.

They eventually found the florist, being somewhat further from the cemetery than Andy had thought. She examined the lilies that she had specified, and then examined various flower holders suitable for a grave. She chose one that had holes for 15 flowers, had a suitably deep bowl that could be buried in the earth, and had a bronze top. *'Very fitting for my beloved Paul',* she thought. She wanted her flowers to stand tall on his grave. She asked that the flowers were cut to suit her selected holder so that she could load the holder at the graveside without needing to cut them.

When she was satisfied that the arrangement in the holder was as she wanted, she had the flowers removed and wrapped. He watched on amazed at the detail that she was applying to this task, and equally amazed with the bill. He said nothing; just paid without any comment.

Chapter 106

When they got to the cemetery, they went directly to the grave to find that it had been prepared for a grave surround and headstone, but currently covered with the wreaths and flowers from the funeral. Andy could see a cemetery worker close by. He told Cis to wait there a moment whilst he took the flower holder. Waving a twenty-pound note in his hand he asked the worker if he could plant the holder in the grave so that she could fill it with her flowers. Seeing the serious nature of his reward for this task he quickly took the holder and the money telling him that he would fill it with water and then plant it for him.

He returned to Cis and told her that the worker would fill the holder and then plant it for her so she should select where she would like it. As the grave was still messy from the soil she cleared a space near the head of the grave such that she could kneel on the grass whilst arranging her flowers. She wanted her flowers to be special so would take care that every flower was properly arranged.

The worker arrived with a trowel and her flower holder, now filled with water. She showed him where she wanted it. He could feel her distress so very solemnly planted the holder where she had indicated and stood back to make sure that it was set properly in the soil. 'Is that as you wish madam', he quietly asked her. She thanked him, and he quietly returned to his duties.

She asked Andy if he would give her some time alone with her task to arrange her flowers. He retreated to the pathway running past the grave. She knelt on the grass and slowly arranged her flowers in the holder. He could hear her speaking but could not hear what she was saying.

Her words were only for her beloved Paul. 'My darling Paul, I feel so lost without you. I have always hoped that one day I would return to your arms. I so miss the touch of your hands, the feelings of being so loved and wanted, and the safety of my valiant knight, lover, and master. I'm so sad that I was not there for you last week, if only to hold you in my arms and let you know how loved you are. Life has been so unfair to us, but you will not be forgotten. Your son will know of his father, and how much I loved him. I've brought Andy with me so that you can see how good and supportive he is, and for him to understand just how much he owes to you. Goodbye my love. Please be at peace in the knowledge that you will live on in your son, I promise.'

She finally stood up and returned to Andy. The tears on her cheeks were evident. She took his hand and took him to stand at the foot of the grave. She lifted his hand to her waist height and put her other hand on top of their already interlocked fingers. She looked straight at the head of the grave, now beautifully draped in her flowers.

She had rehearsed this speech all week as the death of Paul had released all her buried feelings for this man, but she knew that she must not divulge too much to Andy. Life was good, and Andy was fully supportive of her needs during this tragic loss, so she must maintain a picture of happy family, especially as the alternative had now been taken away from her. She had obligations to her beloved Paul, not least in respect of their son.

'My dearest Paul, we have come before you today to express our grief at your untimely and tragic death, and to express our long overdue gratitude for what you so lovingly gave to us. I have brought Andrew with me for both his strength to help me through my profound grief, and so that he can understand better what you did for us.'

The tears were now freely rolling down her cheeks. He held her hand more tightly in an attempt to give her strength to get through what she so clearly needed to say.

'I renew my pledge to you that I will continue to do as you instructed. And I sincerely tell you that Andrew has been a model father to our child, and I love him dearly for this.'

Andy began to well up inside. She had never said anything before about his role as the father to young Paul, but here she was praising him in front of the man who had enabled him to play this role. He felt both proud, and humbled, that she was prepared to recognise him as a model father. He loved young Paul as his own, and until now he had not ever reflected that he was any different.

She continued 'You gave so much but received so little in return. I hope that I continue to live up to your expectations, and I bless you for what you did for me.'

She was now sobbing but he decided to just let her be; let her take her time to get through this.

She finally composed herself. 'I will return each year on the anniversary of your death to sit with you for some time to feel the strength and comfort that you give to me, and to let you know that you are never far from my thoughts. Goodbye my dearest Paul, and I hope that you will now rest in peace knowing that you are loved and will never be forgotten.'

She bowed her head in silence for a few moments, then she looked up at Andy 'I have finished my darling, we can go now.'

Later that afternoon Jane returned to the grave to share a few quiet moments, and to ensure that everything was as it should be. She immediately noticed the flower holder with the beautifully arranged lilies. The cemetery worker saw her and came over to her.

'Hello Mrs Winters. Is everything as you would wish?'

'Yes, thank you Harry. Did you see who left those lilies? They're beautiful.'

'Yes. A couple were here earlier. Asked me to plant the flower holder – it's a very nice one, expensive I should say. I hope you don't mind.'

'No, not at all Harry. Obviously they cared for Paul to be so particular. Do you know who they were?'

'Never seen them before, but they were here yesterday while we were finishing the burial tasks after you had left. Only spoke to him, and he sounded Scottish. She was clearly distressed, and it was all very solemn. They were here nearly an hour.'

'Thank you, Harry. Can you please make sure that when the surround and headstone arrive that you keep that flower holder and place it at the base of the headstone.'

'No problem Mrs Winters, I'll make sure of it.'

Prejudice in Love

'Thank you, Harry. I'm very grateful for your kindness. I have also ordered a park bench in Paul's memory. Can you please be sure to put it on the path here so that I can sit and see his grave when I visit?'

'Consider it done. Leave everything to me.' With that Harry went back to his work knowing that Jane wanted to spend time alone.

Jane stood looking at the grave and thought out loud 'You have admirers who clearly deeply mourn your loss. Why don't I know of these people?'

Chapter 107

That evening Cis was in a much calmer state. She had said her goodbyes to her beloved Paul, and she felt his calming presence.

They had decided to quietly dine at the hotel just in case she needed to escape.

Andrew wanted answers to questions he had, albeit it he was not about to question anything she had done to get where they were today. Life was good for them, and he was not about to cause any problems. The speech at the graveside increased his compassion for the moment, and her praise for him as a model father had really moved him.

'Cis, my darling', he started, 'now that I know who Paul Fulton is, and the role he played in our life, could I ask you some questions that would help me to understand this whole situation. I'm not going to question your actions or judgement at any time since you met him as I've fully reaped the benefits of that meeting. I just want to understand your grief. Any question that is too raw for you to answer at this time, just say so.'

She looked lovingly at him. He had completely supported her throughout this past week without hesitation or question.

Perhaps it would be good that he knows a little more; enough to allow her to continue her relationship with her beloved Paul. But her deepest feelings for Paul were very much on her mind, rekindled by this tragic loss. She must be careful to ensure that she deals with questions as taught by her master in Parent or Child mode and use her knowledge of rhetoric where necessary to tell her story in a way to secure Andrew's full support. She put her hand over his 'of course you can my darling. You have been so good to me this past week. Ask me whatever you wish and I'll try my best to answer'.

'Cis, you tell me that everything that has happened to us since that meeting was due to his teachings, but you were only with him a few days. How did you get so much out of just those few days?'

She started reflectively, just looking at the table 'We had 7 actual days together in all.' And then with some intensity looking directly at him 'but they were long days. My education started from the moment I got up in the morning, which was always early, until I went to bed. Even throughout mealtimes. Andrew, I can best describe him as a font of knowledge, experience, and wisdom. When you started to drink from that font you wanted more, and more, until you were exhausted with tiredness. But when you awoke again you wanted yet more. It was exciting to listen and learn. He started off as a reluctant valiant knight who saved a damsel in distress from a storm, and quickly became my master of knowledge and wisdom. There were rules and objectives that must be followed, but he could explain the most complex of subjects in very simple ways. We even studied some of the works of Aristotle. He took a wimpish, inexperienced girl, sleepwalking her way through life, and transformed her into a confident woman capable of achieving her ambitions in life, and he energised me with the courage to go make things happen – which I did.'

'Wow Cis, I can feel the heat in that answer. Phil, my business partner, always tells me that Paul Fulton's financial and economic articles could take the most complex of issues and rationalise them into understandable arguments, so I can easily believe you, and understand your thirst.'

'Andy, I had a total makeover. He changed my thinking, my philosophy, my lifestyle. He showed me how to transform our mere existence into a loving relationship. How to transform our house into a loving home. Do you remember how much I de-cluttered everywhere and changed our furniture and style of living?'

'Yes, I do remember you transforming our house from a magazine style-house into a home, and it was great.'

'But what happened afterwards. Did Paul know you had a son?'

She chose her words carefully 'yes he did, but you need to know why. If you remember back when I first told you that I was pregnant I told you that he did not want to help me because of the problems and pain he endured with the two children he already had, and who had been turned against him by his vengeful ex-wife. As a result both children suffered behaviour and psychology problems, and he had little or no contact with them. This was a great pain to him, and part of the sadness I told you about. You may have noticed at the funeral yesterday that they did not even speak to each other. The rules he laid down for me as part of his agreement to help us were very strict and designed to ensure that our son was brought up in a happy home with loving parents. I had to pledge to him that this would be the case, and he gave me goals that I must fulfil. Remember, I showed you the photograph at Gleneagles, and the one of us at Christmas, just 3 months later. That was one of my goals. Each time I completed a goal I would text him to confirm that I was fulfilling my pledge to him.'

'But did you never speak again after your time together?'

'The intention was not to speak, or meet, because he did not want to cause any problems with you over your role as father, so just text or email. However, if I had a problem with fulfilling a goal I did contact him a couple of times to better understand how to achieve what was required of me. But that was a long time ago. I have not spoken with him since before the first birthday of Paul when all my goals were essentially completed. I have only sent him occasional pictures since then, and he was true to his word by not contacting me.'

He put his hand over hers as a show of comfort. 'Thank you. I now understand much better what you went through to turn our lives around. I can only applaud your courage and determination to honour your agreement with him. I would like to have met him. He sounds like a special man, and his credentials are obviously impeccable.'

'My darling, he was a very special man. He gave us everything, and we gave him nothing in return.' Tears came to her eyes 'but that's my cross to bear.'

He knew that he had gone far enough. In any event he was completely satisfied with her answers and could understand why she wanted to take him to meet Paul, and to thank him.

'No more questions Cis. You have told me what I need to know to help you through this, and I pledge to you that I will do everything I can to help you to come to terms with this loss, and to continue to honour your pledge to him.'

'Thank you my darling. I'm glad that you now understand why this man is so important to me.' And inside her thoughts *'thank you my beloved Paul, a little Aristotle to the rescue.'*

He fell silent for a while pondering what he had just heard. He gave her a puzzled look. 'Just out of interest what did Aristotle bring to your education? I know he was a philosopher from ancient Greece, but what did his works contribute?'

She looked at him, noticing the puzzled look on his face. *'Aristotle to the rescue again, and so soon'* she thought to herself with a little smile. She could lighten and deflect any further conversation about her time with Paul, yet spend some time explaining the role of Aristotle to him whilst reflecting in her own mind that wonderful morning she spent with Paul understanding how

Prejudice in Love

to convince him of the benefits to them of her pregnancy using Logos, Ethos, and Pathos.

She reached over to him and covered his hand with hers, and with a playful inner smile started, 'Andy, my darling, Aristotle convinced you that my pregnancy was the blessing that it has proven to be for our marriage.' She looked into his eyes and waited to see his reaction.' She had made her peace with Paul. Now it was time to exert her influence over Andy to regain control of their situation.

He looked at her confused. 'How did Aristotle convince me?'

'It was Friday morning, and raining. We were at breakfast. I was full of the joys of spring because I knew, somehow – probably female intuition – that I was pregnant. But then the reality dawned on me – how to convince you that what I had done was good for us. Part of the conditions laid down by Paul was that I could not deceive you. I must tell you the truth as soon as I knew that my pregnancy was established and past the danger points that can occur during the initial 10 – 12 weeks. You said yourself that we had enjoyed so much sex that I could have kept quiet. But the rules were that I must tell you, and I had no desire to deceive you. There is no room for deception in a good marriage. But how to do this? I panicked. But as with everything else my valiant knight had the answers.'

She was reflecting on how good she felt that morning. Instead of clinicals they had made love and dwelt in the shower so long that they nearly missed breakfast.

She continued 'We spent the whole of that morning with me sitting at a table like a schoolgirl with my paper and pen listening to my sage explain the constructs of political rhetoric, as devised by Aristotle. I was learning how to formulate Logos, Ethos, and Pathos to construct elegant statements of reason and argument. I remember thinking why don't I know this? I'm a writer with a degree in journalism sitting here learning how to construct sentences with every word balanced to deliver the message, but with no wasted words. It was incredible and exciting to see, with just a few rules, how to develop very elegant and persuasive argument. When he finished, I went straight to my notebook and keyed it all in to ensure that I understood everything and asked him for clarification when needed.'

'After I thought I understood what I had learnt, he started to coach me in the construction of my speech for you. Then I was coached in how to prepare you, how to find the right moment, and how to deliver my speech uninterrupted to minimise any distress to you but maximise the possibility of success. I continued this study throughout those first three months, practicing my speech more times than I can remember to ensure that I focussed on what had to be said, and the delivery. I was really scared that night, but my new found friend, Aristotle, successfully guided me through.'

'Wow. After I calmed down, I remember thinking that you would make a great politician. Your speech that night was brilliant. I was so proud of you. Now I know why. You made me feel such a coward that I had not told you about my problem, but your courage gave me the strength to come clean.'

'My darling, I have used this knowledge in all of my writing. Although devised for spoken rhetoric, I have found that it allows me to develop written argument that is so much better than my original style.'

Having now seized the initiative she felt tired. 'My darling, it has been a long and emotionally exhausting day. Would you mind if we retire now as I'm feeling very tired?'

With that he called for the cheque, and they returned to their room and quickly were settled for the night.

Chapter 108

When Cis awoke she could see that Andy was lying, looking at her. He smiled at her.

'I'm ready to go home now my darling. Thank you for bringing me here, but now I need to get back to our family.'

He held her close and kissed her. 'Could I offer you shower service before breakfast?'

'That would be lovely; if it's possible in a bath with a shower over it.'

'Let's go make it possible. I need to make you feel loved again.'

After breakfast they packed, and during checkout she booked a room for the 23rd June next year when she would return to start her annual sojourn to spend a few hours with her beloved Paul.

She spent the drive back to Edinburgh deep in her own thoughts very much as she had when she travelled to Glasgow with Paul. But this time she was mourning the fact that she would never see him again, would never again feel his magic touch on her body, and would never share any more time in his arms feeling loved and wanted.

When they arrived home the front door opened before they could put a key into the lock. Their beautiful son was standing in the doorway with an excited smile on his face.

'Mammy, mammy you're back' as he rushed into her waiting arms. She lifted him, held him close, and closed her eyes. *'My beloved Paul lives on in our son'* she thought *'and who, one day, will know of his real father.'*

PART IV

10 Years Later

Chapter 109

Cis was sitting at her desk looking through her diary appointments. One event beamed out at her, not that she needed any reminder of this date. This date was the 23rd June, the anniversary of the death of her beloved Paul, father of her son. She knew it was totally irrational, but she still could not forgive herself that he died alone, no-one with him to hold his hand, comfort him. She wanted to hold him in her arms as he did with her so many times when she needed his comfort all those years ago. Why could she not be there for him? Thinking about this always made her sob uncontrollably.

Every anniversary she made the journey to his grave to lay flowers, and sit and talk with him for a while, reflecting on the good fortune that he had made possible for her.

Andrew had died in an air crash in Central Asia a little over two years ago. Again, she gave thanks to Paul for showing her the way to put her life back together with Andrew, and, in return, Andrew had been a wonderful father to their son knowing that he was not his biological son. Although he did prove to be sterile with no possibility of him fathering additional children, and refusing IVF for her with an unknown donor, or adopting another child because it would expose his problem and thus holding her to her promise to him, it was of no real consequence in their relationship as she had her darling son by her beloved Paul, and that is all that mattered to her. He did everything a good father could do for a son, and she would be forever thankful that he was such a rock for her when Paul died, and completely supported her annual sojourn to his grave to which she always went alone knowing she would be too upset to return home that day.

It was now the tenth anniversary of the death of Paul. Their son was now seventeen, but just one week from his eighteenth birthday. He had recently finished his high school exams and preparing himself for university in October. Since the death of Andrew, he had taken over as the master of the house whilst his mother grieved her loss. The two most important men in her life had been taken away from her, and now she needed her son, the person who kept the flame burning for the men she had so loved. He decided he would go to university in Edinburgh so that he could live at home to be there for a mother who had given him so much love throughout his childhood. It was too soon to desert her even though she still had her journalist career, and many friends. He had detected a sadness in her, something deep inside her, that he could not tease out of her. He could not leave her alone at this time.

Paul disturbed her solace with a request to go somewhere or other on this special day, but she was so engrossed in her thoughts that the words did not register with her. She turned and looked at him. He immediately saw the sadness in her eyes. 'Mom, what's the matter?' he exclaimed, moving towards her to give comfort.

She asked him to sit beside her and held firmly onto his arm as she would her beloved Paul. 'The 23rd June is a very special day for me, a day of great sadness. And this year I want you to share it with me. You will be eighteen in a few days and it's time for you to know some things about yourself' she quietly told him. She looked him straight in the eyes 'I want you to come with me to meet your father.'

This statement thundered in his head, *'what is she saying?'*

Prejudice in Love

'Paul, my darling boy, my rock for these past two years, your dad was not your biological father. Your dad could not have children. And before you jump to any conclusions your dad knew from the beginning that he was not your father, but wanted you as a son, and he loved you as his own. For reasons I'll explain to you when we are with your father, it was not possible for him to be a part of your childhood other than in the background. He died suddenly ten years ago on the 23rd June, and I go to visit with him every year. Do you remember when I was very sad just before your eighth birthday, and nanny and grandpa came to stay to look after you while your dad took me to the funeral? And every year, on the anniversary of his death, I go to visit his grave.'

'This man, your father, is the greatest man I've ever known. Knowing him was a privilege, and without him your dad and I would probably have foundered, and you would not be here. I promised him that I would love you as I loved him, and I continue, and will always continue to fulfil that pledge.'

She started to openly cry. He put both his arms around her, just as his father would have held her. She sobbed 'every time I look at you, I see your father, and he would be so proud of you.'

'Where are we going' he gently asked her.

'We will fly down to Stansted on the morning of the 23rd. I hire a car at Stansted, and I have a hotel near to the cemetery where I stay overnight to be with my thoughts of him. We'll need to book flights, and I'll book an extra room at the hotel for you.' She still had tears in her eyes.

He knew that this is something he must do. His mother needed him. Was this the deep sadness that he had noticed so often? He comforted his mother. 'Whatever you need me to do will be done Mom, have no fear.'

'What can you tell me about my father?'

'Nothing more today. It's only two days away and I'll tell you all when we are there, I promise.'

'Mom, I love you so much. You have always been there for me, so it will be as you wish. My father obviously meant a lot to you, and I want to know who he is, and the bond between you.'

She looked at him 'You are most certainly part of that bond my darling, you will see.'

Chapter 110

Jane decided that this tenth anniversary of the death of Paul could not pass without some proper remembrance. The families of both Paul and Jane were fragmented and mostly dysfunctional. His children, a son, James, and a younger daughter, Sarah, were from a previous marriage. The breakdown of that marriage resulted in both children slowly but surely being alienated against him by their vengeful mother. He was very resentful of this as he loved his children and would have been a great father to them.

James had dropped out of University with serious psychological problems and was now a junior banker in an administrative role. He had at least followed his father into banking but would never aspire to the heights achieved by his father who, at the age of 29 years, was already an executive of the largest bank in the world. Paul did reach out to James some years before his death, but James, who was not then married, was lost in a superficial world of social media without any ambition in life other than to have a good time, and still living with his mother, because he could not afford otherwise. At the funeral Jane detected an enormous chip on his shoulder towards both his father and his sister. *'What a waste'* she thought.

Sarah, having successfully secured a good honours degree under the guidance of her father, started post-graduate studies in London as an intern, but dropped out after just three months. She had sought her father's advice in a roundabout way, but then ignored it, following instead the wishes of her mother. He did not find out that she had dropped out until about a year later when he looked at her Facebook page and saw that she was back at home in an administrative job in the local Chamber of Commerce. Jane reflected that he was so disappointed as he had great hopes for Sarah who, generally, seemed more independently minded than James. She had subsequently married a lawyer and was herself a clerk in a major law firm in London.

She could never fathom why two such privately educated children were still dominated by their mother, someone who had never achieved anything in life herself, not even as a good mother. What was this hold that she had on these children that blinded them to the real world?

They were now grown up and had families of their own. After much ado she got them to the funeral but had not seen much of them since. It was time to bring as much of his family together as possible, and celebrate this quiet, unassuming, great man who had given so much to her during their 27 years together. The fact that he had won the lottery just two weeks before he died was typical of his life. He had real ambitions to activate projects to help people in need to achieve sustainable development in their lives but needed the finance. His reason for being in the City of London that fateful day was to organise the Trust he would need to fund his projects.

He was always so far ahead in his thinking that by the time he was shown to be right everyone was too embarrassed to acknowledge that he was right, having generally ignored or lambasted his ideas at the time. Thus he rarely enjoyed the value of his contribution.

She had contacted James and Sarah. They had both agreed to come on the morning of the 23rd and be part of a remembrance dinner at a local hotel that evening. She had offered to pay for their hotel bills as a sweetener to get them there. Although Paul had left a legacy to both in his Will it was at the discretion of Jane when they got it. She had not yet considered it appropriate to give the legacy to either James or Sarah albeit that she still had over £10 million in the bank from the lottery win. There was also a substantial legacy for a Paul Duncan, but she had no idea how to find this person, albeit she became aware after his death that he was his son.

In all she had assembled about twenty close friends and family, and which was enough for the hotel. She felt that she owed this to Paul as she had a special gift for all of them, something they needed to know about him, and now was the time to present it to them albeit typically long after he could benefit from it.

Chapter 111

It was the morning of the 23rd June. Cis and Paul were up very early to get to the airport for their flight. She could not get her usual 7:30am flight, so had to settle for the 9:20 flight which would get them to Stansted around 10:30. It was about a one hour drive to the village so she did not expect to get there much before midday. She had usually finished her talk with her beloved at his graveside by between 12:30 and 1 o'clock just in case anyone else came. She did not want to be detected, remembering his desire never to upset Jane. Today she would have to take her chances as it would take time to tell their son the story of his father. A bench had been located opposite his grave in his memory, so she usually used it to sit and reflect her loss. She could do the same with Paul as she had much to tell, and she felt comfort when she was near her beloved.

He decided to wear a suit and tie for the first time since the death of his dad, in honour of his mother. He noticed that she was wearing a sober grey jacket and skirt suit, but with an ivory silk top which looked like a camisole, and although she kept her jacket closed, it looked like she was not wearing a bra.

Cis, who was now 47 years old, was still a stunning looking woman, and even though her son enjoyed unfettered and generous use of her breasts as a baby she knew that her beloved would still be excited to undress her and savour her body.

Prejudice in Love

Her son was very confused by what she wore, or did not wear but, on reflection, he had seen her dress like this before – was it for her anniversary visits, and what did this mean? Little did he know that underneath her skirt she had the matching silk French nickers that her beloved so loved. After all this was a special occasion. It was what she wore when her beloved agreed to help her to conceive a child, a child that now stood before her as a grown man.

On warmer June days in previous years she was very tempted to remove her jacket and skirt to show her beloved that she still remembered their time together. She invariably settled to discretely open her jacket so that she revealed to him her bra-less breasts under her silk camisole.

When she saw him in his suit she felt so proud. How quickly he had grown into this tall and handsome man in her life. If only her beloved could see his son and share in the joy he had given to her over the years. 'Thank you' she told him. 'You don't know just how much this means to me.'

Their taxi arrived, and Paul put their overnight luggage into the car. she carried one of her larger handbags. He noticed that there was a leather-bound book, looked like a photo album in her bag, but he had never seen it before. He chose not to inquire as he knew that his role today was to help his mother through the sadness of this day for her, and in the process find out who this man was who has been declared as his father.

Their flight was on time and uneventful. He did not disturb his mother during the flight as she was clearly deep in her own thoughts. At Stansted she went straight to the car rental desk, secured the keys, and off to the car park. They were soon on their way out of Stansted, and on to the M11 motorway, north.

When they arrived, she drove to her usual florist, and then to the hotel. She explained to him that securing an extra room had been difficult as there appears to be a function on this evening with the people staying over. Not quite what she wanted as she sobs the night away, but it is within walking distance of the cemetery, and she has a standing booking for this date every year.

They were permitted to check in early, a pre-ordered light lunch taken, and she took his arm as they left for the cemetery.

Chapter 112

Jane had suggested that everyone assembled at the hotel around one o'clock where she would meet them. They could have a quick lunch and then visit Paul's grave. She wanted to give them a present after the visit to the cemetery. She had put this present together especially for today to give time for those interested to absorb the content before dinner. She had arranged to stay over at the hotel so that she was a part of the whole remembrance dinner.

She was currently driving towards the hotel as she had moved from the house she occupied with Paul – the memories of that house were just too much. With Paul's lottery windfall she found a house that she knew would be favoured by him. She had not co-habited with anyone else although she did have eligible suitors, and she knew that he would be happy for her to get on with her life. However, she lost her mother within two years of losing him. Her world had been shattered and she was still slowly, but surely putting her life back together.

She noticed a well-dressed, dark-skinned women carrying flowers, and what looked like her son, walking towards the cemetery, but thought nothing of it. It was just unusual to see coloured people around this area.

She arrived at the hotel to find that James and his family had arrived. She was happy to see that his attire was suitably sober and respectful. Her mind reflected on how his father had really tried to reach out to him, but he had been so brainwashed by his mother, that he could not see the wood for the trees. She greeted them and showed them into the hotel where they were checked in. She pointed them to a reception room which she

Prejudice in Love

had hired, and which had a display of canopies, salads, and a variety of dishes for lunch.

It wasn't long before others started to arrive, much to her relief. She had no expectations that everyone would arrive, even though they said they would. It was important that Sarah attends because of what she wanted to give to both her and James. She was especially pleased that two nieces of Paul had travelled from the USA, and a former colleague and his wife from Australia were visiting London so agreed to be part of this remembrance. At Paul's funeral the wife of this colleague openly stated to Jane that Paul had been an inspired leader of people and was certainly the best influence in her husband's career.

She was relieved to see Sarahcoll enter through the door, but she was alone. She greeted her and asked her where her husband and children were. Sarah was sombre. She told her that, having given it a lot of thought, and feeling responsible for the breakdown of her relationship with her father, she wanted to have time alone with him at the grave. It occurred to her that she had lost a father who really cared for her. She was very much daddy's girl before she betrayed him at the age of 12 years. She said that it was time for her to make her peace with her father. Jane gave her a big hug. 'He'll really appreciate that', she told Sarah. 'I'll make sure you have the time you need.' During the few years that Sarah did visit with her father Jane and Sarah developed a good relationship together, and Jane detected that this relationship was still intact.

Sarah started to sob. 'What went wrong in this family?' she asked Jane, under her sobs. Jane wanted so much to answer this question, but she thought better of it as accusing her mother on this important day would not be helpful. She would realise who was responsible soon enough on her own.

Jane comforted Sarah, took her to her room, and told her to relax and come down when ready. A buffet lunch was available, and they would leave for the cemetery around 2:30.

Chapter 113

It was only a 10-minute walk to the cemetery from the hotel. It was a bright June day and Cis was grateful for the warmth from the sunshine as it would take some time to tell Paul about his father. She had her private journal with her recording their time together, and as much as she could find out about her beloved including their photo in the kilt shop, her special photo taken on their last night at Gleneagles, and his departing letter to her. Paul's blog took off after they parted, probably as a result of making his work known to her editor as part of her disclosure to her of her liaison with him, resulting in him publishing work in a number of online newspapers and magazines – she had all of them, including his bibliography from Who's Who. She also had the tributes paid in various media after his untimely death. She wanted her son to see all of this so that he would understand that his father was a great contributor to society and was respected for his views.

Paul was carrying the beautiful bunch of lilies that she collected on their way to the hotel. As they approach Paul's grave, she handed her bag to him, and took the flowers. She turned to him 'give me a minute will you please'. He backed away, saw the bench overlooking Paul's grave, and decided to park himself there. He soon noted that the bench had been donated in the memory of a Paul Fulton.

He could read the headstone from the bench.

Paul Fulton
Beloved partner of Jane Winters
Truly loved and admired

There was some scripted text further down, but he could not read it from the bench.

He could not recall hearing this name anywhere, but why should he at his age? Only the names of film stars, rock stars, and sports celebrities were on the lips of people his age. His mother knew lots of important people, especially in the fashion

Prejudice in Love

world, but she clearly put this man, his father, above all of them. He knew his mother and knew that this was very important to her. He must be patient.

He watched his mother approach the grave, unbutton her jacket, and then get down on her knees in front of his headstone to put her flowers in the flower holder still at the foot of his headstone. She was grateful that Jane had kept this flower holder as she had bought it for this purpose. She moved slowly and carefully making sure that every flower was in its right position. She was talking, but he could not make out what she was saying.

After some minutes had passed, she pointed back to him, and then beckoned him to join her. He rose from the bench and joined his mother at her side. He could hear her say 'this is your son, Paul. Look how he is grown. As promised, I bring him to you in his eighteenth year, and now will sit here with him, in your presence, and tell him the story of how two completely different strangers were brought together in a storm, and which changed my life forever. You gave me our son, and he is the living embodiment of our love for each other. I hope that you can hear me and see that my love for you will never wane.'

She held her son's hand very firmly, looked up at him proudly but with tears in her eyes. She bent down and kissed the headstone, re-buttoned her jacket, and led him back to the bench.

She took a minute to compose herself. When she started to speak it was clearly with a quiver in her voice. She started the story. 'As you can see your father's name is Paul Fulton – the source of your name. He was a very senior banker, economist, philosopher, and wonderful man. We met during a storm when a terrified young woman needed a knight in shining armour to rescue her and protect her.' She continued to relate the story of their relationship, having regular breaks for her to re-compose herself after remembering special, tender moments, censored where necessary, and why he could not play a part in his childhood.

She referred frequently to items in the book that she carried informing him that she had compiled this book over the years for him to know his father. She let him read some of what she had assembled, including the letter her beloved had written to her, so that he could see the nature of what had happened those eighteen years ago. She used these interludes for her own reflections, and to compose herself for the next part of the story. The process was taking some time, but she had waited a long time for this moment, and she was in no hurry on this special day.

Chapter 114

Back at the hotel Jane was surprised to see that everyone who said they would come had indeed arrived, and where necessary, were introducing themselves. Sarah had reappeared. Jane told her to stay close, and she would take her with her to the cemetery. It was 2:15 and everyone looked like they had taken whatever lunch they wanted.

She tapped a glass with a spoon to get attention. 'As we are all here shall we make our way to the cemetery, it is only about 10 minutes on foot.'

Off they went with Jane and Sarah in the lead.

Cis could hear the chatter of a group of people approaching but was too engrossed in her story to take any notice. Her story was a slow and painful process, but she wanted her son to know as much as possible whilst here with her beloved. As was always the case, from the first moment they met, she felt stronger in his presence, and wanted him by her side when she told this story to their son.

The voices were getting nearer but this bench was on a pathway – probably a funeral in progress. Suddenly the bench was surrounded by this noisy crowd. Jane quickly noticed the fresh flowers beautifully arranged as was the case every year when she arrived. She then looked at the two people sitting on the bench behind her. Cis looked up and found herself looking into the eyes of Jane, whom she immediately recognised. She realised that there was nowhere to go, and really did not want to in any case. Today was about introducing her son to his father and she was not finished.

Jane realised that this dark-skinned woman had been crying, and was with, what looked like, her son. These were the people she had noticed on her way to the hotel. Her mind went back to Paul's biography. Jane walked to Cis and said 'excuse me, are you Felicity Duncan?'

She could not hold back her tears 'yes' she responded under her sobs, 'and this is my son, Paul.'

Jane could see the distress in her eyes, sat down next to her, put her hand on her arm, and said 'it's alright, I know all about you, and I'm very happy to meet you at last.'

Cis just unwound so much grief and relief as Jane took her into her arms to comfort her.

The rest of the party just stood there confused by this event. Sarah had quietly gone to the grave of her father and placed a lone flower below his headstone in-front of the flowers left by Cis. Sarah was shedding her own tears as Jane spoke to her.

'Sarah, this is your half-brother Paul.'

'Paul this is Sarah, your half-sister. You also have a half-brother', whilst she tried to locate James who was in the background trying to keep his inquisitive children from disturbing this situation.

Paul got up to say hello to Sarah who burst into tears, walked towards him and hugged him 'I have a half-brother?' realising that he was half her age, 'you could be my son. Let me look at you. Like the tan' she laughed under her sobs and trying to wipe her eyes.

Cis had calmed a little and looked at Jane. 'How do you know about me? Paul gave up any contact with his son to ensure that you did not suffer any feelings of betrayal.'

Jane responded 'come back to the hotel where we are having a remembrance dinner this evening, and all will be revealed. Can you stay this evening?'

'We're staying overnight at the hotel just along the road.'

'Sounds like the same place. If it's any comfort I didn't know anything about you before Paul died, but I wish that he'd told me your story. But I'm really pleased to meet you now that I know your place in Paul's life.'

Seeing that Cis was now calmer Jane stood up and assembled everyone around Paul's grave with Jane standing at the foot of the grave looking straight at the headstone. Jane did not want to distress Cis further by introducing them to each of the assembled party in turn. Cis was by her side, with Paul standing on the other side of his mother, and Sarah still hanging onto his arm realising that she did need someone with her on this emotional day. Jane looked directly at the headstone of Paul and started:

'Today, my love, on this tenth anniversary of your untimely death, I bring together family and friends who want to remember the great man you are. Things did not go so well with family whilst you were alive, but I hope that, in your memory, people will be united again. If you brought Felicity and Paul to us today, I'm very pleased because they shared your great love and affection for those around you. I wished you had told me about your son many years ago. I know the pain that you suffered when you lost access to James and Sarah, and the despair you felt not being able to participate in their youth. Knowing the story of your liaison with Felicity I would have fully supported your involvement in the development of this fine-looking young man. In celebration of your life I will ensure that all the people assembled know who you really are,

Prejudice in Love

and how much you touched their lives. You are still my big bear, my rock, and I miss you so much.'

Jane was now sobbing, and Cis was comforting her.

Others said their silent words as they stood with their heads bowed. More flowers were added to those already placed by Cis and Sarah. Sarah had adopted Paul as her companion. He was now comforting her as the words spoken by Jane hit her hard, and she was now sobbing. Even he could feel tears welling within. This day was just too much for him to absorb, but he felt the moment and knew there was much to know about this man, his father. He felt proud to be there, even though he had never knowingly met this man.

After some minutes people started to move back to the pathway and the bench.

Jane turned to Cis. 'Please come back with us to the hotel, I have so much to tell you, and I would love to hear your story from you.'

'Let me speak with my son as this is the first he knows of his father, and I was telling him the story when you arrived.'

She turned to Paul. 'We are invited back to the hotel with these people, some of them family you are not aware of. I've not finished my story. Would you like to wait here a while longer while I finish my story, or shall we join with these people and go back to the hotel?'

Sarah was still on his arm and heard this exchange. 'Please come with us, I have a new brother, and at this moment of grief for our father I need you by my side.'

Paul turned to his mother. 'I now feel the great love that you have for this man, my father.' He paused to compose himself. 'I feel overwhelmed, and we are obviously about to learn more than even you know about my father. We can come back another time, and another time, and as many times as you wish to finish your story. This lady obviously wants to include us in the celebration of my father, so for now let us stay with this party.'

Cis thought, *'my son is a man in his father's image'*, and she loved his repeated use of the words "my father". Her job was done. Her pledge to her beloved honoured. A sadness had been lifted now that she could openly speak with her son of her love for her beloved Paul.

She smiled at Paul and took his hand, 'thank you so much my beautiful son. Your father would be very proud of you.'

With that she turned to Jane, 'we would be honoured to join in with this celebration'.

'Good' said Jane reassuringly, 'we have much to share, and the honour is mine. I have waited ten years to meet you and Paul.'

Chapter 115

Cis and Jane talked all the way back to the hotel. Jane had noticed the same attention to detail in the fresh flowers under Paul's headstone that she had witnessed in previous years. She asked her if this was her first visit, but she told her that she had come to the funeral, but in the background, and visited every year around 11:30 and spent at least an hour at the graveside. Jane asked her if it was she who left the flowers each year. She confessed that it was her. She also explained that it was she who had the flower holder planted in Paul's grave, and thanked her for keeping it there. Jane explained that she always arrived around 3:30 but was always confronted with these beautifully arranged fresh flowers, and always wondered who had left them.

Jane was staggered that they had not met before, but Cis told her that she stayed true to her pledge to Paul that she would not find out about their liaison. It was only because she had decided to bring her son with her this time, they could only get a later flight, and she needed time to tell her story, that they were still at the graveside when Jane arrived. 'We lost track of time and thought that the people approaching would be attending a funeral' she explained. 'I never thought for a moment that such a crowd would be visiting Paul. In any event, having kept my secret from my son for so many years, I was not about to be rushed away from the graveside at which I find so much solace.'

Jane told her that some weeks after his death she had found his biography. She knew it existed because she knew that he started to write it whilst recovering from his cancer treatment.

Cis was amazed. 'Paul had cancer?'

'Yes. And his resolute determination to beat it prevailed. But the treatment did leave side effects, including to the arteries in his neck. He fought with these problems for some years, but they resulted in his early retirement as he was unable to control some of the adverse effects.'

She went on to explain that it was only when she sat down to read his biography that she found out about his time with her, and her resulting son.

'Would you consider letting me have a copy of his biography for my son?' Cis pleaded.

'I have had a number of copies printed and will distribute them at tea when we get back to the hotel, not least because James and Sarah need to read it.'

'You mean that they do not already have a copy?'

'No, you will see when you read it that there is a very distressing section for me. Facing this truth has been very difficult for me, and it's only now that I'm prepared to accept the pain that I caused him.'

'The section on your relationship with Paul is very touching, and typical of his generosity.'

'I would very much like to read his account of our time together as it was he who gave me so much during those seven days. I have my own account of our time together to give to my son, but we did not get that far.'

'Do you have your account with you?'

'Yes. It's part of the tribute that I've compiled for my son so that he will know what Paul did for him even though my son never knew him. Paul stopped visiting with us as soon as my son was starting to recognise people. It was a very sad day in my life.'

'Can I read it?' asked Jane, 'as his account is very moving, but I would like to see your version.'

Cis agreed to exchange their books when they got back to the hotel.

During this walk Sarah had pounded Paul with questions, but he could not provide answers because he was only being introduced to this situation and his father today.

James introduced himself to Paul welcoming him to a family of dysfunctional people. Sarah pounced on him and told him that it was his lack of respect for his father, and this situation, that needed to be addressed. It was clear to Paul that there was no love lost between his brother and sister and wanted to know why. Sarah told Paul not to take any notice of James as he was totally screwed up and needed a wakeup call. James retorted back that Sarah was always daddy's girl and got all his attention. James had always been jealous of the relationship between her and her father although, in realty, there was no foundation to his insecurity. 'He loved us both', she exclaimed loud enough for James to hear, 'but we were not bright enough to realise it.'

They were now back at the hotel, and Jane realised that the structure of the evening needed to be changed. The inclusion of Cis and Paul required a major rethink of her layout. She directed everyone to the room that had been booked for afternoon tea, and she went off to speak with the catering manager.

Chapter 116

The intrigue of the presence of Cis and Paul, not least because of their skin colour but also because of her youthfulness, broke the assembled people into two groups. The first group were the people who wanted to meet these strangers and find out where they fitted into the story, and the other group who were pathetic enough to draw their own conclusions and re-evaluate their own view of Paul. Sarah was very alive to this and kept Paul within reach to ensure that no-one did anything to offend him. She had become unusually protective of this stranger, her brother, and wanted so much to know his story.

Jane reappeared carrying what appeared to be a heavy box. James stepped in to take it from her and place it in a space on the server table. Jane looked around to see how the inter-relationships were working. She was not impressed, but not surprised.

She could see that Cis was engaged with two nieces of Paul who had flown in from the USA for this event, Paul's youngest brother, and Paul's colleague, David, and his wife, Jennifer, from Australia. She knew Cis would be safe with them. Jane was surprised to see the nieces as Paul did not have much to do with them. But she did know that they knew and respected Paul. They were the daughters of one of his brothers, but even Jane would not allow this brother into her house for the problems he created for Paul and his mother resulting in years of no real contact with his mother.

Jennifer explained to Cis that her husband had worked for Paul as his financial controller. She expressed that Paul was a great mentor and inspired David to his subsequent achievements. She wanted her son to hear this as Jennifer had already stated that their trips to the UK would become less frequent as David's parents, the main reason for their visits, had now both passed away. She attracted Paul to join her, and naturally his new appendage, Sarah, stayed at his side. Jennifer explained to both that her husband had worked for Paul. She also stated to Sarah that David had worked with her mother before working for Paul, and they both attended the marriage of Paul and her mother. She told them both that Paul was an inspired leader to his staff, a great mentor to her husband, and happy to attribute the subsequent success of David directly to his time with Paul. On hearing that Sarah had lost contact with her father Jennifer expressed how sad she was as she could not imagine that any of the some 300 staff who worked for Paul when she knew him would have anything other than a strong affection for her father, even today. Sarah, with tears in her eyes, acknowledged that it was obvious to her how much her father touched and inspired people around him and regretted her lack of any contact with him.

Jane called everyone to attention. She opened the box. 'Paul wrote a biography that he started during his treatment for cancer. I've decided that the contents of his biography are so important to a number of people here that I've had copies printed. Anyone interested may have a copy.'

She took a copy out of the box to reveal a fully bound book about 2" thick. Sarah moved forward to take a copy and took a second copy for Paul. Most of the other people also moved forward to take a copy. Jane took a copy for Cis, and they exchanged her journal with Paul's biography. She agreed to return her journal to her before dinner.

Jane announced that everyone should be in this same room for dinner by 7:30.

Chapter 117

Cis had been reading Paul's biography for about 2 hours. She had first read his account of their encounter, and then the years relating to Jane and his children. She then went back to his childhood to find a boy who was so abused by his father just for wanting an education. What she read was shocking to her, so much pain throughout his life. *'This story has to be told.'*

Prejudice in Love

She went back to the account of their time together, and specifically to one passage. Paul had recorded that she pressed them to stay together, and how agonising this was for him. But having not told her about his cancer and the continual health problems thereafter from the side effects of the cancer treatment, all of which required lengthy treatment, he could not expect her to take care of him and a child. He had met her in a rare period of relatively good health. Indeed, he noted that their encounter had been very good for both his mental and physical well-being. But he could not burden one so young with his problems as he would fight one problem thinking he was through it only to be inflicted with another soon after in a seemingly endless fight for survival.

'Oh, my darling Paul', she cried, 'always thinking of others before yourself. Had I known that this was your conflict you would not have left me. It would have been a privilege for me to care for you. And Jane told me that you did not suffer much after our time together in any event. So much happiness lost.'

She was now sobbing bitterly. She did not know whether to be angry with him or respect his compassion. 'We could have had eight years of bliss, especially with our son. Although Andrew was very good to me and our son, we never had the love I shared with you. You deprived both of us of so much happiness together. Why didn't I push you to tell me the conflicts within you? Lovers are supposed to share such things.'

Although she knew in her heart that he had made a rational decision typical of such a man, she also knew that there are times when rational is not the best way for all concerned. She remembered the Adult, Parent, Child philosophy that he had taught her thinking that he needed to get off his Adult pedestal into Parent mode for that decision. The outcome would have been so much better for all three. Yes, including their son.

She changed out of her camisole into a regular top including a bra. Her dress code for her visits to his grave was nothing to do with anyone other than her beloved.

She went along the corridor, clutching Paul's biography, to the room occupied by Jane and knocked on the door. Jane answered. When she looked at Cis she could see that she had been crying again and welcomed her in.

Jane had also read her account of her relationship with Paul and completely understood the devotion that she showed towards Paul. What a selfish fool she was to put Paul into a position where he could not enjoy his new son. She felt so guilty.

'We need to publish this biography', she said, 'and I know how to do it. This is a story which should be told. Although I don't agree with Paul's version of our liaison, the events are correct. He is far too generous towards me. If I resolved those problems for him, I was only aware of maybe two or three. It was his devotion to my problems that filled those days. He told me nothing of his cancer and the toll it took upon him, both physically and mentally, over those years.'

Her editor had already approached her to publish her story of her time with Paul now that Andrew was no longer alive. But she did not want her son to find out about his father through such an article. Now she had the whole story and felt sure that her editor's husband, who was a publisher, would relish the opportunity of such a book.

'I've read your account, and it certainly paints a view of the Paul that I knew. You don't need to convince me of his love for you. I saw the photograph of you both at some dinner. The power of the love between you both radiates from that photograph, and that picture needs to be included in his biography.'

'Please sit down, Felicity because in your account there are some answers to questions that I had, not least why he came back to me. In your account you state that, before he took you home, that he suggested he was staying overnight in Edinburgh to think things through, and he may come back for you. Is that correct?'

'Yes, it is. He was agonising what he should do. I thought I had convinced him to stay with me. But he did not come back for me.'

'If it's any consolation to you Felicity I'm now sure that if it had been a straight choice between you and me, he would have chosen you. You are everything he wanted. Just look at that photograph and you know this to be true.'

'Then why didn't he come back to me?'

'I'm now sure that his agonising that night was what was best for your son. Without a child his decision would have been simple. He obviously thought that his son needed two young loving parents in a loving family environment, and I can see that you have done a wonderful job with Paul. He's such a well-balanced boy. You only need to look at Sarah and James to understand his dilemma that night. His thoughts would have accounted for his possible premature death leaving a young child fatherless with potential devastating impact. I saw him with his own children when they were young. They were very close, far closer than with their mother, and thus her selfish, insecure need to break this relationship. The loss of such a loving father could have had a serious impact with your child, as it did with his when contact was lost. Therefore, I think, as was usual for him, that his decision was brilliantly intuitive, and the best overall option for everyone, and at great personal sacrifice to himself.'

'Why do you think this?'

'After Paul died, I slowly went through all of his papers. I found a book that contained his usernames and passwords for internet sites that he used. There was an unknown one to me with a reference of "Cis". When I looked at the site it was a site that you must have set up for him to monitor the progress of young Paul. His visit log showed that he visited this site at least once every week. He was devoted to your son and wanted what he thought was best for him having suffered so much with his other children. And you can see how dysfunctional they are.'

'I did ask a friend of mine skilful in all thinks internet to put a message up on that site to tell you of his death, and that I wanted you to contact me. But by the time he tried to load my message to you the site had gone.'

'Yes. After I'd finished my grieving, I asked the person who managed it for me to remove it as it was only there for Paul.'

Jane reached out for her hand. 'My sorrow is that he felt that he could not tell me about you. We had been together for so long, but he had lost trust in me, and suffered great pain as a result. I cannot tell you how much I regret the situation that I created for you both.'

Jane was now sobbing reflecting on the pain she had caused not only Paul, but also this lovely lady who so obviously has so much love for Paul.

Jane regained her composure. 'Can you spend an extra day here? I would like you and Paul to come back with me tomorrow to my home and spend the day with me. Paul left a substantial legacy for your son, and I would like you both to read it for yourself, and for me to give it to Paul. I have also kept his dress kilt that he bought whilst with you. I would like to give this to you, or Paul. Your son is a rightful heir to wear his kilt, and it looks like it might even fit him. I also have many photographs and memorabilia that I would like to show to Paul so that he can really understand the achievements of his father.'

Cis looked at Jane speechless, listening to this woman, the woman who stood between her and her beloved Paul, now inviting her to her home and sharing memories of Paul. She would certainly like his kilt as she still had the dress she wore that night, and would like to put them together in her wardrobe. But was she right that Jane did not stand between them, it was her desire to have a child, their son? This is where it all started with Andrew.

Finally, Cis said that she would very much like to stay. She would rearrange her flights for the following day.

Prejudice in Love

Jane also invited her to stay with her for future visits. Cis explained that she liked to be alone with her memories. Jane assured her that she could have as much space as she liked, and Paul would also be welcome to come with her. She added that they shared the love of Paul, and it was time for them to share it together, as it should have been before he died.

With that Jane returned her journal and they agreed to go to dinner together at 7:30.

Cis returned to her room to get ready. She was totally confounded with what she had heard. Paul gave up his happiness with her because he thought it best for his unborn son. *'What is it with men and babies? My desire to have a child caused the problem that provoked my guardian angel to connect us, and then my need for a child lost me the man of my dreams.* Well Paul you told me you can't always get what you want, but if you try, you get what you need. We needed each other, and we could have had both.'

Chapter 118

Within minutes of returning to her room there was a knock on her door. It was Paul. 'Come in my darling. You're early, but this is good because I need you to do something for me. I want you to change our flights. We need to change them from tomorrow to the following afternoon. I'll give you my credit card.'

'Could you also go online and change the car hire to match the new flights. Jane has invited us to spend tomorrow with her. Your father left you a legacy, and she wants to give it to you herself.'

'Mom, I'm so confused and overwhelmed with the events of today. I have so many questions I need to ask you.'

She hugged him. 'I know that it has been a big day for you, but please just help me through this, and I'll help you to make sense of it all. It's proving overwhelming for me also. I did not expect any of this. I've learnt so much today about your beloved father. So please change our reservations for me. You're better with the technology than I'll ever be.'

'No problem Mom, whatever you say.'

She remembered how clever Paul was with technology, how he could make hotel reservations on the fly with just a few keystrokes on his iPad.

Paul had noticed that his mother was no longer wearing her camisole top. Whilst waiting for the airline to answer his call he asked his mother if there was any significance to her camisole top at the cemetery.

'Yes, there is', she replied, 'but some parts of this story are just between your father and myself. Please change our reservations as I need to compose myself for this evening.'

He noticed her book on the table. There was what looked like a photograph hanging out of the last page. He pulled it out and looked at it. It was a picture of his mother looking stunning in a shimmering evening dress looking at an older man dressed in a kilt. He could not help, even at his tender age, to notice the way they looked at each other.

Paul changed the flights, and the car hire. He then looked at this photograph more closely. It radiated togetherness. 'Mom', he said, 'this picture is you and my father?'

She looked to see which picture he had. 'Yes, my dear, we were having dinner at Gleneagles on our last but one night together. I was probably one or two days pregnant with you. We were so happy.'

'You two are joined at the hip', he proclaimed.

'If you mean that it shows two people deeply in love, having created a new life in the form of you, then you are very observant for someone of your tender years.'

'I read his account of your time together. You helped him through a number of difficulties in his life.'

'When you read my account you will see the measure of the man. I was not even aware of most of the issues he raises in his account. Believe me my precious son, it was he who saved me.'

It was 7:30. Jane knocked at the door. Cis was ready, but asked Paul to go ahead. She and Jane would be down in a moment.

Cis told Jane that all was good to spend the day with her tomorrow. They hugged each other.

She collected her own journal and his biography, held them close to her, and waited with Jane just a few minutes longer so that everyone would be in the private dining room before they arrived.

Chapter 119

When they reached the dining room arm-in-arm everyone was already there. Glasses of Prosecco, Jane's favourite fizz, were in the hands of most of the assembled group.

Cis immediately noticed that the long table for dinner had another table at one end in the form of a 'T'. Two places had been set at this table. All places had place name tags. She went to the table to see that she was sitting on the left of Jane at this table. Protocol would deem that her place at the table was the place of honour. Paul was placed directly in front of her on the long section, with Sarah next to him. James and his wife were seated on the other side of the long table in front of Jane.

Cis went to Jane. 'You honour me at this table. This is your celebration, and I'm just a visitor.'

'You and Paul are our honoured guests. We two shared the love of Paul, and we share this celebration and remembrance of his life. You are in your rightful place.'

'Would you mind if I say a few words before dinner?'

'Felicity, or can I call you Cis?

'Cis is fine with me.'

'Thank you.' Jane held her hands 'Whatever you want today, you will have. I'll alert the waiting staff.'

Jane explained to the lady in charge of the hotel catering staff that she would like all glasses charged when everyone is seated, and then wait until after Felicity has spoken before serving dinner. She further alerted the lady in charge that what Felicity had to say could be emotionally charged so if she could keep noise to a minimum. The lady in charge understood and made appropriate preparations.

Jane invited everyone to be seated.

With everyone seated, and all glasses charged, Cis rose to her feet, placing her hands on the table for support. The room went silent.

Cis, having gathered her thoughts and her courage, stood upright and started 'Firstly can I thank Jane from the bottom of my heart for allowing myself, and my son to be part of this celebration of the life of our beloved Paul, and to thank you all for your kindness today. This is the first time that my son has been made aware that the wonderful man that we are here to celebrate is his real father.'

Jane put a reassuring hand over her hand.

'Also I want to express my gratitude to Jane for inviting me to sit with her tonight to share with her this remembrance of the love we both had for Paul. I was totally unaware until today that Jane knew anything about me, or my son, as Paul was fiercely protective of his devotion to Jane.'

She picked up the biography and clutched it close to her breast. 'I'm so grateful to Jane for this biography of Paul. It has already filled a number of holes in my knowledge and understanding of him; and will be invaluable for my son to know the great and compassionate nature of his father.'

She continued to clutch the book but looked up to the heavens.

'Paul, I want to tell these people how you found a very distressed 28-year old stranger in a motorway service station trying the escape a terrifying storm. You scooped her up in your loving arms and changed her life forever. So please, can I call upon your strength to help me lest I flounder into a jabbering, sobbing wreck.' Tears were in her eyes as she lowered her eyes to the assembled people.

She tried to compose herself. 'I assume that Paul touched the lives of everyone at this table at some time. I don't know to what extent any of you feel that his love, strength, and generosity affected your lives, but I would like to tell you how much he touched my life.'

Sarah, already welling up inside, grabbed the hand of Paul.

'I have read the account of our time together in his biography, but, as was his generosity, he writes it as though I helped him with some of the issues that troubled him. Other than I noticed sadness in his eyes on occasion during our brief time together, and he did disclose some discrete details of issues in his life to me in order to placate my inquisitiveness, or even to explain his actions, I can assure you that he was my valiant knight protecting a damsel in great distress. He not only protected me from the storm, but took a woman sleepwalking through her life, and completely turned her around, and for which I will be eternally grateful.'

'Paul told me that we are defined by the decisions we make and moulded by our experiences. Those brief seven days together were the most important days in my life. The courage he gave me to make much needed decisions in my life, and the experiences he shared with me, moulded my whole future.'

'I visit with Paul every year on this date, and I stay in this same hotel to spend the evening alone with my thoughts and memories of our brief, but wonderful time together, and my unwavering gratitude for what he did for me. And not forgetting the much wanted son that he gave to me.'

'It's important that you know that my son is not the result of some covert liaison. I had already left Paul and returned to my home in Edinburgh only to realise the following day that I was ready to conceive. I knew that fate had dealt me a hand with my valiant knight that I must pursue. My darling husband could not give me children, and it was breaking us apart. So I went back to Paul that very day and begged him to help me. He was very reluctant, not least because of the pain he suffered with the lack of contact with his own children, but also in the knowledge that he could not be an active father to my child because of the pain this would cause to Jane. My own darling husband Andrew accepted this gift with open arms and fulfilled the role as father to our son as if his own. This gift brought Andrew and I back together until his untimely death some two years ago in a plane crash. Until two days ago my son knew nothing of this. I don't want him to forget Andrew, or the love they shared for each other, but I do want him to know my beloved Paul who gave me so much. I have lost the two important men in my life, but they live on in the son for whom both played their part.'

'I hope very much that Sarah and James, and their respective families will find it in their hearts to embrace my son as their brother, and together learn about the man you all carry in your DNA, and hopefully in your hearts.'

Sarah squeezed Paul's hand lovingly. She had already embraced this lovely young man and wanted to quickly introduce him to her own young children.

She continued, 'Jane has kindly allowed me the opportunity to publish his biography despite the pain it will cause her, as this is the story of a great man. I'm from the literary world and know a publisher who is already aware of what he did for me. For me it's ironic and distressing to realise that the world knew of the greatness and goodness in this man more than some of the people around him. I want the world to see how this man had to suffer a loneliness for much of his life, even at the end when no-one who loved and cared for him was able to comfort him during his last breaths. He gave so much to those he touched yet received so little in return.' Tears were now running down her cheeks, and she needed a moment to compose herself.

By now there was not a dry eye in the room as they all realised that there was much truth in what she said.

'However, this book is not finished. His life was ended too abruptly for him to finish it himself. I propose to add a tribute about my own love for, and gratitude to this man, especially for the wonderful son he gave to me. If anyone else here wants to add their own tribute, I will happily include it.'

Sarah, with tears running down her cheeks, raised her free hand. James quickly followed suit.

She continued 'I will also ensure that none of his words are edited. He had a great way with words, as seen in his blogs and other media articles, and the little that I've read this afternoon conveys the character, wit, pain, and wisdom of this beloved man.'

She raised her glass and looked up to the heavens once again. 'I celebrate your life, your love, and your compassion. I miss you so much.' Tears were now flowing from her eyes has everyone simultaneously stood and raised their glasses 'Paul'.

After the toast Jane comforted her as she unleashed the sadness that she would normally shed alone in a room upstairs. 'You did very well Cis', whispered Jane, 'and I'm so grateful that we finally meet on this special day.'

The lady responsible for service in this private function room was standing at the door. She could see that she was witnessing a very solemn moment so ensured that it could not be disturbed. What she heard brought tears to her eyes, and she had to step outside to collect herself before indicating to the waiters that they could now start to serve dinner but alerted them to the solemnness that she had witness and asked them to be invisible.

It took some minutes before Jane and Cis resumed their seats, both of them needing a good supply of Kleenex which the service lady had had the forethought to find a box and put it on the table between them.

Paul reached over and held his mother's hand. 'Are you okay Mom?' he said soothingly.

She smiled at him 'you must think your mother a silly woman with all these emotions and tears.'

'Absolutely not Mom, how could you think that?' He could feel tears welling in his eyes. 'Your words were from your heart. If I ever wanted to know what my father meant to my mother, I just heard it. All these years you have carried your sadness, but now it is out, and you can openly share your thoughts and memories with me.'

She smiled lovingly at her precious son, and thought *'as soon as we get home I'll put the canvas picture of us at Gleneagles on my bedroom wall where I can see it every night when I go to bed. I so want him near to me.'*

'Did my father ever come to see me?'

'Yes, he came a few times when you were just a small baby. I wanted him to see what a bonnie son he had, and that I was living my pledge to him regarding my love for you. As soon as you started to identify people, he decided to stop so that your dad became the only father figure in your life.'

She reflected on Paul's visits to Edinburgh to see her and his son. The first was about three months after the birth of their son. Andy was away on business, as was Jane. He drove up to Edinburgh and stayed in a hotel close to where she lived. She remembered the full day they spent together. It was a rainy September day, so they spent most of their time in his hotel room.

Although she posted regular pictures of the development of her pregnancy bump on her special web site for him, she had taken pictures of her completely naked at 8 months. She wanted to show him what this pregnancy had done to the body he so loved, especially how her breasts had ballooned. However, she thought better of posting these online as she knew that once posted she could never really delete them. So she shared them with him on that day.

When it was time for her to breastfeed their son, he gently stripped her to the waist and then sat her in his lap whilst their son suckled her breast to extract her milk. He stroked her, including the breast not being suckled whilst their son was feeding. It was a lovely way to feed her baby, and she quickly introduced this into her routine with Andrew.

Later, when their son was asleep, she issued the magic code 'let's get naked' followed by 'stroke me'. He duly undressed her and stroked her in the way that only he could. The thought of him stroking her, sitting at this celebration table, brought a warm glow to her. Andy never did master the skills to really electrify her with his hands. He did not have the benefit of her masterful teacher. He slowly stroked her all the way to orgasm, after which she was desperate to issue the code 'pussy is hungry'. Alas her menstrual cycle had returned, and she knew that she was not far from ovulation. She could not risk another pregnancy although she, herself, would not mind.

Although he visited twice more, the latter to her house for just two hours during a business trip, she happily gave him access to her breasts whilst she fed their son, but there was no opportunity for any more than this. She so missed the way he touched her.

Appetites had been diminished by the emotional content of what they had heard, but the people at the table started to reminisce their experiences with Paul with a more circumspect view having listened to what Cis had said. The people who really knew him were not surprised by the emotions expressed by her, but those who only thought they knew him were re-examining their views.

After the main course Sarah, who had only picked at her food, left her seat to speak with Cis.

'Felicity, in just seven days you know my father better than I ever knew him. He tried so hard to keep contact with me, but in the end, I betrayed him. Even when he reached out to me whilst at university, I made it hard for him, and then pushed him away. I was so stupid, and now, so ashamed. I have, today, read the pain and sorrow that I caused him. I want to write down what he did for me when he was given the opportunity as I know he loved me. He was the one who took care of me when I was seriously ill as a baby, not my mother. He tried so hard to be a father to me. Can I have your details so that I can send you my contribution? And would you act as editor and tell me if I need to change anything?'

'Sarah', she responded warmly, 'the words should come from your heart, and be your voice. Certainly I'll comment from a purely literary viewpoint, but I hope not to change anything you write. I'll give you my contact details tomorrow morning at breakfast.'

Sarah continued 'I would like to introduce Paul to my children as soon as possible. I would like both of you to come and stay with us for a few days as I have so much I want to ask you.'

'Will you please agree some dates during the summer with Paul as he starts at university in October. I'm happy to whatever dates you both select, and I thank you for your kind invitation. I can tell you that your father loved you very much.'

Tears welled up in the eyes of Sarah, 'thank you, I know, and I'm so ashamed.'

Sarah then went to Jane.

'Jane, I'm so sorry for my behaviour. I'm so ashamed of myself.' Sarah burst into tears. 'Can you ever forgive me?' as she sobbed uncontrollably.

Jane stood up and comforted Sarah. 'All of us need forgiveness my dear, even me. I also betrayed him without realising the pain that I caused. And then, because of my betrayal, your father thought that he could not participate in young Paul's life. That would have been the least that I could have done for him.'

James apologised to Paul for his poor behaviour on the way back from the cemetery. He explained that having read parts of the biography of his father, it made him realise how stupid he had been. It was time to confront his mother with the truth and break the chain of lies that had been his childhood.

The conversation around the table was concentrated on the revelation during the day, and intense enough for most not to notice James rising to his feet. It took a little time for the noise of conversation to hush wondering what this embittered son had to say. His head was lowered as he composed himself, but he was clearly distressed. He started to speak with some nervousness.

'Looking around this table I see people who have travelled from as far as the USA and Australia to celebrate the life of a man who has been dead for 10 years, but who still hold his memory in great affection. The experiences of today, and the truly heart wrenching words spoken by Felicity, has moved me to question who I am, and where I have been for the past 20 years? I find it truly staggering that Felicity had just 7 days with my father, yet some 18 years later still holds this man so close to her heart for what he did for her. It makes me feel empty, wretched, and unworthy to be called his son.'

His wife reached over to hold his hand as he composed himself to continue.

'I've read the part of my father's biography that relates to Sarah and myself. I remember that last Christmas and New Year that we spent with him and Jane. It was as he describes, and when my mother came to collect us neither of us was ready for her, or indeed wanted to go home. We had such a great time and did not want it to end. My mother was furious. That is when the alienation towards my father started. I was a ready victim because I so craved the affection of my mother. Sarah held out for about another 3 years, but she suffered as a result. I can see it all so clearly now, and I'm so ashamed that when I was older, I did not realise what had happened. It has taken until now, today, for me to see that I was totally beguiled by my mother. What was the expression used by Felicity? Sleepwalking.'

'When I first read words like "honey trap" and "black witch" with reference to my mother I was angry that he could use such words, albeit David', looking at Paul's former colleague from Australia,' assures me that the "black witch" label was attributed to her in the workplace before meeting my father. Having read further, and explored my own real memories of him, I cannot vilify my father for his choice of words. He had a right to be angry with my mother.'

'More importantly, and I think that I can speak for both myself and Sarah, we failed him. We should have realised in later years that our father was not as described to us, and we had the memories to know this if only we explored them.'

He turned towards Jane. 'Jane, I feel awful about the way I've treated you over these past 20 years. You were so good with us when we stayed with you. Here, in front of my wife and children, and everyone else here, I humbly apologise for my disgraceful behaviour towards you, and would like to welcome you into our family. If my children experience just half of the love and care you showed to myself and Sarah, they will be truly blessed.'

Jane reached for his hand in appreciation.

James then looked at Cis and Paul. 'As for the revelation that I have a brother, and having heard your moving story, I would be truly honoured to welcome you to our family. Other than childhood memories I have little to offer you in relation to our father as I don't even walk in his shadow, let alone his image. But we can learn together how to aspire to his expectations of us. And as an uncle closer to the age of my children your sure footedness may inspire them to greater things in the image of their grandfather. James reached over to Paul offering his hand.

Paul stood and took it in thanks for such invitation. He was totally confounded with these revelations. He needed to know so much more about the life of his father.

James sat down to great applause from the table, and proud comfort from his wife.

Sarah immediately jumped up as the applause subsided. 'I don't want to take more time with speeches but would like to add a few words of my own to this special day. As with my brother James I'm so ashamed about my behaviour towards my father, especially as I was more aware of the alienation of our mother towards him. My guilt is knowing about it but taking the soft option.'

'I can remember the day I saw a copy of Who's Who on the shelf in his study. At that time, I was at boarding school with the children of supposedly the great and the good. I found my father's entry which made me feel so proud, especially as my name was listed as his daughter. I then went through the surnames of all my classmates at school, and then as many other names as I could recall in the school, and search for entries relating to their parents. I did not find one. I knew that day that my father was special.'

'Even after I caved into the wishes of my mother not to see him anymore, I knew he was always there for me. When I was deciding what subjects to do for my first degree at university, I made sure he found out what I was proposing or, more accurately, what my mother was driving me to do. He wrote to me arguing against my choice and providing me with arguments I should consider when making my own choice. I listened and enjoyed my life at university. After university, my mother was driving me into law. Again, he argued against this and gave me alternative arguments, but without direction, just guidance. I ignored him thinking I knew better, and I fell flat on my face. I have gone back to that letter. It's not too late for me to follow his guidance and try to make amends for my disrespect.'

'As for my new brother, I have already welcomed Paul into my family with open arms. I can share much more of the love he had for me.' She put her hand fondly on his shoulder.

'The most important acknowledgement for today is the relentless effort by Jane to bring this family back together in his name, and for that I'm most eternally grateful. The sorrow of today has invigorated me to be a better person in the hope that, one day, I might walk in the image of my father. Please, a toast to Jane whose steadfast love for my father has made this day possible.'

'To Jane'.

Sarah sat down, put her arm through the arm of Paul. 'Thank you and your mother for shining such a bright light here today.'

Jane looked on thinking, *'it looks like we have unity at last. If you are watching Paul, my darling, I think your namesake will finally bring this family back together, and they will know who you are, and how much you loved them – a little late, as was much of the story of your life, but you can be very proud of Cis. She walks in your image, and she has certainly raised young Paul to do the same. I also now have the great hopes for Sarah that you so desired for her, and James might well surprise us. In honour of today I propose to double the legacy that you left for Paul and will now pay the legacies to Sarah and James. I will also help Cis and Paul to know the man that I feel so privileged to have known. Rest well my darling.'*

After desert Jane stood, and everyone went quiet in expectation of what she would add to the proceedings.

She began. 'We are here today, on this tenth anniversary of his untimely death, as a remembrance to Paul, loving father, partner, uncle, and friend to everyone at this table. This day has been made more special with the presence of Felicity and her son by Paul. I have wanted to meet Felicity since I found evidence of her and Paul's son in his biography, a copy of which you all now have.' Looking at Cis, 'I'm so happy to meet you both at long last.'

'I went to his grave the day after his funeral to find the flower holder that is still there today, planted, and full of beautifully arranged white lilies. The cemetery attendant told me he had planted it for a couple who were clearly distressed at his death. Every anniversary since Paul's death I have visited his grave in the afternoon to find fresh, beautifully arranged lilies at his headstone. Each year I wondered who left these flowers as whoever laid them clearly took great care in how they were arranged. Today the mystery is over. It was Felicity who was at his funeral, and who makes the trip from Edinburgh each year to spend some time with the beloved Paul she knew. We have briefly heard their story from Felicity, and I have been privileged to read her full account of their time together. It is a truly moving account, and I hope that Felicity adds it to Paul's biography exactly as written, including a photograph that she has which clearly tells its own story in the love they shared together for that all too brief period.'

'It's interesting to hear from Felicity that she declares that, at 28 years of age, she was sleepwalking through life when she met Paul, and he completely refocused her life. I can easily relate to this as when I met Paul at the age of 29 years I too was sleepwalking, and he completely transformed my life. This is the measure of the man we celebrate today.'

'What also gives me great pleasure today is for Sarah and James to finally realise just how much he loved them both, and the pain caused to him during their childhood. I hope that they will now realise that he really suffered trying to ensure that their childhood was as conflict free as possible. And of course, they now have a much younger brother in Paul. I hope that all three will engage in understanding their father. He was a very complex man, but you could never question his love and commitment to those he cared for.'

'Felicity has offered to have Paul's biography published, and I think that she is right. His story needs to be told. You all now have a copy of his unfinished biography. For anyone who feels that they want to contribute, or even question events as described, to the extent that I can, I'm happy to meet with any of you to go through events described during the time I knew him. It's possible that some of you may have recollections that differ from his account. However, I've not found any material differences to my own recollections, just much pain that I don't think any of us realised. Felicity mentions a sadness and loneliness within him in her account, and I think she has now identified a great deal of the origin of his pain. Clearly, I'm aware of my contribution to his pain, and I've already asked his forgiveness. We have an opportunity to repair much of the pain which consumed him during his life, and I hope that we will use it well.'

'I would like to invite all interested to meet here again next year where we can celebrate the unity that has resulted from the unusual encounters of today.'

'My home is open to any of you at any time, and it would be nice to think that I can be a focus for Paul's memory.'

'Can I thank you all for sharing this remarkable day in remembrance of Paul. Could you please raise your glasses to Paul.'

After the toast discussion went on for some time but was more upbeat. It was as though a cloud had been lifted on the memory of Paul, with everyone now realising that something special had occurred today, very much as with his achievements in life. An encounter of two strangers at his graveside had changed everything, yet again.

Sarah asked Paul if she could see the photograph mentioned by Jane. Paul asked his mother who extracted it from her memoires. Sarah looked at it aghast. She looked up at Paul and Cis 'There is no doubt about the love between you, but what's with the kilt? Why was my father wearing a kilt?'

Cis smiled at Sarah. 'Do you not know that your father is entitled to wear a kilt by heritage of his grandmother? However, the Frazer of Lovatt tartan that he can wear is primarily red, and your father preferred blue. After establishing that he would not offend his heritage, he purchased his own tartan, the Fulton Blue, and which he is handsomely wearing in that photograph taken at Gleneagles in Scotland.' Pointing to the photograph, 'That kilt is the only one made from the Fulton Blue tartan to date. In years to come when Paul is ready for marriage, I hope he will be proud to wear his father's tartan at his wedding.'

Paul quickly interceded 'Do you mean that I can wear this Fulton family tartan?'

'Of course you can. It's restricted to family and direct descendants, and you are his son. Jane has offered to give me this dress kilt tomorrow. You can try it to see if it fits you as you are about the same size as your father.'

'Wow, my own family tartan. I'll be honoured to wear it.'

Sarah turned to Cis 'Does this mean that I can wear it as well?'

'Yes, my dear, you are his daughter, and your children are his grandchildren.'

'But how do I get hold of the material?'

'When you are ready to explore your family tartan I know where it is held, and can take you there, albeit it is traditional that they will make what you want.'

Sarah saw James taking a great interest in this conversation. She passed him the photograph. He looked at the picture, and then at Cis. 'This is a beautiful photo of you both. I would love to have a copy. And I would be proud to adopt the Fulton Blue tartan in honour of my father.'

Cis reflected on the day. *'Yet another adventure with my beloved, with more to come tomorrow, and thereafter for our son with his newfound family.'* However, she still felt empty without him. No man had touched her for two years, and she felt so devoid of the special intimacy she enjoyed with him. Their son was now a grown man and will soon start to live his own life. She had fulfilled her pledge to her beloved. But what was left for her? She voiced in her head a short prayer *'Please, my guardian angel, it's time for you to find me another Paul who will love me, want me, and know how to touch me. And this time please let me keep him. Amen.'*

AFTERWORD

In developing this book I called upon real events over a six year period relating to four women of completely different backgrounds and career paths but with one problem in common, they were sleepwalking their way to relationship breakdown because their relationship problems were always someone else's fault. The female on the cover closely resembles one of these women, and who, despite her beauty, suffered frequent prejudice because of her colour.

One of these women was a lifestyle editor for a well-known women's magazine, hence the profession of Cis, so consumed with her work that her relationship with her partner was incidental although her desire was to get married. She also considered cooking and laundry as tasks for others. For anyone who thinks the reaction of Cis in a storm a little exaggerated the real event occurred whilst driving with this lady along the autostrada through the mountains of Italy from Firenze to Venice. We were suddenly engulfed in a fierce storm of thunder and lightning. She freaked so much that she reached for the steering wheel and came close to steering us off the edge of the road into a deep ravine to certain death. We did not make Venice that day.

The woman desperate for a child after two years of marriage refused to tell her husband about her method of conception leaving him to think he had sired ·a son. During routine surgery on the then teenage boy blood tests revealed the truth. The husband divorced her and when the son was old enough, he also deserted her leaving a lonely and bitter woman who thought she could control events.

Of the other two, one rebuilt her relationship with her husband, and the other found a loving relationship albeit with a different man.

But this book was never intended to be about Cis who merely spent some 18-years using others to solve her problems. Paul had lost his way in life having his successful career in the City truncated by health issues. He had lost any sense of purpose until he happened upon Cis through whom he could reveal his own sad personal story.

ABOUT THE AUTHOR

His life has been filled by one adventure after another having started as a Nuclear Physicist at the Atomic Energy Research Establishment, Harwell, UK. During the 'brain drain' of the mid-1970's he transitioned into the world of international banking using his skills with computers and mathematics and where he ultimately participated in developing the Global financial village post deregulation of capital movement and the breakdown of communism with special emphasis of engaging with developing economies to better the lives of their people. When Stephen's career as a noted International Banker was truncated by health issues, his adventurous spirit turned to writing to fill the downtime, both recording his adventures and using novels to comment on observation of social issues in today's world.